P9-DMD-088

Joan of Arc

by the same author

BLOOD & ROSES:
The Paston Family in the Fifteenth Century
SHE-WOLVES:
The Women Who Ruled England Before Elizabeth

JOAN OF ARC
A History

HELEN CASTOR

HARPER

An Imprint of HarperCollins*Publishers*

JOAN OF ARC. Copyright © 2015 by Helen Castor. All rights reserved. Printed in the United States of America. No part of this book may be used or reproduced in any manner whatsoever without written permission except in the case of brief quotations embodied in critical articles and reviews. For information, address HarperCollins Publishers, 195 Broadway, New York, NY 10007.

HarperCollins books may be purchased for educational, business, or sales promotional use. For information, please e-mail the Special Markets Department at SPsales@harpercollins.com.

First published in Great Britain in 2014 by Faber and Faber Limited

FIRST U.S. EDITION

Library of Congress Cataloging-in-Publication Data
Castor, Helen.
  Joan of Arc : a history / by Helen Castor. — First edition.
      pages cm
  "Originally published in England in 2014 by Faber & Faber"—Title page verso.
  Includes bibliographical references and index.
    ISBN 978-0-06-238439-3 (hardcover) — ISBN 978-0-06-238440-9 (trade paperback)
  1. Joan, of Arc, Saint, 1412-1431. 2. Women soldiers—France—Biography. 3. Soldiers—France—Biography. 4. Hundred Years' War, 1339–1453. 5. Christian women saints—France—Biography. 6. Women heroes—France—Biography. 7. France—History—Charles VII, 1422-1461. I. Title.
  DC103.C37 2015
  944'.026092—dc23
  [B]
                                    2014029053

ISBN: 978-0-06-238439-3

15   16   17   18   19   OFF/RRD   10   9   8   7   6   5   4   3   2   1

For Luca

At that time the English would sometimes take one fortress from the Armagnacs in the morning and lose two in the evening. So this war, accursed of God, went on.

AN ANONYMOUS CITIZEN OF PARIS, 1423

You men of England, who have no right in this kingdom of France, the king of heaven orders and commands you through me, Joan the Maid, to abandon your strongholds and go back to your own country. If not, I will make a war-cry that will be remembered forever.

JOAN OF ARC to the English at Orléans, 5 May 1429

Contents

CONTENTS

Illustrations

The War Within France: Cast of Characters

FRENCH ROYAL FAMILY

Charles VI, the Well-Beloved, king of France

His uncles:

    Jean, duke of Berry

    Philip the Bold, duke of Burgundy

His wife:

    Isabeau of Bavaria, queen of France

Among their children:

    Louis of Guienne, dauphin of France

    Jean of Touraine, dauphin of France

    Catherine of Valois, queen of England

    Charles, dauphin of France, later King Charles VII

ARMAGNAC (ORLÉANIST) LORDS

Louis, duke of Orléans, brother of King Charles VI

Among his children:

    Charles, duke of Orléans

    Philippe, count of Vertus

    Jean, Bastard of Orléans, later count of Dunois

Bernard, count of Armagnac

Louis, duke of Anjou, titular king of Sicily and Jerusalem

His wife:

    Yolande of Aragon, duchess of Anjou, titular queen of
    Sicily and Jerusalem

Among their children:

    Louis, duke of Anjou

    René, duke of Bar and Lorraine, later duke of Anjou

Marie of Anjou, queen of France
Charles of Anjou
Jean, duke of Alençon
Jean d'Harcourt, count of Aumâle
Charles, count of Clermont, later duke of Bourbon

BURGUNDIAN LORDS
John the Fearless, duke of Burgundy, son of Philip the Bold and
cousin of King Charles VI
His brothers:
Anthony, duke of Brabant
Philip, count of Nevers
His wife:
Margaret of Bavaria, duchess of Burgundy
Among their children:
Philip the Good, duke of Burgundy
Anne of Burgundy, duchess of Bedford
Margaret of Burgundy, countess of Richemont
Agnes of Burgundy, countess of Clermont
Jean de Luxembourg, count of Ligny
His sister:
Jacquetta de Luxembourg, duchess of Bedford

ENGLISH ROYAL FAMILY
Henry V, king of England
His brothers:
Thomas, duke of Clarence
John, duke of Bedford
Humphrey, duke of Gloucester
His uncle:
Henry Beaufort, bishop of Winchester, cardinal of England
His wife:
Catherine of Valois, queen of England

Their son:
   Henry VI, king of England

ENGLISH LORDS AND CAPTAINS, ALLIES OF THE
BURGUNDIANS
Thomas Montagu, earl of Salisbury
William de la Pole, earl of Suffolk
Richard Beauchamp, earl of Warwick
Thomas, Lord Scales
John, Lord Talbot, later earl of Shrewsbury
Sir John Fastolf, captain

SCOTS LORDS AND CAPTAINS, ALLIES OF THE ARMAGNACS
John Stewart, earl of Buchan
Archibald Douglas, earl of Douglas, later duke of Touraine
   His son:
      Archibald Douglas, earl of Wigtown
Sir John Stewart of Darnley, captain

ARMAGNAC COUNSELLORS, CAPTAINS AND CHURCHMEN
Tanguy du Châtel, counsellor
Robert le Maçon, counsellor
Jean Louvet, counsellor
Georges de La Trémoille, counsellor
Étienne de Vignolles, known as La Hire, captain
Ambroise de Loré, captain
Poton de Xaintrailles, captain
Raoul de Gaucourt, captain
Gilles de Rais, captain
Jean Gerson, theologian
Jacques Gélu, archbishop of Embrun
Regnault de Chartres, archbishop of Reims

BURGUNDIAN COUNSELLORS, CAPTAINS AND CHURCHMEN
Jean de La Trémoille, counsellor
Hugues de Lannoy, counsellor
Perrinet Gressart, captain
Pierre Cauchon, theologian, later bishop of Beauvais, then of Lisieux
Louis de Luxembourg, bishop of Thérouanne, brother of Jean de Luxembourg

INDEPENDENT LORDS AND CHURCHMEN
William, count of Hainaut, Holland and Zeeland
   His daughter:
      Jacqueline, countess of Hainaut, Holland and Zeeland
John, duke of Brittany
   His brother:
      Arthur, count of Richemont
Cardinal Niccolò Albergati

Family Trees

English and French Claims to
the Throne of France

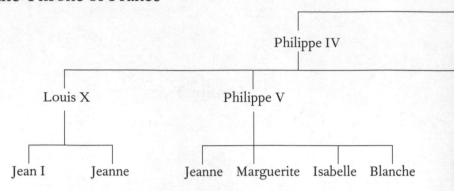

After Louis X of France died suddenly in 1316, his queen gave birth to a son, Jean I, who lived for just five days. The king's only remaining child was his four-year-old daughter by his first wife. That marriage had been annulled on suspicion of her adultery. Both his daughter's young age and the question marks over her parentage made her a less than ideal heir to the throne, and the crown was taken instead by Louis's brother, Philippe V. When he too died without sons, the precedent of his own case was used to secure the succession of his brother, Charles IV, rather than one of his daughters. When Charles then also died leaving only daughters, the crown passed to his male cousin, Philippe VI, beginning the line of Valois succession.

But Edward III of England, the son of Charles IV's sister Isabella, disputed the developing custom that the crown could not be inherited by or through a woman, and claimed that the French throne was rightfully his. This was the basis on which he began what was later named the Hundred Years War, winning great victories at Sluys in 1340, Crécy in 1346 and Poitiers in 1356. It was also the basis on which Edward's great-grandson Henry V sought to emulate his military success in France and to secure the French crown for himself.

In early fifteenth-century France, meanwhile, the combination of these fourteenth-century precedents with the urgent need to invalidate the English claim to the French throne produced the enduring myth that female royal succession was forbidden by an ancient 'Salic Law'.

Philippe III

Charles of Valois

Charles IV

Isabella
=
Edward II
of England

Philippe VI

Maric   Blanche

Edward III

Jean II

Edward, the
Black Prince

John of Gaunt

Charles V

Richard II

Henry IV

Charles VI

Henry V = Catherine
of Valois

Charles VII

Henry VI

The Valois Kings of France

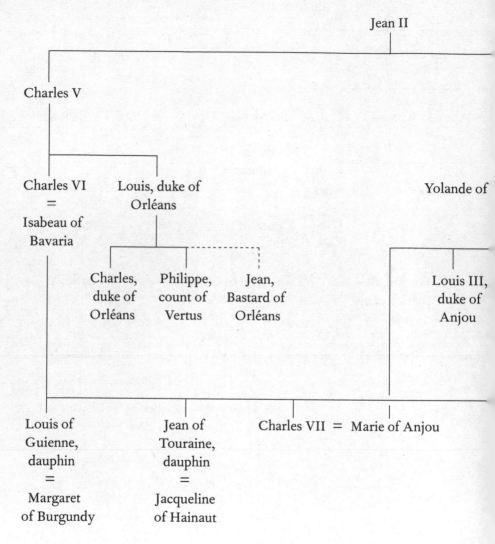

Jean II

Charles V

Charles VI = Isabeau of Bavaria   Louis, duke of Orléans   Yolande of

Charles, duke of Orléans   Philippe, count of Vertus   Jean, Bastard of Orléans   Louis III, duke of Anjou

Louis of Guienne, dauphin = Margaret of Burgundy   Jean of Touraine, dauphin = Jacqueline of Hainaut   Charles VII = Marie of Anjou

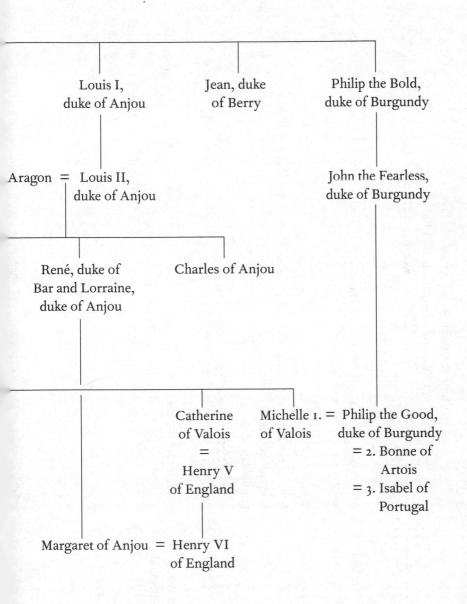

Louis I,
duke of Anjou

Jean, duke
of Berry

Philip the Bold,
duke of Burgundy

Aragon = Louis II,
duke of Anjou

John the Fearless,
duke of Burgundy

René, duke of
Bar and Lorraine,
duke of Anjou

Charles of Anjou

Catherine
of Valois
=
Henry V
of England

Michelle 1. = Philip the Good,
of Valois   duke of Burgundy
              = 2. Bonne of
                   Artois
              = 3. Isabel of
                   Portugal

Margaret of Anjou = Henry VI
of England

The Dukes of Burgundy

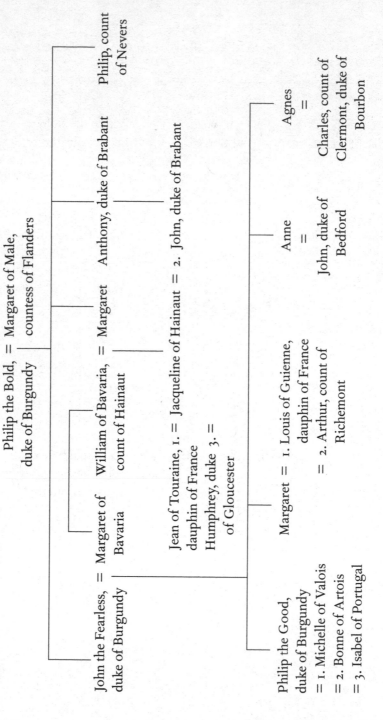

The Plantagenet Kings of England

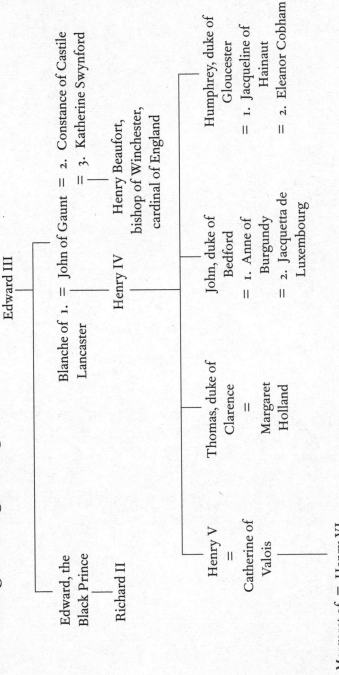

Joan of Arc

Introduction: 'Joan of Arc'

In the firmament of history, Joan of Arc is a massive star. Her light shines brighter than that of any other figure of her time and place. Her story is unique, and at the same time universal in its reach. She is, famously, a protean icon: a hero to nationalists, monarchists, liberals, socialists, the right, the left, Catholics, Protestants, traditionalists, feminists, Vichy and the Resistance. She is a recurring motif, a theme replayed in art, literature, music and film. And the process of recounting her story and making her myth began from the moment she stepped into public view; she was as much an object of fascination and a subject of impassioned argument during her short life as she has been ever since.

In outline, her tale is both profoundly familiar and endlessly startling. Alone in the fields at Domrémy, a peasant girl hears heavenly voices bringing a message of salvation for France, which lies broken at the hands of the invading English. Against all the odds, she reaches the dauphin Charles, the disinherited heir to the French throne, and convinces him that God has made it her mission to drive the English from his kingdom. Dressed in armour as though she were a man, with her hair cut short, she leads an army to rescue the town of Orléans from an English siege. The fortunes and the morale of the French are utterly transformed, and in a matter of weeks she pushes on, deep into English-held territory, to Reims, where she presides over the coronation of the dauphin as King Charles VII of France. But soon she is captured by allies of the English, to whom she is handed over for trial as a heretic. She defends herself with undaunted courage, but she is – of course – condemned. She is burned to death in the market square in Rouen,

I

but her legend proves much harder to kill. Nearly five hundred years later, the Catholic Church recognises her not only as a heroine, but as a saint.

One of the reasons we know her story so well is that her life is so well documented, in a distant age when that was true of very few. In relative terms, as much ink and parchment were expended on the subject of Joan of Arc by her contemporaries as print and paper have been in the centuries that followed. There are chronicles, letters, poems, treatises, journals and account-books. Above all, there are two remarkable caches of documents: the records of her trial for heresy in 1431, including the long interrogations to which she was subjected; and the records of the 'nullification trial' held twenty-five years later by the French to annul the previous proceedings and rehabilitate Joan's name. In these transcripts we hear not only the men and women who knew her, but Joan herself, speaking about her voices, her mission, her village childhood, and her extraordinary experiences after she left Domrémy. First-hand testimony, from Joan, her family and her friends: a rare survival from the medieval world. What could be more reliable or more revealing?

Yet all is not as simple as it seems. It's not just that the official transcripts of their words were written in clerical Latin, rather than the French they actually spoke – a notarial translation alerting us to the fact that this first-hand testimony is not quite as immediate as it might initially appear. It's also that, as befits such a star, Joan exerts a vast gravitational pull. By the time those who knew her spoke as witnesses in the nullification trial of 1456 about her childhood and her mission, they knew exactly who she had become and what she had accomplished. In recalling events and conversations from a quarter of a century earlier, they were grappling with the vagaries of long-treasured memories and telling stories that were deeply infused with hindsight – which by that stage included knowledge not only of her life and death, but also of the final defeat of the

English in France between 1449 and 1453, events that served to vindicate Joan's assertion of God's purpose beyond anything achieved in her lifetime or for years thereafter. In many ways, then, the story of Joan of Arc as told in the nullification trial is a life told backwards.

The same could also be said of Joan's account of herself at the 'trial of condemnation' of 1431. The unshakeable conviction in her cause and the extraordinary self-possession that had brought her to the dauphin's presence at Chinon in February 1429 only grew as time went on. We call her 'Joan of Arc', for example – taking her father's appellation, 'd'Arc', and transferring it to her – but that was a name she never used. Just a few weeks after her arrival at court, she was already referring to herself as '*Jeanne la Pucelle*', 'Joan the Maid' – a title redolent with meaning, suggesting not only her youth and purity but her status as God's chosen servant and her closeness to the Virgin, to whom she claimed a special devotion. And the sense of herself that she expressed at her trial was no 'neutral' account of her experiences, but a defence of her beliefs and actions in response to prolonged questioning from hostile prosecutors intent on exposing her as a liar and a heretic. As such, it's a rich, absorbing and multilayered text, but one that is as difficult to interpret as it is invaluable.

Unsurprisingly, the effect of Joan's gravitational field – the self-defining narrative pull of her mission – is equally apparent in historical accounts of her life. Most begin not with the story of the long and bitter war that had ravaged France since before she was born, but with Joan herself hearing voices in her village of Domrémy in the far east of the kingdom. That means that we come to the dauphin's court at Chinon *with* Joan, rather than experiencing the shock of her arrival, and as a result it's not easy to understand the full complexity of the political context into which she walked, or the nature of the responses she received. And because all our information about Joan's life in Domrémy comes from her own statements and those of her friends and family in the two trials, historical narratives which start there are infused from the very beginning with the same hindsight that permeates their testimony.

Distortion, then, is one risk; but, beyond that, what lies at the centre of this gravitational field is immensely difficult to read. On closer investigation it can seem, unnervingly, as though Joan's star might collapse into a black hole. When we go back to the trial transcripts, at almost every point in her story there are discrepancies between the accounts of different witnesses – and sometimes within the testimony of a single witness, including that of Joan herself – about the detail of events, their timing and their interpretation. The accounts we have, in other words, don't straightforwardly build into a coherent and internally compatible whole. That's hardly surprising: after all, eyewitness testimony can differ even about recent events and in relatively unpressured circumstances. Joan, we must remember, was interrogated over many days by prosecutors she knew were seeking to prove her guilt; and the nullification trial sought to clear her name by asking those who knew her to recall what she had said and done more than twenty-five years after the fact.

Even if they aren't surprising, however, these inconsistencies and contradictions raise the question of how the evidence should best be understood. Sometimes, historians have picked their way through the different accounts, choosing some details to weave into a seamless story and glossing over other elements that don't fit, without explaining why one has been preferred to another. Sometimes, too, parts of a single testimony have been accepted while others are dismissed, apparently more on the basis of perceived plausibility than anything else. (Of the information that Joan offered only at her trial, for example, her identification of her voices as those of Saints Michael, Margaret and Catherine has been taken seriously; her description of an angel appearing in the dauphin's chamber at Chinon to present him with a crown, by contrast, has not.) And, in general, much less attention has been paid to the questions witnesses were asked than to the answers they gave, despite the extent to which the latter were shaped and defined by the former. At the heart of both trials was the question of where the dividing line lay between true faith and heresy. Witnesses, therefore, were not offered a general invitation to describe their experiences of Joan (or, in her case, her own experience), but were instead asked to respond to precise articles of investigation framed – whether the respondents understood it or not – by particular theological principles.

That's also a difficulty for us: whether we, with the mindset of a very different age, can understand not just the finer points of late medieval theology, but the nature of faith in the world that Joan and her contemporaries inhabited. There seems little purpose, for example, in attempting to diagnose in her a physical or psychological disorder that might, to us, explain her voices, if the terms of reference we use are completely alien to the landscape of belief in which she lived. Joan and the people around her knew that it was entirely possible for otherworldly beings to communicate with men and women of sound mind; Joan was not the first or the last person in France in the first half of the fifteenth century to have visions or hear voices. The problem was not how to explain her experience of hearing something that wasn't real; the problem was how to tell whether her voices came to her from heaven or from hell – which is why the expertise of theologians took centre stage in shaping responses to her claims.

Similarly, it might seem to us as though part of Joan's power lay in bringing God into play within the context of war; that, by introducing the idea of a mandate from heaven into a kingdom exhausted by years of conflict, she made possible a new invigoration of French morale. But in medieval minds, war was always interpreted as an expression of divine will. The particular trauma for France in the 1420s was that its deeply internalised status as the 'most Christian' kingdom had been challenged by the bloodletting of civil war and overwhelming defeat by the English. How were the disaster of Azincourt (as the French knew what the English called 'Agincourt') and the years of suffering that followed to be explained, if not by God's displeasure? This was the context in which Joan's message of heaven-sent salvation was so potent, and the need to establish whether her voices were angelic or demonic in origin so overwhelmingly urgent.

And this is the reason why I have chosen to begin my history of Joan of Arc not in 1429 but fourteen years earlier, with the catastrophe of Azincourt. My aim is not to see Joan's world only, or even principally, through her eyes. Instead, I've set out to tell the story of France during these tumultuous years, and to understand how a teenage girl came to play such an astonishing part within that history. Starting in 1415 has made it possible to explore the shifting perspectives of the various protagonists in the drama, both English and French – and to emphasise the fact that what it meant to be 'French' was profoundly contested throughout these years. Civil war threatened France's identity geographically, politically and spiritually; and Joan's understanding of who the French were, on whom God now intended to bestow victory through her mission, was not shared by many of her compatriots.

What follows is an attempt to tell the story of Joan's France, and of Joan herself, forwards, not backwards, as a narrative in which human beings struggle to understand the world around them and – just like us – have no idea what's coming next. Of course, in the process I too have had to pick my way through the evidence, choosing what to weave into a seamless story; but in the notes at the end of the book I've tried to give a sense of how and why I have made my choices, and where the pitfalls might lie within the sources themselves and in the testing process of translation from the Latin and French in which most of them are written. Among all the challenges presented by this mass of material, the most difficult is dealing with the trials, which were defining events in Joan's life and afterlife at the same time as providing evidence through which to interpret them. My aim has been as much as possible to let them take place as events in Joan's story – in other words, to allow the testimony of Joan herself and of the other, later witnesses unfold as it was given and recorded, rather than to read their memories and interpretations backwards into the earlier events they were describing.

The result is a history of Joan of Arc that is a little different from the one we all know: a tale in which Joan herself doesn't appear for the first fourteen years, and one in which we learn about her family and childhood at the end of the story, not the beginning. Many historians have taken, and will undoubtedly take, a different view of how best to use these remarkable sources for the life of a truly remarkable woman. But for me, this was the only way to understand Joan within her own world – the combination of character and circumstance, of religious faith and political machination, that made her a unique exception to the rules that governed the lives of other women.

It is an extraordinary story; and, at the end of it, her star still shines.

Prologue: The field of blood

It was the day of victory.

First light dragged, cold and sodden, over a camp of exhausted men. Exhausted from unpredictable weeks of forced march, parrying the enemy's manoeuvres along the banks of the river Somme, or moving at speed to this urgent rendezvous. Exhausted from a fear-filled day with the enemy in sight, waiting for a battle that had not come before sundown. Exhausted, now, from a wet night bivouacked in the fields, or billeted nearby with the terrified villagers of Tramecourt and Azincourt. Exhausted, but expectant.

This was the feast of Saints Crispin and Crispian, brothers who had spread the gospel at Soissons more than a millennium before. Holy martyrs, they had given their lives for their part in making this land the 'eldest daughter of the Church', ruled by *le roi très-chrétien*, the most Christian king. But their blessed sacrifice was not the only reason to be certain of heaven's favour.

As aching feet sank into liquid earth, these tired men knew that the enemy was suffering more. Across the fields, near the hamlet of Maisoncelle – within earshot, though somehow they had been almost silent in the rain-lashed darkness – stood an English army steeped in mud. It had seeped into bowels as well as baggage in the two months since the invaders had set foot on the coast of Normandy; the bloody flux – dysentery – had been the price of the success they had found at the port of Harfleur. They had left an English flag flying there, and an occupying garrison – and hundreds of sick and dying soldiers waiting for ships to take them home. The troops still standing had marched here, under the command of their grim and

9

purposeful king. He carried the scars of battle – from an arrowhead embedded inches deep in his face when he was just sixteen – and scars, too, of a different kind, from his father's sin in taking the English crown from his cousin Richard II. Now, here in France, retribution was almost upon him.

The weary men preparing to fight this presumptuous intruder were not led by their own monarch. Almost six decades earlier, amid the chaos of another battlefield near Poitiers – and despite the diversionary presence of nineteen identically dressed doppelgängers – the French king's royal grandfather had been captured by the English. Four years had passed before his freedom could be secured, an unhappy interlude during which his kingdom had been convulsed by political crisis. It was hardly surprising that his son and successor had declined to lead France's army in person, instead preferring to direct military operations from a safe distance behind the front line.

But even that was not an option available to the present king, Charles VI. He had been riding with his troops on the fateful August day back in 1392 when, under a blazing sun, he had exploded into psychotic violence, killing five of his attendants before he was overpowered, his eyes rolling in his head and his sword broken in his hand. His body soon recovered from this horrifying seizure, but his mind remained fragile. At times, as the years went by, he was calm, lucid and rational; but he could lapse without warning into episodes of derangement and paranoia in which he believed that his wife and children were strangers, that he was not called Charles, that he was not king, even that he was made of glass and might shatter into a thousand pieces.

So he could not lead his people to war; but this troubled man – with his wide, uneasy gaze and fair hair combed forward to disguise his baldness – was still *le bien-aimé*, France's well-beloved king. And luckily there were many royal princes to lead his people for him. Not, however, his eldest son, the eighteen-year-old dauphin Louis, an overweight, handsome boy with some political nous and many dazzling outfits, but by no means a warrior, and too precious to the kingdom's future to be put at risk. Not his uncle, the duke of Berry, at almost seventy-five the *éminence grise* of the regime, but too old to bear arms. And not his cousin, the duke of Burgundy, for reasons that were painful even to articulate, let alone explain.

At forty-four, John of Burgundy had in abundance the military capability that the king so clearly lacked. '*Jean Sans Peur*', they had called him for his commanding part in an earlier battle: John the Fearless. The difficulty, then, was not personal, but political. His father, the old duke, had dominated the government of France until his death in 1404. With his brother of Berry, Philip of Burgundy had seized the responsibilities – and the lavish rewards – of rule during the minority of their royal nephew in the 1380s and his madness thereafter. When Duke Philip died, John of Burgundy expected to inherit his place at the king's right hand, but he found himself thwarted by the king's vain and ambitious brother Louis, duke of Orléans, who had spent years chafing under his uncle's yoke and was determined now to snatch the reins of power for himself.

For three years, the conflict between the cousins of Orléans and Burgundy smouldered. Louis of Orléans chose as his badge the threatening emblem of a wooden club; John of Burgundy's arch response was to adopt the device of a carpenter's plane, a tool with which an Orléanist cudgel might be smoothly whittled away. He was so taken with the conceit that soon his planes were everywhere, embroidered on his robes, engraved on his armour, and fashioned in diamond-encrusted gold and silver, complete with golden wood-shavings, to be distributed to his servants and supporters. His assault on Orléans's control of government was equally thoroughgoing. He set himself up as the champion of the people against Orléanist taxes, and brought the kingdom to the brink of civil war before an uneasy peace was brokered, satisfying no one and settling nothing.

And then, in 1407, John of Burgundy decided that the time had come to put the blade of his plane to more than metaphorical use. On the evening of 23 November Louis of Orléans was in Paris, returning from a visit to the queen, with whom he shared oversight of the incapacitated king, along a street in the east of the city known as the Vieille-du-Temple. The torches held by his attendants threw pools of light onto the cobbles, but the shadows were deep, and their assailants were upon them before they knew what was happening. Blows rained down so fast and so hard that the duke's left hand was severed as he sought desperately to shield himself from the onslaught. Within moments his skull was gaping and his brains spilled onto the ground. And when news of this terrible murder was brought to the royal council, it was clear that, to the duke of Burgundy, it came as no surprise.

If the duke had believed that a single act of ruthless aggression might cut the knot of dynastic ambition and personal rivalry that restrained him from his political destiny, he had been utterly mistaken. Instead, he found himself wound in the coils of a blood feud. The wife and young sons of Louis of Orléans demanded vengeance on his murderer. John of Burgundy admitted responsibility for the killing but claimed – through his mouthpiece, Jean Petit, a theologian at the university of Paris, who took four dogged hours to read his formal defence of his patron in the presence of the royal court – that the assassination was not only justified but meritorious, because Orléans had been a tyrant and a traitor. This piece of breathtaking casuistry – combined with the armed troops at Burgundy's side and the support of the Parisian populace – was enough to win the duke a pardon from the tattered and brittle remains of the regime, and by the end of 1409 he had succeeded in enforcing a pantomime of reconciliation and in establishing his hold on king, queen and government in Paris.

But in 1410 the opposition to his rule took threatening shape once more. In a league formed at Gien on the Loire, fifteen-year-old Charles, the new duke of Orléans, won the promise of military support from the ageing duke of Berry and a powerful alliance of other noblemen, including young Orléans's new father-in-law, the forceful count of Armagnac, who gave his name to this anti-Burgundian confederacy. By now John of Burgundy, who had once been named 'the Fearless', lived so much in fear of the same bloody end he had devised for his rival that he built a magnificent new tower at his residence in Paris – emblazoned, of course, with his badge of the plane – at the very top of which he slept each night under the careful watch of his personal bodyguard.

Sides had been chosen, and by the summer of 1411 armies were in the field. 'Burgundian' and 'Armagnac' were terms now fraught with fear and loathing; each called the other 'traitor', trading lurid accusations of injustice, corruption and brutality. Campaign followed truce and truce followed campaign until, in the summer of 1413, John of Burgundy was finally unseated from the capital, and the Armagnac lords took control of government – without, however, bringing an end to the fighting. One despondent Parisian, keeping a journal to record each violent turn of Fortune's wheel, concluded wearily that 'the great all hated each other'.

It might have seemed, then, in the summer of 1415, that Henry V of England had picked a fine moment to invade the fractured kingdom he claimed as his. But that was to underestimate the proud defiance of the princes of France. Both the duke of Burgundy and the Armagnac lords had been willing to solicit English help against their fellow countrymen for as long as England's king remained safely on the right side of the sea. Once he had dared to set sail for France, however, the blood royal would unite in the kingdom's defence. Though the port of Harfleur could not be relieved quickly enough to prevent its fall to the English siege, a call to arms had been sounded across northern France as soon as Henry's army had landed in Normandy.

By 12 October, both the dauphin, Louis, and King Charles himself – a compromised but still iconic figure – had reached

Normandy's capital, Rouen. There they stayed as royal figure-heads while their troops moved into the theatre of war, some shadowing the English army as it moved along the river Somme, others mustering for the battle ahead. The lords in command of these men included dukes, of Bourbon, Bar and Alençon; counts, among them Richemont, Vendôme, Vaudémont, Blâmont, Marle, Roucy and Eu; and the kingdom's foremost military officers, the constable and marshal of France – the renowned soldiers Charles d'Albret and Jean le Meingre, known as Boucicaut. The duke of Burgundy had sent forces to join this imposing rendezvous but had been requested not to come in person – a reassuringly wise decision by the royal council, given his role in the vicious conflict of the previous years. His younger brothers, though, were ready to fight: the count of Nevers already in attendance, and the duke of Brabant on his way. The same policy of absence had originally been applied to Burgundy's sworn enemy, Charles of Orléans, but – once it was clear that neither the king nor his son would be at or even near the battle – a summons had belatedly been sent to the young duke, as their nearest male relative and representative.

So now, in the watery light of early morning, exhausted men prepared themselves, confident in God's purpose. They knew they numbered many more than the bedraggled English, and they knew that honour and glory were theirs to win. As battle lines were drawn, some – lords and others – seized the moment to embrace and exchange the kiss of peace, putting aside past division in the face of a present and greater enemy. The duke of Burgundy was not there to join this rapprochement, but the regret would be all his. The flower of French chivalry waited impatiently, men and horses jostling into the great mass of the front ranks, a steel-clad host ready to humble the English few.

Time slowed as the pale sun rose higher. Suddenly an English cry went up, and their banners began to move. This would be the hour: the French lines launched themselves across the land they had assembled to defend. Then the air shifted with a thrum, and all at once the sky was dark. Razor-tipped arrows, unleashed in a numberless, roiling storm, plunged through breastplates and visors, muscle and bone. Violent death was falling from the clouds; and, in response, spurs kicked screaming horses to charge down the archers from whose bows this slaughter flew. They found only death of a different kind, impaling themselves on the sharpened stakes that – they saw too late – bristled from the ground on which the archers stood, or wheeling in panic and stumbling under the pounding hooves of those who pressed behind.

Dead and living fell together, crushed into suffocating earth, one on top of another, in heaped piles from which none would rise. For more than two hours French soldiers laboured onward, heavy feet struggling in sucking mud or tangled in the twisted limbs of the fallen, and all the while English blades hacked and stabbed and gouged. The sound of reinforcements, faint amid the cacophony of killing, brought a lurching hope of rescue; but the duke of Brabant, racing to reach the battle, had galloped too far too fast, outriding his troops and equipment. He was cut down within minutes of hurling himself into the mêlée, his wounds staining the banner he had wrested from his trumpeter to wear, with a raggedly improvised hole for his head, as a makeshift coat of arms.

When the fighting gave way at last to the dreadful work of excavating the mounds of the dead, Brabant's disfigured corpse was counted alongside those of his brother, the count of Nevers, and the dukes of Alençon and Bar; of Constable d'Albret, and the counts of Vaudémont, Blâmont, Marle and Roucy. It was a noble roll-call rivalled only by the names of those who had lost their freedom rather than their lives: the duke of Bourbon; the counts of Richemont, Vendôme and Eu; the veteran Marshal Boucicaut, and young Charles, duke of Orléans. As these eminent prisoners, white-faced and numb with shock, began the long journey north to

Calais and then London, messengers turned their horses south to Rouen, to bring unwelcome news to their anxious king.

It was the wretched day of victory, and France lay broken on a field of blood.

PART ONE

Before

I

This war, accursed of God

God had spoken. That, at least, was what the English said. In the circumstances, it was hard for the French to argue. Or, rather, it would have been, had they not been too busy arguing among themselves.

For the English, it was simple. Their king's claim to the throne of France – and, for that matter, his dynasty's contested right to wear the crown of England – had been utterly, gloriously vindicated by his astonishing victory at the battle they called 'Agincourt'. Only God's will could explain how so few Englishmen had vanquished so many great knights of France, and how it was that so little English blood had been spilled when so much death had been visited on their adversaries. This was heaven's mandate in action: the triumph of another David over the might of an arrogant Goliath, as one of the royal chaplains who had formed the spiritual corps of the English army now solemnly noted in his account of the campaign. These clerical conscripts had sat behind the English lines as the fighting raged, praying furiously for divine intervention, and its undeniable manifestation in 'that mound of pity and blood' in which the French had fallen could lead to only one conclusion. 'Far be it from our people to ascribe the triumph to their own glory or strength,' wrote the anonymous priest with palpable fervour; 'rather let it be ascribed to God alone, from Whom is every victory, lest the Lord be wrathful at our ingratitude and at another time turn from us, which Heaven forbid, His victorious hand.'

Clearly, the English king was waging a just war. He had given his French subjects every chance to acknowledge his rightful claim to be their ruler by descent from the French mother of his royal

ancestor Edward III. Outside the walls of Harfleur, following the
prescription for the conduct of righteous war laid down in the Old
Testament book of Deuteronomy, he had patiently explained that
he came in peace, if only they would open the gates and submit to
his authority as their duty demanded. Their obstinate refusal meant
that he had no choice but to take up the sword of justice to punish
their rebellion. In doing so he was, explained his chaplain, the 'true
elect of God' – 'our gracious king, His own soldier' – at the head
of an army that, thanks to the king's stern instructions, conducted
itself soberly and piously, without resorting to pillage or indulging
in vengeful or wanton violence.

The exposition of this analysis by the anonymous royal chaplain
in his *Gesta Henrici Quinti*, 'The Deeds of Henry V', was intended in part to persuade an international audience of the merits of
the king's cause: specifically, the great Council of the Church
then meeting in the German city of Constance. There was also a
domestic constituency that needed reminding of the imperative to
lend practical support to Henry's divinely sanctioned project – the
representatives of English boroughs and shires in parliament, and
the representatives of the English Church in convocation, whose
responsibility it was to assent to the taxes that would pay for the
king's future campaigns in France.

But heaven's judgement had been made so plain that it seemed a
source of irritation, in some quarters at least, that such campaigns
would have to be fought at all. The bishop of Winchester, England's chancellor, in his opening address to the parliament that
gathered in March 1416, noted testily that God had, in fact, already
spoken three times over: once in England's great naval victory
over the French fleet at Sluys in 1340; then in 1356, when France's
king had been captured at Poitiers; and now, on the killing field of
Agincourt. 'O God,' remarked the royal chaplain as he recounted
the tenor of the chancellor's speech, 'why does this wretched and
stiff-necked nation not obey these divine sentences, so many and

so terrible, to which, by a vengeance most clearly made manifest, obedience is demanded of them?'

The wretched and stiff-necked nation itself, however – while accepting that God had indeed spoken – was much less certain of what He had actually said. Clearly, the English cause was not just. After all, the English king had no lawful right to the throne of France, since claims through the female line had no validity in the most Christian kingdom, and the French had no wish to be his subjects, which made his attempt at conquest an act of unwarranted aggression and his proposed rule a tyranny. The conflict between the two kingdoms would hardly have lasted so long, nor would it have encompassed French successes as well as English ones, had God's judgement been quite so overwhelmingly obvious as the English king was pleased to suggest. The inference of the accursed day of Azincourt, therefore, was not that God supported England's unjust claims. Instead, He had chosen to use England's unjust claims as an instrument with which to punish France for its sins.

Sin was the heart of the matter, that much was clear; but exactly what sin, and committed by whom, were questions on which it was more difficult to agree. Perhaps, suggested the chronicler Thomas Basin half a century later, the blessed saints Crispin and Crispian had abandoned the French to the carnage unleashed on their feast day at Azincourt because their town of Soissons had been sacked and their shrines plundered only a year before, in the course of the civil war between Burgundians and Armagnacs. 'Everyone', he said with sorrowful resignation, 'can think what they will.' For himself, Basin preferred to stick to the facts, 'leaving the discussion of the arcane workings of the divine will to those who presume to do so'.

There were plenty of them. The monk who chronicled the events of 1415 from the abbey of Saint-Denis outside the walls of Paris attempted a pass at the same kind of historical humility – 'I leave it to those who have given the matter careful consideration', he said, 'to decide if we should attribute the ruin of the kingdom to the French nobility' – but he could restrain himself only momentarily from a thunderous verdict of his own. It could hardly be denied that the great were no longer good. The lords of France had fallen into sybaritic luxury, into vanity and into vice, and their impious abuse of Holy Mother Church was matched only by their mortal hatred of each other. 'All these crimes', the chronicler of Saint-Denis declared, 'and others worse still, to put it briefly, have justly stirred up the wrath of God against the great men of the kingdom, so that He has taken from them the power to defeat their enemies, or even to resist their attack.'

But even if it could be agreed that divine retribution was patently at work, questions still remained. Were all of France's sinful noblemen equally guilty in the eyes of God, or were some among them more reprehensible – and therefore more responsible for the desperate straits in which the kingdom now found itself – than others? Supporters of the Armagnac cause knew that one crime above all had cast a shadow dark enough to blot out the light of heaven's grace: the bloody murder of Louis of Orléans by his cousin, the duke of Burgundy. That unnatural act had precipitated a civil war which not only turned the realm upon itself, but opened the door to English aggression. John of Burgundy, the Armagnacs were well aware, had had dealings with the king of England both before and after Henry had inherited his father's throne. Now, the fact that the duke had not taken the field at Azincourt provided proof positive that Burgundy had entered into secret negotiations with the English, and – with horrifying treachery – had agreed not to resist their invasion. About the dreadful outcome of the battle and the slaughter of the duke's countrymen, the Armagnac chronicler Jean Juvénal des Ursins reported, 'it was commonly said that he did not seem angered in the slightest'.

Pierre de Fenin, on the other hand – a writer whose noble family came from the Burgundian-dominated region of Artois – was no less confident that Duke John had been 'much enraged by the French loss when he was told of it'. Those who supported the duke in his efforts to secure the stake that was rightfully his in the government of the kingdom knew that he had wanted nothing more than to fight at Azincourt, until he had been refused permission in the name of the king himself. The deaths of the duke's two brothers, Anthony of Brabant and Philip of Nevers, had been a shattering blow which struck at the heart of his family and his dynasty. And to Burgundian eyes, it was remarkable how many of those who had escaped with their lives, if not their honour, from that field of blood were members of the Armagnac confederacy; chief among the English prisoners, after all, was young Charles, duke of Orléans.

What, then, should John of Burgundy do, as he surveyed the devastation that the crimes of his Armagnac enemies had wrought on the kingdom? From the safety of his duchy of Burgundy, he contemplated his options and calculated his odds. To his French followers, the duke was a distinctively imposing figure, his shrewd brain working behind languorously hooded eyes, the long nose sketching an inimitable profile beneath the rich black folds – piled forward and pinned with a ruby of extraordinary price – of his trademark *chaperon* hat; all in all, as unlike their beloved but pitiful king as it was possible to imagine. But the frontiers of France, as the Armagnacs well knew in accusing him of treachery, were not the limits of the arena across which Duke John now aimed to manoeuvre.

Great prince of France though he was, the territories of Burgundy itself extended his political reach beyond the bounds of the kingdom. As the duke of Burgundy he was a vassal of the French king, sworn to serve and obey; but as the *count* of Burgundy – holding the lands immediately to the east of his duchy, a fief which lay outside the French king's dominions – he owed allegiance and homage to the Holy Roman Emperor. Nor were the 'Two Burgundies', as they were known, his only stake in the complex, shifting geography of western European power. From his mother, the heiress Margaret of Male, he had also inherited the rich counties of Flanders and Artois, territories which made him a force to be reckoned with in the Low Countries.

The colossal figure of the Burgundian duke, towering over the French political landscape, therefore had one foot planted within the kingdom and the other without – a separation of powers which, at times, required him to perform spine-twisting acts of political contortionism. Back in 1406, for example, he had been appointed as the French king's captain-general to command an assault on the English-held port of Calais. He mustered his forces, ready to begin the campaign – and at the same moment, even as he buckled on his armour and rode out to review his troops, his ambassadors were busily negotiating a treaty with the English in which their master guaranteed that his Flemish fortresses would offer no military support of any kind to the French attack that he himself was about to lead.

But, despite the dark suspicions of the Armagnacs, this was not treachery, or even duplicity, in any unequivocal sense. As count of Flanders, the duke had a duty, and a political imperative, to support the economic interests of the wealthy Flemish towns of Ghent, Bruges and Ypres – and that required him to maintain a relationship with England close enough to safeguard the supply of English wool to those who produced fine Flemish cloth, and to protect commercial shipping in the waters between England and Flanders. It did not mean that, as duke of Burgundy, he was any the less a prince of France. In 1406, his outrage had been unmistakable when the order to attack the English at Calais was countermanded from Paris at the eleventh hour for lack of funds: 'My lord has been and is as saddened and angered by this as it is possible to be in all the world, and no one can placate him,' the duke's treasurer told his colleagues in Burgundy. And in 1415 – whatever the insinuations made in the aftermath of the slaughter at Azincourt – he had come to no accom-modation with the English invaders.

Instead, in the weeks and months after the battle, Duke John's sights were fixed as firmly as they had ever been on the prize that still eluded him: control of the government of France. During November 1415 he advanced on Paris, 'very distressed by the deaths of his brothers and his men' (explained the anonymous and by now pro-Burgundian Parisian who kept a journal throughout these years), but prevented from reaching the helpless king by the Armagnac 'betrayers of France'. For the Armagnacs who controlled the capital, meanwhile, the duke's distress was less immediately striking than the heavily armed troops at his back. The gates of the city were closed against him; and his hopes were dashed in December by the death of the dauphin Louis – a young man with a reputation for indolence and self-indulgence who had nevertheless exerted himself in the search for a lasting settlement with the duke, to whose daughter he was married. A year earlier, Louis had attempted to forbid 'the use on either side of injurious or slanderous terms such as "Burgundian" or "Armagnac"'. But now that the dauphin was dead, the count of Armagnac himself was appointed constable of France: a man of wisdom and foresight, said the monk of Saint-Denis; as cruel as Nero, exclaimed the Parisian journal-writer. And by February 1416, the latter reported in horror, he was 'in sole charge of the whole kingdom of France, in spite of all objections, for the king was still not well'.

As the Armagnac grip on government tightened, the duke of Burgundy had little choice but to withdraw his forces northward to his strongholds in Flanders and Artois. His castle at Hesdin, thirty miles west of Arras, lay only seven miles from the field at Azincourt where the English had killed his brothers, and where the Armag-nacs – he believed – had failed to defend France. Hesdin was not only a fortress and a ducal residence but a curiosity, housing a suite of rooms filled with ingenious contraptions, finely wrought

automata and galumphing practical jokes. Visitors to the castle's
gallery might be distracted by a misshapen reflection in a distort-
ing mirror, only to find themselves drenched in jets of water trig-
gered by a footfall or squirted from an innocently impassive statue.
Those who avoided the buffets of a mechanical contrivance that
dealt unexpected blows to the head and shoulders at the gallery's
exit found a room filled with rain and snow, thunder and lightning,
'as if from the sky itself', and beyond that a wooden figure of a
hermit, an uncanny presence that became truly unnerving when it
began to speak.

This cabinet of wonders had been part of the fabric of the castle
at Hesdin for more than a hundred years. By the spring of 1416,
however, John of Burgundy could have been forgiven for thinking
that life was beginning to imitate artifice. The gathering of inter-
national opinion at the Council of the Church in Constance was fast
becoming a hall of mirrors: every theological and political dispute
in Europe was reflected there – often in ludicrous disproportion, at
least in relation to the council's ostensible task of seeking an end to
the long-running schism in the papacy. The delegates sent by the
Armagnac government in Paris expended a great deal of energy in
the attempt to deny any kind of hearing to their English adversaries, but their assault on their French enemy, the duke of Burgundy,
was equally vitriolic. The formidable chancellor of the university
of Paris, an eminent theologian named Jean Gerson, railed against
the justification of the murder of the duke of Orléans proposed in
1407 by Jean Petit, demanding that it now be formally condemned
with the full weight of the Church's authority; but the duke of Burgundy had sent a delegation of his own to the council, and his men
– led by the bishop of Arras, with the support of Pierre Cauchon,
another Paris-trained theologian, and as passionate a Burgundian
as Gerson was an Armagnac – railed back, meeting every attack
with a blistering compound of argument, bribery and barely disguised threats.

While the ecclesiastics wrangled, Duke John tested his footing on uncertain ground by entering into a diplomatic dance with the 'elect of God' himself, Henry of England. In July 1416 duke and king agreed a treaty by which they promised not to make war against one another in the duke's northern territories of Picardy, Flanders and Artois, and a face-to-face meeting in English-held Calais was planned for the autumn. The situation was so delicate and the lack of trust so grave that elaborate arrangements were put in place to guarantee the duke's safety. On 5 October, he left his town of Saint-Omer to arrive at Gravelines, near Calais, at low tide, where the river Aa flowed into the sea as a shallow stream. With his household men and an armed escort, he took up position on one bank of the river; on the other, similarly attended, was the duke of Gloucester, the English king's youngest brother. After a moment, both men advanced, until their horses stood side by side in the middle of the water. The two dukes shook hands and exchanged the kiss of peace, before Humphrey of Gloucester rode on, a lavishly entertained hostage, to Saint-Omer, while John of Burgundy made his way to Calais to meet the king.

By 13 October, when the exchange was effected in reverse, the duke had successfully negotiated both this ad hoc water feature and a week of English hospitality without obvious mishap. But if King Henry had hoped that their private discussions would persuade the Burgundian duke to support his divinely sanctioned claim to the throne of France, he was to be sadly disappointed. 'What kind of conclusion these enigmatic talks and exchanges had produced went no further than the king's breast or the reticence with which he kept his counsel,' reported Henry's chaplain in some frustration; '. . . the general view was that Burgundy had all this time detained our king with ambiguities and prevarications and had so left him, and that in the end, like all Frenchmen, he would be found a double-dealer, one person in public and another in private.'

The difficulty was indeed the duke's French identity, albeit not quite in the way the royal chaplain suggested. Tempting though the acquisition of such a powerful ally against his French enemies might be, and necessary though it always was to protect Anglo-Flemish trade, a military pact with England would vindicate the Armagnacs' allegations of Burgundian treachery and spell the end, once and for all, of the duke's claim to be the rightful defender of his king and country. He turned instead to a French ally who would serve to bolster that claim: the new dauphin, eighteen-year-old Jean of Touraine, who — as it happened — was married to his niece Jacqueline, heiress to the rich and strategically vital counties of Hainaut, Holland and Zeeland in the Low Countries, where the young couple lived at her father's court. In November 1416 the duke followed his inconclusive English conference at Calais with another at Valenciennes in Hainaut, and this time a definitive agreement was the result: Burgundy and Hainaut would work together to establish Dauphin Jean — naturally, with his wife's uncle of Burgundy at his side — at the head of government in Paris.

It was a good plan, but it could not survive the sudden deaths in April and May 1417 of the young dauphin and his father-in-law, the count of Hainaut. Again there was a new heir to the throne, this time the king's youngest son, fourteen-year-old Charles; but he was already in Paris with his father, at the heart of the Armagnac regime, and, unlike his dead brothers, he had no links by marriage to the Burgundian dynasty. Quite the reverse: he was betrothed to the daughter of Louis, duke of Anjou and titular king of Sicily, who, until his death in April 1417, was one of the closest confederates of the count of Armagnac and a personal enemy of the duke of Burgundy. And Charles, who had spent much of the last four years at the Angevin court under the wing of Duke Louis and his formidable duchess Yolande of Aragon, was hardly likely now to reject the political embrace of his surrogate family.

Still, John of Burgundy had regrouped before, and he could do so again. From his castle at Hesdin, he issued an open letter to the people of France, each of the many copies signed with his own hand. The Armagnacs, he said, were 'traitors, destroyers, pillagers and poisoners'; they had murdered the king's sons Louis and Jean, and their treacherous plans lay behind the English triumph at Azincourt. Put simply, they were dedicated to the destruction of the kingdom of France. He, on the other hand, was determined to protect and preserve the French king and his people, a 'holy, loyal and necessary task' in which he would 'persevere until death', and – in case the appeal of his manifesto were not yet sufficiently apparent – he would abolish all taxes to boot. This was no search for a settlement; this, it was clear, was war.

As spring turned into summer, and summer into autumn, Burgundian forces moved into towns and cities around Paris: Troyes to the south-east, Reims to the east, Amiens to the north, Chartres to the south-west. Some townspeople opened their gates; others tried, and failed, to hold out. By October, the noose was drawing tighter. The duke and his army were just ten miles from the capital and, as food ran short and prices rose, 'Paris was now suffering extremely', noted the despairing journal-writer within the city's walls.

To strengthen his white-knuckled grip on government, the count of Armagnac sought to rally his supporters behind a royal figurehead by appointing the young dauphin Charles as lieutenant-general of his father's kingdom. But two could play at that game. Charles's mother, Queen Isabeau, had once been so closely associated with the dead duke of Orléans in the attempt to rule on behalf of her distracted and unstable husband that – as so often happened when female hands touched the reins of power – breathless whispers of innuendo had begun to curl around her reputation. Since then, however, her attempts to preserve some neutral ground on which her husband and sons might stand had provoked growing hostility within the embattled Armagnac regime, and in April 1417 the count of Armagnac had sent her into political exile at Tours, more than a hundred miles from the capital. That, it turned out, was a mistake. When John of Burgundy arrived at her gates in the first week of November, she had no option left but to welcome him — murderer of the duke of Orléans though he was — as a liberator and a protector. Now the duke of Burgundy could draw on the authority of the queen to speak for her husband, the king, while the count of Armagnac could draw on the authority of the dauphin as the heir to his father's throne. France, in effect, had two governments, each committed to the obliteration of the other.

And while they fought, Henry of England slipped through the open door behind them. By January 1418, as Burgundian troops pushed westward into Rouen, the capital of Normandy, the rest of the duchy was being quietly dismembered by the return of the English invaders. Henry had moved inland from the coast with characteristically inexorable purpose, taking the great castle and town of Caen and with it Bayeux, then Alençon, Argentan and Falaise. And almost the greatest shock of this violent assault was that — little more than two years after the wretched day of Azincourt — it no longer seemed the worst of the horrors France had to face. 'Some people who had come to Paris from Normandy, having escaped from the English by paying ransom or some other way,' reported the Parisian in his journal, 'had then been captured by the Burgundians and then a mile or so further on had been captured yet again by the French' — that is, the Armagnacs — 'and had been as brutally and as cruelly treated by them as if by Saracens. These men, all honest merchants, reputable men, who had been in the hands of all three and had bought their freedom, solemnly affirmed on oath that the English had been kinder to them than the Burgundians had, and the Burgundians a hundred times kinder than the troops from Paris, as regards food, ransom, physical suffering, and imprisonment, which had astonished them, as it must all good Christians . . .'

The greatest of all good Christians, Pope Martin V — newly installed by the Council of Constance — sent special envoys in May to treat for peace, but John of Burgundy was not interested in peace when victory was within his grasp. He paid lip service to the cardinals' mission, but his attention was elsewhere: his siege of Paris was about to bear bloody fruit. In the rain-swept darkness of the early hours of 29 May, Burgundian sympathisers within the blockaded capital opened the gate of Saint-Germain-des-Près to a detachment of Burgundian men-at-arms. They had surprise as well as deadly intent on their side, and they were brutally effective. Some seized control of the Hôtel Saint-Pol, the royal residence in the east of the city, and with it the bewildered person of the king. Others hunted down the count of Armagnac and his captains, to put them in chains. By the early afternoon, there could be no doubt that Paris was theirs. For years it had been politic to wear a white sash, the symbol of the Armagnac confederacy, in the city's streets. Now thousands of Parisians daubed or chalked their clothes with the Burgundian saltire – the diagonal cross of St Andrew, one of the duke's badges – to demonstrate their support for their new ruler, or to ward off dangerous accusations of Armagnac collaboration.

'God save the king, the dauphin, and peace!' the Burgundian troops had cried. God had given them the king, but peace was not, it seemed, part of His plan. 'Paris was in an uproar', reported the journal-writer; 'the people took up their arms much faster than the soldiers did.' This was the chance, at last, for those who hated the Armagnacs – those who supported the duke of Burgundy, or resented the oppressions of Armagnac rule, or loathed the count and his captains as 'foreigners' from the south – to take their revenge. The city turned on itself, and in the streets bludgeoned corpses lay heaped, stripped almost naked ('like sides of bacon – a dreadful thing'), their clotting blood washed into the gutters by the pouring rain. Worse was to come. Two weeks later, false alarms at the city gates roused the mob to new fear, and a new fury. They broke into the prisons, mutilating and killing all those they found inside, or lighting up the night by torching any building from which they found their entry barred. Among those who died – his body later identified not by his disfigured face, but by the cell in which he had slept – was the captive count of Armagnac. A band of flesh had been hacked from his torso, from shoulder to hip, in savage mockery of the sash his partisans had worn so proudly.

It was another month before the city was quiet enough for the duke of Burgundy to stage his own triumphant arrival, with Queen Isabeau at his side. Their cavalcade was greeted by crowds who wept, cheered and called '*Noël!*', the traditional cry of celebration and welcome. At last, king and capital were in Duke John's hands, along with the power they represented. But the brightness of this new Burgundian dawn, glittering with the sharpened steel of the plane-engraved lances carried by the duke's soldiers, was shadowed by two menacing clouds. The English were on the march: by the end of July their ominous advance had brought them to the walls of Burgundian-held Rouen, France's second city and the key to upper Normandy. The presence of England's army on French soil had once exerted useful diversionary pressure on France's Armagnac government, but now that the duke himself ruled in the name of the king, he could not afford to be complacent in the face of this growing threat. And the uncomfortable truth was that one vital component of the royal authority he claimed to represent still eluded his grasp. As Burgundian troops had stormed into the sleeping city on 29 May, Armagnac loyalists led by the provost of Paris, a former servant of Louis of Orléans named Tanguy du Châtel, had spirited fifteen-year-old Dauphin Charles away in his nightclothes.

Duke John could reassure himself, of course, that Charles was young and inexperienced, and, with only the stricken rump of the Armagnac regime left at his disposal, he could not match the grandeur of Burgundy's resources. The dauphin was surrounded still by a coterie of loyal supporters: not only Tanguy du Châtel, but men such as Robert le Maçon, his chancellor, and Jean Louvet ('one of the worst Christians in the world', said the Parisian journal-writer) – former servants, respectively, of his prospective mother-in-law, Yolande of Aragon, and his mother, Queen Isabeau. These counsellors were shrewd, ambitious and driven, but among their number were no princes of the blood, ready to rally their *pays* to his cause. With the count of Armagnac so violently dispatched to join the dead of Azincourt, and the dukes of Bourbon and Orléans still prisoners in England, Charles could look little further among the front ranks of the nobility than to the latter's younger brother, the count of Vertus, and his illegitimate half-brother Jean, known, with respectful acknowledgement of his lineage, as the Bastard of Orléans. And, limited in leadership as the dauphin's cause undoubtedly was, it was limited too in cold, hard cash. Thanks to John of Burgundy's show-stealing promise to abolish taxation, the dauphin could hardly attempt to levy the sums required to raise a great army without haemorrhaging support he could not afford to lose.

But his cause was not lost. He could turn, always, to the deep pockets and the formidable political brain of the woman who had become a mentor as well as a second mother to him: Yolande of Aragon, the dowager duchess of Anjou, whose daughter Marie was to be his wife, and whose young sons, the new duke Louis and nine-year-old René, were his companions and friends. With her backing, the dauphin established himself a little more than a hundred miles south of Paris in the city of Bourges, the capital of the duchy of Berry that he had inherited after the death in 1416 of his aged great-uncle – and now, of necessity rather than choice, the new capital of Armagnac France.

It was a motley approximation of a royal court, with a hurriedly organised *parlement* at Poitiers and exchequer at Bourges to mirror those in Burgundian Paris, and at its head a fifteen-year-old boy calling himself the 'regent of France'. But there could be no doubt how much it mattered. However loudly the duke of Burgundy claimed to be the loyal counsellor of the king, and however firmly the queen supported the Burgundian regime, the dauphin refused to accept that a government led by Duke John was anything other than a treasonable usurpation. The unhappy fact was that, while the daily reality of conflict between Armagnacs and Burgundians simmered in towns and cities across the country, the indissoluble sovereignty of France's most Christian king had been raggedly torn into three. The duke of Burgundy dominated the north and the east; the dauphin controlled the centre and the south; and all the while Henry of England – who, like his royal predecessors, already held Gascony in the south-west – continued his relentless advance across Normandy into the heart of the kingdom.

In January 1419, after a five-month siege, the English finally starved Rouen into submission, and two weeks later Henry's forces were at Mantes, only thirty miles from Paris. 'No one did anything about it', noted the journal-writer, matter-of-fact in his misery, 'because all the French lords were angry with each other, because the dauphin was at odds with his father on account of the duke of Burgundy, who was with the king, and all the other princes of the blood royal had been taken prisoner by the English king at the battle of Azincourt . . .' This Parisian remained stalwartly hostile to the Armagnacs, but his faith in the duke of Burgundy had not survived his recent experience of Burgundian rule. 'So the kingdom of France went from bad to worse . . . And this was entirely, or almost entirely, the fault of the duke of Burgundy, who was the slowest man in the world in everything that he did . . .' In fact, by the time news arrived of the fall of Rouen, Duke John had already left his troops to hold the beleaguered capital while he removed the king and queen to the greater safety of the town of Provins, fifty miles from Paris in the opposite direction from the English army's approach.

It seemed possible, now, that France was not just broken, but lost. The kingdom was ancient – but perhaps not eternal, and certainly not immutable. It had, after all, changed shape before, its frontiers ebbing and flowing with the cross-currents of inter-national diplomacy and the rip tides of war. Kings of England had been instrumental in that process already, and might be again; and now a duke of Burgundy whose powers were not confined by France's borders exerted a new and unpredictable gravitational pull. By the summer of 1419, the rival forces wrenching and tearing at the body politic had reached a jittery, precarious impasse. Like wrestlers grappling in search of a winning hold, envoys embraced at summits convened in all possible combinations: the king of England and the duke of Burgundy; the duke of Burgundy and the dauphin; the dauphin and the king of England. Henry hoped that he had won John as an ally to his cause, only to find that Charles had agreed a temporary truce with the man Armagnac propaganda had previously dubbed the 'dearest and well-loved lieutenant' of 'Lucifer, king of hell'.

The forty-eight-year-old duke and the sixteen-year-old dauphin came face to face three times in the first half of July, but their publicly declared promises – that they would join hands to resist the English, and henceforth govern France together as friends – proved as insubstantial as their smiles; meanwhile the crashing thunderstorms that lashed the country with rain and great hailstones were seen by many (said the monk of Saint-Denis) as a sign that these ill-starred negotiations would come to nothing. It was not until the end of the month – when King Henry's troops stormed Pontoise, less than twenty miles from Paris, and much too close for comfort – that minds were concentrated and another personal conference arranged, this time for September at Montereau-Fault-Yonne, south-east of the capital.

The pressing concern for security amid the heightened threat of the English advance meant that the duke of Burgundy now faced another diplomatic meeting in the middle of a river. At Montereau a many-arched bridge spanned the waters where the river Yonne gave into the Seine. On one bank stood the town, held by the dauphin; on the other, the castle, which Charles now made over to the duke of Burgundy as a gesture of goodwill, to facilitate an encounter on which the future of France might stand or fall. By swearing an oath to do one another no harm, and then advancing from opposite sides onto the bridge with only ten men each for company, both the duke and the dauphin could be reassured that their counsels would not be overheard, nor ambushed by some hidden army. The dauphin and his advisers – cautious and painstaking hosts, who had had to work hard to persuade Duke John to accept their invitation to Montereau – gave meticulous thought to the practicalities of the meeting. A stone tower already stood halfway along the bridge, between castle and town, but now a new wooden enclosure was constructed on the town side of the tower, within which the two deputations could safely speak without fear of attack from outside.

By the afternoon of Sunday 10 September preparations were complete. Under the crisp autumn sky, the duke of Burgundy – sleek in his magnificence, hooded eyes unreadable – took the winding path from the castle onto the bridge, past the tower and into the newly built palisade, the gate clicking shut as the last of his men was ushered inside, a key turning in the lock behind them. Ahead stood the short, scrawny figure of the dauphin, an ungainly adolescent who had not inherited the good looks of either of his royal parents, and with him ten of his most senior attendants, including Jean Louvet and Tanguy du Châtel, the latter a familiar face from the frequent embassies of recent weeks. As the duke knelt, doffing his black velvet hat in obeisance to his prince, he could hear the water moving softly all around, but he could see only the craftsmanship of the carpenters who had enclosed the bridge with wooden walls. Did he think of his cabinet of curiosities at Hesdin? The moment was fleeting. Then the buffet struck: the steel blade of a war axe, driven deep into his skull.

There was blood, pooling around the falling body of John of Burgundy, dripping in great gouts from the axe in the hands of Tanguy du Châtel. In blind shock, in churning panic, the duke's counsellors started forward, only to find themselves caught by soldiers pouring through the open door at the far end of the palisade. In their ears, voices shrill with hate shouted, 'Kill! Kill!' – and as they were bundled away they saw, in an uncomprehending blur, a man kneeling over the prone figure of their lord, and the bright blade of a sword plunging down. Then, suddenly, came a roar of explosions, as Armagnac troops concealed within the stone tower on the bridge turned their guns on the bewildered Burgundians in Montereau's castle, waiting in vain for the duke's return.

It was an assassination more precisely planned and more ruthlessly executed than the murder of the duke of Orléans in the streets of Paris twelve years earlier. And as the mutilated corpse was carried away from the bridge – stripped of its finery and blood-smeared, with one hand dangling, almost severed, in a mess of mangled tendons – it was clear that the consequences of this duke's death would be still more terrible. For the veteran Tanguy du Châtel it was an eye for an eye, a reckoning at last for the loss of his former master. For the teenage dauphin, who had been just four years old when Louis of Orléans died, it was the striking down of the devil's lieutenant, the man who had raised war in the kingdom for as long as the young prince could remember. But this killing, in one bloody moment, had irretrievably altered the essence of the conflict. Now – however subtle the diplomacy between the lords of France, and however implacable the onslaught of the English – there could be no hope of reconciliation between Armagnac and Burgundian.

In public, the dauphin acknowledged no conspiracy against the duke. Instead, he explained, the first sword drawn on the bridge had been that of John of Burgundy himself, or perhaps – he later remembered – the duke's attendant Archambaud de Foix, lord of Navailles. (The princely finger was pointed at de Foix only after he had died of head wounds sustained during the mêlée, and was therefore conveniently unable to contest the accusation.) It was this unprovoked Burgundian aggression that had caused the sudden outburst of violence, to the dauphin's utter consternation, and it was only thanks to the quick thinking of his loyal servants that — God be praised — he had not been taken hostage. But no amount of wide-eyed protestation — nor the suggestion to his 'dear and well-beloved brother', the duke's son and heir Philip, that he should remain calm in the face of these unfortunate events — could disguise the fact that John of Burgundy had died under the dauphin's safe-conduct, at the hands of the dauphin's men.

And that, for the Burgundians, changed everything. Two hundred miles away in the Flemish town of Ghent, twenty-three-year-old Philip, the new duke, was overwhelmed with 'extreme grief and distress' at his father's death, his counsellors reported. For Duke John's widow, Margaret of Bavaria, her husband was a Christ-like figure, entering the palisade on the bridge to be betrayed by Tanguy du Châtel's Judas. Not everyone would be prepared to endorse that particular image, perhaps; but in Burgundian eyes there could be no doubt that the dauphin — the heir to the throne of the most Christian king — was guilty of perjury and murder. As a result, Philip of Burgundy was confronted with a decision more fateful, more extreme, than any his father had faced. The hapless king, with Queen Isabeau at his side, remained under Burgundian protection at Troyes, ninety miles south-east of Paris, 'where they are with their poor retinue like fugitives', said the journal-writer bleakly. But Charles the Mad and Well-Beloved was already past his fiftieth birthday — and after him, what then? There were two claimants to his crown: an Armagnac dauphin, or an English king. And for Philip of Burgundy, after Montereau, that was no choice at all.

Still it took time to accept that the next monarch of France might be an English invader. As autumn faded into the beginnings of a bitter winter, Duke Philip remained in the north, in Flanders and Artois, deliberating with his counsellors and arranging a magnificent service for his father's soul in the abbey church of Saint-Vaast in Arras. From Dijon, his indefatigable mother marshalled the resources of the two Burgundies to gather all possible evidence of the crime perpetrated against her husband, and to lobby the great powers of Europe to support her quest for justice. Meanwhile, as the marauding English devastated the countryside to the north of Paris, the dauphin did what he could to exert pressure of his own on the Burgundian-held capital, declaring his commitment to peace even while his troops plundered and burned the lands to the south.

It was not enough. By the spring of 1420, both the Parisian journal-writer and the monk of the abbey of Saint-Denis, four miles north of the city walls, were convinced that the English were the lesser of the two evils that menaced the kingdom. Duke Philip of Burgundy agreed. Negotiations – conducted in a series of taut, delicate exchanges between the duke at Arras, the queen at Troyes, the *parlement* of Paris and the English in Rouen – had taken months, but finally, on 21 May, the sovereign powers of England and France came together in the incense-clouded cathedral of Troyes for the sealing of a treaty.

That sacred space bore witness to the terrible force of the divine will: half a century earlier the spire that reached towards heaven from the crossing of the nave had been smashed into rubble by a tornado, and two decades after that a bolt of lightning had made an inferno of the wooden roof. But still the cathedral endured, an architectural testament to the possibility that, with the blessing of the Almighty, restoration might follow destruction. Not, perhaps, for King Charles of France himself, whose unsound mind had evaded all attempts to make it whole; but it seemed at last that his war-torn kingdom might find a new future. At the high altar, amid the press of lords and prelates, retainers and servants, stood France's enemy-turned-saviour: Henry of England, scarred and self-possessed, with his eldest brother Thomas, duke of Clarence, by his side. Before him was the majesty of the French crown, as embodied by the queen, Isabeau, and the young duke of Burgundy, a loyal counsellor ready to speak for his faltering king. Both sides knew the terms of the peace which had brought them together, but this was the solemn moment at which those provisions became inescapably binding.

Charles, by the grace of God king of France, recognised Henry of England as the rightful heir to his throne. Because of his own unfortunate indisposition – gracefully acknowledged in the ventriloquised text of the treaty – Henry would take control of the kingdom's government with immediate effect: he was now France's regent as well as its heir. He would marry the king's daughter Catherine, their union a physical incarnation of this perpetual peace, and their descendants would wear a double crown as monarchs of the twin realms of England and France, which would thus be joined forever in concord and tranquillity.

And so, not quite five years after the horror of Azincourt, the English king was clasped in the political embrace of the sovereign lord of the French as *notre très-cher fils*, 'our dearest son'. The adolescent who until this moment would have claimed that title went almost unmentioned: the 'horrible and enormous crimes' of the 'so-called dauphin' were such, the treaty declared, that King Charles and his dear sons Henry of England and Philip of Burgundy (the latter being already the husband of another of the royal daughters of France) now swore to have no more dealings with him. Instead, Henry – acting in the name of the most Christian king as heir and regent of France – would do everything in his power to restore to their rightful allegiance those rebellious parts of the kingdom that still held for the party 'commonly called that of the dauphin, or Armagnac'. Royal seals were pressed into soft wax; and, as preparations began for the wedding to come, heralds set out to inform the French people of the identity of their next monarch, and to demand oaths of their loyalty.

Truly, it seemed, God had spoken.

2

Like another Messiah

This was not how it was supposed to be. Charles of Valois, the seventeen-year-old *dauphin de Vienne*, knew that he was the heir to France. He had been the last born of his father's sons, but by the will of God he now stood as the next successor to an unbroken line of illustrious kings reaching back to the glories of Charlemagne, and before him to the saintly Clovis, the first of France's Christian monarchs.

It was to Clovis, almost a thousand years before, that God had sent the Holy Ampulla, a miraculous vial containing the sacred oil with which every *roi très-chrétien* was anointed during his coronation – a sacramental rite held by long tradition at Reims, where the Ampulla itself was guarded with the utmost reverence. It was Clovis, too, the dauphin knew – or had it been Charlemagne? – who first rode into battle bearing the *oriflamme*, a banner of vermilion silk hung from a golden lance which rallied the people of France to fight to the death whenever the kingdom was in mortal danger.

And the protective powers of the *oriflamme* were more than simply military, since this hallowed flag had been a gift from St Denis, the holy man who had converted pagan Gaul to Christianity. Exactly who Denis had been, and when he had brought the gospel to France, were questions of some complexity and much learned debate, but the answers mattered less than the evident fact of his support for the kingdom and his special relationship with its king. The *oriflamme* itself was kept in the saint's own abbey, just north of Paris, ready for when the king should have need of it, along with the priceless regalia that were transported to Reims whenever a coronation took place: Charlemagne's imperial crown and his great sword, called Joyeuse, as well as the crown of the dauphin's great-great-great-great-great-grandfather Louis IX, the crusading king who had been recognised as a saint within three decades of his death. His circlet – fittingly, for this blessed monarch – contained a fragment of Christ's crown of thorns and a lock of the Saviour's hair.

St Louis himself, like all the kings of France of the last two hundred years, was buried in the abbey that belonged to St Denis. From there, these two patron saints of the French crown watched over Louis's royal descendants in nearby Paris, the capital founded long ago by noble Trojans fleeing the sack of their own city, that had since become – in wisdom, might and holiness – a new Athens, Rome and Jerusalem. And from Paris, in turn, the French king watched over the chosen people of a holy land, a kingdom full of clerics, scholars, relics and saints.

All of this was the dauphin's birthright. Yet now, it seemed, his inheritance was being ripped from his fingers. The fire-red blazon of the *oriflamme* had been trampled into the mud at Azincourt, where the sacrifice of French lives had brought only defeat and humiliation, not God-given victory. Paris, the pillar of faith and the seat of the French crown, had fallen into the grasping hands of Burgundian traitors. The consecrated precincts of the abbey of Saint-Denis had welcomed Henry of England – an upstart and a ruthless predator whose device of a fox's brush, elegantly embroidered, could not disguise the fact that his teeth and claws were sticky with French blood – on his journey to Troyes; and in the cathedral there he had been greeted by the dauphin's royal parents as their newly adopted son.

Meanwhile, the dauphin himself stood accused of murder most foul. Henry of England and Philip of Burgundy had agreed, in a bilateral treaty five months before Troyes, that they would work together to ensure that Charles and his accomplices were appropriately punished for their evident crimes. Even his own father – or those who now spoke on the distracted king's behalf – had issued letters patent proclaiming the fact of the prince's guilt and declaring that, as a result, he no longer had the right to use the title of dauphin. Instead, he was simply 'Charles the ill-advised, who calls himself "of France"'.

The dauphin himself, of course, did not acknowledge that he bore any form of responsibility for the death of John of Burgundy. But even if he had, he would not have accepted that disinheritance was its necessary consequence. *Monseigneur le dauphin*, declared an Armagnac pamphlet written in 1420 in response to the treaty of Troyes, was the only true heir of the king and the kingdom. The treaty was therefore no peace, but instead a fount of discord, war, murder, plunder, bloodshed and horrible sedition – an act of tyrannical usurpation that was 'most damnable, most unjust and abominable, and contrary to the honour of God and faith and religion . . .'

Still, in order to stop that usurpation in its tracks, some improvisation might be required. If the guiding light of the *oriflamme* had dimmed, then the dauphin's army would fight instead under a banner depicting the golden fleurs-de-lis of France on a background of celestial blue, a venerable flag laden with meaning – the lily standing for the purity of the Virgin, its three petals for the Trinity, and the whole for the greatness of the French crown – which had also, handily, been presented to Clovis by an emissary from heaven. Some people said that it was St Denis who had brought the fleurs-de-lis to the holy king, but now that Denis had faltered in his role as guardian of the kingdom, it seemed more likely that the gift had come from the hands of the archangel Michael, God's own standard-bearer, whose abbey at Mont-Saint-Michel in Normandy was even now holding out against the English invaders. And so the dauphin ordered two new standards to be prepared for his army, each showing the heavenly knight St Michael with his sword unsheathed to kill the devil that writhed before him in the form of a serpent.

The naked blade of a sword, clasped in an armed hand, was also the dauphin's personal device, painted delicately onto the silken banner of white, gold and blue that hung from his lance. But in practice, despite the money that he lavished on suits of golden armour, the prince could not lead his soldiers himself. It was not just that he was 'not a warlike man', as the Burgundian chronicler Georges Chastellain later remarked, noting his puny frame and unsteady gait. It was also that he was irreplaceable. Though the newly married Henry of England had, as yet, no son to succeed him, he could rally his troops on the battlefield in the knowledge that he had three royal brothers – the dukes of Clarence, Bedford and Gloucester – fighting at his side, ready to take his place if he fell. But the brothers of the dauphin Charles were all dead; the runt of the Valois litter was now the last hope of the Armagnac cause. As a result, when the next confrontation came, the Armagnac army would have to look elsewhere for its captain.

While the English and the Burgundians had been occupied with the making of their diabolical compact to deprive him of his inheritance, the dauphin and his troops had moved together through the south of the kingdom to secure the obedience of these Armagnac lands with a show of strength. But the ceremonies at Troyes – the sealing of the Anglo-Burgundian treaty, and the wedding of Henry of England and Catherine of France a little less than two weeks later – did not keep the English king from the field for long. On the day after the triumph of his marriage, the knights of England and Burgundy proposed a tournament in celebration; instead, the king ordered that they should leave immediately for Sens, forty miles west of Troyes, where, he said, 'we may all tilt and joust and prove our daring and courage' – not in the lists, but by besieging the Armagnacs.

A week later, Sens had fallen. A fortnight after that, Henry's army stormed into Montereau-Fault-Yonne. There, the mutilated body of John the Fearless was exhumed from its shallow grave in the parish church, and reverently laid with salt and spices in a lead coffin for its journey back to the dead duke's capital at Dijon. Then the English and Burgundian troops marched north-west to the fortified walls of Melun, a key staging-post in the campaign to sweep the Armagnacs out of the region immediately to the south of Burgundian Paris. But the soldiers of the Armagnac garrison dug in their heels, and by the middle of July it was clear that Melun would not so easily be taken. Now, if ever, the Armagnac cause needed an inspirational military leader to come to the town's rescue and put a stop to the English king's inexorable advance – and the seventeen-year-old dauphin knew just what to do. He ordered himself two new suits of gilded armour, mustered an army of fifteen thousand men and put his cousin, the count of Vertus, at the head of it.

At twenty-four, Philippe of Vertus carried the weight of his world on his young shoulders. His elder brother, the duke of Orléans, was still under lock and key in England, so it was to Philippe that the responsibility of safeguarding the family's future had fallen. And now his prince, the dauphin, required him to lead the army that would rid France of English invaders and Burgundian traitors alike. The count had made his base at Jargeau, ten miles east of Orléans, and the dauphin joined him there in early August, ten thousand newly stitched pennons fluttering in the breeze above the heads of their massed troops. But by the end of the month, they had made no move to advance. The count, it emerged, was unwell. On 1 September, he succumbed to his illness – and all prospect of stemming the Anglo-Burgundian tide died with him. The dauphin immediately turned tail, retreating southward to his luxurious palace of Mehun-sur-Yèvre near Bourges, and six weeks later the town of Melun – with no hope, now, of rescue – was starved into surrender.

The stage was set for the triumphant English king to take possession of his new French capital. On 1 December 1420, Henry of England, Philip of Burgundy and the pitiful figure of Charles of

France – 'our French lords', as the journal-writer approvingly called them – rode into Paris. It was a hard winter, and food was so scarce that beggar children were dying in the streets, but still the city's hungry inhabitants turned out in their thousands to welcome the royal procession, many dressed in red, the colour of the cross of Henry's heavenly patron, St George. The next day it was the turn of the queens to make their magnificent entrance, Henry's wife Catherine riding through the Porte Saint-Antoine between her mother, Queen Isabeau, and her newly acquired sister-in-law, the duchess of Clarence, while cheering Parisians toasted the coming of peace in the wine that flowed day and night from the city's conduits.

Nineteen-year-old Catherine had been at her husband's side at the siege of Melun, where – in the only nod to romance this battle-hardened bridegroom was prepared to make – he had ordered musicians to play for her every evening as the sun went down. She was with him in Paris when, two days before Christmas, he and her father sat on the same judicial bench to hear a Burgundian demand for justice against her brother, 'the so-called dauphin', and his accomplices in the murder of John the Fearless. The dauphin was summoned to answer the charges before 6 January; to no one's surprise, he failed to appear, and was sentenced in his absence to exile from the realm and disinheritance from the crown. And by then, Catherine and Henry were on their way to England to show the new queen to her people, and to raise more money and men for the final defeat of the Armagnac rebels.

The dauphin, however, had other ideas. He had lost his cousin of Vertus, but his protector St Michael – to whose shrine at Mont-Saint-Michel, still holding out against English siege, he had just sent a pilgrim's offering – would provide him with new champions. The Burgundian traitors might have the help of the English, France's ancient enemy, in their attempt to dismember the kingdom, but the dauphin could call on France's ancient ally, the Scots, who had recognised in him the true line of French sovereignty. For more than a century, Scotland had taken every opportunity to support France in its conflicts with England: whenever English armies moved south across the Channel to ravage French lands, Scots soldiers had launched raids across England's northern border, hoping to inflict debilitating wounds while English backs were turned. Now, with France convulsed on itself, the Scots saw their chance to fight the English at a safer distance from their own frontier, side by side with the Armagnac French.

The first few hundred Scots soldiers – archers, in the English style, as well as men-at-arms – had arrived in France in the spring of 1419. But by the end of that year a major force of six or seven thousand troops had made landfall at La Rochelle under the command of John Stewart, earl of Buchan, and his brother-in-law Archibald Douglas, earl of Wigtown, along with other captains including Buchan's distant relative and namesake, Sir John Stewart of Darnley. This Scottish army had not been sent by the Scots king, James I; he had been captured by the English as a boy of eleven, fourteen years earlier, and the governor of the kingdom during the long years of his absence – Buchan's father, the duke of Albany – had no particular enthusiasm for the prospect of curtailing his own power by securing the king's release. The English response to the arrival of Scottish troops on French soil was to summon the captive King James to join the English army. The dauphin's forces therefore found themselves confronting not one but three kings – Henry of England, the ailing Charles of France and the prisoner James of Scotland – in order that the Armagnacs and the Scots could be accused of treachery in bearing arms against their own sovereigns. This grandstanding from the moral high ground, always Henry's favoured terrain, had dangerous implications for troops who could expect no mercy in defeat if they were deemed to have broken their allegiance. But the Scots remained unmoved, and by February 1421 another four thousand men had sailed from Scotland to join the contingent under Buchan's command.

Marching against them was not Henry himself, who was by now back in England for the first time in more than three years, but the lieutenant-general he had left behind, his brother Thomas, duke of Clarence. Clarence was eager to seize this chance to emerge from his older brother's shadow as a hero of the war, and – apparently looking for a fight in which he might cover himself in glory to rival Henry's – he led a detachment of the Anglo-Burgundian forces south from Normandy into Anjou. But there, on 22 March, just outside the town of Baugé, he encountered the fresh troops newly arrived from Scotland, with Buchan and Wigtown at their head. Clarence charged into the attack, neither listening to his captains' advice nor waiting for his archers to catch up – and found himself overwhelmed in a bloody rout. He died on the field with hundreds of his men; and the Scottish earls wrote in exultation to invite the dauphin to advance immediately into Normandy 'because, with God's help, all is yours'.

At last, divine favour had been restored to the true heir of the most Christian king. The dauphin, giddy with euphoria, hurried to give thanks in the great cathedral at Poitiers, and set out the same day to meet the victorious Scots at Tours. Until now, these inter- lopers from a tiny kingdom far to the north had been received with disdain by some at the dauphin's court: 'drunken, mutton-eating fools' was the phrase whispered, with lips curled, behind elegant French hands. 'What do you think now?' the dauphin demanded after news came of the triumph at Baugé, one Scottish chronicler proudly reported; and 'as if struck on their foreheads by a hammer, they had no answer'. Instead, the earl of Buchan 'seemed to have arisen like another Messiah among and with them'. Within days, this saviour of France had been named constable of the kingdom – the highest military post in the gift of the crown, which gave Buchan authority second only to that of the dauphin himself. And the dauphin ordered some more armour – this time in the Scottish fashion – and another banner of St Michael, and prepared for an assault that would surely drive the English and their Burgundian allies from France for ever.

With the image of the warrior archangel borne before them, the Armagnacs and the Scots pressed northward into Normandy and then turned east, in the direction of Paris; by the beginning of July the dauphin's army was camped outside the walls of Chartres, just fifty miles south-west of the embattled capital. They were poised, at last, for a climactic confrontation with the traitors and invaders who had so grievously usurped the birthright of France's heir. But amid the exhilaration of their triumph at Baugé, they had forgotten, for a joyous, fleeting instant, that defeating the duke of Clarence was one thing; facing his brother, the victor of Azincourt, quite another. After almost six months' absence, Henry had returned to France in June, with fresh soldiers at his back. He arrived in Paris on 4 July, and the very next day – citing sickness among his troops, and the difficulty of feeding an army in the field after an exceptionally long and bitter winter – the dauphin began a southward retreat to the safety of his castles in the valley of the Loire and his court at Bourges.

The hunger and disease were real, but so, unmistakably, was the loss of nerve. Military operations would continue under Buchan's command, but the moment had been lost – and when manoeuvres resumed, the dauphin would no longer be there to witness them. Meanwhile, the serene and implacable elect of God, Henry of England, moved to besiege Meaux, a heavily fortified and strategically vital Armagnac town twenty-five miles east of Paris, whose garrison had long been a thorn in the capital's side.

This time, there would be no musical interludes as night fell on the siege: Henry had come back without his wife, Catherine. Instead, he brought news to strike dread into her brother's heart. She was carrying a baby with Plantagenet and Valois blood mingled in its veins. The treaty of Troyes would soon be made flesh in an heir to the twin thrones of England and Burgundian France; and though the dauphin might be safe, for now, in his refuge behind the protective waters of the Loire, the glorious promise of the victory at Baugé was fading like the sunlight as summer gave way to a sodden autumn.

With rain falling from leaden skies, the besiegers at Meaux needed all their king's relentless determination to sustain them when illness took hold in the camp and food ran punishingly short. But Henry knew that God's purpose was unfolding on both sides of the Channel. He sent a messenger riding sixty miles west to the abbey of Coulombs, near Chartres, to take possession of the foreskin of Christ, a sacred relic that offered special protection for women in childbirth, so that it could be dispatched to England for the approaching confinement of his young queen. Just before Christmas, word came that this holy object had done its work. On 6 December, Catherine had given birth to a healthy boy, named Henry after his royal father.

While bells rang and bonfires were lit in the streets of Paris, the journal-writer in the city contemplated the future of the divided kingdom this infant had been born to rule. His hatred of the Armagnacs, whose treachery had caused 'these bitter troubles, this intolerable life, this accursed war', burned as fiercely as ever, but he saw little reason to celebrate. The cause of the Burgundian duke and the English king might be just, but peace had not come, and on every side it was the poor, betrayed by their rulers, who suffered. 'It is not one year or two,' he wrote in despair, 'it is fourteen or fifteen since this dismal dance began . . .'

That much the dauphin knew: those fourteen or fifteen years were all he could remember. But the salvation of his people – he was certain, even if they were not – lay in the vindication of the Armagnac cause. His Scots captains could not save Meaux from its fate; it fell after seven months of siege, through the grimmest of winters, in early May 1422. What he could, however, do for himself – even from the sheltering valley of the Loire – was offer a response to the dynastic threat of his nephew's birth. He was eighteen, plenty old enough to be a husband and father, and the identity of his bride had been fixed years earlier, when they were both children: Marie, the seventeen-year-old daughter of Yolande, the dowager duchess of Anjou, who had done so much to establish Armagnac power in the south, in what some now disparagingly called the 'kingdom of Bourges'. The dauphin had been encouraged by a visit the previous year from a holy hermit, Jean de Gand, who told him of a vision sent from heaven that he would wear the crown of France and father an heir to the throne. Now preparations were put in train, and in a magnificent ceremony in April 1422 the kingdom of Bourges acquired its dauphine. By the autumn, Marie was pregnant. But by then, everything had changed.

After the fall of Meaux, Henry had spent some time in Paris with his wife. They kept great state at the palace of the Louvre, dining in their jewelled crowns, while on the other side of the city her father and mother – who were still, hard though it might be to remember, the king and queen of France – were left to wander amid the gardens and galleried courtyards of the Hôtel Saint-Pol. But beneath the pomp of Henry's court, a new vulnerability became suddenly, shockingly apparent. In June, the king set out southward in blistering heat to help relieve the siege of the Burgundian town of Cosne by Armagnac forces. He never arrived. He was only twenty-five miles south of Paris when it became clear that this unyielding soldier was too weak to stay in the saddle.

Hollow-faced, Henry was carried in a litter to the castle of Vincennes, south-east of the capital. There, in the cool of the *donjon* tower that loomed against the blue summer sky, his terrified physicians found that they could do nothing to relieve his fever. The elect of God, invincible though he was in the face of the enemy, was not immune, it appeared, to the gnawing, cramping flux that had ravaged his army in the mud outside Meaux. In the will he had written when he left England for the last time fourteen months earlier, he had commended his soul to God, Christ, the Virgin and the saints, his patron St George chief among them. Now, on 26 August – as always, facing what lay ahead with lucid control – he dictated a list of the silver and gold plate he wished to bequeath to his wife Catherine and to the baby son he had never seen. He left altar hangings to the abbey of Saint-Denis outside his French capital and to the abbey of Westminster beside his English one. And on 31 August 1422, in the darkness of the early hours, Henry died.

It seemed impossible that the ferocious energy that had bent two kingdoms to his will could be so abruptly extinguished, but the shocked observers who watched the imposing cortège that bore his body north from Vincennes had no choice but to believe it. On the large lead coffin, draped in crimson cloth of gold, lay an effigy of the king himself, fashioned out of boiled leather, delicately painted and dressed in royal robes, with a golden crown on its head and orb and sceptre in its hands – an embodiment of Henry's majesty as an anointed sovereign, which endured even on this journey to the grave. The stately procession made its way first to Saint-Denis, the necropolis of the monarchs of France, and then, by water, to Rouen. There, three hundred mourners, men of England and Normandy, all dressed in black with torches blazing in their hands, attended the corpse as the tolling of church bells hung heavy in the city air, and everywhere voices were raised to sing the psalms and masses of the Office of the Dead, until the king reached Calais, and the sea, and England.

It was 5 November by the time Henry entered London for the last time. The coffin was drawn through the streets to rest for a night in the great cathedral of St Paul's, before its final journey beyond the city walls to Westminster. There, on 7 November, the requiem mass was sung. A knight dressed in Henry's exquisite armour rode through the west door of the abbey and spurred his warhorse on to the choir, where – in a startling moment of spiritual theatre – man and horse were stripped of their arms, which were offered up, symbols of the king's earthly power, at the high altar. And then, at last, Henry's mortal remains were laid to rest in the tomb he had chosen, nestling close to the shrine of Edward the Confessor, England's royal saint.

Henry of England was in his grave at Westminster, and four days later another funeral rite was enacted, for another sovereign, at Saint-Denis. On 21 October, just seven weeks after Henry's death at Vincennes, Charles of France had taken his last breath in the Hôtel Saint-Pol. For two or three days his body lay where he had died, 'the room full of lights', the journal-writer said, so that all those who wished could see him, and offer up their prayers. Then, on 11 November, he too was carried through crowded streets, with a crowned effigy dressed in ermine-lined robes lying on his coffin, for burial beside his ancestors in the hallowed vaults of France's royal abbey.

Henry had been feared, and poor, perplexed Charles had been loved. Both were succeeded by an heir who was neither: 'Henry of Lancaster, king of France and of England', as the herald proclaimed at Saint-Denis – the nine-month-old baby, son of Henry and grandson of Charles, now in the care of his nurses at Windsor Castle. In him the provisions of the treaty so carefully enacted at Troyes had been fulfilled, but with dangerous prematurity. Despite the obvious hazards of war, no one had truly expected the English king, God's own soldier, to be struck down so young and so abruptly, before even his fragile father-in-law. Now that both were gone in the space of two months, the lords on either side of the Channel who had committed themselves to the union of the two crowns were shaken to find themselves suddenly responsible for securing the rule of this double monarchy.

In England, the younger of the dead king's two surviving brothers, Humphrey, duke of Gloucester, established himself at the head of a council of nobles as protector of the realm and of the infant Henry VI. But in France it was his elder sibling, John, duke of Bedford – a steadier and more conscientious figure than either Gloucester or Thomas of Clarence who had died at Baugé – who was named regent on his nephew's behalf. Charlemagne's Joyeuse, the great sword of state of the French sovereigns, was carried upright before Bedford when he rode in procession from Saint-Denis back to Paris after the old king's funeral, in token of his new authority – 'at which the people murmured very much', reported the Parisian observer, 'but had to endure it for the time being'.

Their disquiet was prompted by the absence of Duke Philip of Burgundy, the prince of the blood whose support had made a French heir out of the English monarch. But Philip – who had been a solemn presence, in the black velvet of mourning for his murdered father, at the wedding of Henry and Catherine and their triumphal entry into the capital two years earlier – did not appear at either of the royal funerals in the autumn of 1422. His interests and ambitions, much more clearly than his father's, now lay principally in the Low Countries, where civil war had broken out over the disputed succession of his cousin Jacqueline to the counties of Hainaut, Holland and Zeeland that bordered his own rich territories of Flanders and Artois. While he was occupied there in the north, and his redoubtable mother kept a watchful eye from her court at Dijon on the fortunes of the two Burgundies in the east, his concerns within the war-torn kingdom of France centred on the protection of his own lands, rather than the quest for control in government that had consumed his father's life. The onerous task of leading the campaign to defeat the dauphin was therefore one he was happy to leave to Bedford. From this secondary position 'in the service of the king of France', as his financial officers had pointed out in 1421, he could demand that his military costs be paid by the regime in Paris; he also retained enough elbow-room to renegotiate the terms of his engagement with the Armagnac enemy should the passage of time and political circumstance require.

For now, however, the duke of Bedford was his ally – not least because Jacqueline of Hainaut had fled from her unhappy marriage to a Burgundian husband, Philip's cousin John of Brabant, into the arms of Duke Humphrey of Gloucester in England. To keep Gloucester out of the Low Countries and his inexhaustible ambition in check, Philip of Burgundy needed the help of the duke's elder brother, John of Bedford; and so, in the spring of 1423, a treaty was sealed at Amiens by which Bedford married Burgundy's favourite sister, Anne. Bedford was thirty-three, an imposingly powerful man both physically and politically, while Anne of Burgundy was just eighteen, one of four girls who were all, one ungallant observer reported, 'as plain as owls'. But she had charm, grace and an impressively quick mind, and soon, it was said, Bedford would go nowhere without her. By the same treaty, her sister Margaret married Arthur, count of Richemont, the brother of the duke of Brittany, and through these two marriages Bedford and Richemont stepped forward into the breach left in the Anglo-Burgundian front line by the sudden loss of England's warrior-king.

Supporters of the kingdom of Bourges, meanwhile, were preoccupied not simply with the practical consequences of Henry's death, but with its meaning. Armagnac chroniclers could not deny that there had been much to admire in a man who had been a brave soldier, a formidable leader and a prince whose justice was dispensed with unbending rigour; but for his life to be cut short in the midst of his triumphs, when he was just thirty-five, suggested something other than the divine mandate Henry had always claimed. Perhaps, they thought, he had been punished for disturbing the holy shrine at Meaux that held the relics of St Fiacre, whose feast day, tellingly, had been the last full day of his life.

The dauphin – whose daily routine included two or sometimes three masses, so unstinting was his devotion – knew that God's will could also be revealed to the world through the movement of His heavens. Among the gifts he had bestowed on the earl of Buchan after the victory at Baugé were the services of an astrologer named Germain de Thibouville, who (it was later reported) had immediately foretold the imminent deaths of the kings of England and France. Even for those less confident in the science of the stars than their royal master, it hardly mattered whether this was skilful prognostication or wishful thinking, now that it had come to pass. Whatever grief the dauphin felt for the father who had disowned him, France's future depended on one overriding truth: that, in the moment when Charles VI's soul had left his body, his son had become Charles VII, the new *roi très-chrétien*.

His title was proclaimed in the sumptuous surroundings of the royal chapel at Mehun-sur-Yèvre on 30 October, but his difficulty was that the crown itself remained physically out of reach. The circlets of Charlemagne and St Louis rested, as they always had, in the abbey of Saint-Denis, under the usurping power of the duke of Bedford. Although the coronation of the most Christian king could perhaps be performed in their absence, the sacred rite could only take place in the cathedral at Reims, with the holy oil of Clovis that was guarded there. And Reims – eighty miles north-east of Paris in the county of Champagne, where only a few hardy Armagnac garrisons held out in beleaguered isolation – lay beyond the current borders of the kingdom of Bourges.

In the circumstances, unction from the Holy Ampulla would have to wait. But there were, at least, other signs of God's blessing. In the last week of September, while his father languished in his final illness at the Hôtel Saint-Pol, the dauphin had set out westward from Bourges to muster the threatened defences of La Rochelle, the only seaport on the Atlantic coast that remained in Armagnac hands. There, on 11 October, he sat in state to receive his supporters in the great hall of the bishop's palace. Suddenly, with a heart-stopping lurch, the floor collapsed beneath their feet into the void of the chamber below. Amid the choking dust and splintered debris, many died and more were badly hurt – but, apart from a few scratches, the dauphin was miraculously unharmed. A fortnight later, when reports arrived of his father's death, the divine purpose for which he had been saved became clear. And the new king knew where thanks were due: he made a generous donation to the abbey of Mont-Saint-Michel to provide that each year, on the anniversary of the accident, there should be sung a mass of St Michael, 'the archangel whom we venerate and to whom we entrust the greatest confidence'. St George might fight for the English, but St Michael, the standard-bearer of heaven, would protect the true king of France. From now on, Charles and his court would put aside the white sash of the Armagnacs in favour of the white cross – not just the ancient badge of the French crown, but the emblem of St Michael himself.

Even with the archangel's help, however, it was apparent that the task of driving the English into the sea would take some time. The renewed sense of purpose within the court at Bourges was matched by the duke of Bedford's determination to defend his brother's legacy, and military operations continued with fresh energy, but to inconclusive effect. In the summer of 1423, an Armagnac army commanded by John Stewart of Darnley besieged the town of Cravant, which lay seventy miles north-east of Bourges, within the duchy of Burgundy itself. Bedford's troops were occupied elsewhere, to the north and west; but, from Dijon, Philip of Burgundy's mother sent for help from her son's allies, and on 31 July four thousand men, English and Burgundian, appeared at Cravant like lightning from the clear sky. Their effect was as deadly: Darnley's soldiers were slaughtered, and Darnley himself lost an eye in savage fighting before he was taken prisoner. If the Scots were the saviours of France, their intervention, clearly, would not always be as miraculous as it had been at Baugé. Charles quickly wrote to reassure his faithful subjects in Lyon that very few French noblemen had been party to the defeat – only Scots and Spaniards and other foreign soldiers, he said – 'so the harm is not so great'.

Smoothly dismissive words might be necessary in public to maintain confidence in his cause, but that did not mean the Scots were any less vital to his plans. Darnley had been in command at Cravant only because the earls of Buchan and Wigtown had sailed for Scotland that summer to raise more troops, and by October there was good news to report: Buchan was about to return with eight thousand men, Charles told the people of Tournai cheerfully. The recovery of Normandy was in hand, and once this new Scots army stood on French soil, he intended to defeat the traitors and rebels, reclaim his kingdom and make his way to Reims for his coronation. And in the meantime, it had pleased God to provide France with an heir. On 3 July, at Bourges, his young queen had given birth to a fine son, named Louis after France's royal saint.

Despite Cravant, then, the omens were good when Buchan made landfall at La Rochelle in the spring of 1424, bringing with him not only fresh soldiers but Wigtown's father, Archibald, earl of Douglas, a fifty-five-year-old veteran of the wars between Scotland and England, who had already lost an eye and a testicle in earlier battles. The grand old man had decided to take his son's place on the front line in France in part because the rewards on offer were so great. When he arrived at Bourges in April to kneel before the twenty-one-year-old king, Douglas was immediately granted the royal duchy of Touraine and named Charles's 'lieutenant-general in the waging of his war through all the kingdom of France'.

This was unprecedented honour and extraordinary power to bestow on a foreigner, but if it resulted in the expulsion of the English and the defeat of the Burgundians, it would be a price worth paying. Appalled though they privately were at the prospect of their uncouth Scottish duke, the citizens of Tours welcomed Douglas with stiff-necked public ceremony, and watched, grim-faced, while he set about plundering the city's treasury as thoroughly as his troops were pillaging the countryside round about. Sooner or later, they knew, he would have to earn his extortionate keep; and on 4 August – having extracted another small fortune from the city to pay his soldiers – he led his army north towards Normandy, and the war they had come to fight.

Marching beside the Scots were French troops under the command of two lords whose own Norman lands had been overrun by the English: seventeen-year-old Jean, duke of Alençon, whose father had died at Azincourt, and Jean d'Harcourt, count of Aumâle, the experienced captain of Mont-Saint-Michel, who had struck deep into Normandy the previous autumn and had begged his king to launch this campaign. And riding to join this Franco-Scottish force was another contingent from outside the realm: heavy cavalry, two thousand strong, recruited from the duchy of Milan. These Lombard riders and their horses – men and animals all plated in steel, thanks to the superlative skill of Milanese armourers – were equipped to withstand English arrows, and the archers within the Scots army stood ready to return English fire. This, Charles and his commanders could be certain, would be no Azincourt.

The thought had almost been enough to bring the king to the battlefield. In the weeks before his troops moved north, Charles had once again ordered new coats of arms and trappings for his warhorse. Now that France had an heir – his baby son, kicking in his cradle – should he ride with his men to reclaim his kingdom? But St Michael's protection had already been tested once at La Rochelle, and by August all were agreed that prudence was the better part of royal valour. The army of France would be led by Alençon and Aumâle, Buchan and Douglas. Their target was Ivry, a castle on the Norman frontier reclaimed a year earlier by an Armagnac garrison, but now close to breaking point under English siege. Knowing how few cards they had left to play, Ivry's defenders had negotiated a truce according to the chivalric laws of war: fighting would stop while they appealed for help from their king, but if reinforcements did not arrive by 15 August, they would lay down their arms and surrender the castle into English hands.

While Charles's army marched to save Ivry, therefore, the duke of Bedford mustered his troops to stop them. On 14 August the duke arrived outside the walls of the castle and picked his ground for battle. But the next day the summer sun rose and fell, and the Armagnacs did not come. Instead, there were riders, breathless and terrified, from the town of Verneuil, twenty-five miles further west, with shocking news. Alençon, Aumâle, Buchan and Douglas had realised that the Lombard knights, still behind them on the road, could not reach Ivry in time, and too much was at stake to risk meeting the English without them. It would mean grave dishonour if the army of France failed to appear at Ivry on the appointed day, but honour had not saved the princes of the blood at Azincourt. So, while Bedford waited, they had turned west to Verneuil. They had called for volunteers from within the Scots ranks – men who spoke English – and bound them backwards on their horses, spattered with blood, as if they were prisoners. Before Verneuil's walls they paraded these bogus captives, who shouted to the townspeople that the English at Ivry had been slaughtered, and there was no hope of help. In consternation and fear, the people of Verneuil opened their gates and gave up the town without a fight. And when Bedford heard of this brazen trick, he set out in furious pursuit.

On 17 August, the English army reached the broad plain just outside Verneuil to the north-east, to find the might of France – or at least the part of it that the kingdom of Bourges could command – ready for battle. Together, the French and the Scots outnumbered the English almost two to one, and in front of their lines stood the newly arrived Lombard cavalry, a wall of muscle and bone encased in steel. This time, lowborn English archers would not preside over a field of blood; this time a noble French assault – in the ominous shape of Milanese mercenaries – would break them where they stood. At a signal, the cavalry wall began to move, faster and faster, hooves pounding into tinder-dry earth. When the shuddering impact came, the English ranks buckled and staggered. Sharpened stakes, too quickly planted, could not bring down horses in armour, and the Lombard riders carved a path of devastation, of trampled, broken bodies, through the heart of the English army. The cavalry had done its work. But, as the Lombards fell upon the spoils of the English baggage-train, they did not see the battered ranks of the enemy taking shape again behind them.

It was the French and the Scots, in shock, who saw English men-at-arms advancing out of the dust-storm kicked up by the horses' heels. Braced though they were, the assault was brutal. In dense, chaotic fighting so ferocious that the earth was dark and slippery with blood, no one could tell who was winning – until, with a great roar, the English archers who had flung themselves out of the way of the Lombard charge regrouped to join the mêlée, daggers and axes in hand. English pressure began to bite, and, at last, the French line broke. Panic spread, and men fled for their lives, only to be trapped and butchered in the deep ditches outside the town walls. The count of Aumâle died where he fell; the young duke of Alençon was captured on the field. Of the few who escaped, almost none were Scots. As the plain of Verneuil became a killing ground, Douglas, Buchan and the army they led were hacked to pieces.

Outside Ivry two days earlier, Bedford had ridden before his troops wearing a blue velvet robe emblazoned with a red cross of St George within a white cross of St Michael. Two saints, two kingdoms, England and France; the claim could not have been clearer. Now it was vindicated in the bloody triumph of Verneuil. Bedford himself – who 'did that day wonderful feats of arms', said an admiring Burgundian chronicler who fought with the English army – returned to Paris, to be greeted with processions, songs and pageants by elated crowds all dressed in the red of St George. Relief at the defeat of the vile Armagnacs was so profound, the journal-writer observed, that the duke was welcomed to the great cathedral of Notre-Dame 'as if he had been God'.

While celebrations continued in Anglo-Burgundian France — lubricated, fortuitously, by the best and most plentiful vintage any-one could remember — the kingdom of Bourges occupied itself with more sombre tasks. The city of Tours received the lifeless bodies of its duke, Archibald Douglas, and his son-in-law, John Stewart of Buchan, and buried them quietly in the choir of the cathedral. 'Dearly loved and delightful they were in life', said the Scottish chronicler Walter Bower, 'and in death they were not divided.' The people of Tours made no comment, other than to blockade the garrison of Scots soldiers that Douglas had left in the castle until they agreed to go away.

It was clear to the *roi très-chrétien*, contemplating the state of his kingdom, that France was going to need another saviour.

3

Desolate and divided

It seemed strange, to the people of Paris, that their country now appeared to have two capitals, neither of which was their own incomparable city.

Bourges, more than a hundred miles to the south, was home to the court of the disinherited dauphin, Charles the ill-advised. Loyal Parisians knew that he was surrounded by traitors and murderers – not just the killers of the good duke John of Burgundy, but all those evildoers who had inflicted years of barbarous suffering on the people of France. But, disconcertingly, the righteous lords to whom France's greatest city had been so conspicuously faithful were not resident in Paris either. The duke of Bedford, regent of the kingdom on behalf of the infant king Henry, had moved into the Hôtel de Bourbon, just beside the palace of the Louvre on the westernmost edge of the city, and held a great feast there before Christmas 1424; but then, as was his habit, he returned to Rouen, the capital of English-held Normandy, and the centre of English government in France since before the treaty of Troyes.

Duke Philip of Burgundy, meanwhile, had been at his Parisian home, the Hôtel d'Artois, earlier in the autumn for the lavish wedding of the master of his household, Jean de La Trémoille, to one of Queen Isabeau's ladies; then, said the journal-writer in the city, he 'went back to his own country'. 'His own country' – his *pays* – meant his own territories, not his own kingdom; but even the most steadfast Burgundian adherent, which this observer had once been, could not help noticing that 'Burgundian' no longer straightforwardly meant 'French'. The duke – a lean, long-nosed figure whose habit of dressing entirely in black emphasised the unhappy circumstances in which he had inherited his title – had replaced his dead father's emblem of a carpenter's plane with his own personal badge, a flint and steel producing sparks and flames. But after the conflagration that his father's determination to rule had fuelled in the most Christian kingdom, the fires of Philip's ambition burned elsewhere, in the new Burgundian state he was forging in the Low Countries. As a result, his visits to Paris – 'a city which had loved him so well and which had suffered so much and still was suffering for him and for his father', lamented the disillusioned journal-writer as early as 1422 – dwindled almost to nothing.

By 1424, then, it seemed that there were two Frances. One, in the north, was ruled from Rouen by the regent Bedford, who decreed that none of King Henry's loyal subjects should refer to the so-called dauphin as 'king', or to the Armagnac traitors as 'French', on pain of hefty fines. Meanwhile, the other France, in the south, looked to the government of King Charles VII in Bourges, from where he promised to sweep the usurping English into the sea and to reduce those of his subjects who had rebelled against him to the obedience they owed.

These, obviously, were incompatible claims. In theory, each kingdom of France was dedicated to the annihilation of the other. In practice, they were locked in a deathly embrace, a stalemate sustained by devastation and bloodshed. 'At that time', the Parisian had written wearily in his journal in 1423, 'the English would sometimes take one fortress from the Armagnacs in the morning and lose two in the evening. So this war, accursed of God, went on.' Though the kingdom of the north had been strengthened by victory at Verneuil, and English forces were pushing southward from Normandy into Maine and Anjou, neither side had yet shown themselves capable of making a decisive move across the great natural boundary of the river Loire, which now, in effect, divided the Armagnac kingdom of the south from English France to the north and its ally, the duchy of Burgundy, to the east.

It even seemed possible that a decisive part in this bloody struggle might now be taken by a different war, fought for different reasons on different soil. In the summer of 1424, while Bedford hammered the Scots into the dust of Verneuil, his brother Humphrey, duke of Gloucester, was mustering troops in England for a continental invasion of his own. At Gloucester's side was his new wife, Jacqueline of Hainaut, whose previous unhappy marriage to the duke of Brabant had not yet been annulled to the satisfaction of the Church – nor, indeed, of the duke of Brabant himself, who was not prepared to relinquish Jacqueline's counties of Hainaut, Holland and Zeeland along with his unloved bride. Gloucester, however, was not about to let matrimonial technicalities stand in his way. He and Jacqueline were married by the beginning of 1423, their union blessed, since Rome refused to sanction it, by the last remaining antipope, who had been living in Spanish obscurity ever since the rest of Europe had ended the papal schism without him. And in October 1424, the duke and his new duchess landed at Calais with an army, ready to reclaim her inheritance.

This irritating intervention was not what Philip of Burgundy's alliance with England had been designed to achieve. Even before Gloucester's expedition had reached the Low Countries, its potential repercussions within Anglo-Burgundian France were beginning to be felt. As news of Gloucester's military preparations spread that summer, tentative diplomatic approaches – the first in years – took place between Burgundian Dijon and Armagnac Bourges. Wild rumours that Duke Philip had already made peace with the man who had murdered his father reached Bedford on the eve of battle at Verneuil, and as a result he decided at the eleventh hour to send away the Burgundian troops under his command, preferring to fight with a smaller number of soldiers on whose loyalty he could depend absolutely, rather than run the risk of treachery from within. There was, of course, no chance that John the Fearless's blood could be washed so easily from the hands of the young king of Bourges, but it was clear that the reordering of Burgundian priorities might at last mean that the stain was starting to fade. That September, Duke Philip put his seal to a truce with the Armagnacs to protect the frontiers of his lands in eastern France – thereby freeing himself to tackle Gloucester's aggression in the north – which acknowledged for the first time the claim of the 'so-called dauphin' to style himself a king. Instead of this disparaging Burgundian circumlocution, the text of the treaty called him simply '*le roi*'.

It took only months, however, for Gloucester's assault on the Low Countries to reveal itself as a damp squib. The English duke discovered that he faced not only a Burgundian army but a public challenge to fight in single combat. Young knights like themselves, Duke Philip declared, should risk their own lives to settle such a quarrel, rather than spill the blood of their followers. This was an offer Gloucester could not, with honour, refuse. At his suggestion the date was set for St George's day, 23 April 1425. In preparation, Philip retired to his castle at Hesdin, where he took lessons to refine his swordsmanship and spent the eyewatering sum of nearly £14,000 on new armour, pavilions, coats of arms, banners and horse harness in embroidered silks and velvets. Humphrey of Gloucester, meanwhile, sought a safe-conduct to return to England to make his own preparatory arrangements, leaving his wife, Jacqueline, in Hainaut. He took with him one of his duchess's most beautiful attendants, an Englishwoman named Eleanor Cobham; and gradually it became clear that he was not coming back.

Thwarted though Philip of Burgundy might have been in his desire to win chivalric glory – or, at least, having comprehensively called Gloucester's bluff – the duke knew that the Low Countries were within his grasp. By the summer of 1425 he had secured custody of the abandoned Duchess Jacqueline and, with her, the chance to consolidate his hold on Hainaut, Holland and Zeeland. But that September, one morning before dawn, Jacqueline escaped from house arrest in Ghent, disguised as a man for her headlong ride to

Holland and freedom. As she mustered support to resist Burgundian rule, Philip gathered his armies for the fight ahead. And for
the duke of Bedford, relief at the retreat from this battleground of
his foolhardy brother Gloucester was tempered by the knowledge
that his greatest ally's interest in France was now subsumed in the
overriding demands of war elsewhere.

From Rouen, Bedford did everything he could to keep his partnership with the absent duke of Burgundy alive, and he had his
beloved wife, Philip's sister Anne, to help him in his task. But the
treaty at Amiens that had brought Bedford and his duchess together
had been a double marriage alliance, and now the duke discovered
that the other union made there – that of Anne's sister Margaret
and Arthur, count of Richemont, brother of the duke of Brittany –
would no longer share the burden of sustaining the political bond
between England and Burgundy.

Richemont's relationship with England was a complex one. His
title was English in origin, but this earl of Richmond, as he was
known on the northern side of the Channel, held no lands there.
Instead, it was a name associated since the eleventh century with
the independent duchy of Brittany, whose dukes now used it as of
right within their own family, whatever the current state of their
dealings with the English crown. His widowed mother had married
King Henry IV of England in 1403, but Richemont had grown up
in France, and it was for France that he had fought at Azincourt.
Wounded on the field, he was found after the battle, covered in
blood, under a pile of corpses. For five years he remained Henry
V's prisoner until, at twenty-seven, he won his freedom on *parole* –
that is, on his word that he would do nothing against the interests
of the king of England or the duke of Burgundy.

That stipulation was a mark of the changed world into which
Richemont emerged from his captivity. He had close ties from
his earliest years in Paris with the houses of both Burgundy and
Orléans, but when the civil war first erupted he had fought for

the Orléanist Armagnacs. By 1420, however, the Armagnac dauphin was the killer of John the Fearless, and Richemont's childhood friend Philip of Burgundy was the ally of the English king. Richemont committed himself to the Anglo-Burgundian cause, and helped to persuade his elder brother of Brittany, who had previously tacked between the two sides, to do the same. His decision was reflected and underpinned in 1423 by his marriage to Burgundy's sister, and he was rewarded by the regent Bedford with a grant of the royal duchy of Touraine, the province that – lying as it did across the great fault-line of the Loire – would also be granted, from the other side of the divide, by King Charles VII to the earl of Douglas.

But despite these years of service to English France in the north, in October 1424 Richemont rode to Angers to kneel before the young king in the south. There Charles proposed that the count should take the place of the dead earl of Buchan as the constable of his kingdom, the military leader of Armagnac France. In March 1425, at Chinon, Richemont swore an oath of homage to his new king and received the constable's sword from his hands. For Charles and the Armagnacs, the reasons to rejoice at this defection were as numerous as the causes for English disquiet: not only was Richemont an experienced and proficient soldier, but his service was offered as one part of a wider realignment of Breton loyalties that, by the autumn of 1425, included a treaty between the kingdom of Bourges and Richemont's brother, the Breton duke. Most alarmingly of all, Richemont had insisted that he could not accept his new command without consulting his brother-in-law, Philip of Burgundy. The fact that Duke Philip did not prevent him from taking up arms for the Armagnac king represented no simple reordering of Burgundian diplomacy, not least because by now there was nothing simple in the Burgundian position; but that conclusion in itself offered little comfort to the English.

More significant even than the presence of Richemont at Charles's side, meanwhile, was the means by which he had been drawn back into the Armagnac fold. The first meeting between the king and his new constable had taken place at Angers, the great capital of the duchy of Anjou, because it had been brokered by Anjou's dowager duchess, Charles's mother-in-law, Yolande of Aragon. The kingdom of Bourges owed its very existence to Yolande's support: in the dark days of 1418, after Charles's escape from Burgundian Paris, she had established his court in the south and surrounded him with loyal supporters. In the years since then, however, this formidable politician had occupied herself with other battles.

The dukes of Anjou held an impressive array of titles scattered across hundreds of miles of territory. Their duchy of Anjou and county of Maine, just south of Normandy, lay on the bitterly fought front line of the war with the English, but their county of Provence, four hundred miles further south-east, was lit by the stronger sun of the Mediterranean, and its trading revenues from the port of Marseille helped to fill Angevin coffers with gold. More impressive still, though infinitely less substantial, was their hereditary claim to the crowns of Sicily and Jerusalem. The latter kingdom was long gone and the former split in two, but one of these paper titles – the mainland kingdom of Sicily, consisting of the lands in southern Italy that were ruled from Naples – remained tantalisingly close to Angevin hands. Yolande's husband had tried and failed to retrieve this Italian realm, but the wife who had governed his French territories during his absence on campaign was still known to her contemporaries as 'the queen of Sicily'.

Nor, after her husband's death in 1417, had Yolande herself given up on this Angevin dream. In 1419, once she had established her royal son-in-law Charles in safety at Bourges, she had travelled south to Provence to prepare a new military expedition through which her sixteen-year-old son, Duke Louis, might secure his Italian birthright. She also had plans for her second son, René. From her mother, Yolande had inherited a claim to the duchy of

Bar in eastern France, which was currently ruled by her uncle, the cardinal-bishop of Châlons-sur-Marne – but as a priest, he could father no children of his own. Yolande persuaded him to adopt René as his heir; and René would also, she hoped, rule the neighbouring duchy of Lorraine through the marriage she negotiated for him with its young heiress, Isabelle.

These were complex and ambitious schemes, but by 1423 they were bearing fruit. René was now married to Isabelle and living in Bar as the cherished heir of Yolande's uncle, and in June Louis took ship for his kingdom of Sicily at the head of the army his mother had raised. It was time to return her attention to the kingdom of France. On 26 June 1423, just a few days after Louis's departure from Marseille, Yolande left Provence for the first time in four years to ride north to Bourges, where her daughter, Charles's queen Marie, was about to give birth to France's heir. And there, after a brief moment of domestic communion with her new grandchild, she addressed herself to the next political task at hand.

Her goals were clear. Her commitment to the future of her son-in-law, Charles, as king of France was matched by her determination that Anjou and Provence should flourish while her son Louis secured his Italian throne, and that Bar and Lorraine should pass peacefully into the hands of her younger son, René. All three objectives required that the English should be expelled from French soil, and the kingdom reunited under Charles's rule. It was no use to Yolande if France were to remain torn in two, its back broken along the valley of the Loire: that would maroon Anjou and Maine on the ravaged frontier of war with the English, and leave Bar and Lorraine struggling in a Burgundian vice, lying as they did between the duchy of Burgundy to the south and the Burgundian territories in the Low Countries to the north. The way forward, then, could not be achieved through military force alone. No matter what had happened in the past, Yolande knew that the princes of the blood – including Philip of Burgundy – must come together under the rule of their king, Charles VII, in the joint interests of the kingdom of France and her Angevin dynasty.

She had already begun a private correspondence with Duke Philip by the time of her return to Bourges in June 1423, but the diplomatic offensive she launched within weeks of her arrival had, as its first target, the duke of Brittany. That autumn she spent a month visiting him at his castle at Nantes, only fifty miles from Angers, and the following spring she returned there with a deputation from her son-in-law's court at Bourges. The result of this elegant intervention was the political détente between Bourges and Brittany that led to the defection of the duke's brother Arthur of Richemont from the Anglo-Burgundian alliance, and his appointment in 1425 as constable of Armagnac France.

Richemont arrived in Bourges, as Yolande had planned, still armed with his Burgundian connections, and as part of the deal by which he took up his sword in the Armagnac cause, some of the men most hated by Duke Philip – those who were directly implicated in the murder of John the Fearless – were removed from Charles's court. Tanguy du Châtel, whose axe had struck the first blow, and Jean Louvet, who had stood beside him to watch the duke die, were exiled from the king's side in the summer of 1425 to positions in faraway Provence. Their destination alone would have revealed the guiding hand of Yolande, even had Charles himself not made her role explicitly clear: his decision had been taken, he said, by 'the good advice and counsel of our dearest and most beloved mother, the queen of Jerusalem and Sicily'.

This reconfiguration of the Armagnac court demonstrated her pragmatism as a politician, but Yolande also knew that divine providence would shape her country's future. She had direct experience, after all, of its role in healing a rupture in the fabric of creation even more cataclysmic than the current division within the kingdom of France. In 1400, when she had first arrived as a young bride in her husband's county of Provence, two rival popes simultaneously claimed dominion over Christendom, one in Rome and the other in the city of Avignon, just twelve miles from her new home at the castle of Tarascon. This great schism in the Church was finally ended, after four decades of bitter wrangling, by the Council of Constance in 1418. During that time, holy voices had been raised across Europe to demand an end to the Church's agony – and Yolande had learned at first hand that these spiritual leaders might be female as well as male.

In the 1390s, for example, her mother-in-law, Marie of Brittany – another strikingly formidable dowager duchess of Anjou – had known a peasant woman named Marie Robine, who had begun to receive messages from God. Originally from the Hautes-Pyrénées, in 1388 Marie Robine had travelled more than two hundred miles to Avignon in the grip of an intractable illness, seeking help at the shrine of a young cardinal who had died a year earlier at the age of just eighteen, and whose grave in Avignon's cemetery of St Michael was developing a reputation for miraculous cures. There, in the presence of Avignon's pope, God's grace had restored her to health, and from then on she remained as a holy recluse within the cemetery.

It was ten years later, on 22 February 1398, that Marie Robine first heard a voice from heaven, telling her that she must direct the king to reform the Church and end the schism. By April, Duchess Marie was taking so close an interest in this divine instruction that she was present in St Michael's cemetery when Marie Robine had another vision, this time of a burning wheel bearing thousands of swords and innumerable arrows, poised to descend from heaven to earth to destroy the wicked. At her voices' urging – and perhaps with the help of the duchess – she left her cell to travel to Paris, but failed to secure a hearing before the ailing king's council. By 1399, back in Avignon, her voices became more outspoken in rejecting the corrupted authority of the earthly Church and more apocalyptic in the face of the king's failure to heed her words, until in

November, fifteen days after her last revelation, Marie Robine died.

Memories of her were still fresh when Yolande arrived in Provence in the following year, and when the young duchess travelled north to the valley of the Loire, she herself encountered another female visionary. Jeanne-Marie de Maillé was a woman of noble birth who, after her husband's death in 1362, had embraced a life of poverty and prayer as a recluse under the protection of a convent in Tours. On occasion, her visions enabled her to make prophecies – one, at least, concerned with the profound trauma of the schism – and her words could command the ear of the powerful. Her connections with the Angevin dynasty were so close that she stood godmother to one of Duchess Marie's sons, Yolande's brother-in-law, and she was twice granted an audience with the king, first when Charles VI visited Tours in 1395, and again when she travelled to Paris in 1398. These were private conversations, their content unrecorded, but Jeanne-Marie spent time too with Queen Isabeau, whom she reprimanded for living in luxury while the people suffered and starved. When Yolande met her, she was already in her seventies, but the two women spent enough time together that when Jeanne-Marie died in 1414, Yolande was a witness at the canonisation hearing held to consider evidence that she might be recognised as a saint.

It seemed, then, in 1425 that Yolande had what Armagnac France needed: vision of a different kind – not the revelations granted to Marie Robine and Jeanne-Marie de Maillé, but the insight to perceive God's plan that France should be reunited under Charles's kingship, and to comprehend how it might be brought about. She was at her son-in-law's side when he called his subjects to arms once again at the beginning of 1426, and established herself at the head of his council in an attempt to bring royal finances under strict control. Constable Richemont stood ready for the double task of fighting the English and facilitating peace with Burgundy, and meanwhile efforts were made to retain old friends as well as welcoming new ones. John Stewart of Darnley, for example, received a grant in November 1425 to help him pay the ransom demanded after his capture by the Burgundians at Cravant, so that he could resume his role as 'constable of the Scots army' (or, at least, what little remained of it after the massacre at Verneuil).

And yet as the months went by, despite all Yolande's efforts, concrete progress in pushing back the frontier of English France or persuading Burgundy into the embrace of the kingdom of Bourges seemed as remote a prospect as ever. At the end of 1425 the duke of Bedford was called back to England to deal with his brother of Gloucester, whose talent for causing trouble had been unleashed at home after his ignominious retreat from the Low Countries. As his lieutenants, Bedford left the earls of Salisbury, Suffolk and War-wick to launch a campaign in 1426 against the duchy of Brittany – in English eyes an ally that had turned traitor with the diplomatic realignment of the previous year – as well as pursuing operations in Maine and Champagne. But Armagnac forces, with Richemont at their head, proved unable to take advantage of the regent's absence. Instead, the court of Bourges was otherwise occupied in turning on itself.

Yolande had hoped that the arrival of Richemont and the ban-ishment of Louvet and du Châtel would enable Charles's regime to settle into a new order focused on rapprochement with Burgundy. In practice, however, the removal of the controversial figure of Jean Louvet from the king's side in 1425 had only been achieved after an astonishing moment of violence, when Louvet himself, in a last desperate ploy to save his position, took the young king to Poitiers with as many soldiers as he could muster, and prepared to hold the city against Richemont, who advanced against him with an army of his own. Civil war among the Armagnacs had eventually been avoided, thanks in large part to Yolande's intervention, but much too narrowly for comfort, and it remained unclear whether Charles was vulnerable to manipulation by the ambitious and grasping men around him, or whether he played some deliberate part in setting them against one another. Either way, the relationship between the king and his new constable had got off to a poisonous start – and the result was escalating conflict within the Armagnac establishment.

By the summer of 1426 the man who had replaced Louvet at the eye of the developing storm was Pierre de Giac, a former Burgundian loyalist who had defected to the Armagnac court and risen high in Charles's affections. That August, Giac launched an extraordinary assault on Robert le Maçon, who had served the king ever since Yolande had first established the court at Bourges. Now in his sixties, le Maçon was taken prisoner on Giac's orders, and kept in confinement for two months until he paid handsomely for his freedom. But Giac's confidence that the favour in which he stood with the king made him untouchable proved entirely misplaced. Richemont had not been recruited to serve at the king's right hand simply to tolerate the antics of men as rapacious as Giac; and in February 1427 Giac was arrested, sentenced to death and killed by Richemont's men. Such summary justice had been necessary, the constable explained in a public letter to the people of Lyon, because the king was 'badly advised, and unaware of the great disloyalty and treason of the said Giac', so that he, Richemont, had been forced to remove him, on the king's behalf and in the interests of good government.

This was remarkable frankness: clearly, the twenty-four-year-old king did not enjoy full control over his own administration, and his most powerful servants were now entirely capable of taking his law into their own hands. Nor did the death of Giac bring greater calm to the court. Another favourite, Le Camus de Beaulieu, was brutally murdered in June 1427, and few doubted that the constable had ordered his dispatch. Meanwhile, Richemont himself introduced a new face into the crowd jostling for position around the king. Georges de La Trémoille – another former Burgundian, whose brother Jean remained master of the duke of Burgundy's household — had been instrumental in Giac's execution, and married his widow five months later. Almost immediately, La Trémoille began his own ascent in Charles's confidence, and soon he and Richemont, in their turn, were at daggers drawn. Yolande, bruised by the self-destructive violence of this bloody heaving and shoving, retreated from court for the first time in three years. And all the while, the people of France endured the effects of a war that now seemed to have no beginning, and no end.

The people of Paris — a city that had once been the centre of the conflict, these days all but abandoned by the powerful — had to find their own moments of distraction in this grimly uncertain world. In the late summer of 1425, the journal-writer there reported, two entertainments had been devised for the diversion of the citizens. On the last Sunday in August, an enclosure was set up in the Rue Saint-Honoré in which a large pig was placed, along with four blind men, each of them wearing armour and carrying a hefty club. Whichever man could kill the pig would win its carcass as a prize, and 'they fought this very odd battle', the anonymous Parisian said, 'giving each other tremendous blows with the clubs. Whenever they tried to get a good blow in at the pig, they would hit each other, so that if they had not been wearing armour they would certainly have killed each other.' Then, the following Saturday in the Rue Saint-Denis, a long pole was set up, more than thirty feet tall and thoroughly greased, with a basket on the top containing a goose and a handful of silver coins. Whoever succeeded in reaching the basket would win its contents; but the greasy pole defeated all comers, until at last the boy who had climbed highest was given the goose, though not the money. The other news of note was that, a little earlier in the year, a painting of the *Danse Macabre* had been unveiled along the cloister walls of the city's cemetery of the Holy Innocents. The grinning figure of Death led a grotesque carnival in which king, beggar, pope and peasant were swept up all together, the pomp and power of the great exposed as worthless vanity by this inexorable procession to the grave. The dance of death; the greasy pole; a battle of the blind. If the journal-writer felt any temptation to suggest that these moments in Parisian life might echo the wider state of the kingdom, it was one he heroically resisted.

By the spring of 1427, when the duke of Bedford at last returned to the city, Paris was in the grip of dreadful weather: heavy frosts, constant rain and storms of hail. The regent's mood was little better. He had knocked heads together in England, but fifteen months of work had produced no permanent solution to Gloucester's truculence, and in France every step forward seemed to be matched by another reverse. There was cause for English celebration that autumn, when many months of campaigning in Brittany at last persuaded its duke, always a versatile player in this endless game, to abandon his alliance with the Armagnacs and pledge his renewed loyalty to the English king. But just seventy-two hours before the treaty was finally signed on 8 September, cheers died on English lips when Armagnac forces won two substantial encounters in a single day. At Montargis, sixty miles south of Paris, a besieging English army was driven off by Armagnac troops under the command of the Bastard of Orléans (illegitimate brother of the duke who, twelve years after Azincourt, still remained a prisoner in England) and a captain named Étienne de Vignolles, known to all by his nickname as 'La Hire'. And 150 miles further west, another Armagnac captain named Ambroise de Loré wiped out an English force almost within sight of the fortress of Sainte-Suzanne, headquarters of Sir John Fastolf, the English military governor in Maine.

For the kingdom of Bourges, meanwhile, these moments of triumph were shafts of light in a lowering sky. The loss of the Breton alliance was a grievous blow. Not only that, but the perfidy of the duke of Brittany compromised the standing of his brother, Richemont, as the military leader of Armagnac France – a circumstance that might have mattered more had Richemont not been busy doing his own extraordinary damage from inside the Armagnac regime. In more than two years since he had sworn homage to the king at Chinon, the constable had yet to lead his troops to victory in an engagement with the enemy. Now, with the English in Maine, and Brittany to the west once again a hostile power, Yolande's duchy of Anjou stood in need of urgent reinforcement. Richemont, however, was yet again arming himself not to confront the English, but to remove an 'evil counsellor' from the king's side – this time his own former protégé, La Trémoille.

And this time, Charles had had enough. La Trémoille's determination not to be prised from his place was matched by the king's resolve not to lose another favourite to sudden death or distant exile. Together, in the spring of 1428, king and counsellor seized the great castle at Chinon, which had been in Richemont's hands ever since his appointment as constable. There, they set about rallying the resources of the kingdom, calling once again on the presence of Yolande to foster confidence in their efforts, while Richemont – his energies now focused entirely on internal rivals rather than the enemy without – installed himself in the fortified citadel of Parthenay in Poitou, forty miles to the south-west. But that autumn, alarming reports arrived of a new and unexpected threat. Orléans was under siege.

Technically, Orléans should never have been an English target. According to the laws of war, the lands of a prisoner – and the duke of Orléans was still a captive in London – had protected status, being reserved from combat to produce the money that would pay his ransom. But there was good reason for the English to make a strategic exception to this honourable rule. Orléans was the northernmost town on the great curve of the river Loire. If the English were ever to make a decisive push across this natural boundary, to break the stalemate that held the war in brutal and costly stasis, Orléans would have to fall. And if it fell, the doorway into Armagnac France would be wide open.

The man behind this plan was Thomas Montagu, earl of Salisbury, at forty a gifted and vastly experienced commander with an exemplary record of service to Henry V and the regent Bedford – 'a thorough soldier, an excellent fighter, and very astute in all his dealings', the Parisian journal-writer noted approvingly. But his march on Orléans was not unequivocal evidence of renewed purpose on the part of the English. Salisbury himself was intent on securing the Loire crossing there, but that had not been Bedford's strategy; the regent and the council over which he presided in Paris in the spring of 1428 had decided that the newly recruited troops the earl was bringing from England should be used to advance the English line from Maine into Anjou, consolidating the conquest slowly and carefully, piece by piece, with a push from English-held Le Mans to the gates of Yolande's capital, Angers.

But when Salisbury and his army landed in France that July, it was to Orléans, not Angers, that they headed; persuasion, or insubordination, or some combination of the two had deflected the regent from his chosen path. And this would not be a momentary diversion. More than thirty watchtowers studded the ancient walls that surrounded Orléans on the north side of the Loire. A massive stone bridge, more than two hundred years old, reached from the town's great gate to an island in the river and then on – a span of nineteen arches in total – to a fortified tower known as the Tourelles, from which a wooden bridge gave access to the river's southern bank. It was a daunting prospect, but Salisbury showed no sign of intimidation. His first move was to launch a storming campaign to isolate the town by water, with the capture of Jargeau, ten miles upstream, and Meung and Beaugency, ten and fifteen miles downstream, among dozens of other nearby settlements and strongholds: '. . . the fare and speed since our last coming into this land has been so good', he reported, 'that I am ever beholden to thank God, beseeching him to continue it for his mercy'.

By 12 October, he was ready to take up position outside Orléans itself. Lacking enough men to surround it on all sides, he settled on an attack from the south; the bridge, he believed, was the key to possession of the town. For twelve days the Tourelles held out against English bombardment and assault until at last, on 24 October, its defenders withdrew across the river to take refuge behind the town walls. English triumph, however, was short-lived. As the besiegers advanced to secure the bridgehead, they saw that the Orléanais had somehow succeeded in mining the bridge across which they had just retreated. The English might hold the Tourelles, but their route into Orléans was gone. Not long after, Salisbury stood at an upper window in the fortress, gazing out across the fast-flowing water at the town he could not reach. Suddenly, a stone cannonball fired from one of the watchtowers on the opposite bank smashed into the wall beside him. When his shocked attendants reached the earl amid the rubble, he was still breathing; but, where one side of his face had been, there was only a gaping, bloody hole. He died eight days later.

This double loss, of the earl of Salisbury and the bridge he had hoped to cross, changed the essence of the English campaign. Instead of a bold strike under a brilliant commander to force their way over the Loire, they found themselves facing a grinding, protracted siege directed by a substitute leader, the earl of Suffolk, an intelligent but cautious man who had little of Salisbury's daring or charisma. Suffolk strengthened the blockade that Salisbury had established round the town, so far as he could. Earthworks reinforced with wood, known as *boulevards*, topped with fortifications known as *bastilles*, were built at intervals outside the walls, but much of the territory to the north and east of the town remained open, because – as Salisbury had known – the English were too few for their grip to become a stranglehold. English guns continued to fire on Orléans, and reinforcements under the command of the lords Scales and Talbot were summoned, but the strategy of the siege was now simply to wait, in the hope that hunger and despair would do their work.

It was a plan fraught with risk. Winter was coming, and the same circumstance that made Orléans a prize to be won – its key position on the frontier between English and Armagnac France – left the army encamped around its walls exposed to danger. Bourges itself was only sixty miles to the south, and the task of maintaining supply lines to the besiegers was almost as difficult as that of doing the same, from the other side, for the besieged. Not, of course, that the English would have swapped places. There was no doubt that Charles was doing what he could to relieve the siege; he was determined to defend Orléans with all his power, reported the Burgundian chronicler Enguerrand de Monstrelet, 'believing that, if it were lost into the hands of the enemy, that would mean the total destruction of his frontiers and country and of himself too . . .'. He sent the Bastard of Orléans to take command of the town, together with La Hire, who had helped the Bastard to victory at Montargis, John Stewart of Darnley, the constable of the Scots, and other captains including an experienced professional soldier named Poton de Xaintrailles. With them, the king sent specialist gunners, and his personal surgeon to tend to the wounded.

At Chinon, he had also gathered a meeting of the estates-general, representatives of their regions who were authorised to make grants of taxation for the defence of the realm. This they did, but they also appealed to the king for the restoration of good government, imploring him to reunite the princes of the blood around his throne, and especially that, 'by all good means possible', he should find a way to make peace with the duke of Burgundy. But this was palpably a plea made in hope rather than expectation. While the truces that offered some form of protection to the lands on the frontier between Burgundian territory and Armagnac France were still holding, the duke himself had paid a rare visit to Bedford in Paris that spring, and there was no sign that his preoccupation with the Low Countries – where he was in the process of securing his victory over Jacqueline of Hainaut – would produce any significant reordering of his alliance with the English in France, however equivocal that relationship might now be. Nor did the prospects of unity among the Armagnac lords seem any brighter. Their ranks had at least been reinforced by the return of the young duke of Alençon, newly ransomed from his captivity after Verneuil, but Richemont was still plotting against La Trémoille behind the walls of Parthenay – and the destructive manoeuvring of the constable Yolande had helped to appoint could only compromise her chances of mitigating the destabilising effects of La Trémoille's presence within the court itself.

As the cold set in, and the weeks of the siege began to turn into grim and frozen months, the impasse at Orléans seemed to encapsulate the plight of the whole kingdom. Across great swathes of France, the oppressive and violent reality of armies moving through the countryside, of battles and sieges, pillage and plunder, had left behind scorched earth, torched homes, and lives and livelihoods destroyed. And over the long years of suffering, as the war slowed to an attritional struggle, the stakes for which it was being fought had begun to blur and fade. Once, this had been a conflict between two anointed sovereigns: Charles the Well-Beloved, who was, whatever his failings, the most Christian king of France, and Henry of England, hailed by his subjects as the true elect of God. Now, the rhetoric might remain, but neither of the two kings for whom so much death and devastation were being wrought had received unction from heaven – one, another Henry, because he was only a child, and the other, another Charles, because he had been disowned by his father, and the holy church at Reims where the most Christian king should receive his crown had been taken from him.

Now, too, there was no question of a king leading his troops in battle. Henry was too young, and although his uncle Bedford was a man of integrity and skill, in the conduct of the war one hand was tied behind his back by the fact that any policy deviating from that set by his dead brother – the release of significant prisoners, for example, or the negotiation of a treaty that might involve territorial concessions – could not in practice be pursued without the guaranteeing authority of an adult monarch. And on the other side it had become clear, to the point where it was no longer questioned, that Charles, at almost twenty-six, would not fight. He had a son to succeed him should he fall, but, all the same, the combined effect of the continuing fragility of the Armagnac regime with his own lack of military capability meant that there would be no repeat of the gestures towards equipping himself for the battlefield that he had made as a teenager.

So that winter, while the king remained at Chinon, it was the Bastard of Orléans who led the resistance to the English siege. His task – apart from directing dangerous but ultimately ineffective skirmishes and sorties, which the chronicler Monstrelet felt moved to declare were 'too long and boring' to describe – was to find a weakness in the English position. And it was clear to the soldiers in the town that the length of the English supply line was one such point of vulnerability. Most of the besiegers' food came from Paris, seventy miles to the north, and at the beginning of February a convoy bound for Orléans was assembled in the city, consisting of more than three hundred carts packed with provisions – mainly flour and salted fish, because it was almost Lent, the season of fasting when eating meat was forbidden. The people of the countryside around Paris watched as the supplies they had been forced to give up began their journey south with a guard of archers under the command of Sir John Fastolf.

They were not, however, the only ones who knew the food was on its way. The Bastard of Orléans, with La Hire, Xaintrailles and Darnley, had succeeded in leading a detachment of troops from within the besieged town past the English blockade to meet a relief force approaching from Blois under the command of the count of Clermont, son and heir to the duke of Bourbon who was, like the

Bastard's brother, still a prisoner in England. On 12 February, after a bitterly cold night, they closed on the English convoy outside a village named Rouvray, thirteen miles north-west of Orléans. Across the plain, Fastolf saw them coming. Realising that his men were heavily outnumbered, he drew his carts into a defensive circle and ordered the civilians in his company to lead the horses into the shelter of this makeshift encampment. The archers drove their sharpened stakes into the ground where they stood guard at the only two points of entry left in this wall of wagons, while the men-at-arms took up position nearby. Then they waited.

Two hours passed while, at a distance, the Armagnacs prepared for battle and attempted to decide on their tactics. In the end, they could only agree to disagree, Darnley's Scotsmen preferring to fight on foot, the French to prepare a charge on horseback. The details, after all, hardly mattered, given the crushing weight of their numbers. When Fastolf sent a messenger to ask if they would ransom prisoners, the answer was chilling: 'if a hair of them escaped', Clermont declared ringingly, 'if they were not all put to the sword', then he himself would give up all claim on God's help for the future. And then, at three in the afternoon, the attack began. Fastolf's archers were ready. Within moments, horses and men were falling, arrows tearing through flesh, animals screaming in pain and panic as longbows and stakes did their deadly work. Soon the frozen ground was sodden with Armagnac blood. More than four hundred men died that day, among them one-eyed John Stewart of Darnley, and with him the very last of the Scots army in France. In total, the English casualties numbered four.

The victory was remarkable. It mattered to the hungry English soldiers at Orléans, who would eat well that Lent, and it mattered that God had smiled on troops loyal to Henry, the true king of France. All the same, this triumph of English archers against overwhelming odds did not resonate with the grandeur of Agincourt, nor even of the 'second Agincourt' of Verneuil. Instead, people spoke of it, in tribute to the contents of Fastolf's convoy, as the 'Battle of the Herrings'. And the journal-writer in Paris drew his account of the fighting to a close with a heartfelt lament. 'How dreadful it is, on both sides, that Christian men must kill each other like this without knowing why!'

If God's purpose no longer seemed clear even to the winners, the losers stood little chance of making sense of their defeat. While the Bastard of Orléans, who had only narrowly escaped the field with an arrow wound in his foot, limped back to the besieged and hungry town with La Hire, Xaintrailles, Clermont and the rest of the battle's survivors, their king, ninety miles away at Chinon, struggled to retain any vestige of hope that his right to his father's throne might one day be vindicated beyond doubt or hesitation. His constable was making war on his courtiers; those among the great lords of his realm who were not still prisoners in England had all but left him to his fate; and the military fortunes of his kingdom were turning, it seemed, from bad to worse. After the deaths of Douglas, Buchan and now Darnley, the promise of salvation from Scotland appeared to have been no more than a vain imagination. Rumours began to fly that, if Orléans were to fall, Scotland itself, or perhaps Castile, might at least offer some kind of safe haven for the fugitive king.

Whatever the whispers, though, it was clear to Charles and his council that it was too soon to think of abandoning the realm. Retreat, on the other hand – perhaps to the Dauphiné in the far south-east, from where he could seek to defend the Lyonnais, Auvergne and Languedoc – might have much to recommend it. There, some suggested, he would be able to wait in greater safety for God to show His grace; but others warned that this was a counsel of despair, and that to give ground, however great the threat, would only incur heaven's wrath and give heart to the enemy. The discussions, and the siege, went on. And every day the king heard his masses, calling constantly to mind (one chronicler suggested) 'that the persecutions of war, death and famine are the rods with which God punishes the crimes of people or princes'.

And then, on 23 February, just eleven days after the massacre at Rouvray, a little band of six armed men arrived, dusty from the road, at the great castle of Chinon. With them rode a girl, dressed as a boy, her dark hair cut short. Her name was Joan, and she had come with a message from God.

PART TWO

Joan

4

The Maid

At Chinon, they were expecting her. She had sent ahead when she and her companions had reached the town of Sainte-Catherine-de-Fierbois, twenty miles to the east, to tell the king she was coming – a letter she had to dictate, since she could not write for herself. But, as Marie Robine and Jeanne-Marie de Maillé had discovered before her, divine instruction by itself was not enough to secure access to the royal presence. For that, she needed friends in high places on earth as well as in heaven – and, like Jeanne-Marie de Maillé before her, she would find one in the dowager duchess of Anjou.

Yolande had had warning of the girl's existence weeks earlier. During the previous year Joan had appeared at Vaucouleurs, a walled town held by an Armagnac garrison in the far east of the kingdom, and asked the captain there, a man named Robert de Baudricourt, to take her to the king, for whom, she said, God had given her a message. De Baudricourt sent her away with a flea in her ear, but at the end of the year she came back, and this time the nature of the message she brought attracted more influential attention. Vaucouleurs – like the girl's home village of Domrémy, a little more than ten miles further south – lay on the frontier between the duchy of Bar and the duchy of Lorraine, and at the beginning of 1429 the duke of Lorraine himself decided that he should hear what she had to say.

Avignon and the valley of the Loire had had no monopoly on visionaries during the duke's lifetime. Thirty years earlier, in Champagne, the neighbouring county to the duchy of Bar, a poor widow named Ermine had been visited by both angels and demons in a case that had raised such troubling questions about how to tell one from the other – a process known as the 'discernment of spirits' – that they had been referred to the great theologian Jean Gerson. Now, as word of Joan's insistent claims began to spread, the duke summoned her to his court for a private conversation. And when she returned to Vaucouleurs after this audience, she discovered that, whether as cause or consequence of the duke's interest, Robert de Baudricourt had changed his mind: he was prepared to send her to Chinon.

By now, some of the inhabitants of Vaucouleurs, an Armagnac town in a region surrounded by Burgundian territory, had developed such hopes of Joan's mission to their king that they offered help for this perilous journey. She was given a horse to ride and an outfit of men's clothes – tunic, doublet, hose and breeches, all in black and grey – as a practical replacement for her rough red dress. When she left, with a black woollen hat pulled down over her cropped hair, her small escort included a royal messenger named Colet de Vienne, whose presence indicated that someone – perhaps the duke of Lorraine himself, or his son-in-law René of Anjou, twenty-year-old heir to the duchy of Bar – had already sent to Chinon to prepare her way. And there could be no doubt that any communication between the duchy of Bar and the royal court in the Loire, especially concerning a matter as weighty as a message from heaven, would come to the attention of René's mother, Yolande.

Colet and his companions did their job well. Despite the dangers of the route – more than 270 miles across country, through Burgundian lands, with the constant risk that someone might take too close an interest in their strange little fellowship – Joan reached Chinon safely. Amid the luxury and ceremony of the court, she was an utterly incongruous sight: a village girl, not yet out of her teens, dressed in clothes that no reputable woman should ever have worn. But the guiding hand of Yolande – unseen but unmistakable in the very fact of her arrival – brought her to the presence of the king, and, though their meeting was witnessed only by his chief counsellors, the clarity of her message and the conviction with which it was delivered meant that news of her mission soon raced from the castle through the town and beyond. It was as startling as the girl herself. Joan, it seemed, had been sent by God not simply to instruct the king, but to help him in the recovery of his kingdom. If Charles – whom she sometimes addressed as 'Dauphin', because he was not yet God's anointed – would give her an army, she would drive the English out of France, and lead him to Reims for his coronation.

The proposition was utterly extraordinary. Robert de Baudricourt, back in Vaucouleurs, had begun by treating this peasant girl as a fantasist whose family, he said, should give her a few slaps to snap her out of her delusions. But Baudricourt had eventually been persuaded to do as she asked, and now that she had reached the king, her words could not be dismissed so lightly. Still, the utmost caution was essential in responding to anyone who claimed prophetic insight or a special revelation of God's will, since it was not easy to tell the difference between true revelations from heaven and trickery unleashed from hell. The devil, after all, could speak with a fair face as well as foul. In this case, it was also necessary to remember that Satan's deceptions were practised more easily on women, whose moral and intellectual frailties made them more susceptible than men to demonic influence. Their fervour, Jean Gerson had written, was 'excessive, overeager, changeable, unbridled, and therefore not to be trusted' – and Joan, who was young, inexperienced and uneducated, was an especially fragile vessel.

There were other reasons, too, to be wary of her claims. Even before she opened her mouth, the girl's virtue and modesty were called into question by the extraordinary outfit she wore. Her hose and breeches, both tightly knotted with many cords onto her doublet, undoubtedly served a useful purpose in allowing her to ride quickly through dangerous country, and in offering a measure of protection against sexual assault when she found herself alone among men, as she had been on her journey from Vaucouleurs. But it could not be denied that, according to the prescriptions of the Old Testament book of Deuteronomy, a woman in men's clothing was 'an abomination unto the Lord'. And Joan not only dressed like a man, but dared to say that she had been sent to make war on the English. This was no humble recognition of a woman's place, no acknowledgement of the proper order of God's creation, but a rash boldness in which it was all too easy to guess that the devil might have taken a hand.

And yet. For Charles and his counsellors – encouraged, as always, by the wise advice of his mother-in-law Yolande – the possibility that God might at last, in his mercy, have been moved by the plight in which the holy land of France now found itself could only be intoxicating. At the same time, the profound risks that the girl embodied were clear, and terrifying. France had already been brought to the brink of destruction by God's punishment for its sins. If the most Christian king now ordered his people to follow a false prophet, an instrument of the lord of hell, he would deliver them to certain disaster. But the outcome would be equally catastrophic if he were to reject the counsel of a true prophet inspired by the king of heaven. It was well known that God would not send a miracle until all human remedies were exhausted. Fourteen long years after the wretched day of Azincourt, might He have decided that the kingdom had suffered enough, and sent help?

The only possible way forward lay in seeking expert assessment of the girl's claims. France's great repository of theological knowledge was the university of Paris, a community of scholars of international influence that was already two centuries old. But the university, like the kingdom, had been torn apart by the war between Armagnacs and Burgundians. The academic battle to demonstrate the theological truths that underpinned each side's position had already raged more than a decade earlier at the Council of Constance, where Jean

Gerson, the university's chancellor, had clashed publicly and bitterly with the Burgundian Pierre Cauchon over John the Fearless's killing of the duke of Orléans. Now, however, the university was divided physically as well as intellectually: the theologians who remained in Paris were loyal to the Anglo-Burgundian regime, while those who offered their allegiance to the Armagnac heir had fled south to his kingdom of Bourges.

Gerson himself was not among the clerics around the king at Chinon. For a year after the Burgundian seizure of the capital in 1418 he had wandered in political exile in Germany. Then, when news came of the death of John the Fearless at Montereau, he returned to France to settle at Lyon. Ten years later, now in his mid-sixties, he was still there, and still writing with his characteristic speed and intensity while living the contemplative life of a hermit. But, even in his absence, the theologians at the Armagnac court could look to his three great treatises on the discernment of spirits, the most celebrated of which – *On the Proving of Spirits*, written in 1415 – provided a checklist of the principles on which theological investigation of mystical revelations should proceed. Amid his learned discourse, Gerson summed them up in a Latin jingle: 'Ask who, what, why; to whom, what kind, whence.' In other words, he proposed an interrogation of both vision and visionary: what could the nature of the revelation itself show about its origin, and what could the nature of its recipient show about its authenticity?

The first step was to test Joan's integrity, her wholeness, in the literal sense of her physical being. Despite her alarming immodesty in wearing male clothes, she was a young unmarried woman who claimed to live a pious and God-fearing life – and if that were true she should by definition be a virgin, an unsullied state which would make it less likely that she had been suborned by the devil. A private examination by two ladies of the court, one the wife of Chinon's military captain, Raoul de Gaucourt, the other the wife of the king's counsellor Robert le Maçon, confirmed that she was indeed what she claimed to be: a maid, *pucelle* in French, from the Latin *puella*, meaning 'girl', a word that had come to signify the transitional state of chaste adolescence before a woman became a wife and mother. And *pucelle* was the word used to describe her when the clerics at court wrote to the archbishop of Embrun, the eminent theologian Jacques Gélu, to seek his advice about the next stage of investigation: testing Joan's spiritual integrity.

She was, they said, a maid from the region of Vaucouleurs, about sixteen years old, who had been brought up among the sheep, but who had come to the king with predictions and prophecies of great advantage to the kingdom – if, of course, they were true. In the attempt to find out, they had questioned her on her faith and her habits, and found her in all things devout, sober and virtuous. Might she, perhaps, be an instrument of God's will comparable to the biblical precedents of the prophetess Deborah, or Judith who had saved Israel from Assyrian invaders, or the sibyls who had foreseen the coming of Christ?

Archbishop Gélu's response was equivocal. A staunch Armagnac, he had no doubt that God might well decide to send help to the king, given that the English invasion – as he pointed out with some passion – was contrary to every kind of law, divine, natural, canon, civil, human or moral. But that undeniable fact did not mean that credence should be given quickly or lightly to the words of a peasant girl whose youth and simplicity made her so vulnerable to the power of illusions, and who came from a frontier region so near to the influence of the Burgundian enemy. The king must be cautious, Gélu said, and should redouble his prayers, keeping Joan at a distance while she was questioned at length by learned men of the Church. If there was evil in her, it could not stay hidden forever. But however unlikely it seemed that divine assistance should come in female form, given that it was not the part of a woman to fight or preach or dispense justice, it was also essential to retain an open mind, since God might bring victory through any instrument He chose.

Further inquiries were clearly necessary before any firmer judgement could be reached and decisions made about what exactly should be done. The clerics around the king knew that greater theological expertise was available at Poitiers, the administrative centre of the kingdom of Bourges, which the Armagnac scholars who had fled the university of Paris in 1418 had adopted as their new home. And so the girl Joan, who had so far been lodged with care in the great keep of the Tour du Coudray at Chinon, was dispatched forty miles southward to Poitiers for more detailed questioning by the greatest gathering of theologians that Armagnac France could muster, under the leadership of the king's chancellor, Regnault de Chartres, archbishop of Reims. For three weeks from the beginning of March, as they later explained, they observed and tested the girl 'in two ways: that is, by using human wisdom to inquire about her life, her behaviour and her aims . . ; and by devout prayer, seeking a sign of some actual or hoped-for divine deed through which it could be judged that she has come by the will of God'.

These were Gerson's principles put into action by the most skilled practitioners of the discernment of spirits in the kingdom of Bourges. And still, as the weeks passed and the conversations continued, no definitive verdict could be returned. The difficulty was that so much hung on an investigation for which there were no easy precedents. Female visionaries in the Church's recent history had experienced their revelations when they were already under the care of a spiritual adviser, a confessor perhaps, who could testify to their morals and the nature of their claims. Joan, by contrast, had appeared alone, apart from her escort of armed men. And, rather than simply conveying a message from heaven, she – a teenage girl – wanted to lead the king's troops into battle. Even when considered against a dossier of past cases that were by definition extraordinary, this one was exceptional.

But as the spring days gradually started to lengthen, some conclusions at last began to take shape. Under pressure though she was, in a place far from home and family, the girl's conduct could not be faulted. 'She has conversed with everyone publicly and privately,' the doctors and prelates reported, 'but no evil is found in her, only goodness, humility, virginity, piety, integrity and simplicity . . .' It was just as clear that her belief in her mission could not be shaken. She continued to speak with the astonishing resolve that had brought her, against all the odds, from a distant village to the royal court, and, out of her unwavering insistence that she had been sent to repel the English and lead the king to be crowned at Reims, there emerged a plan to tackle the second of the theologians' concerns. They were looking for a sign to confirm that her assertions might truly be sent from God. It was far from obvious what form such a sign might take, but when it was pointed out to Joan that her mission to lead the king from Chinon or Poitiers to Reims would be very difficult to achieve, given that the besieged town of Orléans lay directly in the way, her reply was immediate. She would raise the siege herself.

This was promising. An attempt to relieve Orléans would be a finite task, requiring only a minimum of resources to be committed by the king, that could stand as a practical test of the girl's mission. Success, if it came, would be a miraculous vindication of her claims; failure would provide an incontrovertible judgement against her. Either way, God would have spoken – and, even if the verdict were negative, there was relatively little to lose by trying. Orléans would still be under siege, just as it was now, and there would be no shame for the beleaguered kingdom of Bourges in having sought to prove Joan in the furnace of war. Archbishop Gélu had worried about exposing the king to ridicule if she were welcomed with too much credulity; the French, he said nervously, already had enough of a reputation for being easily duped. But, especially given the desperate state in which the kingdom now stood, there could be no dishonour in sending her to Orléans to discover whether her inspiration truly came from heaven. 'For to doubt or discard her, without there being any appearance of evil in her,' the theologians at Poitiers argued, 'would be to reject the Holy Spirit and render oneself unworthy of God's help.'

When the learned doctors presented their conclusions, it was with palpable relief at having found a way forward. 'The king', they said, '. . . should not prevent her from going to Orléans with his soldiers, but should have her escorted there honourably, placing his faith in God.' One last check on Joan's continued virginity, the physical embodiment of her spiritual purity, was supervised by Yolande of Aragon herself. The approval of the queen of Sicily confirmed, once again, that Joan was a true maid, and that word now began to define the public persona of a girl from a background so humble that she did not use a family name to identify herself. She was not simply *a* maid, but *the* Maid – or so the theologians at Poitiers called her in reporting their findings. And when she was given her first chance to declare her mission to a wider audience than the counsellors and theologians who had so far heard her speak, it was a title she claimed for herself with astounding assurance.

Her opportunity came shortly before the court moved back from Poitiers to Chinon to make preparations for the test she now faced. On 22 March, the Tuesday before Easter, Joan dictated a letter to be sent to the English enemy. While she was growing up in Domrémy, more than 250 miles to the east, the hostile forces she had seen close at hand were the Burgundians. But she had come to rid France of the invading English, and the challenge she now issued showed how much she had learned about the war, and about the reality of the mission she had come to fulfil, in the month since she had first arrived at Chinon. At the head of the letter, she instructed the clerk to write two words in the Latin she heard in church: *Jhesus Maria*, 'Jesus' and 'Mary', bounded on either side by the sign of the cross. And then she began.

'King of England, and you, duke of Bedford, who call yourself regent of the kingdom of France; you, William de la Pole, count of Suffolk; John, lord of Talbot; and you, Thomas, lord of Scales, who call yourselves lieutenants of the said duke of Bedford: submit yourselves to the king of heaven. Restore to the Maid, who is sent here by God, the king of heaven, the keys of all the fine towns that you have taken and violated in France.' She herself stood entirely ready to make peace, she declared, just as soon as the armies of England left Orléans, and all of France, and returned to their own country, and paid for what they had taken; but if they did not, they would shortly find that the Maid would do them great harm. 'King of England, if you do not do this, I am the military leader, and wherever I find your men in France, I will make them leave, whether they want to or not, and if they will not obey, I will have them all killed. I am sent here by God, the king of heaven, to face you head to head and drive you out of the whole of France. And if they will obey, I will show them mercy. And do not believe otherwise, for you will never hold the kingdom of France from God, the king of heaven, holy Mary's son; but King Charles will hold it, the true heir, because God, the king of heaven, wishes it, and this is revealed to him by the Maid . . .' There was more. The king, she said, would soon be back in Paris. If the English refused to listen, the Maid would raise a war-cry greater than France had heard for a thousand years. Blows would determine who had the greater right, though it was obvious that God would give victory to the Maid – and it was not too late for Bedford to join her. As prose, it was rambling and repetitive, looping in circles, veering from third person to first and back again. As a statement of intent, it was electrifying.

Singularity of purpose had brought this girl more than half-way across the country, and singularity of purpose had won her the chance to turn fighting words into action. Of course, men of experience knew that the war was not so simple, and opinion was still divided about the merits of her claims. But the disputations between the doctors of theology were not made public, nor the wranglings within the king's council; only the careful conclusion that she should be sent to Orléans. And once that decision had been taken, however short-term its focus and however provisional its rationale, Joan's utter conviction in her cause began to lend a new clarity to the actions of the kingdom of Bourges.

Once the court was back at Chinon in the last week of March, she was at last presented publicly to the king, in a piece of political theatre designed to set the scene for the launch of her mission. The story reached La Rochelle (where the town clerk noted in his register all the information that reached him) that Joan was first directed to the count of Clermont, who had recently returned from the siege, and then to one of the royal esquires, under the pretence that each was the king, only for her to declare that she knew it was not, and to recognise Charles as soon as she saw him. If this was pantomime, it nevertheless served as a dramatic demonstration of the Maid's claim to more than human insight. And after pantomime came propaganda. Not only were the conclusions of the theologians at Poitiers copied many times over and distributed as far as Armagnac diplomacy could reach, but the king's secretaries searched long and hard among the archives to find prophecies that might prefigure Joan's coming. An otherwise incomprehensible chronogram – a verse in which letters became a date when read as Roman numerals, this one attributed to Bede – made mention of a maid bearing banners: surely a foreshadowing of Joan, and all the more significant from the pen of this venerable English writer? Most pertinently, the twelfth-century text of Geoffrey of Monmouth's *History of the Kings of Britain* contained a telling prophecy by the great sage Merlin: 'A virgin ascends the backs of the archers, and hides the flower of her virginity.' What had once been obscurely allusive now clearly referred to the Maid, and a new Latin poem was hurriedly composed and disseminated, expanding on the theme of Merlin's original in the attempt to explain the king's decision to put a girl in armour at the head of his troops, and encourage loyal Frenchmen to join her.

Joan, too, played her part in elaborating the symbols of what the poet called the 'maidenly war' that she was about to undertake. She asked the king to send to the town of Sainte-Catherine-de-Fierbois, where she had stayed on her way from Vaucouleurs, to fetch a sword that, she said, lay hidden in the church there. Sure enough, and to general amazement, the weapon was discovered – according to the clerk at La Rochelle, inside a coffer at the high altar that had not been opened for twenty years. Christian warriors, contemporaries knew, carried holy swords, from King Arthur's Excalibur to Charlemagne's Joyeuse, and wise heads nodded at the thought that Joan's should come to her from St Catherine, the patron of young virgins, who was so often depicted carrying the sword through which she had met her martyrdom.

At Orléans, though, Joan would need more than a symbol to defend herself. A full suit of fine armour, handmade for her slender shape, was ordered from the king's master armourer, and a painter, a Scotsman in Tours, was commissioned to make the banners mentioned in Bede's chronogram. On the Maid's standard the golden fleurs-de-lis of France were sown across a white field, with the words *Jhesus Maria* and a painted Christ sitting in judgement over the world with an angel on either side; on her white pennon was an image of the Annunciation. During the first week in April Joan herself left Chinon for Tours, twenty-five miles further to the northeast, towards Orléans. The presence among the city's inhabitants of a Scots painter was a reminder that Tours had seen the coming of saviours before; if it was a relief that this one was French, however extraordinary she might be in other ways, no one was prepared to say. She was, at least, accumulating the attributes of a military commander: she now had a squire, Jean d'Aulon, and two pages, Louis and Raymond, who at fourteen or fifteen were only a year or two her junior, as well as a chaplain, Jean Pasquerel, who travelled with her to sing mass and hear her confession. And, impatient though she was to pursue her mission, these weeks at Chinon and Tours gave her much-needed time to learn about managing the weight of plate armour on foot and on horseback, about balance in the saddle with a lance or banner in hand, and about the war she had come to fight and the siege that lay ahead of her.

There was time, too, for the men around her to get the measure of their new companion-in-arms. The twenty-two-year-old duke of Alençon had secured his freedom from five years of captivity after the defeat at Verneuil only to find Orléans under siege and the court in turmoil. It was perhaps a measure of his disillusionment that, in the early spring of 1429, he had turned his energies to the hunting of quail, but news of Joan's arrival drew him back to Chinon. When he heard her speak and saw her ride with a lance, he was so impressed that he made her a gift of a horse for the campaign to come; then he set himself to help Yolande, with the assistance of the captains Ambroise de Loré, La Hire, Raoul de Gaucourt and the Breton knight Gilles de Rais, to prepare the supply train and the troops that Joan would lead to the besieged town.

There were influential interventions of other kinds. In Lyon, the great Gerson at last took up his pen to consider this most urgent case of *discretio spirituum*, the discernment of spirits. His strength was failing but, careful as ever, he compiled six propositions in favour of Joan's claims, and six against. His purpose, he said, was to 'invite the finest minds to reason more deeply', but his introductory remarks began with a reference to Amos, the biblical shepherd called to prophesy to the people of Israel, and went on to describe at some length the chastity, piety and conviction of this young shepherdess who said she had come to restore France to its obedience to God. It was not difficult to detect the hopes of the Armagnac partisan beneath the scholarly rigour.

And the tantalising possibility of hope had also reached the scarred and hungry town of Orléans. After the disaster at Rouvray, the prospects of repelling the English at the point of a sword had appeared vanishingly remote; so much so that the future seemed to depend on an appeal to the 'false French' – the Burgundians who fought with the English – to remember their true loyalties. Shortly after the battle, a delegation led by the captain Poton de Xaintrailles made its way past the English blockade and rode to the court of Philip of Burgundy, to offer him a deal. They would surrender the town into his hands, they said, on condition that he should hold it in the name of his cousin, the captive duke of Orléans. The English could come and go freely, and half of the town's revenues would be paid to the king of England, but the other half must be reserved for the duke's ransom. Duke Philip was pleased to agree, but when he arrived in Paris in early April, he found that the regent Bedford refused to countenance the possibility that territory belonging to the crown of France should be given over into the hands of anyone but its rightful king. Towards the end of the month, after heated words had been exchanged, the duke of Burgundy left for Flanders, and news reached Orléans that the treaty could not be concluded. But the embassy had not been in vain. In Xaintrailles's company on his return to the town was a herald from Duke Philip, bringing orders that the Burgundian forces present at the siege should withdraw. And, as the people of Orléans watched a part at least of the enemy at their gates melt away, rumours raced through the battered streets of a miraculous maid who was coming to save them.

From Chinon, Charles and his counsellors had been observing events at Orléans closely. On 21 April, four days after the Burgundian contingent abandoned the siege, Joan left Tours for Blois, another thirty-five miles along the Loire towards Orléans, and the place where her soldiers and supplies were gathering. From there, the letter in which she issued her roaring challenge to Bedford, Suffolk, Talbot, Scales and all the English in France was at last dispatched to the enemy. Carts were loaded, weapons polished, and the Maid's discipline imposed on her men; even Jean Gerson, far away in Lyon, had heard that 'she prohibits murder, rape and pillage, and any other violence' towards those who were willing to submit to the justice of her cause. On the night of 25 April she slept in her armour. And the next morning, without looking back, the Maid rode to war.

5

Like an angel from God

It was an odd sort of an army, the English soldiers thought. They had had a hard winter, stretched as they were to keep a grip on the town. There had been too few of them from the start, and many of the men who had been there at the beginning were now gone, home to England when their contract of service was up, or called away by their master, the duke of Burgundy. They were the besiegers not the besieged, but still they found themselves hungry, especially when – as had happened in the first week of April 1429 – a sortie from within the walls robbed them of a mouthwatering consignment of wine, pork and venison. Now they watched from their posts in the *bastilles* on the north bank of the river and the Tourelles tower at the southern end of the broken bridge, as more provisions, grain, cattle, sheep and pigs, approached the town from the south. For once, though, the food was not the focus of attention. Instead, English eyes were fixed on the military escort, which looked for all the world like a religious procession. From out of the forest on the southern side of the Loire walked priests, carrying a banner of the Crucifixion and singing the hymn *Veni Creator Spiritus*, 'Come, Holy Spirit'. Only then came the men-at-arms, with the carts behind; and riding among them, her fine armour gleaming in the April sun, was the girl.

They had heard about her, this blasphemous whore, even before the herald had arrived with her letter. A challenge to the enemy to surrender was nothing new; great King Harry had done the same outside the walls of Harfleur. But he had been an anointed king, God's own warrior, not a lowborn scrap of a peasant girl. She was threatening to kill them all, which made her touched in the head, or a witch, or both. And she called herself 'the Maid'. Was she daring to compare herself to the blessed Virgin, the holy mother of God, while she ran around with soldiers, her hair cut short and her legs on show like a shameless little tart? It had been clear before that the Armagnacs and their so-called dauphin were desperate, but this was ludicrous. And so they looked on, howls of derision and insults of epic profanity hanging in the spring air, while the girl and her men moved to cross the river at Chécy, upstream to the east of the town.

On that side, English defences were so thin as to be almost negligible, even before the Orléanais launched a raid on the *bastille* of Saint-Loup, the lone English fortification to the east of the gates, to buy time for the convoy of supplies to make its way past. By the time the losses were counted – several dead, injured and captured on either side, and an English standard now in Armagnac hands – the girl, as well as the provisions, had slipped through the English blockade. Her escort of priests, and most of the troops she had brought with her, had remained on the south side of the river; little point in bringing food, after all, if it came with more mouths to fill. While they turned back towards Blois, and darkness fell, the English soldiers could hear the sound of cheering carried on the wind from within the town – but any fleeting moment of unease in the English camp was soon dispelled with some well-chosen anatomical vocabulary and more mocking laughter.

Inside Orléans, meanwhile, there was delirium. Men, women and children crowded the streets, their voices raised with the exhilaration of hope after six fear-filled months of suffering, as the Maid rode among them on her white horse, her armour shining in the torchlight, her banners carried before her. Accompanied by her squire and her pages, with the town's commander, the Bastard of Orléans, and the captains La Hire and de Gaucourt beside her, she made her way slowly through the press of people – hands reaching out towards her all along the way, as though a touch would bring a blessing – to the comfortable house that had been prepared for her lodging. And, once she was safely inside, it became clear that Joan was incandescent with fury.

She had come at God's command to fight the English, with soldiers who had not simply rallied to her cause but joined her mission, making confession of their sins and forswearing pillage and prostitutes, as she required, while they marched under her standard. Raising the siege of Orléans was her task and her sign. She knew what she had to do; yet, now that she was here, she had been prevented from going immediately to confront Talbot and Scales and the rest of the English to start her work. Not only that, but her troops had been sent back to Blois against her will. The Bastard and La Hire, de Gaucourt and the others talked of tactics and strategy, of food supplies and calculation of risk, but why need she think in those terms when she had the will of God to guide her? And if God was her guide, on what grounds could these men contradict her?

It was becoming uncomfortably clear that the operational realities of the Maid's mission had not occurred to the theologians debating her case. 'The king', they had said, '. . . should not prevent her from going to Orléans with his soldiers, but should have her escorted there honourably, placing his faith in God.' That he had done; but he had failed to consider in any practical detail what might happen when she got there. As a result, Joan – the 'military leader' of France, as she had called herself in her letter to the English – now found that her first battle was with the commanders she had come to rescue.

The next day, 30 April, La Hire led a raid against the *bastille* of Saint-Pouair to the north of the city, but Joan was not interested in a skirmish; she wanted a war. The herald who had taken her letter to the enemy had been held prisoner by the English, so she wrote again to their captain, Lord Talbot, to demand the man's release, and to repeat the terms of the challenge he had carried: the English must raise the siege and return to their own country, or face defeat at the hands of the Maid. The herald was freed, but the answer with which he returned came dripping with contempt: she was a trollop, Talbot said, and should go back to herding cattle. For their part, the English would burn her. Joan was so outraged by their insolence that she climbed the fortifications overlooking the ruined bridge and shouted to the English in the Tourelles tower that they should surrender to God. She succeeded only in provoking more abuse. Did she really think, they jeered, that they should give themselves up to a woman and her pimps?

The chief pimp, the Bastard of Orléans, could see that he had a problem. A saviour had been sent to his town, and he had ridden beside her through streets that were alive with anticipation. People wanted to believe; *he* wanted to believe. But what could one girl do? He had no choice; the following day he left the town by the eastern gate, slipping past the *bastille* of Saint-Loup to ride to Blois to beg that the soldiers the Maid had brought with her should return to Orléans to fight.

He left Joan kicking her heels. For two days she rode through the town and out towards the English fortifications, finding her way around, familiarising herself with the disposition of the defences on both sides, and showing herself to the people who thronged around her everywhere she went, as if she were their guardian angel. On the third day, the burgesses of the town organised a procession in her honour, offering gifts and making a formal request for her help in lifting the siege. But formalities were hardly needed; the fact was that, until the Bastard's return, she could not put her plan – which was, simply, to attack the English – into action. At last, on the morning of 4 May, he reappeared, with Gilles de Rais and Ambroise de Loré at his side, and Joan's troops and her priests at his back. The logic of his position had won the day at Blois; there could be no sign, after all, if Joan were deprived of the means to put her mission to the test. That afternoon, finally, they would take the battle to the enemy.

Their first target was a soft one: the *bastille* of Saint-Loup, the isolated fortification on the eastern side of the city that had proved such an insufficient obstacle to the movement of soldiers in and out of the town. Still, it took three hours of hard fighting, and the intervention of a reserve force from within the walls to beat back an English attempt at rescue from the *bastille* of Saint-Pouair to the north, before Saint-Loup was taken and burned. Joan rode beside the Bastard, but she did not shed English blood herself; she carried her standard, not a weapon, to urge her soldiers on. But for the first time she saw death in battle close at hand. That evening, her mood was sombre. She ate sparingly, as was her habit. And the next day she wrote again to the enemy. 'You men of England,' she railed, 'who have no right in this kingdom of France, the king of heaven orders and commands you through me, Joan the Maid, to abandon your strongholds and go back to your own country. If not, I will make a war-cry that will be remembered forever.' She was forthright as always, but no longer rambling. Now, she was losing patience. 'I am writing this to you for the third and last time; I will write no more.' As she directed, the clerk added the inscription '*Jhesus Maria*' before her name, '*Jeanne la Pucelle*': Joan the Maid. She tied the letter to an arrow, and ordered an archer to shoot it into the English camp. When it dropped to the ground, the shouts could be heard in the distance: 'News from the Armagnac whore!'

Now that Saint-Loup was in French hands, the defenders of Orléans could cross the river unimpeded, and that same day they made their move on the *bastille* of Saint-Jean-le-Blanc, the only fortification on the southern bank of the Loire to the east of the Tourelles bridgehead. But when they got there, they found it empty. After the fall of Saint-Loup the previous day, the English had retreated into the stronghold of the Tourelles and the *bastille* of the Augustins that defended it. For all the derision and abuse they had hurled her way, the enemy, it seemed, had been rattled by Joan's singular presence and her determination to attack. And now the

day of reckoning was at hand, because the Augustins and the Tourelles were the key to the town's safety. Here, at last, the Maid would
lead the assault to raise the siege, and – whether in victory or defeat
– God would give His verdict on her mission.

When dawn came on 6 May, Joan's chaplain heard her confession and sang mass for her and her men. If the English were dis-
comfited, the Armagnac soldiers and the Orléanais they were there
to defend were full of fire and hope. God had sent the Maid to save
France, and this was the moment, here at Orléans, when the salvation she brought would begin. Many loyal Frenchmen would lose
their lives in her service; that much was unavoidable. But to die
doing God's work was an end devoutly to be wished for. It was
with eager purpose that the troops crossed the river once again,
with the Bastard, La Hire and de Rais riding beside the Maid at
their head. Almost at once, they encountered an English contingent
bearing down on them from the Augustins, but Joan and La Hire
led a ferocious charge that beat the enemy back to the fortifications
of the *bastille*. It took all day, and the combat was bloody, but by
sundown the Augustins was in French hands, and the Englishmen
who had held it were either corpses or prisoners.

Suddenly, it was not Orléans but the Tourelles that was under
siege. On the north side of the tower were the waters of the Loire
and the ruins of the stone bridge that had once led into the town.
Immediately to the south lay the Augustins, the *bastille* on the bank
that now threatened rather than protected the English position. The
English garrison was trapped. An Armagnac force remained outside the walls of the Tourelles throughout the night, well supplied
by the townspeople with food and wine to keep up their strength
for the next day's assault. The battle began at daybreak, and, as
missiles fell like savage hail from the ramparts above, it was clear
that this would be a struggle in which no quarter would be giv-
en. The English were fighting for their position, for their lives and
for the belief that God was still with them; but the momentum of

the French attack was driven by a new conviction that heaven had intervened on their side, in the miraculous person of the Maid.

For hours it seemed as though this irresistible force had met an immovable object. Wave after wave of Armagnac assailants broke on the formidable defences of the Tourelles. As exhaustion took its toll and the sun sank lower in the sky, Joan was caught by an arrow between her neck and shoulder, and, at the sight of their Maid staggering and bloodied, the French began to falter. The Bastard prepared to sound the retreat, but Joan stopped him. It was a flesh wound, nothing worse, and she pressed forward into the ditch at the foot of the tower, brandishing her standard. When they saw her rise from where she had fallen, and heard her urging them on, her soldiers pushed again towards the walls and began to climb the scaling-ladders to the ramparts. Sudden fear gripped the English, and when, in the distance, they saw townsmen emerge from the gate on the other side of the river with great planks of wood to bridge the ruined arches, and more soldiers waiting to cross behind them, their frayed nerves finally broke. Their captain, Sir William Glasdale, whose voice had led the chorus of crude invective aimed at Joan over the previous days, lost his footing and toppled, fully armed, into the water. He did not reappear. Panic spread among his men, and by the time the sun tipped below the horizon, the Tourelles was once again an Armagnac fortress.

The carpenters at the bridge had done their work so well that Joan, the Bastard and their troops were able to re-enter the town directly from the Tourelles – the first time the crossing had been made there since the siege had taken hold six months earlier. Through the gate they met a wall of noise, church bells clanging in jubilant cacophony, streets packed with priests and people singing the great hymn of praise, *Te Deum Laudamus*, and calling on the town's patron saints, the long-dead bishops Aignan and Euverte, to bless their living saviour, the Maid. But, while the celebrations continued, she needed to rest and eat and receive treatment for her wound, because her work was not yet over: the taking of the Tourelles had broken the English grip on Orléans, but garrisons remained in the *bastilles* ranged around the town to the north and west. And when first light came next morning, the sentries watching from the town walls reported that the enemy was arming for battle.

The defenders of Orléans mustered to meet them. La Hire, de Rais and the other captains rode out of the town beside the girl who had now, extraordinarily, become their brother-in-arms. They drew up their forces close to the English position and waited, alert and ready. But they did not move. For the first time since she had come to war, Joan did not order her men forward. They should defend themselves with all their power if the English attacked, she said, but they should not start the fight. After the triumph of the previous day, tired though they were, the troops were restive in their eagerness to put the enemy to flight, but they obeyed the Maid's command. Behind the English lines, the *bastilles* abandoned by the besiegers overnight were empty, and some were burning; whatever happened now, it was clear, would be the last act of this brutal drama. An hour passed, and still the armies did not stir. And then, at last, a command rang out, and the English ranks began to peel away. The siege was over.

English casualties had been so heavy and the loss of the bridgehead so grave, the chronicler Monstrelet later reported, that the commanders Suffolk, Talbot and Scales had decided that their wisest option was an orderly retreat from fortifications they could no longer be confident of holding. They would fight the Armagnacs if they had to; but when no attack came, they gave the signal to withdraw. The unnerving matter of the girl sent from God was, it seemed, best left entirely unspoken. The girl herself and her fellow captains, her troops and the jubilant people of Orléans all watched the English go. Only when it was too late for the enemy to turn again and fight did Armagnac soldiers ride to harry them on their way, and to raid the artillery train at the rear of the English convoy for guns to add to the French arsenal.

The miracle had happened. After six months of siege, and with the kingdom of Bourges in disarray, Joan the Maid had freed Orléans in just four days – *four days* – of fighting. The threat that the English might snatch this key to the Loire was lifted. And even more importantly, God had vindicated the legitimacy of King Charles's cause. A seventeen-year-old peasant girl knew nothing of war: how could she? Yet Joan had known what she would do. The learned doctors at Poitiers had asked for a sign, and it had come, heaven-sent.

In Orléans itself, the churches were packed with people giving thanks, in wonder, for their deliverance. Citizens who had once feared the depredations of the soldiers sent to defend their town now embraced them, the chronicler of the siege noted, as if they were their own children. But it was Joan who was the focus of their devotion – and now her fame began to spread. Just two days after the English retreat, Pancrazio Giustiniani, an Italian merchant in Bruges, wrote to tell his father in Venice what had happened at Orléans, and how a 'maiden shepherdess' had promised the dauphin that the siege would be lifted; 'it seems', he said, 'that she may be another St Catherine come down to earth'. In Rome, the bishop of Cahors, Jean Dupuy, hurriedly added a new chapter to his magnum opus, a brief history of the world, to describe the 'maid named Joan' who 'accomplishes actions which appear more divine than human'.

And in Lyon, the frail and elderly Jean Gerson once again applied the principles of *discretio spirituum*, the discernment of spirits, to this most exceptional case. The first treatise he had produced on the subject, with its even-handed exposition of points for and against Joan's claims, was known simply as *De quadam puella*: 'About a certain maid'. That his second became known as *De puella Aurelianensi* – 'About the Maid of Orléans' – or alternatively *De mirabili victoria* – 'About the wonderful victory' – reflected the change in his judgement wrought by the dramatic events of the first week of May. He began with his customary caution, offering an extended discussion of the relationship between probability and truth, and a recitation of a number of theological questions in which disagreement between learned scholars could not be definitively resolved. But, having said all that, a verdict on the Maid was now possible, he believed, because the outcome of her actions – the restitution of the king to his kingdom, and the defeat of France's most obdurate enemies – justified belief in their divine inspiration. She did not resort to spells or superstitions; she took risks to pursue her mission; she inspired faith in the king and his people and fear in his enemies; and she did not tempt God by acting imprudently. Her story found parallels, he pointed out, in the holy lives of Deborah, Judith and St Catherine. And, if she wore men's clothes despite the Old Testament prohibition, that could be excused because the Old Testament had been superseded by the New, and because her circumstances, as a warrior surrounded by men, made it necessary. His conclusion was simple. 'This deed', he wrote, 'was done by God.'

As manuscript copies of Gerson's new treatise began to circulate across France and beyond, at Chinon the court was celebrating. During the evening of Monday 9 May, the king had composed a letter to the people of Narbonne, three hundred miles away in the Languedoc, to give them the encouraging report that two supply trains had succeeded in breaching the siege at Orléans during the previous week, and that the *bastille* of Saint-Loup had been captured, to the great loss of the English. Heartfelt thanks and prayers were due to God, he said; but then, at one in the morning, a herald came pounding on the castle gates with news that seemed scarcely believable, had the exhausted man not sworn on his life that it was true. The *bastille* of the Augustins and the tower of the Tourelles had fallen, praise be to God who, in His divine mercy, had not forgotten France, and these victories had been accomplished in the presence of the Maid. Charles was busy adding this astonishing postscript to his letter to the Narbonnais when two more messengers arrived, sent by Raoul de Gaucourt to tell him that the English had fled, and Orléans was free.

Three days later, the Maid herself rode with the Bastard to meet the king, to report on what they had achieved, and petition for more men and money to finish the task. Charles must go to Reims, Joan insisted, for the coronation that would give divine sanction to his kingship. She would lead him there; but before that crucial campaign could be undertaken, the route north and east across the Loire would have to be cleared by sweeping away the remaining English garrisons along the river at Meung, Beaugency and Jargeau. After the miracle at Orléans, there could be no question of dismissing the Maid's mission or ignoring her instructions, but her triumph had not eliminated the military and financial challenges facing the kingdom of Bourges. It took the best part of a month for the new troops she needed to be mustered – a frustrating delay, but one during which Joan could, at least, continue to refine her developing skills on horseback and with weapons of war. A young nobleman, Guy de Laval, who met her during a visit to the court, saw her wearing plate armour and riding a great black warhorse with a small axe in her hand. When he visited her at her lodgings, she ordered wine to be brought, and said she would soon be offering him a drink in Paris. His admiration was breathless and fervent. 'It seemed to me a gift from heaven', he told his mother, 'that she was there, and that I was seeing her and hearing her.'

By the time de Laval's letter was written on 8 June, preparations were nearly complete. His encounter with the Maid had taken place at Selles-sur-Cher, a little more than twenty miles south-east of Blois, and she was joined there by the young duke of Alençon, who had helped muster the troops for her first campaign. Now, the duke was ready to fight. He was by her side, along with the Bastard, Xaintrailles, La Hire, de Loré and other captains, when they rode for Jargeau, the English stronghold ten miles upstream from Orléans. Alençon, as the prince of the blood present in the field, was now the king's lieutenant in command of this campaign, but there was no mistaking the fact that it was Joan's relentless purpose – the conviction and the burgeoning charisma that had so dazzled de Laval – which drove the army forward.

On 11 June they laid siege to the earl of Suffolk's forces in Jargeau, beating the English back from the suburbs until they withdrew behind the town's walls. As she had done at Orléans, Joan sent a message that night to tell the enemy they could save their own lives, if they would give up the town to God and King Charles. When the refusal came – notably, this time without the mockery that had been the prelude to so many English deaths at Orléans – French guns began to sound, and by the morning the walls were pitted and damaged, and one of the great towers broken.

Still, the task of taking a fortified town by headlong assault was daunting. Word had come that Sir John Fastolf, the victor of the Battle of the Herrings, was approaching from Paris with reinforcements, and some of the French captains counselled caution: perhaps retreat, or an attempt to meet Fastolf in the open, before he could approach Jargeau itself. But Joan insisted on immediate attack. Again, she carried her standard into the ditch outside the walls; again she was felled by a missile, this time a stone thrown at her head by an English soldier. And once again she got back to her feet, shouting to her men that there could be no doubt of their victory because God was with them. It seemed to French and English alike as though events at Orléans were repeating themselves: after four hours of unrelenting assault, Joan's presence urged the French forward while the English shrank back in fear. When French troops scaled their ladders and hacked their way onto the ramparts, the earl of Suffolk himself was taken prisoner, pausing for a moment to knight the soldier who captured him before surrendering into the man's newly honourable hands. With him, Jargeau fell, and the

Maid, Alençon and the Bastard led their captives back to Orléans, where they were welcomed with wild celebrations.

From there they moved westward to Meung, ten miles down-river – another walled town, this one with a fortress outside its gates where the English lords Talbot and Scales had taken refuge after their retreat from the siege at Orléans. Rather than attempt a double assault on town and castle, the Armagnac army seized the fortified bridge that gave access over the Loire and left a garrison to hold it while they moved on another few miles to Beaugency, leaving Talbot and Scales cut off on the northern side of the river. The siege was set at Beaugency on 15 June, with the French artillery menacingly ranged, but the following day disturbing news reached Joan and the Armagnac captains on two fronts. From the north, Sir John Fastolf and his troops were now very close to their position, while approaching from the south-west – to general consternation – was the count of Richemont, the renegade constable of the king-dom of Bourges, who had not appeared in the field for months, ever since he had taken up arms against his former protégé and chief rival for power at court, Georges de La Trémoille. It seemed that word of the Maid's miraculous exploits had tempted Richemont out of his fastness at Parthenay. If God were to grant famous victories against the English, he wanted a share of the glory.

For Joan and the duke of Alençon, however, the constable's imminent arrival was profoundly alarming, given that the king had barred him from his presence and proscribed him from his service. At the same time, the fact was that Fastolf was the clear and present danger, and Richemont brought with him more than a thousand fresh troops. After fraught discussion within the Armagnac camp, Joan, Alençon and the Bastard rode to meet him. Richemont's admiring biographer later put a carelessly heroic speech into his mouth, made while Joan – supposedly – knelt at his feet: 'They tell me that you want to fight me,' the constable reportedly declared. 'I don't know if you are from God or not; if you are from God, I fear you not at all, because God knows well my good intentions. If you are from the devil, I fear you even less.' Much more plausible were reports that Joan and the other commanders made him swear a solemn oath that he would serve the king faithfully before they would agree to fight at his side. However it was achieved, Richemont's forces joined the siege. And when Fastolf arrived at Beaugency, with Talbot and Scales now in his company, the Armagnac position appeared too strong to attack. The English reinforcements withdrew upriver to the castle outside the walls of Meung, and that night the besieged garrison of Beaugency, despairing now of rescue, negotiated their surrender.

The following day, 18 June, the soldiers from Beaugency left for Paris, with their lives, their horses and little else. When this devastating news reached Meung that morning, Fastolf, Talbot, Scales and their men followed them onto the road north; the fortress there was not worth holding if the river was lost. But behind them, spurred on by the Maid's determination that the English should now be driven out of the valley of the Loire at swordpoint, was the full force of the Armagnac army, moving at speed with La Hire and Xaintrailles in the vanguard, and Richemont, Alençon, the Bastard, de Rais, de Gaucourt and Joan herself at the head of their troops. The English had not quite reached the village of Patay – not far from the scene of Fastolf's triumph at the Battle of the Herrings just four months earlier – when their scouts brought alarming reports of this furious pursuit.

As before, Fastolf took up a defensive formation, with Talbot and several hundred archers holding a forward position, a narrow pass between two woods, to protect the main body of the army behind them. The familiar but formidable plan was that a storm of English arrows would take the Armagnacs by surprise. The troops were almost in place when suddenly a stag erupted out of the woods and plunged into the English ranks, precipitating a great shout of confusion and fear just at the moment when advance riders from the French forces were approaching within earshot. The animal had given away the English position before Talbot's archers had finished planting their sharpened stakes in the ground and making ready their bows; the trap that the English were attempting to lay would be sprung on them, it turned out, by their Armagnac enemy. With a roar, the Maid's soldiers charged into Talbot's position, sharpened steel meeting flesh and bone. As the English collapsed into confusion and panic, Talbot and Scales were captured, and, despairing amid the slaughter, Fastolf turned his horse and fled.

Already before the battle, according to a Burgundian knight named Jean Waurin who fought under Fastolf's command, 'by the renown of Joan the Maid the hearts of the English were greatly changed and weakened, and they saw, as it seemed to them, that Fortune was turning her wheel harshly against them'. Now, the bloodshed at Patay had not only secured the frontier of the kingdom of Bourges, but pushed it back across the Loire into English France. All this had been achieved in just seven weeks since the Maid's arrival at Orléans. 'And by these operations', Waurin wrote, 'she acquired so great praise and renown that it really seemed to all men that the enemies of King Charles would have no power of resistance in any place where she was present, and that by her means the said king would shortly be restored to his kingdom in spite of all those who wished to gainsay it.'

That was what Joan had said all along. And next, she would lead the king to his coronation.

6

A heart greater than any man's

There was one person, at least, in London who received the news from France with pleasure. By now, the duke of Orléans had been a prisoner in England for fourteen of his thirty-five years. He was an honoured captive, allowed to live in the luxury his royal blood demanded and to receive carefully monitored visits from his French servants, but he was powerless to help his town of Orléans during its long months of suffering under English siege. Now it was free, thanks to the marvellous intervention of this extraordinary girl. In tribute, the duke sent her a gift: a fine robe and short jacket in crimson and darkest green, the livery colours of the house of Orléans, to be made up for her by a draper and tailor in the town.

Jean Gerson had believed, when he wrote his first treatise to consider the Maid's case, that she changed back into women's clothes when she was not riding with soldiers; whenever she dismounted from her horse, he said, this peasant girl was as inexperienced in worldly matters as an innocent lamb. Gerson might once have been right on both counts, but no longer. When she took off her armour, she dressed as a man, in silken hose and satin doublets like the one sent by the captive duke. She had servants to wait on her. She could summon wine when she was thirsty, as she did when she drank with the bedazzled Guy de Laval, and she could send Laval's aristocratic grandmother a gold ring, apologising as she did so that it was only a tiny trinket. Now, she was not just a peasant girl but a player on the political stage of the Armagnac court – a position that, day by day, brought with it new experience of a complex and frustrating kind.

After their triumph at Patay, Joan and the duke of Alençon had rejoined the king at Sully-sur-Loire, a moated fortress belonging to his favourite, Georges de La Trémoille, that lay twenty-five miles eastward along the river from Orléans. Charles greeted them with delight, thanking God for giving the Maid such courage in her mission, and extending an elegant welcome to her noble English prisoners. But when Joan knelt to petition the king that Richemont, who had brought so many soldiers to her cause and fought bravely at her side, should be pardoned his previous offences, the reply was much less fulsome. Richemont was forgiven, Charles said, but he should not come to court, nor join the king on his progress to his coronation at Reims. To Joan, this was baffling. God had sent her to reunite France in the service of its true sovereign. Why, then, would the king not embrace a prodigal son returning to the fold? The answer, it was clear, lay with La Trémoille, whose enthusiasm for Joan's victories was diluted by concern that they might reintroduce undesirable influences into the politics of a kingdom in which he currently held such sway. The unhappy lesson Joan was beginning to learn was that even a mission from heaven could not easily repair the rifts in this fractured court.

Still, at least the king had agreed to leave the renewed safety of the Loire to make the journey to Reims for the coronation that the Maid had promised. This would be his first foray into enemy territory since the aftermath of the Armagnac victory at Baugé eight years earlier, when his father and the warrior-king Henry of England had still been alive – and, for a king who had never led his people from the military front line, it was not a reassuring prospect. Reims itself, where the sacred oil of Clovis was kept in the Holy Ampulla, lay under Burgundian control, and much of the hundred miles and more of territory between there and the Loire was in English or Burgundian hands. Other voices at court argued that Reims was a distraction, and pressed instead for a strike into the English heartlands in Normandy, but Joan was adamant that the king must be anointed and crowned. Once God had sanctioned his kingship, she knew, the power of his enemies would wither away.

She had been right at Orléans, a verdict confirmed by glorious victory at Patay. Men were flocking to join the king's army for the first time in years, and towns such as Janville, twenty miles north of Orléans – where Fastolf had attempted to take refuge after the fighting at Patay, only to find the gates closed against him – were spontaneously reverting to Armagnac loyalties. Her mission, in other words, was unanswerable. And so, on 29 June, the royal party set out.

The king rode at the head of thousands, the largest army he could muster; he had summoned all of his subjects who were fit to bear arms to come to his aid, and now he sent letters ahead to warn the Anglo-Burgundian towns that lay in his path of his imminent approach. If they would render the obedience that was rightfully his, the past would be forgotten, with no further thought of royal vengeance for their disloyalty. The scarcely veiled threat did its work at Auxerre, where the Burgundian town governors showed no appetite for armed confrontation, and by the morning of 5 July the Armagnac army had moved on to Troyes, the place where the outrageous sentence of disinheritance had been formally pronounced against France's true heir almost a decade earlier.

But the people of Troyes, it turned out, would not so easily be persuaded to open their gates. They had sworn allegiance to the duke of Burgundy and to King Henry, the lawful successor to King Charles the Well-Beloved by the terms of the treaty that had been sealed in their cathedral, and their garrison of English and Burgundian soldiers stood ready to defend them against the pretensions of the so-called dauphin and his army of traitors. Nor were they cowed by the presence of the girl who called herself the Maid. Within their walls was a man well qualified to judge her claims of divine inspiration: a friar named Brother Richard, who had first come to public attention in Paris three months earlier. For ten days in April he had preached warnings of the coming of the Antichrist to crowds of thousands, summoning up the pains of hellfire with such terrifying immediacy that men burned great heaps of chess-boards, dice, cards 'and every kind of covetous game that can give rise to anger and swearing', said the journal-writer in the city, while women tossed elaborate headdresses and other such feminine vanities into the flames. Now he had brought his apocalyptic message to Troyes, and so the townspeople sent him out to discover whether Joan had come to them from heaven or hell.

When he returned, however, it was not with the answer for which they were hoping. They had thought he might declare her a heretic or a witch, to be condemned like the mandrake roots – kept by the foolish in the superstitious belief that they would bring earthly riches – which he had tossed onto the bonfires in Paris. Instead, Brother Richard had been so impressed by the Maid that he brought back a letter she had dictated the day before her arrival outside the walls of Troyes, addressed to the town's inhabitants. They had received a missive already from Charles, the rightful king of France; now Joan brought them word from the almighty king of heaven. She did not forget that the people of Troyes were Frenchmen, to be welcomed back to the path of righteousness, not Englishmen to be threatened with God's wrath, but her instructions – after her customary invocation of the holy names *Jhesus Maria* – were no less direct.

'Very dear and good friends,' she began, 'if that is what you are: my lords, townsmen and people of the town of Troyes, Joan the Maid brings you a message from the king of heaven, her rightful sovereign lord, in whose royal service she spends each day, that you should submit yourselves in true recognition to the noble king of France, who will very soon be in Reims and in Paris, whosoever may oppose him, and in his fine towns of this holy kingdom, with the aid of King Jesus. Loyal Frenchmen, come before King Charles, and do not fail; and have no fear for your lives or your possessions if you do so.' Her arms were open to receive them, but still there was steel behind her words. 'If you do not do this, I promise and swear to you, on your lives, that we will enter with God's help into all the towns which rightfully belong to this holy kingdom, and we will impose a good and lasting peace, whosoever opposes us. I commit you to God; may God preserve you, if that be His will. Reply at once.'

But the authorities in Troyes felt little inclined to obey this peremptory demand. Brother Richard was not the honourable man they had thought, it was clear, but a sorcerer, and this girl was a madwoman inspired by the devil; not Joan the Maid, but Joan the Braggart. They read her letter and mocked it – it had no rhyme or reason, they declared – and then burned it without responding. As they watched the Armagnac army range itself outside their walls, they wrote urgently instead to the citizens of Reims, asking them to petition the regent Bedford and the duke of Burgundy to come to their aid. In the meantime, they prepared themselves to defend their town to the death.

It was not long, though, before an early sortie by some of their soldiers demonstrated that the army of traitors was unnervingly larger than they had imagined. As the impasse dragged on from one day into two, and from two into three, their hopes of rescue began to fade, along with the certainties of their position. Was it possible that Brother Richard might be right after all that this girl had some kind of authority from God? They could not know, as heralds moved fruitlessly between the two sides, that anxiety was building outside as well as inside the town walls. There were many hungry mouths in the Armagnac army, and little with which to feed them. The besiegers were short of money and artillery, and the town was strongly defended. Perhaps, as the king's chancellor Regnault de Chartres, archbishop of Reims, suggested to a receptive audience of royal counsellors and captains, they should leave Troyes to its intransigence, and move back to the safety and plenty of the Loire. But the veteran Robert le Maçon insisted that one more opinion should be sought: that of the Maid, who rode at the head of the king's troops, but who was not a regular presence among the wise heads of the king's council. She, le Maçon said, was the reason they were there; she should therefore be given the chance to speak.

Joan was duly summoned, and the difficulties of their position explained. Not for the first time, she was mystified. These details were irrelevant. What reason was there, now or ever, to deviate from a course set by God Himself? The answer was simple. Within two or three days she would lead the king through the gates of Troyes, of that there could be no doubt. The counsellors knew they had a choice: either follow her faith, or set it aside in favour of reason. But, if they opted for the latter course, why had they left the Loire for the dangerous journey to Reims in the first place? Put that way, their decision was already made.

And so, with the reluctant blessing of the royal council, Joan rode out on her warhorse in full view of the watching townspeople, directing her soldiers to make ready what guns they had and to fill the ditches around the walls with brushwood. After four days of fear and deepening uncertainty, the sight of these preparations for an assault led by the miraculous Maid finally shattered the town's resistance. The gates opened, a deputation emerged to offer terms for surrender, and the next morning the king rode into Troyes in imposing procession, with Joan and her banner at his side. The following day, 11 July, the governors of the town hastily wrote again to Reims. This time, there was no mention of the regent Bedford and the duke of Burgundy, of their oath to serve King Henry, or of fighting to the death; this time, they explained that King Charles was prepared to forget the past, and that he would bring peace to his realm, just as his ancestor St Louis had done. The people of Reims would surely share the joy that Troyes now knew, once they had submitted to a prince of such discretion, understanding and valour.

It was not long before the people of Reims received another letter offering a rather different version of events. As bad luck would have it, the captain of their own garrison was not with them in the town, but his brother wrote urgently from nearby Châtillon-sur-Marne to tell them that many loyal knights at Troyes had not wanted to capitulate. Despite this firm opposition, and the evident weaknesses in the enemy position, the wiles of Brother Richard – or so the captain's brother had heard – had persuaded the bishop and many of the common people to open the gates to the Armagnacs. The squire who had brought him this news from Troyes had seen Joan the Maid with his own eyes, and heard her speak, and swore that she was so simple as to be almost half-witted; she made no more sense, the man reported, than the greatest fool he had ever seen.

Not everyone, it seemed, was convinced by the peasant girl dressed in armour, talking about God and playing at soldiers. But whatever view the people of Reims now took of her, the fact was – as their returning captain was unwillingly forced to admit – that any prospect of rescue by the dukes of Bedford and Burgundy was weeks away, while the enemy was almost within sight. On 16 July, the inhabitants of Châlons, twenty-five miles south-east of Reims, wrote to inform their neighbours that they too had decided to receive the gracious and merciful King Charles as their sovereign, and to advise that Reims should do the same without delay. In the end, the choice was quickly made. When the king and his army arrived at Sept-Saulx, just twelve miles from the town, they were met by a group of dignitaries from Reims who knelt to offer Charles their obedience as their rightful monarch.

That evening, the king rode through the gates of Reims while crowds cried '*Noël!*' in welcome. The cheers were politic, but their meaning was inscrutable; after so many years of conflict it was impossible to distinguish between expressions of relief and fear, between enthusiasm and exhaustion. Charles was greeted by the town's archbishop, his own chancellor Regnault de Chartres, who had left his side only a few hours earlier to take possession at last of the archiepiscopal seat from which he had been exiled during its years in Burgundian hands. And that night, while the king rested in the sumptuous surroundings of the archbishop's palace, his officers, counsellors and servants worked through the hours of darkness to prepare for the makeshift coronation that would take place in the great cathedral the very next day.

At nine in the morning of Sunday 17 July, forty-nine years after his father's coronation and seven after his father's death, Charles VII of France entered the cathedral of Reims for his own conse-cration. The octagonal labyrinth inlaid in black and white marble in the floor of the nave might have seemed to represent the tortu-ous path which God in His wisdom had required the king to tread, had it not been for the fact that, since the Maid's arrival, heaven had opened the way before him with a new and startling directness. Four months earlier, he had contemplated retreat to the far south of his kingdom in the face of a usurpation that had begun to seem inexorable and irreversible. Now, after the miracle at Orléans and victory at Patay, he had advanced deep into territory held by his enemies, without a blow being struck to resist him. The ancient regalia of Charlemagne still, for the moment, lay out of his reach at Saint-Denis, but a substitute crown and sword had been made ready, and at six o'clock that morning four of his knights, including Gilles de Rais, had gone to the nearby abbey of Saint-Rémi to col-lect the sacred oil of Clovis with which his kingship would, at last, be given sacramental force.

Now the knights rode fully armed on their great chargers through the west door of the cathedral to present the Holy Ampulla to the archbishop at the entrance to the choir. And so the ceremony began. Lacking though it might have been in prepared magnificence, its sanctity was palpable. With prayers and psalms, the king was pre-sented to God, and the holy oil with which he was touched at the head, breast, shoulders and arms consecrated him to the service of heaven as the anointed sovereign of his people. At that sacred moment, and again when the archbishop placed the crown on his brow, cries of '*Noël!*' echoed to the vaulted ceiling that soared high above, and trumpets sounded so loudly, one observer declared, that it seemed the vaults themselves might shatter. And throughout it all, Joan the Maid stood at Charles's side, dressed in her shining armour and holding her white banner in her hand.

Now, at last, the true king of France was truly a king. After the ceremony, Joan knelt at his feet. 'Noble king, God's will is done,' she said, and began to weep, overcome with the magnitude of what heaven had helped her accomplish. As she had promised, she had brought the man she had once called the dauphin to Reims and seen him crowned, with the nobility of the most Christian kingdom gathered around him. The duke of Alençon, the count of Clermont and the Bastard of Orléans were there. The devoted Guy de Laval, who had fought at Joan's side ever since meeting her at Selles, was made a count that day, along with the king's most beloved counsellor Georges de La Trémoille. Gilles de Rais was appointed a marshal of France, under the approving gaze of the captains with whom he and Joan had ridden to war at Orléans and Patay. They had been joined in time for the ceremony by the king's brother-in-law, Yolande's son René of Anjou, heir to the duchies of Bar and Lorraine. And also newly arrived from Bar, along with the young duke-to-be, was a small group of wondering faces that were dearly familiar to Joan: her father, her brothers, her cousin's husband and her godfather, who were given lodgings at an inn at the expense of the townspeople.

But, despite the tears and the jubilation, there were figures missing from this loyal gathering whose absence was a pointed reminder of what still remained to be done. Regardless of Joan's pleas, the constable, Arthur of Richemont, who should have carried the sword of state in procession before the king, had been refused permission to attend, his place taken instead by the half-brother of his enemy La Trémoille. The duke of Orléans, the king's first cousin, was unavoidably detained by the bars of his gilded English prison. And the most significant absentee of all was the duke of Burgundy, the prince of the blood royal whose feud with the newly crowned king lay at the heart of France's self-mutilation. If the kingdom were to be made whole again, and the English driven away for good, then Philip of Burgundy would need to stand at King Charles's side. All parties within the Armagnac court knew that to be true, however wide the rifts between them yawned. La Trémoille, who had been a Burgundian before he was an Armagnac and whose brother Jean remained in Burgundian service, had been involved in diplomatic exchanges with Duke Philip's envoys since the end of June, and at that point Joan too had taken it upon herself to write to the duke to remind him of his duty to come to Reims for the coronation of his rightful king.

Now, on the triumphal day of the ceremony itself, she summoned her clerk once again. '*Jhesus Maria*', she began. 'High and mighty prince, duke of Burgundy, Joan the Maid calls upon you by the king of heaven, my rightful and sovereign lord, that you and the king of France should make a good and lasting peace. Forgive one another entirely, in good faith, as loyal Christians should do; and if you wish to make war, do so against the Saracens.' She was respectful – 'prince of Burgundy, I pray, beseech and call upon you as humbly as I can that you should make no more war in the holy kingdom of France' – but she did not hesitate to make clear how much was at stake, and what the consequences would be if the duke took no account of her words. 'I bring you word from the king of heaven, my rightful and sovereign lord, for your good, for your honour and upon your life, that you will win no battle against loyal Frenchmen, and that all who wage war against the holy kingdom of France wage war against King Jesus, the king of heaven and of the whole world, my rightful and sovereign lord. And, with my hands clasped, I pray and call upon you that you fight no battle and wage no war against us, neither you, nor your men or subjects; and know surely that, however many men you bring against us, they will win nothing at all, and great sorrow will be the result of the great battle and the blood that will be shed there by those who come against us.'

The evident truth of her words was demonstrated by the fates of those to whom she had written before: the English at Orléans, defeated, and the Frenchmen of Troyes, surrendered. And yet Philip of Burgundy had made no reply to her first letter, nor did he respond to this, her second. If any flicker of hesitation had crossed the duke's mind, any moment of questioning whether the gift of prophecy this girl claimed might truly come from heaven, it had been extinguished – in public, at least – exactly a week earlier, when he was welcomed with great magnificence into the city of Paris by his brother-in-law, the duke of Bedford.

These were ceremonies in which Bedford's elegant words of greeting were uttered through gritted teeth. The regent could have been forgiven for wondering how he came to find himself facing such parlous news that summer. He had not wanted to besiege Orléans in the first place; that had been the earl of Salisbury's plan, until a cannonball had torn his face away. Even then, the so-called dauphin and his Armagnac rebels had been almost on the run, until the arrival of this girl, this witch, who was now leading the false king to Reims for a spurious coronation. Back in April, even before Joan had arrived at Orléans, Bedford had written to the council in England to request reinforcements, and to propose that the child-king Henry should himself be crowned as soon as possible. He knew how important it was to demonstrate that God was with this boy who ruled two kingdoms, just as He had been with his glorious father at Agincourt. But the council in England had done nothing. And now, after the extraordinary reverses that had befallen the English in the intervening months, it was left to Bedford to remind his Burgundian brother-in-law of his divinely sanctioned duty to fight the Armagnacs.

The public ritual that marked Duke Philip's five-day visit to Paris included a grand procession and a sermon preached at

Notre-Dame, but at the heart of this political performance was a spectacle that took place on 14 July in the presence of the two dukes at the royal palace on the Île de la Cité. There, reported the journal-writer, it was publicly rehearsed how 'in former times' the so-called dauphin and his perfidious Armagnacs had made peace with the duke of Burgundy's noble father, and had sworn solemn oaths and taken together the sacrament of the Eucharist, 'the precious body of Our Lord', and how then the duke's father – 'desiring and longing that the kingdom should be at peace, and wishing to keep the promise he had made' – had knelt before the dauphin on the bridge at Montereau, only to be treacherously murdered. At this reminder of the crimes committed by the man the Armagnacs dared to call their king, there was uproar in the Parisian crowd, until the regent Bedford called for silence to allow the duke of Burgundy to speak of his sorrow at the broken peace and his father's untimely death. Then the two dukes together swore to defend the city, and called on its inhabitants to swear in their turn that they would be loyal and true.

In the emotion of the moment, it was easy to forget how rare it was these days for the two dukes to be in Paris at all, let alone at the same time. As his interests in the Low Countries grew and his differences with the English multiplied, Philip of Burgundy seemed increasingly to be a sleeping partner in the Anglo-Burgundian alliance. And that was dangerous, if it gave the impression that the war had become a conflict between the English and the French, rather than between the true French loyal to King Henry and the false French of the pretender Charles. To speak simply of the French fighting the English, after all, was to use the language of the girl who had been sent by the devil to break the siege at Orléans. But Bedford's Parisian *coup de théâtre* – reinforced behind the scenes by the help of his devoted wife, Burgundy's much-loved sister Anne – now meant that Duke Philip had no choice but to reassert his commitment to his alliance with England against the Armagnac traitors.

All the same, the continuing fragility of the Anglo-Burgundian coalition was everywhere apparent. Despite their public gestures of solidarity, Bedford was forced to agree that the duke of Burgundy should continue to be paid in full for the military support he provided to English France. And well might the regent have wondered whether an ally who required payment was an ally at all: on the very day that Duke Philip left Paris after his meeting with Bedford, envoys from his court arrived at Reims in time to witness the coronation of King Charles. While they set about negotiating a temporary truce between Burgundians and Armagnacs, the Armagnac king and his army moved on, edging closer to Paris as more Burgundian towns opened their gates and submitted to his authority.

But his heaven-sent champion, Joan the Maid, was not happy with this piecemeal approach. Her renown was growing; though the great Armagnac theologian Jean Gerson had died on 12 July, five days too soon to witness the apotheosis of his king at Reims, other writers of a different stamp took up their pens to record Joan's achievement. One of the king's secretaries, an accomplished poet named Alain Chartier, composed a Latin letter describing the miraculous deeds of this 'she-warrior' who was 'the glory not only of the French, but of all Christians'. And his praise was echoed by the extraordinary figure of Christine de Pizan, the daughter of a Venetian physician at the French royal court who, despite the odds stacked against her by her sex, had become one of the most distinguished writers of her day. In 1418, when the Burgundians seized Paris, Christine had retreated in horror to the abbey of Poissy outside the city walls; now, in her late sixties, she emerged from more than a decade of literary silence to celebrate the renaissance of the Armagnac cause, rejoicing in effervescent verse at the restoration of the rightful king through this blessed Maid. Joan, she declared, was sent by God, 'who has given her a heart greater than any man's'.

Now, however, the Maid's heart was troubled. On 5 August, she sent a letter to her 'dear and good friends', the people of Reims.

They should not have a moment's doubt of her commitment to them, she said, or of the cause for which she was fighting, but it was true that the king had made a truce with the duke of Burgundy, by the terms of which the duke must hand over the city of Paris at the end of fifteen days. Joan was not convinced. 'Do not be surprised,' she told them, 'if I do not enter there so quickly. Although this truce has been made, I am not at all content, and I do not know if I will keep it. But if I do, it will only be to preserve the honour of the king, and also as long as they do not further demean the blood royal in any way, because I will be holding and keeping together the king's army in order to stand ready at the end of the said fifteen days if they do not make peace.' The responsibility God had given her had always been singular, but now – after the euphoria of the coronation, and finding herself suddenly caught amid unpredictably swirling political currents – she sounded newly conscious of how alone she was with her duty. 'My dearest and most perfect friends,' she added, 'I pray you that you should not feel uneasy as long as I live; but I ask that you keep a good watch and protect the good city of the king, and let me know if there are any traitors who wish to harm you, and as soon as I can I will drive them away; and let me know your news.'

Christine de Pizan, finishing her hymn of praise to the Maid six days earlier, had been certain that Joan would soon lead the king into Paris, and to Joan herself the recapture of the kingdom's great capital seemed the obvious next step. Obvious perhaps, but not God-given. She had known she would take the king to Reims from the moment she arrived at Chinon, and at Poitiers, shortly after, she had learned that her sign would be to free Orléans. What now remained was the rest of her mission: to drive the English from French soil. That much God had made clear – but the question was how it should be achieved. Peace with the duke of Burgundy would heal France's wounds, but that, for Joan, required the duke's submission to his king, not the subtle and insubstantial words of diplomats. She also knew that if she attacked the enemy – and to take Paris from English hands would be a great and necessary prize – then God would give her victory. But in this large army that had escorted the king to Reims, she was one among many captains, and a place was not habitually made for her in the arguments about policy and strategy that consumed the attention of the king's counsellors.

She had been an exceptional leader in an exceptional moment – a miraculous anomaly who, by the will of heaven, had transformed the landscape in which she stood. She knew that God was with her, and how much work still lay ahead. But what if those around her believed the moment of miracles had passed?

7

A creature in the form of a woman

It was clear to the duke of Bedford that, if Paris were to be defended, he would have to do it himself. In public – and with the air of one who hoped to make it so, if he said it often enough – the duke insisted that the Anglo-Burgundian alliance was holding strong; Philip of Burgundy, Bedford told the council back in England, was showing himself in this hour of need to be a 'true kinsman, friend and loyal vassal' of the young King Henry.

But the practical fact of the matter was that Duke Philip was not in Paris. Instead, by the first week in August 1429 he was in his palace at Arras in Artois, a hundred miles north, where – as Bedford happened to know – a high-level delegation of Armagnac envoys had just arrived, led by the chancellor Regnault de Chartres, archbishop of Reims, and the veteran soldier Raoul de Gaucourt. Duke Philip did not admit them to his presence straight away, and Bedford had the best of all possible spies, his sharp-eyed wife Anne, to keep him informed of what her brother was up to. Still, the situation was hardly reassuring – and, quite apart from his anxiety about the reliability of his Burgundian partner, Bedford was also distinctly short of English lieutenants, given that Suffolk, Talbot and Scales now languished in enemy hands.

There was little option but to set to work. Already the thirty-foot walls of the city had been strengthened and artillery positions ranged around them, and on 25 July the duke had ridden through the gates in the company of his uncle, Cardinal Henry Beaufort, along with 250 men-at-arms and 2500 archers – fresh troops raised by the cardinal in England for a crusade against Hussite heretics in Bohemia but, thanks to the pressure of events in France, hurriedly diverted instead to Paris. Within days, Bedford and this new force were in the field, moving through the countryside outside the city in the attempt to ward off any closer approach by the Armagnac army. But when the news arrived that Armagnac ambassadors were in Arras to treat for peace with Burgundy, the regent decided that the moment had come for a more dramatic move of his own.

By 7 August he was in Montereau, the fateful place where the blood of John the Fearless had been spilled almost ten years earlier. From there, Bedford issued a ringing challenge to 'you, Charles of Valois, who are accustomed to name yourself *dauphin de Vienne*, and now without just cause call yourself king'. Charles should meet him face to face, he declared, either to make peace or to give battle; but the terms in which this defiance was couched made it clear that his words were intended as much for the ears of his Burgundian ally as they were directed at his Armagnac enemy. 'We are, and we will always be, intent and determined on all good ways of peace that are not feigned, corrupt, dissembling, broken or perjured,' he said – and all those listening could guess what was coming next – '. . . such as that at Montereau-Fault-Yonne, from which ensued, through your guilt and connivance, the most horrible, detestable and cruel murder, committed against law and knightly honour, of our dearest and most beloved late father' – John the Fearless being Bedford's father, according to church law, through his marriage to the duke's daughter Anne. After their oaths sworn in Paris, and now this evocation of the killing on the very spot where it had taken place, it was Bedford's hope that his brother-in-law Philip could not publicly overlook the crimes of the past, however much water had flowed under Montereau's bloodstained bridge since then.

Bedford also had a message for the people of Paris. The so-called dauphin was abusing the trust of the simple and the ignorant, he explained, with the help of two 'superstitious and reprobate characters', both of them 'abominable in the sight of God': one 'a sluttish woman of ill repute, dressed as a man and dissolute in her conduct', the other 'an apostate and seditious friar'. Brother Richard, it seemed, had been won over by his encounter with Joan at Troyes to such an extent that he was now riding with her and the Armagnac army. This news was so unwelcome in Paris, where his thundering sermons had converted many to a new austerity of life, that the citizens went back to playing backgammon, bowls and dice in ostentatious defiance of his teaching, and swapped the tin medallions that he had persuaded them to wear, each one inscribed with the name of Jesus, for Burgundian saltires. Yoking the friar and the Maid together therefore served a useful purpose for Bedford within the city he was trying to defend: Joan's claims to divine inspiration could only be tarnished, in the eyes of the Parisians, if she were the partner in crime of a spiritual leader who had utterly betrayed their trust.

Bedford's letter was long, but its conclusion was clear. God, 'who is the only judge', he said, would recognise the true right of King Henry, whether through peace or war. However much these words were intended for others as well as the newly crowned Armagnac king, Charles could hardly ignore such a challenge to his title and his conduct. By 14 August his army had approached within sight of Bedford's forces north of Paris at Montepilloy, just outside Senlis. Both sides dug in overnight, working quickly to fortify their positions. The English – along with a few hundred Burgundian soldiers mustered at English expense for the defence of Paris – flew the banners of France and England, King Henry's two realms, and the standard of their patron, St George. The Armagnacs were drawn up under their many commanders: the duke of Alençon, René of Anjou, Gilles de Rais and, at the front, the Bastard of Orléans, La Hire and the Maid, her white banner held high. King Charles, escorted by the count of Clermont and the ever-present La Trémoille, rode at a careful distance behind the lines. And so, through the heat of a scorching August day, they all – English, Burgundians and Armagnacs – waited for battle.

The kingdom of France in early 1429, showing the division of territory
between English, Burgundian and Armagnac rule.

Charles VI of France, the Mad and Well-Beloved. Charles retained the love of his people and his title as the 'most Christian king', despite the intermittent psychosis that left him unable to rule and his kingdom in the grip of civil war. This exquisite figure is from an enamelled gold altar-piece which the queen, Isabeau of Bavaria, gave to her husband as a New Year's gift in 1405. The image of the king kneeling before the Virgin and Child not only demonstrates his blond good looks (and his concern to disguise his receding hairline), but seems, in his wide-eyed gaze, to hint at his mental fragility.

Henry V of England, the challenger to Charles's possession of the French throne, and 'God's own soldier', as he was called by one of his chaplains. This profile portrait gives a sense of his stern and implacable will, but shows no sign of the scar left by the wound he suffered in battle when he was just sixteen: an arrow struck him in the face, penetrating deep into the bone to one side of his nose, and it took weeks to remove the arrowhead with a specially constructed surgical device. His recovery from this injury is likely to have fuelled the king's belief in his divinely sanctioned destiny. He sports the cropped, round haircut popular among fashionable young men in the early decades of the fifteenth century.

The powerful dukes of Burgundy, John the Fearless and his son Philip the Good, in their trademark black velvet hats. The distinctive piled-up profile of John the Fearless's *chaperon* hat appears in almost all contemporary depictions of him. The magnificence of the increasingly independent Burgundian court is evident not only in Philip's collar of his chivalric Order of the Golden Fleece (a golden sheepskin hanging from a chain of linked firesteels and flints, Philip's personal emblem), but in the quality of the portrait, from the workshop of the Flemish artist Rogier van der Weyden.

LE TRESVICTORIEVX ROY·LE FRANCE·

CHARLES·SEPTIESME·DE CE NOM·

ABOVE The dauphin Charles, son of Charles VI, here depicted around 1450 as 'the most victorious king of France, Charles VII of that name'. Victorious though he was by that point, Charles was no more prepossessing, robust or charismatic a figure than he had been in the 1420s, when he had failed to lead his army against his sworn enemy Philip the Good of Burgundy and the duke's English allies.

BELOW The great twelfth-century castle of Chinon on the river Vienne, where Joan first appeared at the Armagnac court in February 1429.

The only surviving image of Joan made during her lifetime: a picture drawn in the margin of the records of the Paris *parlement* by its notary, Clément de Fauquembergue, on 10 May 1429, the day when news arrived of the liberation of Orléans. He had heard that the Armagnacs were accompanied by a maid carrying a banner, but he had never seen her, and so depicted her with long hair in female dress.

A late fifteenth-century image of Joan from an illuminated manuscript. Her armour, banner and sword reflect contemporary descriptions of the Maid once she had been equipped for war by the Armagnac regime, but her hair does not; it should be darker and shorter, cut round above her ears in the same style as the portrait of Henry V.

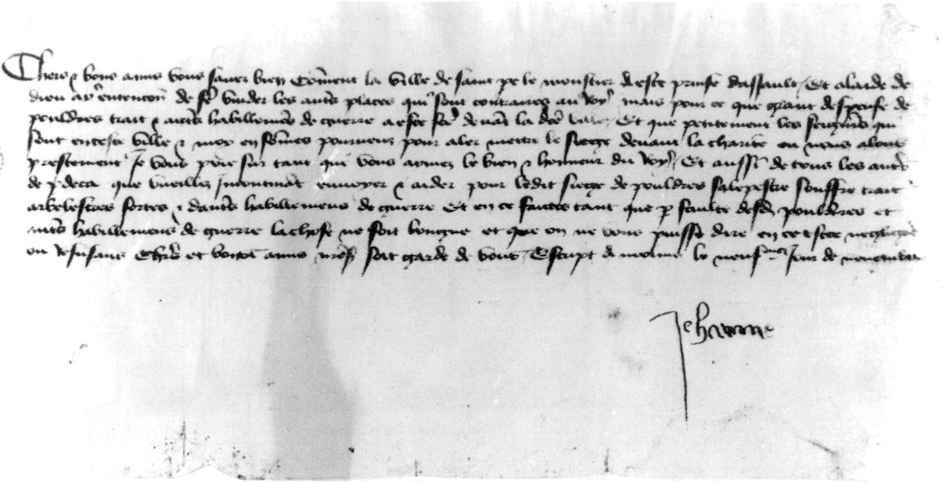

Jehanne

ABOVE Letter from the Maid seeking military supplies for the siege of La Charité from the people of the town of Riom, 9 November 1429. Joan, who dictated her letters to a clerk, had by this stage begun to learn to write, and her own hesitant signature, *Jehanne*, appears at the end of the text. The nineteenth-century scholar Jules Quicherat noted that he saw a fingerprint and a black hair caught in the wax seal of this document.

LEFT Mid-fifteenth-century manuscript illumination of St Catherine of Alexandria, one of the saints who brought messages to Joan – or so she claimed at her trial. St Catherine cradles a book, to symbolise her success in confounding the pagan scholars who interrogated her. Beneath her feet lies the Roman emperor who ordered her execution, along with the spiked wheel upon which, miraculously, she could not be broken. She holds the sword with which she was eventually beheaded. Joan's own sword was brought to her from the church of St Catherine at Fierbois.

John, duke of Bedford, younger brother of Henry V and regent of English France on behalf of his young nephew Henry VI, kneels before St George, the patron saint of England. St George, a warrior saint in armour, wears his emblem of the red cross – which also appears on the English flags behind him – and the blue robe of the English Order of the Garter. The book of hours in which this illumination appears was given by Bedford's wife, Anne of Burgundy, to nine-year-old Henry VI at Christmas 1430, while he was in Rouen awaiting his French coronation, and shortly before the beginning of Joan's trial.

An illumination of St Michael vanquishing the devil in the form of a dragon, from the Salisbury breviary, a manuscript commissioned in Paris by the duke of Bedford as regent of English France. The archangel Michael, a warrior saint to match the warlike St George, had been adopted as the patron saint of Armagnac France, along with his emblem of the white cross – and Joan would claim at her trial that St Michael had appeared and spoken to her, along with St Catherine and St Margaret. This English-commissioned St Michael, however, has been appropriated by Bedford for England: instead of the white cross of the Armagnacs, he carries a shield that much more closely resembles the red cross of St George.

Jean, Bastard of Orléans, illegitimate brother of Charles, duke of Orléans. The duke was captured at the battle of Azincourt in 1415, and remained a prisoner in England for twenty-five years. The Bastard was therefore in charge of the defence of Orléans when Joan arrived there in 1429, and fought at her side to liberate the town. He served with distinction in later campaigns against the English in Normandy and Gascony, and became count of Dunois in recognition of his service. He gave detailed testimony at the nullification trial held to clear Joan's name in 1456.

Cardinal Niccolò Albergati, sent by the pope as an 'angel of peace' to broker a settlement between the Armagnacs and Burgundians after Joan's death. He took a leading role at the Congress of Arras in 1435 where peace was made between the two sides in the teeth of English opposition. This remarkable portrait was painted in the early 1430s by the Flemish painter Jan van Eyck, who lived in Bruges and served Philip of Burgundy.

There were skirmishes, feints and parries, as each side sought to tempt the other into a full-blown assault. Every movement kicked up so much dust from the parched earth that, close as they were, it was hard to keep the enemy in plain sight. But as the hours dragged on, it began to dawn on the Armagnac captains that the English had no intention of leaving the ground they had staked out. At Rouvray, English forces had broken the Armagnacs with a battery of arrows from behind a barricade of herring-filled wagons, but at Patay, with their defences incomplete, they had met bloody disaster. They had no intention of making the same mistake again. And, of all the Armagnac captains, it was Joan who could not contain her frustration. She took her banner in her hand and rode right up to the enemy lines, daring them to attack; when her presence failed to provoke them, she sent a message that King Charles's troops would give them time and space to deploy themselves for battle as they wished. There was no response. Night fell; and the next morning news reached the French camp that the English were marching back to Senlis, and from there to Paris.

Bedford had made his point, but he was not about to risk everything on a single encounter in the open. Let his enemies move against Paris if they dared; meanwhile Normandy urgently required his attention. There, Mont-Saint-Michel still held out, a lone Armagnac outpost off the coast of English France, but across the duchy, as reports spread of the rescue of Orléans and King Charles's coronation campaign, resistance to English rule was growing. So much so, in fact, that the town of Évreux, thirty miles south of Rouen, had been surrounded by Armagnac troops and forced to agree to surrender if help did not come by 27 August. Bedford, who could not afford to see his Norman power base disintegrate, moved at speed to the rescue, and then took up position at Vernon, poised watchfully between his two threatened capitals, Paris and Rouen.

In the duke's absence, King Charles continued his stately and apparently inexorable takeover of the towns around Paris.

Compiègne, forty miles north-east of the city, opened its gates, and Beauvais, another thirty miles west from there, sent a delegation to offer its submission. This was a menacing royal progress, not only pushing towards Paris itself, but moving within striking distance of English Normandy to the west and Burgundian Artois to the north. The Armagnac strategy, however, had two faces. The king's army remained in the field, but on 16 August – the day after the inconclusive face-off with Bedford's forces at Montepilloy – his envoys were finally admitted to the presence of the duke of Burgundy at Arras. They hoped to hammer out terms for peace between the king and his Burgundian cousin, and there was serious intent, it seemed, on both sides: after intensive discussion at Arras, Burgundian ambassadors returned with the archbishop and de Gaucourt to Compiègne, to present the results of their labours at the Armagnac court. By 27 August, the king had agreed in principle to make spiritual reparation for the murder at Montereau (which he had of course, regrettably, been too young to prevent), and to offer financial compensation for the jewels and belongings the duke had had with him when he died. Philip would be confirmed in lands he had been granted by the English, and would be personally exempt from any requirement to do homage to Charles, while Charles himself would grant a general pardon and a general truce.

But it was not enough. Bedford's public summoning of the spectre of Burgundy's dead father had done its work; the duke could not bring himself to make a permanent peace with his murderer. Instead, on 28 August, a temporary truce was agreed, by which the abstinence from war that already protected the southern frontiers between Burgundian and Armagnac territory would now be extended to all lands north of the Seine with the exception of the city of Paris, which the duke of Burgundy could defend if it were to come under Armagnac attack. This, in other words, was a gesture of goodwill that would allow the moment to play itself out. The duke of Burgundy had not abandoned his English alliance, but his door was still open to the Armagnacs, who would, in the meantime, have the chance to find out whether Paris was theirs for the taking.

That was music to the ears of Joan, who had been left in uncomfortable limbo while these diplomatic wheels turned. She had a mission that depended on divine, not human, agency – except for the inconvenient fact that she needed the faith of politicians and the presence of soldiers to put it into effect. And now that the initial momentum of her campaign had dissipated in the aftermath of the coronation at Reims, questions about the nature and limits of the authority she might claim were becoming a little more difficult to answer. Some time earlier, for example, Count Jean of Armagnac – son of the nobleman who had given his name to the anti-Burgundian cause – had written from his lands in the far south-west of the kingdom to seek her advice on the papal schism. Almost all of Europe now regarded the conflict as settled in favour of Martin V, who had been elected to the Holy See at the Council of Constance, but Count Jean was one of the few who persisted in the belief that one of two others might still have a claim. 'I beseech you', he asked her, 'to beg Our Lord Jesus Christ that, in His infinite mercy, He might wish to declare to us, through you, which of the three men is the true pope.' At Compiègne, during the military lull after Montepilloy, Joan gave her answer. '*Jhesus Maria*. Count of Armagnac, my very dear and good friend, Joan the Maid lets you know that your messenger has reached me . . . I cannot reliably tell you the truth of the matter now, until I am in Paris or elsewhere, as required, because I am now too much caught up in the business of war; but when you know that I am in Paris, send a messenger to me and I will then tell you clearly which one you should put your faith in, and what I have learned from my rightful and sovereign lord, the king of all the world . . .'

Joan was prepared to envisage, it seemed, that her instructions from heaven would one day encompass more matters than she had so far spoken of. For the time being, though, she was consumed

— and troubled — by the interruption to her military mission. On 23 August, the day after her reply to the count of Armagnac, she was at last given leave to ride out of Compiègne with her soldiers and her fellow captain, the duke of Alençon. Three days later, they had reached Saint-Denis, the town outside the walls of Paris that housed the holy abbey of France's ancient patron and the blessed bones of its most Christian kings. The English had not thought it worthwhile to install a garrison in a place that had few fortifications, and many of the townspeople had retreated into Paris at news of the Armagnacs' approach. Joan and her men therefore encountered no resistance as they reclaimed the protection of St Denis for a kingdom and an army that had marched for so long under the banner of the heavenly warrior St Michael, before the Maid had come to lead them.

Now the walls of Paris were just four miles away, but still Joan could not launch the attack she wanted. Instead, the king moved slowly south from Compiègne to Senlis while his counsellors continued their painstaking summits with the duke of Burgundy's envoys. Finally, the partial truce was signed that left open the possibility of a fight for the capital, and by the end of the first week in September Charles arrived at Saint-Denis, while Joan and the army pushed on another two miles to the village of La Chapelle. She and Alençon now had the champions of Armagnac France around them — the counts of Clermont and Laval, de Rais, La Hire, de Gaucourt, Xaintrailles and more — and they had spent the days since their own arrival at Saint-Denis engaged in sorties and reconnaissance, gauging the task that lay ahead.

There was no doubt that the defences of Paris were monumental, on a scale far beyond anything that Joan had experienced before. Massive walls were pierced by arrow slits and topped with fortified towers and gun placements, and new-built *boulevards* protected each of the six gates, all of which lay behind an immense ditch that circled the whole city. Not only that, but the duke of Bedford had issued an impassioned summons to his captains in Normandy to come to him at Vernon by 8 or 9 September, with all the men they could spare, to march to the capital's rescue ('. . . and fail not hereof, as you love the conservation of this land, and as you will answer to my lords and us therefore in time coming'). But the threat of Bedford's arrival was all the more reason to do what Joan had always believed she should: to strike, in God's name, without delay.

And so, on Thursday 8 September, the feast of the Nativity of the Virgin, the Maid took her banner in her hand and rode with her troops to the Porte Saint-Honoré, the gate that led to the palace of the Louvre on the western edge of the city. For the Armagnac soldiers, as they set about God's work under the command of the leader He had sent to save France, the holiness of the day could only sanctify their labours. For the Burgundians of Paris, on the other hand, it was sacrilege: '. . . these men were so unfortunate, so full of foolish trust,' railed the journal-writer within the city, 'that they relied upon the word of a creature in the form of a woman, whom they called the Maid – what it was, God only knows – and with one accord conspired to attack Paris on the very day of the Holy Nativity of Our Lady.' This time, clearly, there would be no faction among the besieged pressing to open the gates. This time, the city would be taken by assault, or not at all.

Even for Joan, there was a familiarity, by now, to the workings of the military machine. The noise was deafening. The roar of the Armagnac cannon was answered by artillery blasts from the walls above; whenever a Parisian gunner struck his target, the screams of mutilated horses and men added a nerve-shredding counterpoint to the shouts of the soldiers who toiled in the moat, hurling bundles of wood into the standing water at the bottom in an attempt to build a makeshift pathway to the foot of the walls. As always, Joan led the way into the ditch, brandishing her banner and urging on her men, while arrows and stones fell from above in a piercing, bludgeoning storm. Long hours passed, until muscles were cramped in agony and eyes stung with blood, sweat and dirt, and still the walls loomed high above them, impenetrable and impassable.

As the sun dipped below the horizon, Joan called urgently to the unseen enemy in the fortifications above. 'Surrender to us quickly, in the name of Jesus! For if you do not surrender before nightfall, we will come in there by force, whether you like it or not, and you will all be put to death without mercy!' 'Shall we, you bloody tart?' came the reply, and a crossbow bolt ripped through her thigh. As she staggered, another arrow pinned the foot of her standard-bearer to the ground beside her. When he lifted his visor so that he could see to free himself, a third shot split his skull between his eyes. He died where he fell. Darkness was coming. Joan was losing blood, but still she shouted till she was hoarse: her exhausted soldiers should move forward, onward, to the attack. At Orléans and at Jargeau she had been hurt only to rise again, her resilience a sign to her troops that God would give them victory. Paris was next, of that there could be no doubt. And then, over the cannon blasts, she heard the sounding of the retreat. She did not stop insisting that the city could be won as she was dragged from the ditch and carried to safety. Only when the tail of the Armagnac army disappeared into the night did the Parisian guns stutter, at last, into silence.

It had been worth a try, the king and his counsellors knew. To take Paris by assault – to overwhelm the defences of the strongest city west of Constantinople without help from inside the walls – would have been a miracle; but the Maid, after all, had worked miracles before. Then again, to ask for more might test the patience of heaven. God's help might come when all human remedies had failed, but now, thanks to Joan's intervention at Orléans and Reims, the newly crowned King Charles could hope to help himself. The Maid had had her chance, but Paris had not fallen, and the imminent arrival in the capital of the duke of Bedford's troops made it all the more certain that it was time to take stock, to pursue the peace with Burgundy that would unite France against the English invaders. A truce had been agreed with the Burgundians, to last until Christmas, and in a time of truce – as Charles explained in a letter to the people of Reims a few days later – the king could not keep an undeployed army in the field without risking the 'total destruction' of the countryside across which they ranged. Privately, too, he knew that his cash-strapped regime did not yet have the money to pursue a full-scale campaign against the English in Normandy. He would therefore return to the Loire, leaving the count of Clermont to hold the lands north of the Seine, and prepare himself and his forces for the new year to come.

Joan was distraught. Wounded though she was, she had woken in the camp at La Chapelle on 9 September determined to renew her assault on Paris. She asked the duke of Alençon to sound the trumpets and ready the troops; only then did she learn that Charles had given the order for wholesale retreat. While envoys returned to the city walls under safe-conduct to collect the Armagnac dead, she travelled the two miles to Saint-Denis in pain and despair to rejoin the king who had betrayed her. How was she – how was anyone – to understand such a reverse for Joan the Maid and her mission from God? The great theologian Gerson had foreseen this very problem. The 'party having justice on its side', he had concluded after her triumph at Orléans, must take care not to render the help of heaven useless through disbelief or ingratitude; 'for God changes His sentence as a result of a change in merit,' he wrote, 'even if He does not change His counsel.'

One possibility, then, was that she had failed at the walls of Paris because her king had not shared her conviction that, with God's help, victory was certain. But there was another interpretation, and the Burgundian scholars of the university of Paris were quick to find it. Perhaps – ran the argument of a theological treatise written a few days after her retreat from the capital – she had failed because her inspiration came not from heaven, but from hell. 'It is not enough', wrote the author of *On the Good and the Evil Spirit*, 'that someone claims purely and simply to be sent from God, since this is the claim of all heretics; but it is necessary that this invisible mission should be confirmed by a miraculous work or by a particular testimony drawn from holy scripture.' For the supporters of English rather than Armagnac France, the relief of Orléans was no miracle – and therefore, in the absence of theologically sufficient proof, anyone who accepted Joan's assertions was rejecting the judgement and the authority of the Church itself.

Not only that, but her claims were demonstrably false. If she had truly been sent by God, she would not wear men's clothes in contravention of God's law and the Church's teaching. The nature of her supposed mission was no excuse for this abomination, since no 'greater' good could ever justify sin – and in any case women were forbidden to fight, just as they were forbidden to preach, to teach, to administer the sacraments, and all other duties that belonged to men. That she did the devil's work was clear from the fact that she incited war, rather than bringing peace; she had even dared to insult God by fighting on the feast day of the Nativity of His most glorious mother. She had allowed children to kneel before her with burning candles, from which she dropped wax onto their heads as an enchantment for good luck: idolatry, sorcery and heresy, all in one. And some poor souls worshipped images of her as though she were a saint, an error of such magnitude that it threatened the true faith – and the Church should do all in its power to excise the danger this Maid represented.

The Maid herself was hardly likely to agree. All the same, she was limping, spiritually as well as physically, as she prepared for the long ride south to the Loire. At the sacred abbey of Saint-Denis, she left a suit of armour as an offering before the image of the Virgin; not a gift of thanks for victory, but a more inscrutable acknowledgement of a task unfinished. And then, because she had no other choice, she followed the king as he retraced his steps around Paris to the east, from Lagny-sur-Marne to Provins, and then southward to Montargis, Gien and Bourges. 'And thus', wrote a servant of the duke of Alençon, 'was the will of the Maid and of the king's army broken.'

A couple of days later Bedford stormed into the capital, and rounded in fury on the remaining inhabitants of Saint-Denis for having accommodated the Armagnac enemy without resistance or protest. For the lodgings they had provided, they had been promised payment from the Armagnac plunder of a conquered city; instead, they found themselves heavily fined for their miscalculation. But Bedford knew that this was a moment in which his principal weapons were diplomatic, not financial or military. On 18 September, ten days after the failed Armagnac assault, King Charles's council belatedly agreed that Paris should now be incorporated into the truce he had already sealed with the duke of Burgundy. The task Bedford faced was to ensure that these negotiations between Armagnacs and Burgundians went no further without him, and instead to wind the coils of English France more tightly around his brother-in-law.

On the last day of September Duke Philip himself arrived in the city, gorgeously arrayed, and accompanied, as always in recent months, by his sister, Bedford's loyal wife Anne. A week later, the two dukes were joined by Bedford's uncle, Cardinal Henry Beaufort, for talks which ended in agreement that the duke of Burgundy should become the new governor of Paris. Not only that, but envoys from England and Burgundy met Armagnac ambassadors at Saint-Denis, and concluded that a truce should be observed between all parties to the war until comprehensive peace negotiations could begin the following April (or, as Bedford suggested to Burgundy in private, a renewed assault on the Armagnacs could be launched). Meanwhile, Bedford's plan to draw the sting from Charles's consecration at Reims by anointing and crowning his nephew, King Henry, was finally coming to fruition. On 6 November, in the soaring splendour of Westminster Abbey, the newly returned Cardinal Beaufort placed the heavy crown of England on the eight-year-old boy's head; and preparations were well under way for the young king's progress across the Channel to his second realm, for a second coronation in France.

Events were leaving Joan behind. The time of miracles had passed, and now even the war she had come to fight had been temporarily suspended. Skirmishes continued, and garrisons needed captains; once her leg was whole again, some occupation could certainly be found for her. And yet the qualities that had made her the saviour of Armagnac France now threatened to undermine her future. She had learned much, but if the course of the war were now to be determined by military strategy, not divine inspiration, there were other commanders with infinitely more experience and skill. Above all, perhaps, if the hand of heaven had once more withdrawn from direct intervention in the world, then a woman on a battlefield became an alarming liability, rather than a unique embodiment of God's will.

Some of the men who had fought beside her did not falter in their belief. Despite the truce, the young duke of Alençon was assembling forces of his own to move in the direction of his ancestral lands in Normandy, of which he had been dispossessed for so long. He wanted Joan with him, but the king's counsellors – among them the archbishop of Reims, La Trémoille and the grizzled Raoul de Gaucourt, all of whom had taken part in the recent rounds of diplomacy – knew that the impulsive aggression of the Maid and Alençon in the field together might undo all their careful work. Instead, after several weeks of convalescence in the home of one of the queen's ladies at Bourges, Joan was sent with Charles d'Albret, La Trémoille's half-brother, to deal with a mercenary captain named Perrinet Gressart who was making a nuisance of himself on the frontier along the eastern reaches of the Loire.

In theory, Gressart served the English and the Burgundians. In practice, his own interests came first. Two years earlier, he had

dared to kidnap La Trémoille himself on the road between Armagnac and Burgundian territory, releasing him only on the payment
of an exorbitant ransom. Now, Gressart ran his own unofficial fief-
dom from the fortified town of La Charité-sur-Loire, thirty miles
east of Bourges, and his brutal grip extended as far south as Saint-
Pierre-le-Moûtier, a further thirty miles upstream. La Trémoille
was determined to break him, and thus it was that Joan and d'Albret
arrived outside the walls of Saint-Pierre in late October. The siege
was set, but it was not long before the Maid turned to the tactics
she knew best. She led the way into the ditch outside the walls,
and called the soldiers to cast bundles of firewood into the water
to make a pathway across to the town. She urged them forward,
towards walls that stood only a fraction as high as the great defences of the capital before which she and the might of the Armagnac
army had foundered. Once again, one of the men who served her
was pierced through the foot by an arrow; but Saint-Pierre was not
Paris. At the Maid's words, her troops surged to the attack, and the
defenders faltered. On 4 November, the town was taken.

It was a small victory, but it was something. Still, La Charité lay
ahead, and that, as the winter began to draw in, was a less comfortable prospect. Joan was in grim mood on 9 November when she
wrote to the people of Riom, sixty miles south of Saint-Pierre, to
seek their help in supplying her little force. She had begun to learn
to hold a pen as well as a lance, and when the message was done she
wrote her name in large, uncertain letters at the end, but for once
she did not begin with the name of Jesus. 'Dear and good friends',
she said, 'you know well how the town of Saint-Pierre-le-Moûtier
was taken by assault, and with the help of God I intend to clear
out the other places which oppose the king. But because there has
been such a great outlay of gunpowder, arrows and other military
equipment in facing that town, and because I and the lords who
are now in that town have minimal stocks left to lay siege to La
Charité, where we are on the point of going, I entreat you, in as

much as you have at heart the welfare and honour of the king and also of all our other men here, to assist with the siege by immediately sending gunpowder, saltpetre, sulphur, arrows, good strong crossbows and other military equipment. And thereby ensure that the matter should not be long drawn out through lack of the said gunpowder and other military equipment, and that you cannot be said to be negligent or unwilling. Dear and good friends, may Our Lord protect you.'

It was focused, practical, and markedly lacking in the glorious certainty that had infused every word of her earlier missives. Who knew, now, what the future might hold? That, at least, was the message sent across Europe from Bruges to his father in Venice by the merchant Pancrazio Giustiniani on 20 November. The Maid was surely still alive, he said, and had even recently taken a strong castle by assault. If what people were saying was true, she was still capable of astonishing the world. The university of Paris had sent to Rome to accuse her of heresy, he reported, but then again the university's former chancellor, Jean Gerson, had written an excellent work in her defence. Some believed in her, and some did not. Meanwhile the king of England had been crowned in London, and would soon arrive in France at the head of a formidable army. 'It seems to me certain', he wrote, 'that great things will happen in the spring.'

Joan could only hope that he was right.

8

I will be with you soon

It was cold. December was always bitter, but in the frozen mud outside La Charité the damp clawed its way through layers of leather and wool and into aching bones. Hunger did nothing to help. The king had sent regretful word from his palace of Mehun-sur-Yèvre, forty miles west and a world away, that he lacked the money to send more supplies. As a result, the soldiers fumbling to load the great iron guns were now labouring with yawning stomachs as well as numb and stiffened fingers.

They had been here four weeks. Four days, it had taken the Maid to free Orléans from siege. A single day, the king had given her for the attempt to storm Paris. And now she stalked, her jaw set, beneath the looming fortifications of La Charité, on which a month's bombardment had left alarmingly little trace. The commander of this huddled troop, the king's favourite's half-brother, did what he could to eke out their stores of food and ammunition, but when the order came to call off the siege, a couple of days before Christmas, they were so weary, and so eager to leave the place, that they abandoned artillery pieces among the debris of the camp, guns that were too damaged or too unwieldy to pull along roads deeply rutted with ice.

If Joan felt relief, it was overlaid with something darker and more difficult. She had not wanted to fight a Burgundian mercenary at La Charité when the English still held so much of her king's dismembered realm. But she did not want to come back with nothing to show for a month of punishing effort, and with nowhere else to go. When the soldiers dispersed, she did not ride to Mehun, to the court that no longer knew what to do with her; instead, she took the road further north to Jargeau, the scene of her triumph over the earl of Suffolk in the summer sun just six months ago. There she heard that the king, in his wisdom, had chosen to reward her for her service. Back in July, Charles had declared – at Joan's request, he said – that her home village of Domrémy should be exempt from the payment of all taxes, in recognition of the extraordinary role she was playing in the recovery of his kingdom. Now, it was a personal honour he had in mind: the Maid and the family from which, by the grace of God, she had so gloriously sprung should be by royal authority ennobled. This was not the gift of a title, but an elevation of status. Not only Joan herself but her parents, Jacques and Isabelle, and her brothers, Jacquemin, Jean and Pierre, and all their descendants, male and (an unusual privilege, this) female, should henceforth rank among those with noble blood in the kingdom of France, even though their birth had not previously qualified them for such distinction.

The royal charter spoke of the Maid's service to come, as well as achievements past. All the same, the tone was unmistakable: this was the closing of a chapter. But Joan, at not quite eighteen, and with her mission from heaven still unfinished, was not ready to lay aside her armour for a comfortable retirement. She made no public mention of her new dignity. Her authority came from God, not the king, and the trappings of aristocracy could not soothe her anger at her enforced inactivity in this hour of France's need. As she moved along the valley of the Loire from Jargeau to Orléans and then back, reluctantly, to join the king at La Trémoille's castle of Sully, all that was left for her to do was respond to those who still looked to her for leadership, however small the request. The daughter of the Scots painter at Tours who had made her banner was getting married: would the city, given their regard for Joan, agree to pay for the bride's trousseau? Even this favour, it turned out, was now beyond the Maid's power. The councillors expressed their profound regret that they could not respond more positively to her letter, because their funds were committed to municipal repairs, but they would pray for the girl, and – for the love they bore the Maid – offer a small gift of bread and wine for the wedding meal.

The painter's daughter was not the only one planning a wedding that January. The duke of Burgundy was preparing to become a husband for the third time, and, for him, expense was no object. Though he was by no means short of female company – the Burgundian court housed a growing family of his illegitimate offspring – Duke Philip had been a widower for five years, ever since the death of his second wife in 1425. Now, he had chosen as his bride Isabel, daughter of the king of Portugal, a match that proclaimed his power as an independent player on the European political stage (albeit with a tactful nod to his English allies, given that she could count King Henry's great-grandfather, John of Gaunt, among her own grandparents).

Her arrival from Portugal had been anxiously awaited for weeks, but the harsh winter weather had blown her little fleet off course, and it was not until 8 January that she made her ceremonial entry into Bruges, accompanied by the sound of 150 silver trumpets through crowded streets festooned with crimson drapery. At the duke's palace, temporary kitchens, ovens and larders surrounded a banqueting hall 150 feet long, decorated everywhere with his flaming flints and steels. The wedding feast combined breathtaking culinary art with slapstick entertainment: the *pièce de résistance* was a vast pie out of which burst a live sheep, its wool dyed blue and its horns gilded, along with a man dressed as a wild beast who ran the length of the table while the terrified animal dived beneath it. Then days of jousting culminated in the duke's declaration that he had founded a new chivalric brotherhood, the Order of the Golden Fleece, an honour to be bestowed upon twenty-four of the finest knights in Artois, Flanders and the county and duchy of Burgundy.

For years, Philip had politely declined the duke of Bedford's invitation to become a knight of the English king's Order of the

Garter. The combined message of his own foundation of the Golden Fleece and his new royal marriage was therefore that Burgundy was more than ever a force to be reckoned with, an emerging state staking its claim to an independent place within the political map of Europe. But how, in practice, that force would make itself felt would depend on what happened after Easter Sunday, 16 April, the date on which the truces between England, Burgundy and Armagnac France would come to an end.

Already, the jockeying for position was well under way. The duchess of Bedford, Anne of Burgundy, was a guest of honour at her brother's wedding, but her husband was absent from the festivities, since he was busy shoring up the defences of English France. The rhetoric of King Henry's two crowns was as strong as ever: in the illuminations of a liturgical book even now being produced for Bedford by sublimely skilled craftsmen in Paris, the warrior archangel St Michael held an exquisitely painted shield bearing not the white cross of the Armagnacs, but the red cross of England and St George. To appropriate a saint with a couple of delicate brushstrokes was one thing; the military reality a great deal more challenging. The truces still held, but they were increasingly unsteady, and in February the Armagnac captain La Hire seized the great Norman stronghold of Château Gaillard on the Seine, just twenty miles south-east of Rouen. A month later, Armagnac troops once again raided Saint-Denis, plundering the town and causing panic among the inhabitants of Paris. It was time, Bedford felt, that his newly married brother-in-law showed himself willing to take to the battlefield, should the projected peace not materialise as planned, and on 8 March he named Philip count of Champagne, in the expectation that this new title and the territorial rights that went with it would encourage the Burgundian duke to retrieve Reims, Troyes and the other Champenois towns from their freshly pledged Armagnac allegiance.

Duke Philip, however, was not quite so sure of his next move. His dilemma was laid bare in the roll-call of his newly dubbed knights of the Golden Fleece: they included Jean de La Trémoille, brother of the Armagnac king's closest counsellor, but also Hugues de Lannoy, whose commitment to the Anglo-Burgundian alliance was so unshakable that he presented the duke with a blow-by-blow military plan for the spring campaign to come. The grant of the county of Champagne, in fact, formed part of a deal by which the duke had undertaken to lead his army for two months against the Armagnacs in the service of King Henry, but at the same time as that contract had been agreed in late February, Philip was also extending his richest and most courteous welcome to a deputation of Armagnac knights, including Poton de Xaintrailles, for five days of jousting at Arras. It was clear, if nothing else, how much now hung on the imminent arrival in France of eight-year-old King Henry himself, at the head of what was planned to be the largest English army to cross the Channel since the glory days of his father's extraordinary campaigns.

Tension was rising, and still Joan found herself caged at the castle of Sully. There she received a series of increasingly frantic missives from the governors of Reims, who were deeply alarmed at the possibility that the duke of Burgundy might seek to reclaim their town – as well they might be, given how quickly they had surrendered to an Armagnac king who had now retreated more than a hundred miles south to the safety of the Loire. She did what she could to reassure them. 'Very dear and good friends whom I greatly desire to see', she wrote on 16 March, 'Joan the Maid has received your letters saying that you fear being besieged. Please know that you will not be, if I can encounter them soon; and if it should so happen that I do not encounter them on their way to you, shut your gates, because I will be with you soon. And if they are there, I will make them put on their spurs in such haste that they will not know what they are doing, and I will relieve you there so quickly that it will seem no time at all.' She dictated another message full of encouragement almost a fortnight later, but the truth was that she could not protect the people of Reims, or even guarantee that she would come to their help, if the king and his counsellors would not give her leave to fight and an army with which to do so.

Her own growing desperation found a voice in a very different letter, composed in Latin on her behalf a week later by the chaplain who had been at her side since Orléans, Jean Pasquerel. The message was addressed to the Hussites, the heretics fighting for control of faraway Bohemia. For years, Pope Martin V had sought to gather a crusading force to crush them, and now – thwarted as she was within the kingdom of France – Joan unleashed her anger for the first time beyond its borders. '*Jhesus Maria*. For some time now, reports and widespread rumours have been reaching me, Joan the Maid, that you have turned from being true Christians to become heretics, and like Saracens . . . Indeed I, in truth, had I not been occupied with fighting the English, would have visited you already. However, unless I hear that you have mended your ways, I may well abandon the English and march against you, so that by the sword, if I cannot do it another way, I shall destroy your empty and abominable superstition, and strip you of either your heresy or your lives. But if you return to the Catholic faith, and to your former enlightened state, send me your envoys, and I will tell them what you should do.'

Whether this was Joan's idea or Pasquerel's, or simply a howl of frustration that it was six months since she had last had the chance to fight the English outside the walls of Paris, it had the effect at least of restating her claim to a unique spiritual authority on the battlefield – an idea that had begun to lose its potency with each moment that passed since the triumphs of the previous summer. Not that Joan herself had any intention of relinquishing it. Before she had set out on her ill-fated winter campaign against the mercenary Gressart, the preacher Brother Richard had asked her to give her verdict on a woman named Catherine de La Rochelle, who wanted to make peace between King Charles and the duke of Burgundy with the help of what she was claiming were heaven-sent visions. Joan was not impressed – Catherine should go back to her housework, she declared – and told the king so, to the displeasure of Brother Richard; but much of her own mission still remained to be completed, and she could not countenance the possibility that this woman's false claims might serve to distract from the truth of the God-given message she herself brought.

By the end of the month, it seemed possible that Joan's time was coming. At last, she rode with a detachment of troops eighty miles north to join the garrison at Lagny-sur-Marne, just east of Paris. With her little band, she ranged around the capital, from Melun, twenty-five miles south, to Senlis twenty-five miles north, skirmishing with the English wherever she could. The Armagnacs, wrote the alarmed Parisian journal-writer, were raiding right up to the city gates: 'The duke of Burgundy was expected daily, but all through January, February, March and April, he never stirred.' In fact, by April Duke Philip was in the field, but not within sight of the beleaguered Parisians. Instead, he was heading towards Compiègne, a town that had submitted to King Charles in the weeks after his coronation, but which – according to the detailed terms of the Armagnac–Burgundian truces – should now have been surrendered again to the duke of Burgundy. The people of Compiègne, however, were not willing to be handed over, and they began to reinforce their defences and build up their stores of food and weapons. If Duke Philip wanted their town, he would have to come and get it.

It would not be an easy task. Compiègne stood on the southern bank of the Oise, with a single stone bridge spanning the river to the north. There were great walls surrounded by a water-filled moat, and turreted gatehouses topped, now, with guns. And, as nerves began to jangle more and more with every April day that passed, all eyes turned to this town that stood at a strategic crossroads between English Rouen to the west and Armagnac Reims to the east, between Anglo-Burgundian Paris to the south and the duke of Burgundy's own town of Arras to the north.

Further north even than that, meanwhile, at Calais, the boy-king Henry VI of England made landfall in his French kingdom at ten in the morning on 23 April, the feast day of his patron St George. With him were his great-uncle, Cardinal Henry Beaufort, and twenty-two English peers, including the dukes of York and Norfolk and the earls of Warwick, Huntingdon, Arundel, Stafford and Devon, along with a lavish household of servants and retainers and more troops to join the advance guard that had already landed earlier in the year. There to welcome him was Pierre Cauchon, the bishop of Beauvais, a stalwart Burgundian partisan who had helped to negotiate the treaty of Troyes ten years earlier and had been a devoted counsellor of the English crown in France ever since. Cauchon had served Henry V; now, it was a moment of personal triumph to accompany that great sovereign's son on his progress to his French coronation.

But for the time being Bishop Cauchon and his eight-year-old king found their journey rudely interrupted. However inexactly they had been observed, the truces that formally required the English, Burgundians and Armagnacs to abstain from war had expired a week earlier, on Easter Sunday, and all parties were pointing accusatory fingers at each other to explain why it was that they were not assembling, as previously agreed, to negotiate a permanent peace. And, if peace could not be guaranteed in the country across which the royal cavalcade had to travel, then the precious and irreplaceable person of King Henry could not be put at risk. He would wait in safety behind the massive walls of Calais until his French kingdom was ready to receive him.

While the young king settled into his new accommodation, guarded by the fortresses of the Calais pale, the duke of Burgundy was moving towards the front line. For weeks already he had been mustering his troops at Péronne, twenty-five miles south of Arras.

Once Easter was safely past, he marched them south to Montdidier, and then on, zigzagging across country with his captain Jean de Luxembourg, another of his knights of the Golden Fleece, to compel the submission of castles and towns along his way. This military advance was enough, at last, to convince King Charles and his counsellors that their policy of Armagnac–Burgundian détente had failed. On 6 May, a royal letter was drafted to warn the king's loyal subjects about the treachery of the Burgundian enemy. Charles, it explained, had sought reconciliation with all his heart, in the hope that he might relieve his people of their suffering. Duke Philip, by contrast, had done nothing but demonstrate his bad faith, trifling with truces when he had no intention of making a lasting peace. Burgundy, it was now clear, still stood with England; the result would be war.

And war was what Joan had been waiting for. If the duke of Burgundy had Compiègne in his sights, she stood ready to defend it. She had seen action in the previous weeks – one skirmish had resulted in the capture of a troublesome Burgundian captain named Franquet d'Arras, who was tried and beheaded at Lagny – but now the task ahead had a comforting familiarity. She would relieve a town that found itself under siege, just as she had at Orléans. Just as at Orléans, her intervention would stop the enemy from securing a vital river crossing. Her opponents this time were the Burgundians, the false French, not the English, and the river was the Oise rather than the Loire, but, just as at Orléans, she had the loyal captain Poton de Xaintrailles riding at her side. The omens were good, even as the Burgundian commanders drew menacingly close: Duke Philip had set up his headquarters at Coudun, three miles north of Compiègne, and Jean de Luxembourg at Clairoix, just across the river to the north-east.

By the third week in May, she had a plan. As at Orléans, it was still possible for the defenders of Compiègne to move in and out of the town on one side, and Joan set out with other captains and a detachment of troops for Soissons, a little more than twenty miles to the east along the river Aisne. Their idea was to use the river crossing there in order to ride north and take the enemy by surprise with an attack from behind their position. In principle the strategy was sound; in practice, the difficulty of fighting the Burgundians across territory that had embraced Armagnac authority less than a year earlier became rapidly and alarmingly clear. Soissons had surrendered to King Charles in the wake of his coronation the previous July, but now the Armagnac king was long gone. Instead, the duke of Burgundy and his army were close at hand, and the prospect of accommodating Armagnac troops within the town walls seemed, to the people of Soissons, to be dangerous foolishness. They gave the Maid a bed for the night, and shut her soldiers out in the fields.

The plan would have to be changed. If she could not cross the river, Joan at least had the chance to seek reinforcements before she headed back to Compiègne, and so she made for Crépy-en-Valois, twelve miles south of the besieged town. When she returned with fresh troops, under cover of darkness on the night of 22 May, she found that the siege had tightened. The moment had come. After a few hours' rest, she called for her banner and gathered her men for an assault on the enemy. With Xaintrailles beside her, she rode across the bridge, out through the fortified *boulevard* on the north bank of the Oise, and on, charging into the heart of the Burgundian position. The onslaught drove the enemy back and back, the shouts of the attackers and the cries of the fallen mingling with the noise of steel striking steel. Joan spurred her horse onward, urging her soldiers forward again and again until, suddenly, something shifted in the din of the battle. A glance over her shoulder told her what it was.

Not all of the enemy stood ahead of her. Another division of Burgundian and English troops had held back from the fighting, out of sight. Now, they had moved into position behind her, cutting her off from the bridge, and safety. Still she cried out to her men till her throat was raw that God was with them. But the pressure was relentless. More and more of the Armagnac soldiers were forced into retreat across the river, until the enemy pushed so close to the *boulevard* that the captain of Compiègne had no choice: on his command, the great gate into the town swung shut. The sunlight was fading as the Burgundians pressed around her, blades and hands closing in, until at last she was pulled roughly from her saddle. Amid the confusion of faces, she offered the nearest Burgundian captain her formal submission, as a noble knight should, in acknowledgement of her new, unlooked-for and unwelcome status. The Maid was a prisoner.

Word spread quickly, with excited shouts and ribald laughter, in the Burgundian and English camps. Duke Philip himself lost no time in riding from the comfort of his lodgings at Coudun to take a closer look at this extraordinary prize. The chronicler Enguerrand de Monstrelet, who was among the Burgundian duke's entourage when he came face to face with the Armagnac whore, claimed not to remember the words that passed between them, but there was no mistaking the duke's delight. He wrote that same night to the faithful towns in France and the Low Countries that were subject to his authority: '. . . by the will of our Blessed Creator, matters have so befallen and He has shown us such grace that the woman known as the Maid has been captured . . . Her capture, we are certain, will everywhere be great news, and it will demonstrate the error and foolish credulity of all those who have let themselves be convinced by the deeds of this woman; and we are writing to give you this news, hoping that you will find therein joy, comfort and consolation, and that you will give all due thanks and praise to our said Creator who sees and knows all things . . .'

The man to whom the captive belonged, according to the laws of war, was Jean de Luxembourg, the commander of the soldiers who had fought the Armagnacs that day. She was taken under guard to his castle at Beaulieu-les-Fontaines, seventeen miles north of

Compiègne, to await the next move in a game in which she had suddenly been transmuted from a knight to a pawn. Joan saw herself as a soldier, that much was clear from the manner in which she had surrendered to de Luxembourg's captain, and, as such, she would expect to be ransomed – perhaps by her king, given that she had no income of her own with which to buy her freedom – or exchanged for another prisoner.

But others saw her very differently. She was an eighteen-year-old girl whose military command derived purely from her mission. For the English and Burgundians – as Duke Philip pointed out with such satisfaction – her capture provided incontrovertible proof that her claim to act on heaven's behalf had always been false. Clearly, the Armagnac king could not accept that misguided interpretation, but neither could he agree with the late Jean Gerson that, if the Maid faltered, the blame might lie with the inadequacies of those around her. Instead, the only possible conclusion was that she had overreached herself. That night, while Duke Philip's missives were dispatched to the Burgundian towns, urgent letters from the archbishop of Reims, King Charles's chancellor, conveyed the news – and its explanation – to Armagnac France. Joan the Maid had been captured, he said, because she was too wilful, too unwilling to listen to wise advice. As it happened, the king had already been approached by another messenger from heaven, this time a young shepherd from the mountains in the south-east of the kingdom. There was no doubt that the English and Burgundian enemy would be defeated, this boy had confirmed; nevertheless God had allowed the Maid to be taken because, consumed by pride and luxury, she had done what she wanted rather than following His commands.

It had been difficult to know what to do with Joan once her miracles had begun to fade. If God had now withdrawn His favour from her completely – which was surely the message of her capture – then that, at least, provided helpful certainty. It was a matter of regret, but it could not be permitted to cast a shadow over the mandate from heaven that had been confirmed so powerfully by the king's consecration at Reims. For the archbishop and his fellow Armagnacs, therefore – politicians, theologians, and those who, like the archbishop himself, were both – there was every reason to leave the Maid to whatever fate God had designed for her, which would surely be a judgement on her own conduct, not on the kingdom she had served.

But that was a conclusion which the spiritual guardians of English France – the parts of the French Church that had taken the Burgundian side from the start of the civil war – could not allow to stand. The failure of the Maid was the failure of her mission. The error into which she had led the so-called dauphin, and the demonic inspiration that had prompted her to contest the God-given rights of King Henry, required investigation and condemnation; so, three days after her capture, the theologians of the university of Paris and the vicar-general of the inquisitor of the faith in English France wrote to the duke of Burgundy, humbly requesting him to surrender the woman known by the enemies of the kingdom as 'the Maid' to ecclesiastical justice. She was vehemently suspected, they explained, of heresy, and – as all good Christians knew – it was under the Church's authority that she should be tried for crimes that had insulted God and risked the souls of the simple folk who had followed her. Six weeks later, having received no response, they wrote again, urging the duke to do his duty to God and Holy Church by handing Joan over to the inquisitor or, if he preferred, to the bishop of Beauvais, within whose diocese she had first been taken prisoner.

The case, they believed, was clear. Joan had been defeated on the battlefield, and now their chance had come to shine the light of the true faith on the manifest scandal of her claims. But their arguments fell on deaf ears. Faithful son of the Church though he was, Jean de Luxembourg still expected to trade such a renowned prisoner for a substantial ransom. And, after the coup of Joan's capture, the duke of Burgundy was beginning to regret his renewed commitment to fight for the English. Bogged down in the mud outside Compiègne, and finding his territories elsewhere under attack, he required room for political manoeuvre much more pressingly than a theological demonstration of the fact that God was not an Armagnac.

The solution, it emerged, lay with the bishop of Beauvais. Pierre Cauchon was a scholar who, back in 1416, had defended the duke of Burgundy's father over the long-ago murder of Louis of Orléans against the Armagnac Jean Gerson at the Council of Constance. Now, he found himself a bishop without a see, since the town of Beauvais had given itself up to the Maid and her king in the wake of the coronation at Reims the previous summer. He was determined to see Joan tried for her crimes, and – as a politician with years of experience among the royal counsellors of English France – he was well placed to bring about such a hearing. If the English, advised by Bishop Cauchon, would ransom the girl from Jean de Luxembourg, then King Henry could hand her to the Church, in the person of Bishop Cauchon, for judgement.

The English military position in Normandy had improved sufficiently that at last, in the second half of July, King Henry himself had travelled the hundred miles south from Calais to join his uncle Bedford at Rouen, where he was met by a deputation of burgesses in red hats, and by crowds who cried '*Noël!*' so loudly that the boy asked if the noise could be made to stop. Henry's presence in his French kingdom, young though he was, meant that Bedford was temporarily relieved of his role as regent, and it was therefore the king's council – under the leadership of Cardinal Beaufort, and counting Bishop Cauchon among its members – that agreed, on the king's behalf, to buy Joan the Maid from the Burgundians. With plans being prepared for Henry's French coronation, there could be no doubt of the virtue of exposing to public view the sorcery and idolatry of the whore who had put a crown on the head of the Armagnac pretender.

Bishop Cauchon opened financial negotiations with the duke of Burgundy and Jean de Luxembourg, while the council set about raising the necessary money from the king's loyal subjects of his duchy of Normandy. It was time-consuming work, but its urgency was evident. At the beginning of September, a follower of Brother Richard, a Breton woman named Pieronne, was put on trial in Paris; she claimed not only that God conversed with her in human form, wearing a white robe and a red tunic – evident proof of her blasphemy, the Parisian journal-writer said – but also that 'the woman Joan who fought alongside the Armagnacs was good, and that what she did was well done and was God's will'. Pieronne was condemned, and a sermon preached outside Notre-Dame to explain her error; then, because she would not abjure her heresy, she was burned alive. But the longer the delay in putting the Maid on trial, the greater the risk that such expressions of support for her might grow – or that the prisoner herself might in some way pre-empt the exposition of her crimes. She had already made one attempt at escape from Beaulieu-les-Fontaines, as a result of which she had been moved in July to the greater security of another of de Luxembourg's castles, the fortress of Beaurevoir, thirty miles further to the north-east; there she had contrived to jump from the window of the tower within which she was locked, and although she survived the fall, it took some time for her injuries to heal.

Finally, in November, the deal was done: the Burgundians had their money, and the English their prisoner. The theologians of the university of Paris sent a letter in icy Latin to Bishop Cauchon expressing their astonishment that it was taking so long for the woman to be surrendered to the jurisdiction of the Church, and another, in more politic French, to King Henry himself to ask that she should be brought to Paris forthwith, where so many learned men stood ready to assist with the investigation into her wrongdoing. But King Henry's council had other ideas. They had only just secured possession of their captive, and they were not about to send her to a city that was too near the reach of the Armagnacs and too uncertainly under English control. The bishop of Beauvais could not hear the case in his own diocese, which lay in enemy hands; it would therefore be moved instead to Rouen, the capital of English Normandy, where the nine-year-old king himself could keep watch over the proceedings, with his council and his army reassuringly close at hand.

And so, on 3 January 1431, an edict in the name of Henry, by the grace of God king of France and England, was issued to his loyal subjects. 'It is sufficiently notorious and well known,' the royal letter declared, 'how for some time, a woman who calls herself Joan the Maid has put off the habit and dress of the female sex, which is contrary to divine law, abominable to God, condemned and prohibited by every law; she has dressed and armed herself in the habit and role of a man, has committed and carried out cruel murders and, it is said, has led the simple people to believe, through seduction and deceit, that she was sent from God, and that she had knowledge of His divine secrets, together with several other very dangerous dogmas, most prejudicial and scandalous to our holy catholic faith.' Because these crimes required that she be examined 'according to God, reason, divine law and the holy canons', the king – as 'a true and humble son of the Holy Church' – ordered his officers to deliver the prisoner to the bishop of Beauvais. What that meant, it transpired, was that Joan would be judged by the Church, but she would be brought to court each day from a cell in a royal castle, and returned there each night. There could be no risk that the prisoner might escape. And 'if it should come to pass that she is not convicted or found guilty of the said crimes', the king's letter went on, 'it is our intention to retake and regain possession of this Joan'. In the unlikely event that her heresy was unproven, she would still, after all, be a prisoner of war.

Joan herself had arrived in Rouen under close guard by Christmas Eve. She had been thirteen months a soldier, and seven months a captive. Now her trial was about to begin.

9

A simple maid

Just after sunrise on 21 February 1431, Bishop Pierre Cauchon took his place in the chapel of Rouen's royal fortress. Assembled around him were some of the finest theological and legal minds in English France: forty-two clerics of the utmost probity and scholarly distinction, most of them trained at the university of Paris, the greatest seat of learning in the most Christian kingdom. They were here, in the half-light of a grey morning, faces taut with anticipation, for the first public session of a case that encompassed the weightiest matter of heresy upon which they had ever been called to adjudicate.

Today, the accused would make her first appearance before the judges and their advisers, but the inquiry itself had opened weeks earlier, on 9 January, when the bishop and eight of his distinguished colleagues had met in the royal council chamber near the castle to decide on the precise form the proceedings should take. Under canon law, the process of inquisition was initiated by the perception of guilt, by public notoriety so well established that it served as an accusation in itself. And in this case, of course, the infamy of the prisoner could hardly have been greater. As the opening of the trial record noted, 'the report has now become well known in many places that this woman, utterly disregarding what is honourable in the female sex, breaking the bounds of modesty, and forgetting all feminine decency, has disgracefully put on the clothing of the male sex, a shocking and vile monstrosity. And what is more, her presumption went so far that she dared to do, say and disseminate many things beyond and contrary to the Catholic faith and injurious to the articles of its orthodox belief.' The bishop was duty bound, it was clear, to investigate these apparent crimes, and to expose them to the scrutiny of theologians and canon lawyers for definitive judgement.

Scrupulous care was required in any inquisition into suspected heresy, but never more so than in this case, given that the accused had had the temerity to suggest that God had sent her to wrest the kingdom from its rightful sovereign. That claim had been noised across Europe; the demonstration that it was false had therefore to be conducted and recorded with unimpeachable propriety and rigour, so that the judges' conclusions could be published equally widely. And a great deal hung on the hearing, personally as well as politically – principally, of course, the fate of the prisoner herself. If her guilt were established, and she remained unrepentant, the Church would have no choice but to abandon her to the secular arm, which would sentence her to die in purifying flames. It was a mark of the singularity of her situation that, if she were not convicted, she would not be freed but handed back to the jurisdiction of the crown, her future to be decided by the king. But that outcome was hardly likely, and a greater preoccupation for Bishop Cauchon was the possibility that she might be drawn to confess her guilt and abjure her heresy. Then she would be spared the fire, to spend the rest of her days behind bars in penitent contemplation of her sin. This trial, the bishop knew, was a chance to save a soul and a life, as well as vindicate the kingdom to which he had devoted his career. And, in doing God's work, he might also win himself an archbishop's mitre; the see of Rouen was vacant, and over the next weeks and months he would publicly demonstrate his credentials as a man of God before the members of the king's council and the canons of Rouen's cathedral chapter.

There was much to be done, and Cauchon set about fulfilling his responsibilities with single-minded determination. On 9 January, he and his eight advisers reviewed the evidence they had already compiled, and decided that more was needed, including some to be sought in the prisoner's home village – not an easy matter, given that Domrémy lay on the border between Armagnac and Burgundian territory, but necessary, the committee agreed. Then there were officials to appoint: Jean d'Estivet, a canon of Beauvais, to act for the prosecution as promoter of the trial; Jean de La Fontaine, a specialist in canon law, to oversee the interrogation as examiner; Jean Massieu, a dean of Rouen, to carry out the judges' instructions as executor; and two experienced clerks, Guillaume Colles and Guillaume Manchon, as notaries. Over the next six weeks, under Cauchon's direction, the case was summarised into articles and a series of questions drafted. On 19 February, a meeting of twelve scholars under the bishop's supervision confirmed that the evidence was sufficient to justify summoning the prisoner for preliminary questioning. The inquisitor of the faith in France, Jean Graverent, was busy, it emerged, with another hearing in Coutances, and his deputy in the diocese of Rouen, a friar named Jean le Maistre, was therefore summoned to act in his place as a judge at the bishop's side. Le Maistre seemed reluctant – or, at least, keen to argue about the technicalities of his appointment – but he agreed that the hearing could proceed while the details of his participation were resolved.

At last, on 20 February, Bishop Cauchon was ready. He gave the order that the accused should appear before him at eight the following morning, 'to answer truly to the articles and questions and to other matters upon which we hold her in suspicion'. Jean Massieu, who delivered this summons, returned to report that she was willing to appear; she asked only to be allowed to hear mass beforehand, and that the bishop should assemble around him 'as many men of the Church from France as from England'. The bishop consulted his advisers, but the response needed little discussion: there could be no question of the woman attending divine service, given the crimes of which she was accused and the fact that she still insisted on the perversion of wearing men's clothing; and, of course, all the holy men gathering in the gloom of the royal chapel were French, even if they recognised a different king from the one to whom the prisoner had offered her allegiance.

Silence fell, and suddenly she was there: a girl, dressed as a boy, with her dark hair cut short. The silks and furs to which she had grown accustomed since Orléans were gone, and she was pale from long months without sight of the sun. But her face was composed, her eyes steady. Within this large and solemn assembly, she was the only woman, and the youngest by years, but, after her adventures since leaving Domrémy, that was no longer such a novel experience. She had faced interrogation before, at Poitiers, where another august company of scholars had sought to investigate the truth of her mission. That had not been an inquisition of the hostility she now faced, but still there was much that was familiar. Once again, the questioning with which she would be confronted today had been prefaced by an examination to confirm that she was a virgin, conducted this time under the aegis of the duchess of Bedford. Her physical wholeness had been proved; now it was time for her spiritual integrity to be tested. The Maid's judges were ready, but so was she.

The first formality was a sacred oath that she would tell the truth, to be taken, Bishop Cauchon explained, with her hand touching the gospels. And, for the first time, the girl spoke. 'I don't know what you want to question me about. Perhaps you might ask me things that I will not tell you.' She was required to tell the truth about matters of faith, and other things that she knew, she was told, and again she demurred. She would gladly talk about her parents and all that she had done after she left home, but her revelations from God were a different matter; those, she had only told her king, and she did not believe she was permitted by heaven to speak of them, even if her head were to be cut off – though she would know more, she said, within eight days. This was a hurdle the bishop had not anticipated. He asked again, and again, and each time she gave the same response, until at last, kneeling before him with her hands on the holy book, she swore to tell the truth about matters concerning the Catholic faith. For now, her revelations would have to wait.

In any case, there were the basics to be established, her light voice following question with answer as the notaries' quills scratched on the parchment before them. Her name was Joan, she said, and she knew nothing of a surname. Her father was Jacques d'Arc, and her mother, Isabelle. She was nineteen years old, she thought, and she had been baptised in the church at Domrémy, the village where she was born. At the judges' prompting, she named her godparents, and the priest who had baptised her; she confirmed that she knew the Lord's Prayer, the Hail Mary and the Creed, all of which she had learned from her mother. But here again the bishop encountered the prisoner's will, which, it was already becoming clear, might prove to be a formidable obstacle. Asked to repeat the Lord's Prayer for the court, she said she would gladly say it, but only to one who would hear her confession. Cauchon pressed her time and again, but she would not concede, until he was left with no choice but to move on.

Still, at least the day's business was almost complete. Before the girl was taken back to her cell in another part of the castle, Cauchon warned her not to attempt to escape, on pain of conviction for heresy. But this too roused her resistance. She would be breaking no oath if she fled, she protested, since she had never given her word that she would not; she complained, too, of the iron chains with which she had been bound. But the shackles were necessary, the bishop reminded her, because she had tried to escape before. That last was true, and she admitted as much, but wanting to escape, she declared, was the right of any captive. In the circumstances, it seemed wise for her jailers to swear on the gospels that they would guard her well and allow no one to speak to her without Bishop Cauchon's permission. And with that, the court was adjourned.

The next morning at eight, the crowd of scholars packed into the robing room at one end of the castle's great hall was even larger: forty-eight men of the Church were there to assist Bishop Cauchon and his officers in the administration of their duty. If the newcomers had decided to attend in the hope of witnessing the girl's defiance, they did not have long to wait. Once again the proceedings opened with the requirement that she should swear to tell the truth, and once again she objected. 'I took an oath for you yesterday; that should be quite enough for you.' And when she was pressed: 'You burden me too much.' In the end she swore as she had done the day before, to tell the truth in matters concerning the faith; but when the theologian Jean Beaupère, whom Cauchon had nominated to conduct the day's interrogation, began to speak, she fixed him with a look. 'If you were well informed about me, you would wish that I were out of your hands. I have done nothing except through revelation.'

Beaupère started slowly, carefully, with her life at home in Domrémy – no one could best her at sewing and spinning, she told him proudly – and her journey to Vaucouleurs. The questions coiled and probed, forwards and backwards through her story: her meeting with the captain Robert de Baudricourt, her letter of defiance to the English at Orléans, then back to her arrival at Chinon, and on to her assault on Paris. Often she answered, but sometimes, from one question to the next, Beaupère met blank refusal. (Had it been right to attack the capital on a holy feast day? 'Move on.') But as they talked, there were moments when those listening found they had forgotten to exhale; because, despite her protests, Joan had begun to speak about her voice from God.

She had first heard it at the height of a summer day in her father's garden when she was thirteen years old. On her right side, towards the church, there came a light, and a voice, and she was afraid, but she heard it a second time, and then a third, and then she understood that it was the voice of an angel, sent to her by God. It told her to be a good girl, and to go to church; then it told her of her mission, even though she was a poor girl who knew nothing of war. When she had arrived at Chinon, her voice had revealed her king to her, among all the lords of his court. Her king and his lords saw and knew that she heard a voice from God, she said, and by now, as the exchanges went back and forth, she was speaking sometimes of a voice, and sometimes of 'voices'. But when Beaupère asked who had told her to wear men's clothes, she refused to say. She blamed no one else, she said, and, besides, she had to do it; 'and she changed her answer often', observed the notaries.

It was enough for one day. When the next session was called to order, two days later, a still greater number of distinguished clerics — sixty-two in all — struggled to find a seat in the robing room to hear the lengthiest argument yet about the swearing of the oath. 'You can leave the matter. I've sworn twice; that's enough,' Joan said. She would not give in, no matter how Bishop Cauchon pressed her, and it was her own provisional oath she swore before turning to face Beaupère, and his questions about her voice. When had she last heard it? Today, and yesterday three times, once in the morning, once at vespers, and again when the bell rang for the Hail Mary at night. In the morning, the voice had woken her from sleep but (this in response to Beaupère's query) without touching her physically. It had told her to answer boldly and God would help her; at that, she turned to the bishop. 'You say that you are my judge. Take care what you do, for in truth I am sent by God, and you put yourself in great danger.'

The self-possession was utterly remarkable, but Beaupère scarcely had time to notice. His work was complex and subtle: how to unravel, step by step, the information required for this most challenging case of the discernment of spirits. The great Jean Gerson, in his last days, had been deceived by the Maid's claims, but his method still provided the template for this court's attempts to reach the truth. Already it was apparent that Joan did not display the necessary humility, the awareness that she, an unlettered girl, required the authoritative judgement of the Church to decide on the nature of her revelations. Instead, she believed – dared to declare, even – that her revelations gave her the authority to resist the Church's judgement. The court would therefore have to rely on Beaupère's skill in eliciting evidence from her reluctant testimony in order to conclude whether she truly heard messages from heaven, or whether they came to her from hell.

Was the voice, he asked, that of an angel, or a saint, or did it come directly from God? 'The voice comes from God,' she said; but as the questions continued she resisted, hesitated, demurred. Could she ask her voice to take a message to her king? She did not know if it would obey, unless it was God's will. Did her voice tell her she would escape from prison? 'Do I have to tell you?' Had the light appeared with the voice in recent days, and did she see anything else when it spoke? The light came before the voice; but 'I will not tell you all; I don't have leave to, and my oath does not cover this. The voice is good and worthy, and I'm not bound to answer about it.' Could the voice see, did it have eyes? 'You won't learn that yet.' Did she know she was in the grace of God? That question, at least, was straightforward for any devout parishioner who had listened to the sermon in church on Sundays. 'If I'm not, may God put me there; and if I am, may God keep me in it. I would be the most wretched person in the world if I knew I was not in the grace of God.'

The day was drawing in, and the session almost over. Beaupère turned to his dossier of evidence from the girl's village – an Armagnac place, she confirmed, even though the neighbouring village was Burgundian. (Had the voice told her to hate Burgundians? She did not love them once she understood that her voices supported the king of France.) But Beaupère's interest in her life in Domrémy focused on the village, not the state of the kingdom: on stories, gathered by the bishop's investigators, of a great beech tree near a spring. Local people called it the tree of the fairies, and believed the waters there had healing properties. Sometimes young girls made garlands to hang in the tree, and danced at its foot. Beaupère knew well that fairies did not exist, and that if there were spirits in the tree they could only be demons, so if Joan shared the old folk's beliefs about the fairies, if she danced around the tree and offered them garlands, it would demonstrate her erroneous thinking and her failure to distinguish a diabolic presence for what it truly was. But Joan showed little interest in his questions. She had made garlands for the image of the blessed Virgin in the village, she said, and danced *near* the tree, but she never saw fairies, nor heard her voices there. Her answer was hardly correct in its grasp of doctrine – she did not know, it appeared, that fairies, unlike angels and demons, were not real – but neither, the judges knew, was it damning. She seemed weary. One last question: did she want a woman's dress? 'If you will let me, give me one, and I'll take it and go. Otherwise, not. I'm content with this, since it pleases God that I wear it.'

This time she had two full days to wait in her cell before she was brought back to the robing chamber. The assembly was slightly smaller – fifty-four ecclesiastics, not counting the officials of the court – but the day began, as always, with the familiar argument about the oath: 'You should be content. I've sworn enough.' Beaupère stepped forward. How had she been doing? 'You see very well how I've been doing. As best I can.' The voice that spoke to her was the subject to which he wanted to return, and again her answers looped and swerved, stopping in their tracks, then starting the dance anew. His questions were variations on a theme already played: what had the voice told her? Did it forbid her to say what she knew? Was it the voice of an angel, or a saint, or did it come directly from God?

Suddenly the room was still. The moment lengthened. What had she said? It was the voice of St Catherine and St Margaret. Their forms were crowned with precious diadems. 'And I have leave from the Lord about this. If you doubt it, send to Poitiers where I was interrogated another time.' Now, the questions came tumbling one after the other. How did she know there were two saints? How did she know who they were? Were they dressed in the same cloth? Were they the same age? Which one came to her first? Again, the answers danced away. She knew very well who they were, and they had told her their names. 'I will tell you nothing else now; I don't have permission to reveal it.' But then: she had received comfort first of all from St Michael. Another silence. Had much time passed since she first heard the archangel's voice? 'I do not name the voice of St Michael to you, I speak rather of great comfort.' But still, she had seen him surrounded by angels from heaven. Had she seen the saint and the angels bodily, and really? 'I saw them with my bodily eyes, just as well as I see you; and when they left me, I wept and truly wished they had taken me with them.'

Beaupère's mind was racing. At last, this was progress. He knew, like all the men in the room who had studied the two-hundred-year-old writings of the saintly scholar Thomas Aquinas, that angels were beings of the spirit, capable of assuming bodily form when they appeared before humans, but not truly corporeal by nature. It was clear that the warrior St Michael might show himself on earth, and the virgin martyrs Catherine and Margaret too, but, if Joan had really seen them, she would need to prove it by describing the true essence of their angelic and saintly selves – and 'real' bodies would give the lie to her claims. Not only that, but the saints would surely have given her a sign through which she could convince others of the truth of their revelations. This, out loud: did she have a sign? 'I've told you often enough that they are St Catherine and St Margaret: believe me if you wish.'

That would do for now; there was much more to ask. A good inquisitor, he knew, should expose the untruths and contradictions in a heretic's answers by changing tack, doubling back, feinting and repeating. Had she been commanded to wear men's clothes? It was a small matter, she said, one of the least. In any case, 'all that I have done is by the Lord's command'. Why had her king believed her? The clergy at Poitiers had questioned her for three weeks, and, besides, he had a sign. Her weapons: Beaupère knew the story of the sword for which she had sent to the church in Sainte-Catherine-de-Fierbois, and of the silken banner that she carried into battle. Her voices had told her the sword could be found at the altar there, she said, but she much preferred her banner, which she carried in order to avoid killing anyone; she never did take anyone's life. And the battles themselves? She had known she would raise the siege at Orléans, and she had known she would be wounded there, when an arrow grazed her neck: St Catherine and St Margaret had told her so. Sorcery and superstition were the words in Beaupère's mind when he talked of special weapons, talismans and foreknowledge of the future. Sorcery and superstition: words worth pursuing in days to come.

Sure enough, when the court reconvened two days later, she was asked again about the fairy tree, and about mandrake roots and healing rings. But she dismissed them all. More difficult – and here the quiet of the room took on a particular intensity – were the questions about her saints. In what shape did she see them? Faces, richly crowned. How did they speak if they had no other parts of the body? 'I leave that to God.' They spoke French, she said. But did St Margaret not speak English? 'Why would she speak English, when she is not on the English side?' Answering questions with questions served her for a while, but the tactic could not be sustained forever, and when it came to the subject of the sign she had given her king to prove that she was sent by God, she resorted to flat refusal. 'I have always told you that you will not drag that out of me. Go ask him.'

The last day of public interrogation was a long one. Beaupère took her through her journey from Troyes to Reims to Lagny, to her encounters with the preacher Brother Richard and the woman Catherine de La Rochelle who claimed to see visions from God. (Joan had stayed up all night watching for the 'white lady' the woman pretended to see, but – as St Catherine and St Margaret had already told her – it was foolish nonsense.) He spoke of her saints, and her clothes, and her failure to enter La Charité despite God's command. ('Who told you I was commanded so by God?') And he talked of her leap from the tower in which she had been imprisoned at Jean de Luxembourg's castle of Beaurevoir. Her voices had told her not to do it, she said, but she had preferred to deliver her soul to God than fall into the hands of the English, so she had commended herself to God and the Virgin, and jumped.

With that, Bishop Cauchon declared that the record of her responses would be studied, and notes made of subjects on which more questioning was required. It took a week; then Joan learned that her inquisitors – or a small group of them, led by the bishop himself and the examiner Jean de La Fontaine – would visit her in the confined space of her cell. There, like Beaupère before him, de La Fontaine wove webs with his questions, moving lightly from topic to topic, retreating and returning as he sought to expose what might be erroneous in her thinking. And at the heart of this inter-rogation, it soon became clear, was the sign that had convinced her king of the truth of her mission.

Of this sign, she had always claimed she was forbidden to speak. Now, closed within the four walls of her prison, she no longer stood before an intent audience of dozens of clerics. Still, she responded boldly – as her voices instructed, she had always said – to the eight men who now faced her. But, little by little, the pressure began to tell. Why would she not reveal her sign, de La Fontaine asked, giv-en that she herself had demanded to know the sign of Catherine de La Rochelle? She would not have done so, she said, if it had already been shown, as her own sign had been, to many bishops and lords – the archbishop of Reims, the count of Clermont, the lord de La Trémoille and the duke of Alençon among them. The sign was a physical thing, then, perhaps, if it could be shown to the king's noble advisers: did it still exist? It would last, she declared, for a thousand years and more – and it lay even now in her king's treasury. Was it gold or silver, a precious stone or a crown? 'I won't tell you anything else about it. No one could describe a thing as rich as the sign is.' Then a flash of the familiar defiance. 'And in any case, the sign you need is that God will deliver me from your hands, and it is the most certain one He could send you.' Had her sign come from God? An angel of God had brought it to her king, she said, and she thanked Him for it many times.

They were getting close. The next time they entered her cell, she told them that this angel – the same one, she said, who always came to her, and never failed her – had directed the king to put her to work. What was the sign the angel brought? That was a subject upon which she would consult St Catherine. And then the next day they pressed her again, and at last, in staccato bursts punctuated by the prompting of their questions, she offered up her story. At Chinon after Easter in 1429, an angel had brought her king a crown of pure gold, its richness unfathomable, wrought so finely that no goldsmith in the world could have made it. The heavenly being had bowed before the king, and Joan could see – though the others present could not – that he was attended by myriad other angels, some with wings, some with crowns, and among them were her own beloved saints, Catherine and Margaret. 'Sire, here is your sign; take it,' Joan had said. And the crown signified, the angel declared, that the king would have his kingdom of France with God's help, if he would give Joan soldiers and put her to work. The angel gave the crown to the archbishop of Reims, who gave it to the king. And why had all this happened to her, instead of someone else? Because it pleased God, she said, to drive back the king's enemies by means of a simple maid.

At last, they had her sign: an angel who could walk up stairs and through a door, and speak to the king's court, and hand a crown to an archbishop. Her king had known it to be an angel because his learned clerics had confirmed it, she claimed. The learned clerics

in Rouen had other ideas; but for now they would keep their conclusions to themselves while their questions continued. For three
of the next four days, Joan faced more deputations in her cell. Had
she meant to kill herself when she leaped from the tower at Beaurevoir? No, she had commended herself to God; she had wanted to
help the desperate people of besieged Compiègne, and it was true
that she would rather have died than fall into the hands of the English – but her voices had told her not to jump. As she lay injured,
St Catherine had comforted her and told her to seek God's forgiveness for what she had done. And, now that she was in an English
prison, St Catherine had reassured her that help would come. Perhaps she would be freed from her cell, or perhaps some disturbance
would intervene in the trial to secure her liberty – one or the other,
she supposed.

Did she believe, they asked, that she had committed a mortal sin
in throwing herself from the tower, in consenting to the execution
of the Burgundian Franquet d'Arras at Lagny, in wearing men's
clothes, in attacking Paris on a feast day? She committed herself
entirely to God, she said, but she knew – because her voices had
told her – that she would come to heaven in the end. Here, the clerics were well aware, they had a duty to act as confessors and pastors
as well as inquisitors and scholars, with tender care for the prisoner's soul. Did she understand that the heavenly Church triumphant – God, the saints, the angels and the saved – was represented
on earth by the Church militant, the pope, the cardinals, prelates
and clergy and all good Christians, a body which, when assembled,
could not err? And would she therefore submit – they entreated her
warmly – to the decision of Holy Mother Church? But it was from
the Church victorious in heaven – from God, the blessed Virgin
and all the saints – that she came to the king of France, she said, and
it was to that Church that she would submit. 'It seems to me that
God and the Church are one and the same, and there should be no
difficulty about that. Why do you make this a difficulty?'

By Passion Sunday, 18 March, Bishop Cauchon and the vice-inquisitor Jean le Maistre – who had finally been persuaded, despite his protests, to take up his official role – had decided that formal articles of accusation based on Joan's testimony should be drafted for the next stage of the trial. Nine days later, after much discussion among the learned assessors about the best and most correct way to proceed, the promoter Jean d'Estivet presented seventy such articles to the court, each one read out and explained in detail to the prisoner. 'Let her be pronounced and declared a sorceress or soothsayer, diviner, false prophetess, invoker and conjurer of evil spirits, superstitious, engaged in and practising the magic arts, evil-thinking in and about our Catholic faith, schismatic, wavering and inconstant in the article "One holy Church" etc, and other articles of the faith, sacrilegious, idolatrous, apostate from the faith, evil-speaking and evil-doing, blaspheming God and his saints, scandalous, seditious, a disturber of peace and an obstacle to it, inciting wars, cruelly thirsting for human blood and encouraging its shedding, wholly forsaking the decency and reserve of her sex . . . A heretic,' d'Estivet declared, 'or, at least, vehemently suspected of heresy.'

But seventy articles was too many, and, at the beginning of April, Cauchon and his colleagues spent three headache-inducing days distilling their contents into twelve. And it was on these twelve articles of accusation that, the following week, sixteen of the theologians who had attended the trial pronounced their expert opinion: '. . . the apparitions and revelations of which she boasts, and which she claims she had from God through angels and saints, were not from God through the said angels and saints, but were instead humanly fabricated stories, or they proceeded from an evil spirit, and she did not have sufficient signs to believe and know this.' The twelve articles showed her, they solemnly and sorrowfully concluded, to be under the gravest suspicion of errors in the faith, of blasphemy and heresy. Further advice was sought from the canon and civil lawyers; they, in their turn, overwhelmingly concurred.

For more than three months, the bishop had conducted a trial more rigorously scrutinised and painstakingly recorded than any other that this assembly of the greatest scholars and clerics in English France could recall. The case had been made. What remained was the attempt to save a soul, to convince the prisoner of her fault, to seek her repentance. No one could know what God, in His mercy, had in store for the girl. But the end – whatever it might be – was near.

10

Fear of the fire

Joan was ill. She had been a prisoner for ten months. For the last two she had been under interrogation, first in the intimidating public theatre of Bishop Cauchon's court, and then in the claustrophobic intimacy of her own cell. She had held her own with the boldness that was her watchword, but the pressure had been relentless, and her initial refusal to speak of her revelations – her voices and her sign – had proved impossible to sustain. The Armagnac theologians she had faced at Poitiers had been well disposed to her mission; they had satisfied themselves of the blamelessness of her life, and then they had put her to the test at Orléans. But Burgundian clerics would never be convinced by a sign that took the form of an Armagnac victory. As a result, she had been driven to tell them more than she wanted, to talk of angels, saints and the gift of a golden crown. And still they did not believe her.

She had last seen the bishop on 31 March, when he visited her cell with seven other theologians in an attempt to convince her to submit to the judgement of God's Church on earth. She had said what she always did: she submitted to the Church, so long as it did not require her to reject the commands that came to her from God Himself. That she would not do for anything. And so they had departed, closing the door of her prison behind them. For more than two weeks, she had been left to contemplate the shackles in which she was bound. And now she was not just bone-weary, but sick.

She was certain, of course, that God's help would come, but sometimes the waiting was hard. 'God helps those who help themselves,' she had told her judges, and she knew the proverb to be true. She had tried to escape from her first prison at Beaulieu, squeezing between the planks in the floor of her cell, until she was caught by a porter, and she had been so filled with anguish during her second incarceration at Beaurevoir — so intent on freedom, and so desperate not to become a prisoner of the English — that she had risked death by jumping from the tower. But it had been God's will that she should live as a captive a while longer, so she had asked His forgiveness, and found comfort in the counsel of her voice — the voice, she had said, of St Catherine, the young and holy virgin who had resisted the interrogation of pagan scholars with eloquence and courage, and who, in statues and stained glass, always carried the sword of her own martyrdom. Joan had found her own holy sword at the altar in St Catherine's church at Fierbois, but here in Rouen she had no weapons. Here, she was alone in an English fortress, guarded by men who ogled and touched, and jeered in a language she did not understand.

At least her clothes — her tunic, doublet and hose, stained and ragged though they were — gave her some protection against grabbing hands. They had been the armour of her mission from the beginning, before she had had real armour to put on, and she would not give them up for a woman's dress — not even in return for the chance to hear mass, something for which she longed, and with which the bishop had tried again and again to entice her. Now, as the bolts were drawn back and the key turned in the lock, she knew he was here again. The faces around him changed — today, eight other clerics filed into the small space of her cell behind him — but he remained the same, in fur-lined episcopal robes, a man of about sixty, old enough to be her grandfather, smiling kindly, chillingly.

They had come, he said, in love and friendship, to offer her comfort and encouragement in her illness. Over the past weeks she had been questioned on great and difficult matters before many wise and learned men, who had studied her answers and had found in them many dangers to the faith. They understood, he said soothingly, that she was a woman, unlearned and ignorant of the scriptures, and they stood ready to teach her, for the salvation of her body and soul, just as they would do for their neighbours or themselves. Holy Mother Church would not close her heart to any strays from her flock who wished to return. But if Joan refused – and here the bishop's voice grew sombre – the Church would have no choice but to abandon her. That was the fate from which he was trying to protect her, with all his power and out of Christian love.

Joan looked up. She was grateful for their concern, she said. 'It seems to me, given the illness that I have, that I am in great danger of death. And if it is so that God wishes to do His will with me, I ask you that I may have confession and the sacrament of the Eucharist, and that I should be buried in holy ground.' The answer came again: submission to the Church was required if she wished to receive the sacraments. She said heavily, 'I don't know what else to tell you.' But the bishop had more to say. The more she feared for her life, he argued, the greater her need to change it for the better – and she could not receive the rites of the Church if she refused to submit to the Church's authority. 'If my body dies in prison, I trust you will bury it in holy ground. If you don't bury it, I trust in God.' She did not understand why the Christian love of which this man talked would not allow him to see that obeying the command of heaven could not be a sin, that the authority of the earthly Church could not trump that of God Himself. But still he would not stop. Holy scripture, one of his assistants said, showing her the verses, taught the necessity of obedience. She had already answered this, over and over. 'Whatever should happen to me, I will not do or say anything other than I have said before in the trial.'

They left her then. Another two weeks passed, of slow and grim recuperation. On 2 May, she was told to make herself ready to face the court once again, while, in the robing room near the castle's great hall, Bishop Cauchon rose to make a preparatory address to an attentive and closely packed audience of sixty-four of his fellow clerics. The woman had been fully examined, he declared, and her confessions scrutinised by doctors of theology and of canon and civil law. For a long time it had been evident that she appeared to be at fault, but before a final decision could be taken, it was necessary to warn her, with love, of the ways in which she had departed from the true faith, and to attempt, with all gentleness, to secure her repentance. Many worthy experts had spoken to her in private, but the devil's wiles had bested them. It was his hope that the public warning of this solemn assembly, given with love and kindness, might succeed where they had failed.

Then Joan was brought in: thinner, paler, a quieter presence than at the start of this long ordeal. To deliver the loving admonition of the court, the bishop had nominated an archdeacon of Évreux named Jean de Châtillon, an aged theologian who now stood, stiffly, to address her. He began at the beginning: did she understand that all the faithful in Christ were required to maintain the articles of the Christian faith? 'Read your book', she said, with a nod at the manuscript in his hand, containing the schedule of charges on which he was about to expound, 'and then I will answer you. I wait on God, my Creator, in everything. I love Him with all my heart.'

And so de Châtillon embarked on his lecture. He explained the infallible authority of the Church militant; the perversion of wearing men's clothes without being driven by necessity to do so, contrary to God's commandment in the book of Deuteronomy; the falseness and presumption of her claims about her revelations; and the grave danger in which she stood because of her obstinate refusal to repent of her errors. Would she submit? She was no longer ill, but she was still weary, and still waiting for the rescue that would vindicate everything she had said. Now, her answers neither danced nor swerved. 'I do believe that the Church militant cannot err or fail; but, as for my words and deeds, I lay them before God and refer in all things to Him, who had me do what I have done.' Did she understand that, though the Church could not take a life, a convicted heretic would be punished with fire by other judges, those of the secular arm? 'I will say nothing more to you about this. And if I saw the fire, I would say all that I am saying to you now, and would not act differently.' Would she submit to the pope and cardinals, if they were here? 'You will get nothing more from me on this.'

Her resistance was impenetrable; only at the end did she raise her voice with scornful defiance. Would she submit, de Châtillon asked, to clerics of her own party, to the Church of Poitiers, if her apparitions were referred to them? 'Do you think you can catch me like this and drag me towards you?' He warned her again: did she truly understand that, if she did not submit, the Church would have no choice but to abandon her, leaving her soul to be consumed by the eternal fires of hell, her body by the fire of this world? This time, all the certainty of her mission was distilled into each word of her response. 'You will not do what you are saying against me', she said evenly, 'without evil seizing upon you, body and soul.' Other learned voices joined in the chorus of warning and entreaty, until at last Bishop Cauchon himself spoke, telling her how carefully she must consider this wise advice. 'Within what time shall I decide?' she asked. She must make up her mind now, the bishop said. But Joan did not reply, and the guards led her back to her cell.

It was another week, but when she saw her judge and tormenter again, everything was different. On 9 May, when Joan was escorted into an unfamiliar room in the great tower of the castle, the bishop was there to greet her, along with ten of his colleagues, including the elderly figure of Jean de Châtillon. With them were other men, their faces blank, and by their sides various tools of worked metal with teeth and blades and pincers. Bishop Cauchon had offered up the best and most magnanimous demonstration of Christian love he was capable of choreographing, and she had refused to respond. Now, it seemed, he had decided to try the opposite of kindness.

She had been shown the proof of her errors many times, the bishop told her sternly, and in response she had lied and lied again, and denied the truth despite the efforts of many learned scholars to teach and advise her. She left them no choice but to put her to the torture, in order to lead her back to the path of righteousness for the good of her soul and body which she had exposed to so much danger. She looked, steadily, at these instruments of pious violence, and at the silent men whose task it was to inflict pain in the name of God. 'In truth', she said at last, 'if you were to have me torn limb from limb and my soul separated from my body, I still won't tell you anything more. And if I did tell you anything else about this, afterwards I would always say that you had made me say it by force.'

This was not, she could see, what the bishop wanted to hear. Fear, yes, and self-doubt in the face of the implacable authority of the Church militant. But not implacable certainty in return. She spoke again. A few days earlier, she had received great comfort from the archangel Gabriel; she was sure it was St Gabriel because her voices had told her it was so. She had asked her voices whether she would be burned, and they had said that God would help her. Cauchon was quiet; then a look at his associates, and a few whispered words. If they could not break her will, then breaking her body might do more harm than good to the progress and the reputation of this most carefully conducted and publicly scrutinised trial. A wave of the episcopal hand, and the session was over.

This time, she had two weeks to wait. Every day that passed, while Cauchon and his advisers deliberated elsewhere in the castle, made it less likely that she would be recalled to that chamber of horrors. But every day that passed was also a day when heaven's help had not yet brought her rescue. Finally, on 23 May, she was taken from her cell, not to the tower room, nor to the robing chamber where the plenary hearings were held, but to another room near her prison. There the bishop sat in state, the vice-inquisitor Jean le Maistre beside him. Around these two judges were assembled nine theologians and canon and civil lawyers, as well as priests belonging to Rouen's cathedral. This would not be just another day in the trial; this was its culmination.

Joan had been asked many questions, and she had given many answers. On that basis, the court could already have proceeded to judgement. But over the past two weeks, Bishop Cauchon explained, he had deemed it expedient to consult one further eminent authority: the university of Paris, and in particular its faculties of theology and canon law. Now, with the benefit of their conclusions, the learned theologian Pierre Maurice would explain once more the position of Holy Mother Church. Maurice was a younger man, not yet forty, whose own brilliant studies at the university were not long behind him, and his address, it soon became clear, had been prepared with erudition and elan.

Point by point, he moved through the twelve articles of accusation, demonstrating in each case Joan's transgression. Either her voices and visions were stories she had invented, or, if she had truly heard and seen them, they were diabolical in origin. If the latter, then not only had she believed in them too rashly, but her reverence for them made her an idolater and an invoker of demons. Her sign of the angel bringing her king a golden crown was 'not plausible', he declared, 'but a presumptuous, misleading and pernicious falsehood, a fabricated matter that diminishes the dignity of angels'. Her claim to know of things to come was an empty boast, full of superstition and divination. Her insistence on wearing men's clothes, against nature, God and the authority of the Church, implicated her in blasphemy, idolatry and transgression of the faith. She had encouraged tyranny and bloodshed. In leaving home without her parents' permission she had broken God's command to honour her father and mother. Her claims about her saints' enmity towards the English and Burgundians were blasphemous, and a violation of the commandment that she should love her neighbour. Her leap from the tower at Beaurevoir showed her sin in risking suicide, and her presumption in claiming to know that she was forgiven. Above all else, there could be no doubt that she was schismatic and apostate, since, by refusing to submit to the judgement of God's Church on earth, she had withdrawn herself from the community of the faithful.

'Joan, dearest friend,' – the man's voice was full of sorrow – 'now it is time, at the end of your trial, to think carefully about what has been said.' Her judges begged her, he said, they urged and warned her in the name of Christ to return to the path of truth by offering her obedience to His Church. 'By so doing, you will save your soul and, I believe, redeem your body from death. But if you do not do this, and if you persist, know that your soul will be utterly damned, and I fear the destruction of your body. From such a fate may Jesus Christ preserve you.' At last, Maurice stepped back. All eyes turned to Joan. She raised her head. What more could she say? 'As for my words and deeds that I spoke of in the trial, I refer to them and wish to stand by them.' The question came again: would she not submit? 'I will maintain what I always said during the trial.' If she saw the fire burning, with wood prepared for the pyre, if she saw the executioner with the torch in his hands, if she herself were in the fire, still, still she would say nothing else, even until death. A moment passed. Then Bishop Cauchon consulted the schedule in his hands, and declared the trial at an end. Tomorrow, she would face her sentence.

The next morning, Joan was taken from the castle to the abbey of Saint-Ouen in the centre of the city, where a scaffold had been built in the open space of the cemetery, upon which she would stand to hear her sentence publicly pronounced. The bishop and the vice-inquisitor were there, and with them an august figure swathed in the red robes of a cardinal: Henry Beaufort, bishop of Winchester, cardinal of England, great-uncle of the child-king, and head of the royal council in English France, a prince of Church and state together. A great gathering of churchmen clustered around them; Joan could see the young orator Pierre Maurice, the venerable Jean de Châtillon, and Jean Beaupère, who had questioned her at the start of the trial all those weeks ago. Below her, at the scaffold's foot, the entire city, it seemed, was elbowing and jostling for a better view of the infamous Armagnac whore. But Joan fixed her gaze on the filigree spires of the abbey church, reaching high into the sky that she had hardly seen during the twelve months of her imprisonment.

She was waiting for the help she had been promised, and that she knew would come. Now she saw one of the clerics stepping forward to deliver a sermon, struggling to make himself heard over the noise of the heaving crowd. There was still time. 'The branch cannot bear fruit of itself', he intoned, 'unless it remain in the vine.' His gospel text told of the true vine of Holy Mother Church, plant-ed by Christ's right hand, and of the withering of those who – like Joan – cut themselves off from its divine sustenance. And now he was talking directly to her, imploring her once again to submit. She had answered so often already, but, out here in the dancing air, she needed more time, so she spoke again. All that she had said and done had been at God's command. She raised her voice. After God, she would yield to the Holy Father in Rome. Let everything be reported to him for judgement; that was her submission.

The judges muttered behind their hands. She had said twice before, at points in the trial when they had pressed her hard on the question of obedience to the Church, that she wished her case to be heard by the pope, but then it had been part of the cat-and-mouse game of question and answer. (Would she submit to her lord the pope? 'Take me to him and I'll answer him.') Now, this was eva-sion of a different kind: a public appeal to Rome as an attempt to stop this moment in its tracks. It could not be allowed, not only because, at a stroke, it would sweep aside the authority of the court that had spent almost five months hearing her case with all pos-sible diligence, but also – and here Cauchon was acutely aware of Cardinal Beaufort's imposing presence at his side – because the English would never allow the prisoner to be removed from their keeping. After a moment, the bishop spoke. Her answer was not a sufficient submission. The pope was too far away to be consulted; her judges were here, and she must accept the authority of Holy Mother Church that they represented. Three times he repeated his warning. She did not speak again. Cauchon shuffled the documents in his hand, and began to read the final sentence.

Joan stood, bound and immobilised. She listened as the bishop declared that her obduracy left the Church no choice but to abandon her to the secular power – the English guards surrounding her, and the executioner with his cart standing by – to be burned alive in purifying fire. Heaven's help was coming, she had been certain. But there was no more time. She spoke. Cauchon hesitated, and a hush stilled the crowd. She spoke again. She wished to obey the Church and her judges. They had said that her visions should not be believed, so she would not uphold them. She said it urgently, over and over. She wished to submit.

There was uproar. As the crowd howled, the bishop stood for a moment, then spoke to the cardinal, who nodded. Cauchon gestured to Jean Massieu, the executor of the court, who stepped forward with a document, a statement of abjuration, which he read aloud. Did she confess her grievous sins – here itemised again in all their wretchedness – and did she renounce her crimes, never to return to them? She did, and, as the court required, she would swear to it by almighty God and His holy gospels. Massieu brought her the text, a quill in his other hand, and, haltingly, she marked the page to sign her submission.

It was a different sentence that Bishop Cauchon was now called upon to deliver. He had thought to preside over the condemnation of a heretic, but, at the eleventh hour, the devil's grasp on the girl had loosened. Now, shouting over the waves of noise, he described again the wickedness of her crimes and the care with which her case had been considered by her judges. At last, with God's help, she had recanted her error with a contrite heart and unfeigned faith. She would be welcomed back into the bosom of Holy Mother Church, and, according to this final sentence of the court, she would live out her days in the penance of perpetual imprisonment, eating the bread of sorrow and drinking the water of affliction as she wept for her sin.

Joan was bundled away. Some hours passed before the vice-inquisitor came to her cell, attended, as always, by an escort of learned clerics. She must be grateful, they said, for the grace of God and the mercy of His Church in receiving her into their embrace. She must submit to the sentence of imprisonment with humble obedience, and never, on any account, return to the invented stories she had previously told. And now, as the Church had commanded, she must lay aside the shameful clothing she wore. A dress was proffered; she put it on at once, taking off the doublet, tunic and hose to which she had clung for so long. Then she bowed her neck for the shaving of her head. As the priests watched, her dark hair – which, dirty and grown though it was, had still recognisably been cut short and round over her ears in the manner of a fashionable young man – fell lock by lock to the floor.

At last, it was over. Many people were filled with rage, Bishop Cauchon knew, at the thought that the slut of the Armagnacs had escaped the fire. But he was a shepherd to his flock, and he had saved a soul for Christ. Her guilt had never seriously been in doubt, but he had drawn it out into public view, step by step, with all the rigour of which he was capable. Many of the English lords – whom she had insulted, threatened and defied, and whose soldiers' blood she had spilled – had wanted her dead. But the bishop could reflect with satisfaction upon the fact that the great cardinal of England had stood with him to receive her recantation. She had publicly abjured her wicked claim of God's support for the so-called dauphin and the false French who dared to follow him. Now, the girl who had seemed to perform miracles would rot in an English jail for the rest of her life, in abject contemplation of the sins she had committed.

Three days later, the bishop received word that his presence was required once more at the castle. The next morning, 28 May, he and Jean le Maistre, with an escort of clerics and guards, were shown to Joan's cell. The black stubble of her shorn hair was rough upon her scalp, and she appeared agitated, but for a moment they saw nothing except her clothes. Why, Cauchon asked, was she dressed as a man, when she had promised and sworn never to do so again? When she spoke, her answers raced and tumbled, slipping and sliding from one to the next. She preferred these clothes, she said, to a woman's dress. She had not understood that she was taking an oath not to wear such garments again. It was more suitable, she thought, to wear men's clothes since she was forced to live among men. She had put them back on because the promise that she might go to mass and be freed from her shackles had not been kept. She would rather die than be bound in irons, but if she could go to mass, and her shackles could be removed, and if she were placed in a more gracious prison, with female company, then she would be good and do what the Church wanted.

There was a pause. Had she, the judges asked, heard the voices of St Catherine and St Margaret in the four days that had passed since her abjuration in the abbey cemetery? She nodded. What had they said? This time her distress was clear in every thread she pulled from the tangled bundle of her thoughts. Her voices said that she had damned her soul to save her life. Before, they had said she should speak boldly on the platform. The preacher at Saint-Ouen had accused her falsely. If she said God had not sent her, she would be damned, because she had truly been sent by God. She had not meant to deny her visions. Her recantation was utterly false. Everything she had done on the scaffold was from fear of the fire. Then what, Cauchon asked, was the truth about her voices, and about the angel with the golden crown? 'I told you the truth about everything in the trial, as best I knew how.' She would rather do penance once and for all by dying than suffer prison any longer.

She had understood nothing in the words of her abjuration, and she had done nothing against God. She would put on women's clothes if the judges wanted, but she would do nothing else.

They left her alone then. The next day, Cauchon and le Maistre called a meeting of their advisers and assessors – nearly forty clerics in all – in the chapel of the city's episcopal palace. There, the bishop rehearsed what had happened: her sentence, her recantation, and the disturbing events of the previous day. One by one, scholarly voices spoke. All offered counsel of one kind or another; some suggested that one final attempt be made to redeem her immortal soul. But every conclusion was the same. Joan was a relapsed heretic, and, as such, she must be abandoned by the Church.

Early the following morning, while finishing touches were put to the pyre and platform in the city's old market square, a last deputation filed into the prisoner's cell. It was Pierre Maurice who took the lead. Her life was beyond hope, he said, on this, the day of her death, but the salvation of her soul was still within reach. He would ask, and she must answer. Had she truly heard voices and seen visions? Today, her distress was quieter, more contained. When she spoke, it was without defiance. Her apparitions were real, she said. 'Whether they are good or evil spirits, they appeared to me.' She heard her voices most of all when the church bells rang for matins in the morning and compline in the evening. (It was sometimes the case, Maurice told her gently, that people heard the ringing of bells and believed they could make out words within the sound.) And truly, she had seen visions: her angels had come to her in a great multitude, in the smallest dimension, as the tiniest things. What of the angel who had brought her king a golden crown? A small silence. There was no angel, she said. She herself was the angel, and the crown was her promise that she would take him to his coronation.

The door opened again: her judges had come. It was Bishop Cauchon who spoke. Her voices had always promised her that she would be freed. They had deceived her, had they not? Another moment. Yes, she said. She had been deceived. Whether they were good or evil, Mother Church must decide. It was enough; time was running out. A friar named Brother Martin stepped forward, at a gesture from the bishop, to hear the prisoner's confession and – as she had wanted for so long – to administer the sacrament of the Eucharist.

The hour was at hand. She was led from her cell to a waiting cart, which jolted through the crowded streets to the market square. There was a sea of people, the morning light catching buckles and blades as English soldiers moved among them. She saw the bishop, the vice-inquisitor, the great cardinal, the clerics and lords, their faces turned, watching intently as she was helped onto the scaffold. Brother Martin murmured beside her, his task to be her last adviser and friend, but she knew the condemned could expect little dignity; onto her shaven head, before she left the castle, they had shoved a cap bearing the words 'relapsed heretic, apostate, idolater'. She must endure another sermon, from a different cleric this time, preaching on a different text. 'If one member suffers, all the members suffer with it,' St Paul had written. And then, once again, Bishop Cauchon recited the litany of her sin. Joan, known as the Maid, was guilty of schism, idolatry, the invocation of demons, and many other crimes. She had abjured her heresy, and the bosom of Holy Mother Church had opened to her once more, but she had returned to her sin, like a dog (said the Book of Proverbs) returning to its vomit. To contain her deadly infection, she must be divided from the body of the Church. From this moment, she belonged to the justice of the secular power.

The executioner was there. English soldiers held her slight figure as she was bound to the wooden stake high above the waiting crowd. Her lips moved in restless, ceaseless prayer. Now the air was shifting: a snapping in the ears; a catch of smoke in the throat. Her voice was high and urgent. 'Jesus. Jesus. Jesus.' The fire burned.

PART THREE

After

11

Those who called themselves Frenchmen

The duke of Bedford had not been in Rouen to watch the Maid die. His wife had overseen the formal examination of the girl's virginity when the trial began in January, but a few days later the duke and duchess had ridden out of the city, leaving his uncle, the cardinal, to supervise the progress of Bishop Cauchon's conscientious work. At the end of the month Bedford had arrived in Paris to a hero's welcome: he brought with him a convoy of around seventy boats and barges packed with supplies, all of which he had shepherded up the Seine from Rouen through lashing winds and torrential rain, dodging Armagnac ambushes along the way. By the beginning of June, in more clement weather, he was back in the field outside the capital when news finally arrived that the Armagnac whore had paid for her crimes with her life.

That breathless messenger was followed, over the next weeks and months, by a stream of documents. There was a letter in Latin addressed, in the name of nine-year-old King Henry, to the Holy Roman Emperor and all other kings, dukes and Christian princes of Europe, and another, in French, to the lords spiritual and temporal of France and to the cities of this most Christian kingdom. Both missives recounted the outrageous heresies of the 'woman whom the common people called the Maid', and sketched the events of the trial that had been conducted by Holy Mother Church 'with great solemnity and honourable dignity, to the honour of God and the wholesome edification of the people'. It was the need for such edification, in fact, which had moved the king (or, at least, his voice as ventriloquised by his noble council) to proclaim the news so widely. Since tales of the woman's exploits had spread 'almost to the entire

197

world', it was necessary that her just punishment be published in the same way, to warn the faithful of the dangers of false prophets.

The prelates, nobles and cities of English France were required by this royal letter to arrange that sermons should be preached so that the common people should know the truth – and in Paris on 4 July the inquisitor of France himself, Jean Graverent, addressed a great crowd at the abbey of Saint-Martin-des-Champs about the trial over which he had been unable to preside in person. He spoke so authoritatively that the journal-writer in the city noted down his dramatic account of the three demons who had appeared to the woman Joan in the forms of St Michael, St Catherine and St Margaret, only to abandon her utterly at the last. But the tale Graverent told was already familiar to the inhabitants of Paris, complete with grim details of the Maid's fate that had raced along the road to the capital from Rouen. After she had taken her last breath, the journal-writer reported, and her clothes were all burned away, the executioner had raked back the fire to expose her charred and naked body, still bound as it was to the stake, so that the people could see beyond any doubt that she was truly a woman. Then, when they had stared enough, he had stoked the flames higher and higher, until her flesh and bones were nothing but ashes. His masters, he knew, would not thank him for leaving fragments of the corpse to be retrieved as holy relics by deluded fools.

In the battle to eradicate such spiritual contagion, there was more work to be done. As soon as the trial was over, Bishop Cauchon had entrusted one vital task to the notary Guillaume Manchon and to Thomas de Courcelles, a theologian who had attended many of the sessions. The notaries had recorded the interrogations, day by day, in the French in which they were conducted. Now, Manchon and de Courcelles were to produce a Latin translation of these minutes as an official transcript of the proceedings. With this text, they were to gather all the correspondence, from the bishop, the university of Paris and the king, by means of which the trial process had been established, and they were to append witness statements from the clerics who had spoken to the prisoner on the morning of her death – a pastoral visit after the end of the formal trial, which had therefore gone undocumented by the notaries – as well as the public letters in which the king announced her execution. Then they were to transcribe this composite narrative into a register and make five official copies, to be signed by the notaries and bearing the judges' seals. And then this detailed record of the trial, written in the Latin that was the lingua franca of Church and state throughout Europe, would stand as an open testament to the diligence of the judges and the enormity of the girl's heresy.

Manchon and de Courcelles worked as quickly as they could, but there was no doubting the urgency of their assignment. It was essential that the rumours sweeping the continent should be corrected at the earliest possible opportunity. Reports reaching Venice from Bruges in the first half of July, for example, alleged that St Catherine had appeared to the Maid just before her death. 'Daughter of God,' the saint had said, 'be secure in your faith, for you will be numbered among the virgins in the glory of Paradise!' Meanwhile, the Armagnac king, the Venetians were assured, was stricken with grief, and had sworn to wreak terrible vengeance on the English.

But this was gossip running wild on the subject of the court at Chinon as well as the court of heaven. From the lips of King Charles, there came no comment on events in Rouen. His enemies had not dignified Joan with a public response while she was winning battles against them; it was not until her capture and execution had confirmed the self-evident truth that God was not an Armagnac that a torrent of their words told the world what she truly was. And, between the lines of each sermon, letter and transcript, the weight of one further conclusion could be felt: that the taint of the Maid's heresy hung heavy on the false king for whom she had fought. Of course, King Charles himself knew that idea to be a ludicrous misapprehension. The archbishop of Reims had already made clear the position of the Armagnac court: Joan's regrettable pride and wilfulness had caused her fall, but her faults could not detract from God's blessing upon her king, as embodied in the holy oil that had touched his brow during the sacred ceremony of his coronation. Nothing more need be said; and, from Chinon, the rest was an echoing silence.

In any case, as the archbishop had told the king's faithful subjects, another envoy from God was presently riding with the Armagnac forces. William the Shepherd, they called him, this boy who could hardly have been less like the Maid: full of wondering innocence, he rode side-saddle on his horse, his holiness made manifest by the bloody stigmata on his hands, feet and side. That August, the Shepherd was with the captain Poton de Xaintrailles when they chased after some English outriders who had dared to approach the walls of Beauvais. Too late, they realised it was an ambush laid by the earls of Arundel and Warwick. And, as the soldier and the boy disappeared into English custody, the silence from Chinon deepened.

The summer was not going well. The autumn, it transpired, was worse. In October 1431, the town of Louviers – a vital staging-post on the Seine between Rouen and Paris, which had been captured by La Hire while Joan was struggling in the mud outside La Charité – fell to an English siege. The mighty Château Gaillard was already back in English hands, and, as a result of these two Armagnac losses, the route along the river from the seat of English government in Rouen to the kingdom's capital now lay open once again. For the duke of Bedford and his uncle the cardinal, there was no time to lose: at long last, eighteen months after his arrival in France, the young King Henry could safely grace Paris with his presence.

On Advent Sunday, 2 December, the boy rode into the city to a rapturous welcome. The guilds took it in turns to hold over his head an azure-blue canopy starred with golden fleurs-de-lis – first the drapers, then the grocers, the money-changers, the goldsmiths, the mercers, the furriers and the butchers – while cries of '*Noël!*' warmed the freezing air. Ingenious pageants were presented at every turn: the beheading of the glorious martyr St Denis, the hunting of a stag in a small wood, and then, at the Châtelet, a doppelgänger of the king himself decked out in scarlet and fur, surrounded by the lords of England and France, with the two crowns of his twin kingdoms glittering above. At the window of the Hôtel Saint-Pol the dowager Queen Isabeau, with tears in her eyes, bowed to the royal grandson she had never met. And at the back of this stately parade, wretched and bound with rope like a common thief, came the holy fool William the Shepherd, now abandoned, it seemed, by his God. The simpleton was not seen again; rumour had it that he was dumped in the Seine and left to drown once the celebrations were over.

Two weeks later, another great procession assembled on the Île de la Cité to accompany the king on the short walk from his royal palace to the cathedral of Notre-Dame. In the vast splendour of the church, a flight of steps broad enough for ten men to stand abreast rose to a newly built platform that led into the choir. There, as heavenly music soared to the vaults above, King Henry VI of England was anointed and crowned King Henry II of France. Notre-Dame was not Reims, and the balm on the boy's royal head was not the holy oil of Clovis – but that could not be helped, since both were in the hands of the usurping Armagnacs. Still, the ancient regalia of the most Christian kingdom had been brought from Saint-Denis, and now the young king received them solemnly from his great-uncle, Cardinal Beaufort, who pronounced God's blessing on his sovereign. After the ceremony the company returned to the palace for a feast, its courses punctuated by elaborately sculpted sugar 'subtleties', one an image of the Virgin with the child-king of heaven, another a golden fleur-de-lis carried by two angels and topped with a shining crown. And there, among the lords of Church and state who drank the health of their newly consecrated monarch, was the gratified figure of Pierre Cauchon, bishop of Beauvais.

And yet, among the smiles and the celebrations, there were signs that all was not quite as it should be in the kingdom of English France. The bishop of Paris did not appreciate being elbowed aside by the English cardinal for a coronation in his own cathedral, and there was a spat between the officers of the king's household and the canons of Notre-Dame over who should keep the silver-gilt cup in which the wine had been offered at mass. The Parisian journal-writer, meanwhile, was scathing about the incompetence with which the English had organised the feast, and how dreadful the food had been. 'Truly,' he wrote, 'no one could find a good word to say about it'; and the half-hearted tournament held the day after the ceremony was similarly underwhelming. 'Really, many a time a citizen of Paris marrying off his child has done more for tradespeople, for goldsmiths, goldbeaters, all the luxury trades, than the king's consecration now did, or his tournament or all his Englishmen. But probably it is because we don't understand what they say and they don't understand us . . .'

This mutual incomprehension was hardly improved when the royal party hurried away from Paris only ten days after the coronation, back through flurries of snow and freezing rain to Rouen, then Calais and England. And with the king's departure from France, all eyes turned to the greatest of his French subjects. Philip of Burgundy had been present in Paris in the proxy form of an actor, bending his knee to his sovereign in the tableau at the Châtelet, but at the coronation the duke himself was nowhere to be seen. It was true that he had been much occupied during the previous eighteen months with the practical challenges of war. Despite the triumph of the Maid's capture, Compiègne had not fallen to the Burgundians in 1430, a failure which the duke angrily blamed on inadequate funding by the English. By that autumn, however, it was clear that Burgundian interests in the Low Countries – where he had just added the duchy of Brabant to his control of Hainaut, Holland and Zeeland – were reclaiming the duke's attention, and observers could not help noticing that his absence from the French capital in December 1431 meant that he was called upon to swear no personal oath of fealty to the young king. Not only that but, more than a hundred miles north in his Flemish town of Lille, he was occupied instead in negotiating a new six-year truce with the Armagnac enemy.

The meteoric moment of the Maid's career – her blazing rise and her dying fall – had briefly hardened the divisions between the two rival kingdoms of France, strengthening the Armagnac position while driving the duke of Burgundy into a closer embrace with the English. Thanks to Joan and the momentum of her mission, both kings had been anointed and crowned; but, now that she was gone, old fault-lines in the political landscape were beginning to open up once again. With every month that passed, the duke of Burgundy's gaze was more obviously fixed on the horizon to the north and east, where his new Burgundian state was emerging into independent being. And the dawning realisation that his policy would be shaped by whatever best served the interests of that autonomous power-bloc left the loyal French subjects of King Henry increasingly uneasy about what the future might hold.

The brittleness of English France was made disquietingly apparent in a series of conspiracies in 1432 that shook the English hold on Rouen, Argentan and Pontoise, and succeeded – through an improvised Trojan horse of soldiers hidden in barrels by turncoat merchants – in delivering Chartres to the Armagnacs. That summer, the duke of Bedford's satisfaction at retrieving the reins of power from the departed Cardinal Beaufort was cut short by his failure to take Lagny-sur-Marne, to the east of the capital, where the Maid had fought before her fateful move to defend Compiègne. Bedford's siege – conducted in a punishing heatwave that had followed the biting winter – had to be lifted in August after the Bastard of Orléans, Raoul de Gaucourt and Gilles de Rais led their troops in a slick manoeuvre to rescue the hard-pressed garrison and thereby maintain the military pressure on Paris. And the autumn, when it came, brought Bedford a body-blow that combined personal tragedy with political disaster.

Plague had been raging in Paris for weeks, and the spectacular luxury of the duke's home in the capital proved no defence against its ravages. In the early hours of the morning on Friday 14 November, his wife Anne succumbed to the epidemic, at the age of just twenty-eight. She was 'the most delightful of all the ladies then in France', lamented the journal-writer, and 'much loved by the people of Paris'. Bedford had loved her too, and so had her brother of Burgundy; and, once she was gone, the remaining bonds of loyalty that tethered the Burgundian duke within the fold of English France began to fray and loosen. She was buried in the church of the Celestines in the east of the city, English singers weaving melodies in haunting counterpoint as her body was lowered into the grave, '. . . and with her died most of the hope that Paris had', the journal-writer said, 'though it had to be endured'.

The cause of Parisian despair could scarcely have been more obvious in a summit at Auxerre convened that same month by Cardinal Niccolò Albergati, a legate sent from Rome, according to his master the pope, as an 'angel of peace'. The English were looking for no more than a truce, since they could not contemplate any permanent settlement which their boy-king might one day see as a betrayal of his God-given rights. But an Anglo-Armagnac truce was unworkable and unenforceable, the Armagnacs declared, and besides, they could decide nothing without the participation of the princes of the blood – the duke of Orléans chief among them – who were still captives in England. The duke of Burgundy had already concluded a truce with the Armagnacs that, in theory at least, took him out of the war; his interest, therefore, lay in securing his own possession of the county of Champagne, to which King Charles (the Armagnac ambassadors said) would never agree. In the end, all Cardinal Albergati could achieve was an appointment to meet again in the spring, 'and they had done nothing,' said the journal-writer wearily, 'but spend a great deal of money and waste their time'.

And when the spring came, the potential significance of the cardinal's reconvened conference was comprehensively trumped by a wedding. On 20 April 1433 in the cathedral at Thérouanne, halfway between Calais and Arras, the widowed duke of Bedford took seventeen-year-old Jacquetta de Luxembourg as his second wife. The bride was not only 'vivacious, beautiful and graceful', the chronicler Monstrelet reported, but very well connected: her father, the count of Saint-Pol, was the brother of Louis de Luxembourg, bishop of Thérouanne and chancellor of English France, and of Jean de Luxembourg, the Burgundian lord who had captured Joan the Maid outside Compiègne. For Bedford, the match seemed to promise both political and military advantage, as well as the hope of an heir – something which his childless marriage to Anne of Burgundy, devoted though it was, had failed to provide. But he had reckoned without the insult that Philip of Burgundy perceived in his remarriage only five months after their beloved Anne's death. There was injury too: the count of Saint-Pol was Duke Philip's vassal, and the see of Thérouanne formed an enclave within the Burgundian county of Artois, yet neither count nor bishop had seen fit to seek the duke's permission for the wedding to take place.

Cardinal Beaufort saw the dangers of this rift, and sought to bring Bedford and Burgundy together at Saint-Omer, just north of Thérouanne, at the end of May. Both dukes duly arrived in the town with much pomp and circumstance. Only then did it transpire that neither would cede precedence by agreeing to visit the other. The cardinal – a man with years of diplomatic experience at the greatest courts in Europe – shuttled between the two households, but neither would give in. The loss of the duchess had never been more acutely felt. And when both dukes left the town in magnificent style without having met, it was apparent that the personal relationship between these twin pillars of English France had been damaged beyond repair.

Within Armagnac France, meanwhile, bridges were being built rather than burned. The king's mother-in-law Yolande of Aragon, queen of Sicily, had retreated from the political front line while the mission of Joan the Maid, which she had helped to unleash, had directed the course of the war. Now that the stark imperatives of those dramatic months had faded, the subtleties of politics and diplomacy were once again to the fore, and, thanks to Yolande, a queen's gambit was already in play. The first move, in 1431, was a treaty between Yolande herself and the duke of Brittany, and that in turn prepared the way for a settlement sealed at Rennes in March 1432 by which the Breton duke's brother Arthur of Richemont, the estranged constable of Armagnac France, was restored to royal favour. Not only had Yolande persuaded the king to set aside his deep antipathy to the constable in order to harness Richemont's support against the enemy, but she had frustrated the duke of Bedford's hopes of securing a lasting alliance with Brittany and the service of Richemont for English France. Now, only the endgame remained: to remove from the board the troublesome figure of the king's favourite, the adversary who had precipitated the constable's rift with his sovereign, Georges de La Trémoille.

June 1433 was the moment chosen for the palace coup. At Chinon, armed men loyal to Yolande and Richemont seized La Trémoille in the middle of the night. The favourite tried to resist, but he was quickly overwhelmed; in the scuffle, he was stabbed with a dagger, but his vast belly absorbed the blow and saved him from mortal injury. King Charles heard the disturbance and started up in fear, but, on being reassured that all was well – that he was in no danger, and La Trémoille was simply being arrested for the good of his realm – he went back to bed. La Trémoille disappeared, unmourned, into internal exile, and, with scarcely a ripple in the glassy surface of the court, his place at the king's side was taken by a charming eighteen-year-old, Yolande's youngest son, Charles of Anjou.

The volatile Armagnac regime had been smoothly reconfigured by the queen of Sicily's expert hand, while in English France tensions between Bedford, his belligerent brother Gloucester on the other side of the Channel, and their uncle, the cardinal, threatened to undermine the cash-strapped government. Fighting continued in Normandy and Maine, around Paris, and – despite the Armagnac–Burgundian truce – in Champagne, Artois and on the borders of the duchy of Burgundy, as a result of which the duke of Burgundy himself decided to take the field once more in the summer of 1433. Nothing was certain, nothing was clear; but that in itself – compared to the dark days before the Maid's coming, when it had looked as though the English might take Orléans and swarm over the Loire into the heart of the kingdom of Bourges – was a source of strength to Armagnac France. King Charles would never inspire his troops on the battlefield. That thought had long since been dismissed. But now he was an anointed sovereign, and his captains – the Bastard of Orléans, the duke of Alençon, La Hire, Ambroise de Loré – had shared the Maid's victories; they knew, at least, what it was to win. And that was a sensation that seemed lost to the people of Anglo-Burgundian Paris. 'The war grew worse and worse,' reported the journal-writer in 1434; 'those who called themselves Frenchmen came every day, pillaging and killing, right up to the gates . . .' Though the city waited, neither Bedford nor Burgundy came to the rescue; 'they might as well have been dead', the Parisian said bitterly.

It would not have consoled him to know that the duke of Bedford felt equally thwarted. Among the reasons for the duke's absence from Paris was a year-long visit to London forced upon him by the need to seek more money and troops, and to counter pernicious accusations, stage-managed by his disruptively self-seeking brother Gloucester, that he had mishandled the war. In a passionately argued document submitted to the young king's council just before his return to France in the summer of 1434, Bedford spoke of the sufferings for which the journal-writer in Paris blamed him and all the noble lords who had failed to relieve the city. Because of the war, Bedford explained, the king's good townspeople of Paris and his other loyal subjects of France could not cultivate their lands or their vines or keep their livestock, and, as a result, they were driven 'to an extreme poverty such as they may not long abide'. More help was needed, and Bedford had no doubt at what point the great enterprise of English France had fallen into uncertainty: '. . . all things there prospered for you,' he told the king, 'till the time of the siege of Orléans, taken in hand God knows by what advice. At the which time, after the adventure fallen to the person of my cousin of Salisbury, whose soul God pardon, there fell by the hand of God, as it seems, a great stroke upon your people that was assembled there in great number, caused in great part, as I think, of lack of steadfast belief, and of erroneous doubt that they had of a disciple and follower of the fiend called the Maid, that used false enchantment and sorcery, the which stroke and discomfiture not only lessened in great part the number of your people there, but as well withdrew the courage of the remnant in marvellous wise, and encouraged your adverse party and enemies to assemble them forthwith in great number . . .'

Bedford had never before spoken in public about the Maid. This was not the carefully calibrated exercise of the months after her death, setting rhetoric to work to advertise heaven's verdict on her sin. Instead, he was giving voice to deeply felt frustration. The duke knew that his brother, the great King Henry, had been God's own soldier, and that his royal nephew's claim to the crown of France was just. Yet the wiles of the devil – finding a foothold in the world in the person of this misguided girl – had dealt an extraordinary blow to the righteous cause to which he had devoted his life. Bedford was forty-five, and, though his commitment to English France was as determined as ever, even the company of his lively young wife could not alleviate the weariness that now dogged his every step.

He was hardly helped, when he finally returned to Paris that December, by the fact that the winter was the coldest anyone could remember. It snowed for forty days without stopping, noted the journal-writer in the city; if he was exaggerating, it was not by much. Back in London the Thames froze over, and in the duke of Burgundy's town of Arras, a hundred miles north of the French capital, the inhabitants decorated the streets with elaborate sculptures carved out of snow. Their subjects were chosen from myth and legend; among these frozen tableaux, laced with the excitement of the supernatural, the only one taken from life was the figure of *la grande Pucelle*, the great Maid, at the head of her soldiers.

The people of Arras had seen Joan in person four years before, when she was brought to their town as a captive on her unhappy journey to Rouen and the stake. Now, this icy representation of the Maid was altogether too inscrutable to reassure the duke of Bedford and his fellow custodians of English France about the loyalties of King Henry's Burgundian subjects. And within weeks it became clear that Arras would soon play host to a meeting that promised them still less in the way of succour.

In January 1435, all wrapped in furs against the perishing cold, an illustrious gathering assembled two hundred miles south of Arras at Nevers, between Armagnac Bourges and Burgundian Dijon. The duke of Burgundy had come to meet the Armagnac count of Clermont – newly elevated to the dukedom of Bourbon after the death of his father, who had never regained his freedom after Azincourt. The two men had spent much of 1434 in a battle for control of the border lands between their territories in eastern France; now, however, they had agreed a truce. The fact that the new duke of Bourbon was Burgundy's brother-in-law, thanks to his marriage years earlier to the duke's sister Agnes, had done nothing to stop the fighting, but now that diplomatic relations had been restored, Bourbon brought with him to the conference at Nevers another brother-in-law, Constable Richemont, the husband of Burgundy's sister Margaret. Along with these two Armagnac princes of the blood, King Charles had sent his chancellor, the subtle and experienced archbishop of Reims. It was a happy reunion: so joyous, one chronicler said, that it appeared as though these lords had always been at peace. (How foolish, a Burgundian knight exclaimed bitterly, were all those lesser men who had risked death to fight a war so easily forgotten by the great.) Out of these personal negotiations came proposals by which it seemed a general peace might at last be secured, and it was agreed that all three parties – Burgundians and Armagnacs, and also, of course, the English, who were not present at Nevers – should meet at Arras on the first day of July in the hope of achieving such a settlement.

Philip of Burgundy had been playing a complex and relentlessly demanding game in the fifteen years since his father's murder. Now, finally, his pieces were aligned. The English duke of Bedford was no longer his brother-in-law. There could be no question of simply jettisoning his commitment, sworn by sacred oath, to his English allies; instead, it was up to his English allies to show themselves willing to make peace on the entirely reasonable terms to be offered at Arras by his Armagnac brothers-in-law on behalf of their king, who would also, naturally, offer restitution for the lamentable death of the duke's father. Peace in France would not only serve the interests of the kingdom's beleaguered people, and find favour in the eyes of the Church, but it would allow the duke to attend to the needs of his rich territories in the Low Countries, and to defend himself against the Holy Roman Emperor, whose long-standing alarm at the expansion of Burgundian power in the north had been transmuted only weeks earlier into a declaration of war.

For Philip, therefore, with his multiple perspectives and multiple priorities, Arras promised much. For the English, it was a prospect that chilled the blood. There could be no compromise between the claims of King Charles and King Henry: only one head could, with God's blessing, wear the French crown. If Burgundy were now to put forward as 'reasonable' a raft of proposals that required the abandonment of the English title to the throne of France, then the English would have no choice but to refuse. And if the duke of Burgundy were determined to see such a refusal as 'unreasonable', then he was already intent on a constructive dismantling of the Anglo-Burgundian alliance.

And so it proved when the first plenary session of the new conference opened on 5 August – a month late, thanks to the time it had taken to assemble all the various attendees – in a hall hung with cloth of gold in the abbey of Saint-Vaast. Arras was swamped with people; every inn, every lodging-house was full. Quite apart from the large delegations from England, Burgundy and the Armagnac court, there were observers sent by the great lords of France and all the towns and territories that owed their loyalty to the Burgundian duke, and ambassadors from far-flung lands including Spain, Navarre, Norway, Italy and Poland. The Armagnacs were once again led by the duke of Bourbon and Constable Richemont, with the diplomatic support of the archbishop of Reims, while the duke of Burgundy, as host to these noble visitors, kept magnificent state; and the warmth and bonhomie with which he entertained his Armagnac brothers-in-law did not escape the despairing gaze of the English.

King Henry was represented by lords spiritual and temporal from his councils in London and Rouen, including the archbishop of York, the earl of Suffolk (now freed from his brief captivity after the Maid's victory at Jargeau, albeit at the cost of a crippling ransom), and the devotedly loyal Bishop Cauchon. But the driving force behind their last-ditch attempts to hold the duke of Burgundy to the alliance he had made almost sixteen years earlier was Cardinal Beaufort. He used all his powers of persuasion, every ounce of the personal credit he had built up with the duke and duchess, to plead his case with such intensity that, during one lengthy private conversation, observers noticed great gouts of sweat standing out on his forehead. A truce – a twenty-year truce, even, bolstered perhaps by an Anglo-Armagnac royal marriage alliance – would relieve the sufferings of the French people, and sidestep the thorny issue of sovereignty without disturbing the friendship between England and Burgundy. But the cardinal was wasting his breath. The conference had been designed from its very inception to present proposals for peace to which the English could not possibly agree. Nothing remained for them to do but leave, and as they rode away on the morning of 6 September in bucketing rain, each man in the cardinal's lavish retinue wore the word 'honour' embroidered proudly – uselessly – on the sleeve of his red livery.

In Arras, the negotiations proceeded without them. Since England had turned its face against a godly peace, the duke of Burgundy could not in law or conscience – as Cardinal Albergati was quick to confirm on behalf of his master the pope – be held to a treaty which now promised only war. Still the duke hesitated. On 10 September a requiem mass was sung in the echoing space of the abbey church, sixteen years to the day after the murder of his father on the bridge at Montereau – a killing which, of course, King Charles had been much too young to prevent, although he would now do everything in his power to pursue those responsible. The one man who had never let Duke Philip forget the horror of that Armagnac crime had not come to Arras: the duke of Bedford lay a hundred miles away at Rouen, sick in body and heart. And then, on 16 September, came the sudden news that he had died. The regent of English France – that sober, cultured and dedicated man to whom the duke of Burgundy had once been so closely bound by ties of marriage and respect and affection – was gone.

It was a mercy, perhaps, that Bedford was spared knowledge of the solemn ceremony that took place in the church of Saint-Vaast on 21 September, exactly a week after he had succumbed to his illness. The treaty of Arras was complete – territorial concessions agreed, and restitution for the devastating loss of the duke's father promised. Now, with his hands touching the consecrated host and a golden cross, Duke Philip swore that he would henceforth live at peace with his sovereign lord, King Charles. Prompted by the love of God, he forgave his king, once and for all time, for his father's death. And then Cardinal Albergati laid his hands on the duke's head and absolved him from the oath he had given to serve the English king of France – a lifetime ago, it seemed – in another church, at Troyes.

This was not peace. Many French men and women, after all, were still ruled by the English, who proclaimed King Henry's right to the crown of France as stoutly as ever. Nor, despite the smiles and embraces at Arras, were the conflicts between Burgundians and Armagnacs that festered across the most Christian kingdom suddenly and miraculously resolved. But it was a movement of tectonic plates that utterly transformed the landscape of the war. The necessity that Yolande of Aragon had always seen, and that Joan the Maid had so forcefully demanded – that all French princes of the blood should recognise the God-given right of King Charles, and reject the false claims of the English invaders – had finally come to pass. At Bourges, Yolande celebrated the news with her pregnant daughter, Queen Marie, and her son-in-law the king; and when her next royal grandson was born at Tours in February 1436, he was named Philip, after his loving godfather Philip of Burgundy.

By then, the subjects of English France found themselves under fiercely intensifying pressure. Once the diplomats had left Arras, Armagnac forces had launched a whirlwind campaign in upper Normandy, seizing ports along the coast from Dieppe to Harfleur before pushing inland in January towards the embattled English stronghold of Rouen. The English lords Talbot and Scales – who, like Suffolk, had had to be expensively retrieved from

French custody after their defeat by the Maid – managed to rebuff this assault on the city; but in the meantime Constable Richemont and the Bastard of Orléans were tightening a noose around Paris.

For the people of the capital, all was confusion. Unlike English Rouen, Paris had been a Burgundian city ever since the bloody expulsion of the Armagnacs by men loyal to John the Fearless back in 1418. Now, the dead duke's son had made peace with the traitors and murderers. The Burgundian governors of the city, who were too deeply implicated in the English regime to reconsider their allegiance – principally King Henry's chancellor Louis de Luxembourg, bishop of Thérouanne, the doughty loyalist Bishop Cauchon and the bishop of Paris – made efforts to rally the people to a cause from which the heart had been ripped by the duke's defection. By March, however, even they were forced to concede that anyone who wished could abandon his possessions and leave. Those who chose to stay, they declared, must take an oath of loyalty to King Henry and wear the badge of St George's red cross.

But, for the journal-writer there, the bishops' defiance was a sort of frenzy that served only to prolong still further 'this evil and diabolical war'. He and his fellow citizens were so desperate for relief from fear and starvation, and so disoriented by the abrupt shifting of the political world on its axis, that the war itself now became the enemy, rather than the Armagnacs whom they had hated for so long. On Friday 13 April, when Richemont, the Bastard of Orléans and the Burgundian lord de l'Isle-Adam appeared with their troops outside the gates, bringing with them a promise of protection from the duke of Burgundy and letters of amnesty from King Charles, there was only a brief flurry of resistance, easily swatted aside, before the city opened to let them in: '. . . the constable and the other lords made their way through Paris as peacefully as if they had never been out of Paris in their lives', the journal-writer noted. And this 'very great miracle' – along with Richemont's declaration of the king's love and forgiveness for the inhabitants of his capital

– did its work in reminding the people of what it now meant, once again, to be French: 'the Parisians loved them for this, and before the day was out every man in Paris would have risked his life and goods to destroy the English'. The pages of the writer's journal themselves bore the traces of this seismic change: quietly, without comment or fanfare, the name of 'the king' was now Charles, rather than Henry.

The euphoria could not last. It became clear all too rapidly that fear and hunger were not, after all, at an end, and by the autumn the journal-writer was back to his familiar disenchantment with all men of power and rank, of whatever stamp. 'There was no news at all of the king at this time, no more than if he had been at Rome or Jerusalem. None of the French captains did any good worth mentioning ever since the entry into Paris, nothing but looting and robbery day and night. The English were making war in Flanders, in Normandy and before Paris; no one opposed them . . .' That last was not strictly true; and when, in November 1437, King Charles finally made his royal entry into the city, for the first time since he had fled in 1418 as a fifteen-year-old boy in his nightshirt, enough relief remained, and enough pleasure at the unfamiliar prospect of the French capital greeting its French king, for the people of Paris to give him a hero's welcome.

It was an unaccustomed sight in more than one respect: the king, as ungainly a figure as ever at the age of thirty-four, riding into Paris clad in the shining armour he had so rarely worn to lead his soldiers. This, at last, was a triumph, not a battle, but still there were reminders of battles past. With Charles and his fourteen-year-old son, the dauphin Louis, were princes of the blood and captains who had fought in his wars, among them Constable Richemont, Yolande's son Charles of Anjou, the Bastard of Orléans and La Hire. Just in front of the king rode Poton de Xaintrailles (who had freed himself from English custody more successfully than the poor drowned Shepherd), carrying the royal helmet on a silver staff braced against his thigh; around the helm was a golden crown, with a golden fleur-de-lis catching the low sunlight in its centre. And holding the bridle of Xaintrailles's horse, between cheering crowds so densely packed that it was scarcely possible to move through the streets, walked Jean d'Aulon, once the Maid's squire, now a gentleman of the king's household.

The officers of the city held a canopy of blue velvet powdered with gold fleurs-de-lis above the king's head, suppressing as they did so any memory of the same service performed for a small English boy six years earlier. As the cavalcade moved into the heart of the city, the king encountered singing angels and gatherings of saints, from France's patron St Denis to St Margaret, springing unharmed from the belly of an artfully painted dragon, while St Michael, the young warrior of heaven, weighed the souls of the sinful in his golden scales. That night there were bonfires in the streets, with music, dancing and drinking in the flickering light of the flames. A few days later the remains of the count of Armagnac, who had died so violently at the hands of the Burgundian mob in 1418, were reverently exhumed and transported to a fitting resting-place in his patrimony in the south. With his bones was buried the name of Armagnac as a badge of division within the most Christian kingdom of France.

The future was not simple, but it had at least begun. No one spoke any longer of the kingdom of Bourges, even if, out of long habit, the court could still most often be found in one of the royal castles south of the Loire. Charles, like his father before him, was an anointed king of France, and now both the idea and the reality of English France were starting to fade. Other English lords stepped forward into the void left by the loss of the regent Bedford, among them the ferocious veteran Talbot, as well as King Henry's new lieutenant-general, the twenty-six-year-old duke of York, and the cardinal's nephew Edmund Beaufort. But, despite some moments of military hope – including the recovery of Harfleur in 1440 – the combined effect of the loss of Paris and continuing pressure on English Normandy meant that the resources and the will needed to defend King Henry's French realm were dwindling.

King Charles, too, had his problems. The divisive figure of La Trémoille had been banished from his court, but division remained: the duke of Bourbon, in particular, resented his own lack of influence compared to the young Charles of Anjou, and he found a partner in dissatisfaction in the impoverished duke of Alençon, who could not yet enjoy the fruits of the reunified French kingdom because his lands in Normandy still lay in English hands. In seeking to assert themselves, Bourbon and Alençon could look to the support of those mercenary captains who had for two decades enjoyed the free rein conferred by a constant state of military emergency. The most infamous mercenary bands were known as *écorcheurs*, 'flayers', a name that aptly conveyed their double threat of violence and extortion. Since the treaty of Arras, their activities had become more obviously freelance, and, while the king might turn a loftily blind eye wherever their depredations ravaged territories belonging to his newly minted ally of Burgundy, he could hardly do so in the heartlands of his own kingdom. Royal efforts to check their worst excesses would therefore have made the *écorcheurs* natural allies of a malcontent nobleman such as Bourbon, even had two of the most notorious mercenary captains not been Bourbon's bastard half-brothers and a third, a Castilian named Roderigo de Villandrando, the husband of his illegitimate sister.

Already, in 1437, Bourbon and Alençon had attempted a show of strength to demonstrate their unhappiness with the regime, but a decisive military response from King Charles drove de Villandrando and his men out of the kingdom and the two dukes into retreat – a disgrace that explained their absence from the triumphal royal entry into Paris that November. In February 1440, however, hostilities broke out again. At the end of 1439, Charles had set in train a programme of reform designed to centralise all powers to raise troops in the hands of the king – a move intended to bring order to his kingdom, but which offered further provocation to resentful princes and mercenaries alike. This time, Bourbon and Alençon were joined in their disaffection by sixteen-year-old Louis, the king's eldest son and heir. The origin of the breach between son and father – the reason why the dauphin was so easily suborned by the rebel lords – was not made public, but it evidently ran deep, and, by lending the proximate authority of the king's heir to the dukes' self-assertion, it magnified the threat of the revolt many times over.

For five months, King Charles found himself at war within the frontiers of his own kingdom. But once again, with the able support of Constable Richemont and his deputies, Raoul de Gaucourt and Poton de Xaintrailles, incisive military action forced the rebels to submit. Bourbon, Alençon and the king's prodigal son were pardoned, in return for the 'humility and obedience' with which they had approached their sovereign, and peace was restored. All the same, the next decade was marked by continuing tensions among the lords and the increasing alienation of the dauphin from his royal father – conflict that was not ameliorated by the death of the *grande dame* of French politics, Yolande of Aragon, in 1442, or by the rapid rise to power from 1444 of the king's influential new mistress, Agnès Sorel.

Still, no rivalrous intrigue at the court of France could compare with the bewildering nightmare that was unfolding on the other side of the Channel. The lords of England had sought to shoulder the weighty legacy of Henry V – the government of their own realm and the war to secure English France – until his son, Henry VI, should be old enough to lead them himself. By 1440, the younger King Henry was eighteen years old, well past the age at which previous kings had sloughed off the tutelage of minority councils – or indeed the age at which the Armagnac whore had defeated his captains at Orléans. But he showed no sign of leading anyone anywhere. He was mild and vague, and generous too, in the sense that he said yes to any request that reached him, but in his gentle artlessness it began to seem – alarmingly – that he might resemble his maternal grandfather, the fragile King Charles the Well-Beloved, rather more than his warrior father. As a result, his lords found that they had no choice but to continue to manage his kingdoms, and his war, on Henry's behalf.

By the early 1440s, the unhappy reality with which they were confronted was that, in the face of the French resurgence and the absence of a king who could rally his faltering troops, it was peace rather than war that presented the best chance of keeping Normandy, at least, in English hands. In 1444 the earl of Suffolk, who had emerged as the leading figure in this hobbled and improvised regime, was sent to France to negotiate a truce and bring home a royal bride. But the English position was now so weak that Suffolk could secure a suspension of war for only twenty-two months, and a bride who was not one of the king's daughters – Charles could not, after all, allow any child of his to marry a rival who still denied his right to his own throne – but a more marginal figure, the queen's fourteen-year-old niece Margaret, daughter of Yolande's son René of Anjou. It was a start, but what remained of English France need-ed more time for retrenchment, and more would have to be offered to get it. And so, in 1445, a secret deal was done by which the county of Maine, which lay precariously between English Normandy and French Anjou, would be handed over to King Charles in return for a truce of twenty years.

If the opportunity had been taken to renew Normandy's battered defences – if the listing English regime had had the galvanising leadership of its king, or the money it needed to seize the moment – then perhaps the plan could have worked. Instead, chaos reigned. Crisis in England consumed the energies of the lords who might have taken command in Normandy, while the captains who had fought for so long to keep Maine for King Henry simply refused to hand over their hard-won territory to King Charles. The English, it became painfully apparent, could neither deliver what they promised nor defend what they held. In February 1448, after repeated demands for its surrender, Charles sent troops into Maine to take by force what was his. Now, it was only a matter of time. An army under the command of the Bastard of Orléans made its move into Normandy in July 1449. A year later, all that remained of Henry V's glorious conquests was the fortress of Cherbourg, perched on a rocky outcrop in a stormy sea. And by 12 August 1450, the French tide had swept the demoralised English utterly away.

Nine years earlier, King Henry's council in Rouen had written to their king to plead for his help. 'Our sovereign lord', they said, '. . . we write to you once more in extreme necessity, signifying that our malady is akin to death or exile, and, as regards your sovereign power, very close upon total ruin . . . we do not know how for the future it is best for you to keep your people nor to manage your affairs in this your lordship, which we perceive to be abandoned like the ship tossed about on the sea by many winds, without captain, without steersman, without rudder, without anchor, without sail, floating, staggering and wandering in the midst of the tempestuous waves, filled with the storms of sharp fortune and all adversity, far from the haven of safety and human help.' Of the most loyal of those counsellors, many had now been overtaken by time: Bishop Cauchon was more than seventy when he died suddenly in 1442, and Louis de Luxembourg had followed him to the grave in 1443. But their despairing verdict stood. England found itself without a captain, and English France was lost.

On 10 November 1449, the captain of the most Christian kingdom of France – who had learned, from unpromising beginnings, how to believe in his God-given sovereignty, how to take the fight to his enemies and how to unite his people around him – had ridden into Rouen. The city had surrendered to his forces only weeks earlier, and now King Charles was taking possession of what had been, for more than thirty years, the citadel of the English invaders. First came his guard of archers, dressed in their liveries of red, white and green, then trumpeters in red with gold on their sleeves, the sound of their silver trumpets filling the pale sky. Just before Charles himself came Poton de Xaintrailles on a great charger carrying the mighty sword of state, Charlemagne's Joyeuse; then at last the king, in plate armour, his horse draped in trailing blue velvet spangled with golden fleurs-de-lis. The standard of St Michael flew over the procession as it passed through the city gate, where the king was joined by Raoul de Gaucourt, who had spent so many of his seventy-four years fighting to defend the realm, and by the Bastard of Orléans, now raised to the ranks of the peerage in his own right as count of Dunois, in recognition of his brave and loyal service to the crown.

Charles of France stopped at the great cathedral of Notre-Dame to give thanks for the victory God had granted him. He was not far from the river, into which the ashes of a nineteen-year-old girl had been thrown almost twenty years before. He prayed; and the quiet waters of the Seine flowed on.

12

She was all innocence

Joan had not been forgotten. In the dazzling city of Constantinople, almost two years after her death, a servant of the Byzantine emperor asked a Burgundian visitor whether it was true that the Maid had been captured. 'It seemed to the Greeks an impossible thing,' the Burgundian reported, and when he told them what had become of her, they were 'filled with wonder'.

Closer to home, her memory had been kept alive by the people of Orléans, whose gratitude for their liberation had not dimmed. Every year celebrations were held in the town to commemorate the miraculous events of 8 May 1429, when the Maid had forced the English into ignominious retreat. In 1435, thanks to Gilles de Rais, the Breton nobleman who had been one of Joan's brothers-in-arms that glorious day, the anniversary was marked with a performance of breathtaking scale and ambition: a play entitled *The Mystery of the Siege of Orléans*. Since 'mystery' was a word that usually signified the depiction of stories from the Bible or the lives of saints, the burden of the drama was clear even before the cast of hundreds made their appearance on stage, speaking twenty thousand lines of verse in which, amid ingeniously constructed scenery, the Maid relived her divinely inspired triumph. In her honour, no expense was spared – and some at least of the extravagant outlay was deliberately incurred, since de Rais had specifically ordered that the actors should be costumed only in the finest fabrics, and that the crowds should eat and drink their fill while they watched. It was an epic spectacle, but its grandeur was fleeting. De Rais's frenzied spending proved part of a vertiginous plunge into financial ruin. Then, five years later, he was tried and hanged for the sexual assault and murder of more than a hundred children. His play was not seen on stage again.

By the time de Rais died, his name indelibly stained with the horror of his crimes, hopes had been raised that Joan herself might return to the world. In May 1436 – a little more than a month after Paris had fallen to King Charles's forces, just as the Maid had always said it would – a dark-haired woman had appeared at Metz, a town fifty miles from Domrémy, outside the north-eastern borders of the kingdom. She looked so like Joan – either that, or the desire to believe that Joan had somehow escaped the fire was so great – that many people claimed they recognised her, including two of the Maid's own brothers. She wore men's clothes and rode a horse with ease and skill, and her brief moment of celebrity brought her a wealthy husband, a knight of Metz named Robert des Armoises. This counterfeit Maid had given birth to two sons, it was said, by the time she moved west to Orléans in the summer of 1439. There, she was wined and dined and given purses of gold 'for the good that she did the town during the siege'. But when she appeared in Paris in 1440, she was publicly denounced as a fraud by the *parlement* and university, and after that, with little prospect of further profit from her imposture, the woman slipped away from public view.

In Paris, as the years went by, the spectre of Joan herself – a wandering revenant haunting the kingdom's memories of the war – was a provocative presence. She had led King Charles to his coronation and proclaimed his God-given right to the throne, but she had also appeared at the head of an army outside the walls of the capital, and died as a heretic condemned by the expert theological judgement of its university's scholars. In such circumstances, the king's silence on the subject of the Maid entirely suited the leading inhabitants of his first city. If the unhappy names of Armagnac and Burgundian were now to be consigned to the pages of history, then surely they should be joined by that of the girl who had claimed the mandate of heaven in defining 'Armagnac' as 'French' and 'Burgundian' as 'traitor'.

But one problem remained. If the verdict of heresy still stood against the Maid, whose victory at Orléans had been the sign of heaven's blessing on her king, then did a shadow still fall on the most Christian monarch? There was nothing to be done while Rouen and the archive of the court that had tried her there remained part of English France, and in any case the argument for letting past divisions rest was a powerful one. But in February 1450, four months after the English had finally been driven from Rouen, and three since the king had entered the city in majesty, Charles spoke, at last, of Joan. 'A long time ago, Joan the Maid was taken and captured by our ancient enemies and adversaries, the English, and brought to the city of Rouen. They had her tried by certain persons who had been chosen and given this task by them, and during this trial they made and committed several errors and abuses, such that, by means of this trial and the great hatred that our enemy had against her, they had her put to death very cruelly, iniquitously and against reason.' Of course, only a trial perverted by hatred could have condemned the Maid, and now the purpose of this royal letter, addressed to a theologian named Guillaume Bouillé, was to discover exactly what form that perversion had taken. 'Because we wish to know the truth of this trial,' the king went on, 'and the manner in which it was carried out, we command, instruct and expressly charge you to inquire and diligently ask about this and what was said. And bring to us and the men of our great council the information that you find concerning this, or faithfully send it in a sealed letter.'

Bouillé was, like so many of the Maid's judges, a professor of the university of Paris, but his career had been in its infancy when she was tried nineteen years earlier, and his standing as a loyal servant of King Charles was unquestioned. He was ideally placed to review the technicalities of the process over which Bishop Cauchon had presided, and he lost no time in beginning his investigation. In early

March, he questioned seven witnesses who had participated in the trial, including the notary Guillaume Manchon, the executor, Jean Massieu, and Martin Lavenu, the friar who had been at Joan's side in her last hours. They had sat among the packed ranks of French clerics who had condemned the Maid, at a moment when the due process of God's law had seemed wholly compatible with the rejection of her claims. Since then, of course, it had become clear that Charles was in fact the true heir to France, exactly as Joan had said, and now these men of God were moved to agree with their king that the defining influence on the trial had been the prejudice of his enemies, the English, in whose castle the hearings had taken place.

Two of them – the friars Isambard de la Pierre, who had been much involved in the judges' deliberations, and Guillaume Duval, who had been there only a little – insisted that the earl of Warwick, governor to the young King Henry and commander of the English garrison at Rouen, had threatened to throw de la Pierre into the Seine if he sought to offer the prisoner any help. Cauchon had been in the pocket of the English throughout the trial, all the witnesses agreed. It was English pressure that had prevented any appeal to the pope, or any possibility that Joan might be kept in ecclesiastical custody rather than guarded by soldiers in a castle cell. The bishop had even sent a spy to extract information from her covertly, Guillaume Manchon explained: a canon of Rouen Cathedral named Nicolas Loiseleur had visited her to offer himself as a confessor and counsellor, gaining her confidence and drawing her out while Manchon and others took notes as they listened through a secret hole from a neighbouring room. And Martin Lavenu remembered that on the day of Joan's relapse into heresy, when Cauchon had emerged from her cell, Warwick and his attendants had greeted him outside the door with applause and celebrations. 'Farewell! It is done,' the bishop had declared.

For several of the witnesses, the visible manifestation of that relapse – Joan's decision to dress once again in men's clothes – was a source of particular anxiety. After all, once she had submitted to the judgement of the court and put on the modest dress of a woman, why and how had she come to change her mind? De la Pierre and Jean Toutmouillé (a friar who, as a young man, had accompanied Brother Martin to attend Joan on her last day) described the intense distress in which they found her; she told them, they said, that, once she wore skirts rather than hose tied with laces to her doublet, she had been violently assaulted by her guards. Martin Lavenu believed that it was an English lord who had tried to rape her. The executor, Jean Massieu, meanwhile, was not convinced that her resumption of men's clothes had been her own choice, even one forced upon her by such brutality. She slept each night, he explained, with her feet bound in irons chained to a great piece of wood, while three English soldiers kept watch in her cell and two more outside. He remembered Joan saying that, when she woke on the third morning after her submission, her guards had taken away the women's clothes she now wore, and instead emptied out the bag in which her old tunic and hose had been left in a corner of the room. For hours she remonstrated with them, insisting that these were clothes she was forbidden to wear, but they would not relent, until by midday she was so desperate to relieve herself outside that she was left with no option but to put on the prohibited garments.

It had always been clear how physically vulnerable she was, a lone female prisoner in a castle full of men. The broader truth of that vulnerability, and the anguish that was its consequence, rang through these diverging stories, just as it had through Joan's own scattered incoherence in the trial record for that fateful day. Equally apparent, through equally shifting narratives, was the overwhelming experience of watching the Maid die. De la Pierre, Manchon and Massieu all agreed that, in the midst of the flames, she had called constantly upon Christ and His saints with such pious devotion that almost everyone there, French or English – even, said de la Pierre, Cardinal Beaufort himself – was moved to tears. Someone (was it de la Pierre or Massieu? Both claimed the honour) had hurried at her request to a nearby church to fetch a crucifix, and held it before her eyes until they were rendered sightless by the fire. Martin Lavenu told of the misery of the executioner, who had been unable to hasten the end of Joan's agony because the platform on which she burned was so high. De la Pierre – whose entire testimony was inflected with drama – described the man's unbearable remorse at having participated in the death of such a holy woman. Though he had heaped up the pyre time and again, the Maid's heart had remained whole and unconsumed, by which he had been dumbfounded (de la Pierre reported), as though it were clearly a miracle.

Only one witness – the veteran theologian Jean Beaupère, who had taken a leading role in interrogating Joan during the early days of the trial – was less than reverent in speaking of her memory. She had had the wiles of a woman, he said, and he believed that her visions derived from human invention rather than a supernatural cause. No one else had yet mentioned the thorny issue of her voices, but Bouillé had the matter in hand, drafting a lengthy treatise in which he painstakingly assembled details from the trial transcript with which he might rebut her judges' conclusions, while reanimating what had once, long ago, been the Armagnac defence of her claims.

There was plenty here to encourage those who, like Bouillé, wished to clear Joan of the calumnies that Bishop Cauchon had heaped upon her – or, as the king's letter had originally instructed, simply to demonstrate that the trial had been filled with error and driven by hatred. For the moment, however, all was in vain. After only two days of testimony, the inquiry was called to a sudden halt, whether because of the pressing demands of the fight to drive the English from the rest of Normandy, or because the rattling of skeletons had proved disturbing to powerful men. The archbishop of Rouen – the man who had succeeded the English royal chancellor Louis de Luxembourg after his death in 1443 – was a canon lawyer named Raoul Roussel. He had led the august deputations who welcomed King Charles to the city in November 1449. He had also been one of Joan's most assiduous judges. After more than thirty years of English rule, wounds were raw in Normandy in 1450, and nerves on a knife edge. Silence, it was clear, still had its virtues.

That was not, however, the opinion of a new player in the complex world of the French Church. Guillaume d'Estouteville was a Norman nobleman of irreproachably Armagnac credentials, a second cousin of the king and now a cardinal, sent by the pope in the spring of 1452 as a legate to the kingdom of France. His principal tasks were to make peace between the English and French – whose soldiers were still fighting, now that Normandy had fallen, in what remained of the English duchy of Gascony in the south-west of the kingdom – in the hope that the military efforts of both realms might be directed instead against the threat of the Ottoman Turks, and to press for the restitution of full papal powers within France after they had been limited by royal edict fourteen years earlier. But it soon transpired that d'Estouteville had another aim in mind. Whether because it was a subject dear to his own heart, or because he thought he detected a chance to accrue valuable political capital, the cardinal reopened the question of Joan's trial, a matter which, he told the king, 'greatly concerns your honour and estate'.

It was far from clear that King Charles was happy to receive instruction, however well intentioned, concerning his honour and estate, still less to see the pope's representative reviving a process it had seemed politic to drop only two years before. But, technically, it could not be denied that a verdict delivered by the Church was the Church's to rescind, should it so wish. In May 1452, d'Estouteville enlisted the newly appointed inquisitor of France, a friar named Jean Bréhal, to preside over a fresh inquiry at Rouen. Twenty-one years earlier, the Maid had stood trial in the city; now, the accused was the trial itself.

Together, d'Estouteville and Bréhal studied the transcript of Bishop Cauchon's hearings and drafted a list of articles by which the proceedings might be condemned. Was it not true that the English had sought Joan's death by every means they could, because of their mortal hatred of her? Had not the judges, assessors and notaries been intimidated by English threats, so that the trial and its record were neither free nor fair? Could it be denied that Joan, a simple and ignorant girl, had been left without advice or help, and confounded with interrogations of such length and difficulty that she could not defend herself? Had she not often said that she submitted to the judgement of the Church and her Holy Father the pope – and, if she had ever said that she would not submit to the Church, had she not meant only the churchmen before her, who had embraced the English cause? Had not Joan died in such a holy and devout manner that all those who saw it wept? And were all these things not commonly noised and known to be true?

During the following weeks, these questions were put to some of the clerics who had participated in the trial, including, once again, Guillaume Manchon, Martin Lavenu, Jean Massieu and Isambard de la Pierre, whose testimony had acquired yet more startling colour in the intervening years. (An English soldier who hated Joan with a passion, de la Pierre said, had been utterly overcome by witnessing her death. After a restorative drink at a nearby tavern, the man declared that he had seen a white dove fluttering from the flames as the Maid's last breath left her body.) Of the thirteen others to whom d'Estouteville and Bréhal now spoke, some enthusiastically agreed with the articles, and some strongly resisted. Many, of both persuasions, were keen to defend the accuracy of the trial record, and to note that Joan had answered questions well, even if she were a simple girl among learned doctors. Some were adamant that Bishop Cauchon had been a lackey of the English; others recalled that, when he was reproved by an English cleric for having accepted Joan's abjuration at the cemetery of Saint-Ouen, he had become angry, and said it was his duty to seek the prisoner's salvation, not her death. And it seemed that some – such as the civil lawyer Nicolas Caval, who had attended many sessions of the trial – could remember very little. 'The English had no great love for the Maid,' was his laconic observation, and he knew, he said, that she had been burned. But whether that was just or unjust he could not say, since it was a matter for the court.

There were others, of course, who did not appear before the cardinal and inquisitor at all, the influential and compromised figure of Archbishop Roussel chief among them. Still, when the examination of witnesses drew to a close, Jean Bréhal found that he had ample material to submit to scholars of theology and canon law for their expert assessment. Over the following months, many hours of intellectual endeavour were expended on the task of elaborating all the ways in which other scholars – those who had advised Bishop Cauchon's trial two decades earlier – were wrong. Meanwhile, Cardinal d'Estouteville returned to Rome. He had failed to make peace between England and France: instead, in July 1453, the aged English commander Talbot and thousands of his troops were slaughtered by King Charles's forces at Castillon, twenty-five miles east of Bordeaux. By the end of the year Gascony, as well as Normandy, was French, and – with the lone exception of the garrison grimly holding on within the fortified pale of Calais in the far north – the English had been driven out of the whole of France, just as the Maid had once told Talbot and his fellow commanders they would be.

This was final vindication for the king, and for the girl who had fleetingly been his champion. And it was good news, it seemed, for those who sought to revoke Bishop Cauchon's sentence against her. So too was the fact that, when Raoul Roussel died on the last day of 1452, Cardinal d'Estouteville was appointed to succeed him as archbishop of Rouen. Still, the wheels turned slowly. Charles himself – now *le roi très-victorieux*, the most victorious as well as the most Christian king – showed no greater inclination to revisit this troublesome moment in his past than he had since the abandonment of Bouillé's inquiry in 1450, while Pope Nicholas V had more pressing matters on his mind, given that the Turks had sacked and conquered the mighty city of Constantinople, the bulwark of Christendom in the east, in the spring of 1453. In 1454 Inquisitor Bréhal made the long journey to Rome to pursue his case, but it was not until June 1455 that he succeeded in securing from Nicholas's successor, Calixtus III, a letter of authorisation for a new trial, in which – following the suggestion of one of the canon lawyers Bréhal had consulted – Joan's surviving family, her mother and two brothers, were to act as plaintiffs. Three papal commissioners would oversee the process in the name of the Holy Father, all of them loyal servants of France: the bishop of Coutances, the bishop of Paris and the archbishop of Reims, Jean Juvénal des Ursins, a talented writer and historian who had been Pierre Cauchon's Armagnac successor as bishop of Beauvais.

And so, on 7 November 1455, an extraordinary ceremony unfolded in the hallowed grandeur of Notre-Dame in the heart of Paris. Had Joan lived, she would by now have reached her forties. As it was, her bereaved mother Isabelle had quietly tended her grief for almost twenty-five years; and now she appeared in the cathedral before the archbishop of Reims, the bishop of Paris and Inquisitor Bréhal. Beside her stood one of her sons, Pierre, and supporters from Orléans, a town which had demonstrated its unwavering devotion to the Maid by providing her mother, who had found herself impoverished in her widowhood, with a comfortable home. While she knelt before the commissioners to proffer the papal mandate, her petition was explained on the old lady's behalf: her devout and virtuous daughter, whom she had brought up in the true faith, had been falsely accused of heresy, a charge which was prompted not by any fault in her, but by hatred and enmity. Despite her innocence, Joan had been iniquitously condemned and cruelly burned, because her trial was riven with injustice and error. Her family had been unable to right this wrong while the kingdom was ravaged by war, but now that, by God's grace, Rouen and Normandy had been restored to France – and the task thereby accomplished that had been started, in Joan's time, at Orléans and Reims – they turned for help, as Joan herself had done, to the Holy See. Beyond these elliptical phrases, there was no mention of the Maid's mission, her voices or her victories. Instead, the commissioners' assignment was delineated with lawyerly precision: to demonstrate that the process by which the girl had been declared a heretic was flawed, and to expunge that verdict from the public record.

An inquisitive crowd began to gather in the cathedral as others among Isabelle's supporters stepped forward to speak, anxious to detail all the many ways in which Joan had been oppressed by the partiality and prejudice of her judges and guards. Her simplicity, her devotion and her actions for the good of the realm, all these, they said, were merits, not crimes, piety, not wickedness – that is, if they were interpreted correctly. The press of people became so great that the commissioners were forced to draw Isabelle and her companions aside into the quiet of the sacristy. There they explained, with care and concern, that they would receive her petition and undertake the inquiry, but that the process would be long and complex, and its outcome uncertain. The solemn judgement of the Church, they warned, could not be lightly overturned. The Maid's mother and her friends should therefore seek learned counsel for themselves, and return to the commissioners' presence in the episcopal court of Paris ten days later. There was much work ahead, but, at last, the case had begun.

Step by step, Inquisitor Bréhal found himself mirroring the meticulous stages through which Bishop Cauchon had moved a quarter of a century before. A distinguished gathering of theologians and civil and canon lawyers considered the grounds on which the verdict of Joan's trial had been called into question. The infamy of those proceedings and the public perception of her innocence, they agreed, could hardly have been greater; it was therefore the commissioners' duty to proceed with the inquiry. A promoter and notaries were appointed. Guillaume Manchon produced his original French notes of the trial, to be compared with the official Latin transcript, and the records of Cardinal d'Estouteville's investigation of 1452 were scrutinised by the court. The learned counsel appointed for Joan's mother and brothers made exhaustive representations detailing the Maid's manifest virtues and the patent injustices of the process against her, which were drafted into a total of 101 articles for the commissioners – or judges, as they now were – to consider. And at the beginning of 1456, the judges dispatched officers to collect the testimony upon which they would form their conclusions. Twenty-five years earlier, there had been a single witness, interrogated on many subjects. Now, the witnesses were many, and the subjects few: in the region of Joan's birth, the court's questions concerned her childhood, her character and the beginning of her mission; in Orléans and Paris, her deeds in the war; and in Paris and Rouen, her trial and death.

In Domrémy, the villagers who had known Joan told the officers what they could, but there was no sign, in this little place far away from the scenes of her extraordinary exploits, that memories had been heightened by the passage of time. At home she had been 'Jeannette' rather than 'Jeanne', it seemed. The older villagers, her godparents among them, recalled a respectable family and a dutiful child, well-behaved, pious and modest, who worked hard – she span with her mother, they said, and guided the plough and tended animals for her father – and liked to go to church. She was as well instructed in the faith, noted one of her godfathers, as the other girls of Domrémy. This was reassuring, if a little non-specific. The reminiscences of the younger generation, who had grown up with the Maid, were scarcely more particular. A woman named Hauviette said she had wept when Joan left the village, because she was good and kind and had been her friend. Sometimes, the local boys had teased her about her displays of devotion to God: when Joan heard the church bells, one of them explained, she would fall to her knees in the fields and pray. And it was the bells that prompted one of the few memories in which the living, breathing Joan could suddenly be felt. Perrin Drappier had been the churchwarden in the village, and when in the evenings he forgot to sound the call to compline, she used to scold him, he said, and promise to bring him cakes if he would be more diligent.

Even if the Maid was a strangely insubstantial presence in their testimony, the villagers had done their work in demonstrating to the court the blamelessness of her early life. But Joan herself came into vivid focus as soon as the inquiry moved to Vaucouleurs, the town where she had persuaded the captain Robert de Baudricourt to send her to Chinon and the king. It was Durand Laxart, the husband of one of her cousins, who had been inveigled into taking her there; several of the younger inhabitants of Domrémy remembered him explaining that, at Joan's insistence, he had told her father that she was coming to stay at his house in the nearby village of Burey-le-Petit to help his wife in her confinement with a new baby.

Laxart himself did not mention this subterfuge. Instead, his focus was the crystalline clarity of Joan's purpose and the irresistible force of her will. She had announced, he said, that she must go to the dauphin and lead him to his coronation. And she knew a prophecy that spoke of her mission: 'Was it not once foretold that France would be devastated by a woman and then restored by a virgin?' Who this first woman might have been was not clear, unless it was the mad king's much maligned wife, Queen Isabeau, but the echoes of the biblical roles of Eve and Mary, and the part Joan believed she was destined to play in the story of the most Christian kingdom, were unmistakable. The couple with whom she had stayed at Vaucouleurs remembered similarly bold and resolute pronouncements. She was sent by the king of heaven to the dauphin, she told Henri le Royer, and, if she had to, she would go there on her knees. She did not fear the journey, because God would open the way before her; she had been born to do this, she said. And she had been full of impatience, Henri's wife Catherine remembered, time weighing on her as it did on a pregnant woman waiting to give birth.

It was this certainty that had overwhelmed the men who accompanied her when she left, at last, for Chinon. Jean de Metz and Bertrand de Poulengy were the soldiers who, with their servants Julien and Jean, the royal messenger Colet de Vienne and another man named Richard l'Archier, had guided Joan for eleven days through enemy country on her way to the court. Jean de Metz was now a nobleman, rewarded by the king for his loyal service, and Bertrand de Poulengy an esquire of the royal household, but still, twenty-five years later, they were struck with awe at the memory of the Maid. It was because they believed she was sent by God to save France, they said, that they had offered themselves as her escort. Despite the hazards of their route, she had assured them calmly that there was nothing to fear. She was young and so were they, but when they snatched what sleep they could, lying side by side with Joan fully clothed in the doublet and hose she had swapped for her rough red dress, neither of them, they said, had felt any stirrings of desire for one so holy.

That claim was echoed, when testimony was received from the witnesses at Orléans and Paris, by the men who had fought beside her when she went to war. When he was with her, said the Bastard of Orléans, he had no carnal impulses of any kind, towards her or any other woman. Privacy was hard to come by in the field, and when she dressed and armed herself on campaign the duke of Alençon had seen her breasts — which were beautiful, he said — while her squire Jean d'Aulon had caught glimpses of her breasts and her bare legs, but neither of them had been aroused. If there was the faintest air of protesting just a little too much, none of these noble knights was prepared to admit it. But Marguerite La Touroulde, widow of the king's counsellor René de Bouligny, in whose house Joan had stayed at Bourges – a witness who was equally convinced of the Maid's holiness, if less perturbed by her physical presence – remembered Jean de Metz and Bertrand de Poulengy saying that they had lusted after her in the beginning, but were so abashed by her purity that they never dared speak a word of it to Joan herself. This sense of her bodily integrity was so strong that it went beyond her evident chastity. D'Aulon believed that she did not menstruate: he had been told, he said, that she never experienced 'the secret malady of women'. And, according to the euphemistic observation of a royal servant named Simon Charles, her soldiers marvelled at the length of time she could stay on her horse without answering the call of nature.

Of course, the Maid's physical virtue was the outward expression of her moral and spiritual merit. Every witness agreed that she was good and devout, simple and humble. She was all innocence, said the courtly sophisticate Marguerite La Touroulde, and knew nothing about anything except for waging war. On the field of battle, she conducted herself with remarkable confidence, as if she had been a captain for twenty or thirty years, the duke of Alençon declared. But there too she required godly behaviour. She could not abide oaths and blasphemy: La Hire and Alençon in particular, who were in the habit of swearing a great deal, had to curb their tongues in her presence. Nor would she tolerate the presence of whores among her men; if she came across a woman in the camp, she would chase her away angrily with the flat of her sword, unless a soldier came forward to marry her. She ate sparingly, and refused food that had been stolen rather than bought; she forbade pillage and plunder, and gave churches her special protection. She required her troops to confess their sins, and wept for the men who died without absolution, whether they were French or the enemy English. There could be no doubt that, as Simon Charles was moved to conclude, 'she did God's work'.

But what of her mission: how could the witnesses be sure that she had been sent by God to save the king and the kingdom? The answer, all agreed, was her victories, which she had known would be won, and which could only be explained by divine intervention. There was no need, now, to speak of Paris, La Charité or Compiègne. It was Patay, Jargeau, Meung and, above all, Orléans that demonstrated the truth of the Maid's claims. The Bastard remembered that, when Joan first arrived with supplies for the besieged town, the wind was blowing in the wrong direction for the boats to carry the provisions across the river. She told him that she brought help from the king of heaven, at the request of the royal saints Louis and Charlemagne, and in an instant the wind changed and the sails filled. The recollection of Joan's chaplain, Jean Pasquerel, was a little different: the river, he said, had been too low for the boats to float, but suddenly, at the Maid's approach, the waters rose and the flotilla began to move. For the duke of Alençon, meanwhile, who had not been at Orléans, the miraculous memories were more personal. The duke's father had died at Azincourt, and he had been captured in bloody battle at Verneuil when he was just seventeen; it seemed that, by the time he fought at Joan's side at Jargeau, fear had become his enemy as much as the English. But she was there to urge him on. 'Noble duke, are you afraid? Don't you know that I promised your wife to bring you back safe and sound?' And she had pointed out a cannon on the town walls, and told him to move before it killed him; a few moments later, he said, he watched another man die on the spot where he had stood.

Alençon was now fifty, in constant pain from chronic disease in his kidneys, and bitterly resentful that he had never been restored to the wealth and power that should have been his birthright. But it was clear that, half a lifetime ago, he had been taken by surprise by the Maid, their brief partnership a gift from God in a golden moment when anything had seemed possible. And in that moment, others had seen her as the fulfilment of a heavenly promise made long before. Jean Barbin, a lawyer then living in Poitiers, remembered Jean Érault, one of the Armagnac theologians who had examined Joan there, speaking of a prophecy that referred to the Maid. Marie Robine, the peasant woman who had received divinely inspired visions at Avignon in the last years of the fourteenth century, had had many revelations concerning the calamities that would afflict the kingdom of France, Érault said. She had been terrified by a vision of great quantities of armour, fearing that she would be required to put it on and fight, but she had been told that it was not for her. Instead, a Maid would come after her, who would bear these arms and deliver France from its enemies. That Maid, Érault had been certain, was Joan.

If the coming of the Maid had been foretold in visions, then what of her own? The Bastard remembered how often she prayed; every day, he said, she would go to church at dusk and ask for the bells to be rung for half an hour. And he had been with the king at Loches when the royal confessor enquired if she wished to explain how her heavenly counsel spoke to her. She had blushed, and said that, when she was unhappy because people did not believe her messages from God, she took herself away to pray; then she heard a voice saying, 'Daughter of God, go, go, go, I will help you, go!' And then she was filled with a wonderful joy, and longed to remain in that state forever. Her squire Jean d'Aulon recalled that, when he had asked about her revelations, she told him she had three counsellors – one who was with her always, another who came and went, and a third whom the other two consulted. But when he begged to be allowed to see them, she said he was not worthy or virtuous enough. He did not ask again.

Questions she had been required to answer, however, were those of the theologians at Poitiers, one of whom, a friar named Seguin Seguin, now offered his testimony to the court. The Maid told them, he said, that she had been watching the animals in the fields when a voice came to her, saying that God had great pity for the people of

France and that she must go to the king. Then, she added, she had begun to cry, and the voice had told her that she must not doubt her mission. But if God wanted to save the people of France, one of the learned doctors objected, surely He had no need of soldiers. 'In the name of God', Joan replied, 'the soldiers will fight and God will give victory.' It was a good answer, they thought. Then the friar himself asked in what language the voice spoke. A better language than yours, she fired back. (Seguin's own tongue, he explained, was the dialect of the Limousin.) Did she believe in God? Yes, she said, and better than you. Why should they believe her, Seguin asked, without a sign to support her claims? 'In the name of God,' came the impatient response, 'I have not come to Poitiers to give signs; but take me to Orléans, and I will show you signs of the purpose for which I am sent.'

Impatience and quickfire confidence were qualities that had helped to press her case with the theologians at Poitiers, for whom the idea that God might wish to help the Armagnacs required no further justification. But they had been no use when she faced theologians at Rouen for whom that most fundamental proposition was self-evidently false. Twenty-five years on, however, their roles were reversed: in the most uncomfortable and challenging sessions of the inquiry, those scholars – or the survivors among their number – had to decide how far they would go in attempting to defend what was now, in the France of Charles *le très-victorieux*, indefensible.

Some elements of the Maid's story were established beyond debate. The piteousness and piety of her death were described in heart-rending detail by those who were there, weeping, they said, in the old market square as she burned – and also, as a matter of common fame, by those who were not. She had been a simple girl, that much was clear, and the judges had tried to confuse, harass and exhaust her, but still she had answered their questions with wisdom beyond her years. And it was the English, out of hatred and fear and with the enthusiastic support of Bishop Cauchon, who had controlled the trial, paid for it, and pressed it to its tragic conclusion.

But other parts of the tale proved harder to tell. Some witnesses found themselves simply unable to remember what they themselves had done during the proceedings. Remarkably, the statement of the laconic Nicolas Caval was even shorter than before, and the bishop of Noyon, an influential diplomat named Jean de Mailly, could recall almost nothing, apart from Joan declaring that, if she had done anything wrong, it was her own fault and not the king's. Thomas de Courcelles – an eloquent scholar who had been present throughout the trial before translating the notaries' French minutes into the official Latin transcript – wove his testimony from weasel words as he attempted to explain his involvement. He had not argued that Joan was a heretic, he said, except in the case that she might obstinately refuse to accept her duty to submit to the Church. When it came to the judges' final deliberations, he believed he had said that Joan was as she had been before – that is, if she had been a heretic before, she was so still, but he himself had never positively declared that she *was* a heretic.

No wonder, given the weight of scrutiny the trial record was now being required to bear, that the notary Guillaume Manchon seemed ill at ease in his own contorted statement. He had served in the trial only under compulsion, he said, because he did not dare resist an order from the royal council, and he complained bitterly of the pressure under which he had been placed by Bishop Cauchon and the English. Yet at the same time he insisted on his own integrity and that of the transcript he had produced. He was particularly exercised by the role of the spy in Joan's cell, Nicolas Loiseleur, who had gained her trust, he said, by pretending to be her fellow countryman from the duchy of Lorraine, and to share her Armagnac loyalties. This was a yarn that, over the years, had evidently stretched in the spinning: another witness testified – though he could not remember who had told him – that Loiseleur had disguised himself as St Catherine in order to bend Joan to his will.

But even in Manchon's own account of this treacherous deception, Loiseleur had tried to save Joan's life by urging her to submit to her judges at Saint-Ouen. Here was the heart of the difficulty for witnesses who now claimed, queasily, that they had only been following orders. What had been right in 1431 in English Rouen – to secure the girl's salvation by persuading her to abjure her heresy and embrace the loving counsel of the Church – was wrong twenty-five years later, in a kingdom from which God had driven the English with their tails between their legs. It all came down to the gift of vision: not revelations like Joan's – since, as Inquisitor Bréhal and his colleagues now sagely noted, 'it is very difficult to reach a settled judgement in such matters' – but the ability to see which facts conformed with God's plan for the world.

That, of course, was where Bishop Cauchon and his fellow judges had allowed their prejudice to lead them so deeply into error. And so, sitting in state on 7 July 1456 in the great hall of the episcopal palace in Rouen, the judges appointed to review Cauchon's work declared that the twelve articles through which the Maid had been condemned had been drawn up 'corruptly, deceitfully, slanderously, fraudulently and maliciously'. The truth, they said, had been passed over in silence, and fabrication put in its place. Information that aggravated the charges against her had been introduced without reason, and circumstances ignored that would have served to justify what she had said and done. As a result, the trial record and the sentence against her were utterly null, invalid and void. Joan had been innocent, and she was justified; and the judges decreed that a cross should be built in the old market square where she had died so cruelly, to preserve her memory forever.

It was done. Charles *le bien-servi*, the well-served as well as the most victorious, received the news in the heartlands of his kingdom, south of the Loire, where he was passing the summer months.

The Maid had not been a heretic, an apostate or an idolater. Now, she could rest in peace, and her unsullied name would be remembered whenever the glorious story of his victories was told. The most Christian king, meanwhile, faced challenges ahead. He had suffered some recent ill-health, and his son, the ungrateful dauphin, continued to flout his authority. Regrettably, it had also become necessary in the previous weeks to dispatch his loyal servant, the Bastard of Orléans, to arrest the malcontent duke of Alençon on a charge of treasonable conspiracy with the English enemy. Still, he could survey with pleasure the God-given realm which he ruled like his royal father before him. And he could gaze with satisfaction across the narrow sea to England, where his nephew, the fragile king Henry VI, looked on distractedly while the princes of the blood, heirs to the great houses of York and Lancaster, tore the kingdom to pieces between them.

Epilogue: 'Saint Joan'

On 16 May 1920, as a hushed crowd of thousands waited outside St Peter's Basilica, Joan of Arc was recognised as a saint of the Roman Catholic Church. The declaration had been half a century in the making: it had been in 1869 that Félix Dupanloup, then bishop of Orléans, first petitioned the Holy See to examine her case. The town of Orléans had never forgotten her, but it was history, rather than memory, that animated Bishop Dupanloup's campaign. He had read the transcripts of her trials after the manuscripts were published by the pioneering scholar Jules Quicherat in the 1840s, and his conclusion was clear. 'She is a saint', he declared. 'God was in her.'

In fact, in several respects Joan made an unlikely candidate for canonisation. Not many saints had been put to death by the judgement of the same Church that was asked to recognise their sanctity. That, of course – said the promoter of the faith, or devil's advocate, assigned to test her case in 1892 – was a reflection of the fact that she had not been martyred for her faith, but killed for political motives, through the enmity of those whom she had defeated in battle. She had been rightly admired for her military achievements, he conceded, but, like Christopher Columbus, for whose canonisation a vocal lobby had argued unsuccessfully in the 1870s, her outstanding spiritual virtue had not been proved. During her life she had shown anger, and arrogance, and a fondness for worldly luxury, and she had not embraced her suffering with patience and heroic fortitude, but abjured her visions out of fear, and met her death with lamentation and anguish.

In 1892, and again in 1901 and 1903, the many pages of the promoter's arguments were met with hundreds more of rebuttal from the defender, who pressed Joan's case on the basis of her divine revelations and advanced counter-proposals to demonstrate that she had indeed displayed all the virtues to a heroic degree. On 6 January 1904, it was the defender's reasoning with which Pope Pius X concurred. Four years later he acknowledged three miracles that had taken place through her intercession: three nuns had been cured of grievous illness after invoking her aid in their prayers. The need for a fourth miracle, the Holy Father accepted, was obviated by her salvation of France in her own lifetime. 'Joan of Arc', he declared, 'has shone like a new star destined to be the glory not only of France but of the universal Church as well.' On 18 April 1909 she was beatified, and in 1920 – after the agonising intervention of the Great War – came her canonisation, as a virgin who had lived a life of saintly virtue. The feast day of St Joan, the Maid of Orléans, was inscribed in the Church's calendar on 30 May, the anniversary of her execution almost five hundred years before.

Over the span of half a millennium, from the trials of 1431 and 1456 to the canonisation hearings in twentieth-century Rome, the events of Joan's brief and extraordinary life have been the subject of legal processes designed to assign her to a category: heretic or saint. In each case, evidence has been sifted, seized and discarded, a winnowing dictated by theological principles which, for the expert assessors, are paramount and all-pervasive. And yet, in theology as in history, answers reached are shaped by questions posed and facts admitted. For all the commissioners' warnings to the Maid's mother about the unpredictability of the outcome, there was no possibility that the hearings of 1456 would uphold the sentence of 1431: the information they sought and the purpose for which they sought it would not allow that conclusion, just as there had been no chance that the trial of 1431 would exonerate Joan from the charges of heresy that defined every moment of that earlier investigation. Both sides were sure that God's purpose was at work in the world, but their shared certainty underwrote diametrically opposed understandings of right and wrong, truth and falsehood. And therein lies the essence of faith: did Joan's king win the war because she came from God, or did she come from God because he won the war?

For those in search of Joan herself, the surviving documents produced by these tribunals present a double challenge. Though their purpose may be clear, their rules of engagement – articles of inquiry, for example, glimpsed only through the responses they elicit – can be disconcertingly elusive. And the difficulty of interpreting the information they contain is compounded by the shockingly vivid presence of a girl who, through the unforeseeable effect of her own unyielding conviction, had achieved what should, for someone of her sex and class, have been impossible. Her forceful charisma is palpable in the transcript of the trial that condemned her to a heretic's death. When dazzlingly displayed through the differently partisan judgement which annulled that verdict, it transformed the Maid into a legend, an icon and a saint.

In gaining a saint, however, we have lost a human being. This ferocious champion of one side in a complex and bloody war has been robbed of her context and her roaring voice. By 2011, Pope Benedict XVI could say, of what he called 'her mission among the French military forces', that 'she sought to negotiate a just Christian peace between the English and French'. It is hard not to believe that Joan herself – who told the English king that 'wherever I find your men in France, I will make them leave, whether they want to or not, and if they will not obey, I will have them all killed' – might have put it in markedly different terms. One of the most eminent of the Maid's historians suggests that 'Joan is above all the saint of reconciliation – the one whom, whatever be our personal convictions, we admire and love because, overriding all partisan points of view, each one of us can find in himself a reason to love her'. But, in becoming all things to all people, the woman herself risks disappearing altogether.

She is still there to be found. If we read the remarkable records of a wholly exceptional life in the knowledge of how those documents came to be made, if we immerse ourselves in her cultured, brutal and terrifyingly uncertain world, assured of nothing but the supreme force of God's will, then perhaps we can begin to understand Joan herself: what she thought she was doing; why those around her responded as they did; how she took her chance, to miraculous effect; and what happened, in the end, when the miracles stopped.

And, still, in the well-worn pages of her trials there are unexpected moments that catch the humanity, the violence and the transcendence of her story. On 7 May 1456, a nobleman named Aimon de Macy gave evidence in Paris in the presence of the archbishop of Reims. De Macy was now in his fifties, but he had encountered the Maid when he was a young man, a friend of her captor Jean de Luxembourg. His testimony was an ugly thing: he told of visiting Joan in her cell at Rouen with de Luxembourg and the English lords Warwick and Stafford, to mock her with feigned offers of ransom, and he could confirm that she was virtuous, he said, because of the force with which she fought him off every time he grabbed at her breasts or put his hands into her clothes. Then he had been at Saint-Ouen to witness her abjuration, with the clerk holding the pen in her hand to put her mark on the paper. The last sentence of his statement appears an afterthought, almost as if he turned back to speak once he had risen to leave. 'And he believes she is in paradise.'

Notes

ABBREVIATIONS USED IN THE NOTES

Beaucourt, *Charles VII*   G. du Fresne de Beaucourt, *Histoire de Charles VII*,
  6 vols (Paris, 1881–91)

Duparc, *Nullité*   P. Duparc (trans. and ed.), *Procès en nullité de la
  condamnation de Jeanne d'Arc*, 5 vols (Paris, 1977–88)

Hobbins, *Trial*   D. Hobbins (trans. and ed.), *The Trial of Joan of Arc*
  (Cambridge and London, 2005)

Journal   *Journal d'un bourgeois de Paris, 1405–1449*, ed. A. Tuetey (Paris, 1881)

Monstrelet, *Chronique*   *La Chronique d'Enguerran de Monstrelet*, ed. L. Douët-
  d'Arcq, 6 vols (Paris, 1857–62)

ODNB   *Oxford Dictionary of National Biography*, ed. H. C. G. Matthew and
  B. Harrison (Oxford, 2004), online edn, ed. L. Goldman (2010)

Parisian Journal   *A Parisian Journal, 1405–1449*, trans. and ed. J. Shirley
  (Oxford, 1968)

Quicherat, *Procès*   J. Quicherat (ed.), *Procès de condamnation et de
  réhabilitation de Jeanne d'Arc*, 5 vols (Paris, 1841–9)

Taylor, *Joan of Arc*   C. Taylor (ed. and trans.), *Joan of Arc: La Pucelle*
  (Manchester, 2006)

Tisset, *Condamnation*   P. Tisset and Y. Lanhers (trans. and ed.), *Procès de
  condamnation de Jeanne d'Arc*, 3 vols (Paris, 1960–71)

INTRODUCTION

For Joan as a protean icon, see M. Warner, *Joan of Arc: The Image of Female
  Heroism* (London, 1981).

Anyone who studies Joan of Arc has reason to be grateful to Jules Quicherat,
  the remarkable scholar who, in the 1840s, edited the transcripts of the trials
  of 1431 and 1456 and gathered them together in five volumes with a vast
  range of other materials relating to Joan's life, including chronicles, poems,
  letters and administrative documents. Since then, the trials have been edited
  and translated many times. The minutes of the trial of 1431 were taken by

the notaries in French, but those original documents do not survive. Instead, we have two partial copies, one from the later fifteenth and one from the sixteenth century. Shortly after the trial had finished, the French minutes were translated into Latin and collated with other relevant documents into an official transcript, of which three of the five copies made and signed by the notaries still exist. I have used the edition of the trial produced by Pierre Tisset and Yvonne Lanhers between 1960 and 1971, which gives the Latin transcript and the French minute in parallel in its first volume, and a modern French translation in its second. Since then, the main substance of the hearings has been translated into English by Daniel Hobbins, and extracts translated by Craig Taylor in his edition of selected sources for Joan's life. The records of the nullification trial of 1456 are entirely in Latin, apart from a single witness statement in French, that of Joan's squire, Jean d'Aulon. I have used Pierre Duparc's edition, published in the 1970s and 1980s, which gives the complete Latin text of the trial in its first two volumes, and a modern French translation in the following two. There is no complete English translation of the nullification trial, but once again Craig Taylor offers translated extracts. I have relied on all these texts (of which full details can be found in the list of Abbreviations, p. 247), and I owe a great debt to their editors and translators; I have sought in these endnotes to cross-reference between the various volumes, so that anyone wishing to investigate further can more easily find their way to the relevant text in the appropriate language. Translation is at the heart of Joan's historical presence, given the multiple layers of text through which her life has been transmitted, and I could not have hoped to calibrate my own readings of the texts I have quoted here without the linguistic wisdom and scholarship of my parents, Grahame and Gwyneth Castor.

'*Joan of Arc*': surnames were not yet firmly established in fifteenth-century Europe. Joan's father's name – which was variously given in contemporary documents as *Darc*, *Tarc*, *Day*, *Dars* – seems to have been based on a place-name. Joan's mother Isabelle was sometimes known as Vouthon – the name of the place near Domrémy where her family lived – and sometimes as Rommée, perhaps because she had made a pilgrimage to Rome. At her trial in 1431, Joan initially said that she did not know her surname; later she mentioned her parents' names, and said that girls of her region usually took their mother's name. See R. Pernoud and M.-V. Clin, *Joan of Arc: Her Story*, trans. and revised J. DuQuesnay Adams (New York, 1998), pp. 220–1; Tisset, *Condamnation*, II, pp. 39–40nn.

PROLOGUE

Rather than give a blow-by-blow account of a military engagement over
which debate still rages, I have sought to evoke the experience of the battle
of Agincourt from the French perspective. For the details of the campaign
and battle, and the complexities of the evidence, see A. Curry, *Agincourt:
A New History* (Stroud, 2005, repr. 2010). An invaluable edition of extracts
from primary sources is A. Curry, *The Battle of Agincourt: Sources and
Interpretations* (Woodbridge, 2000). For a narrative of the battle, see J.
Barker, *Agincourt: The King, the Campaign, the Battle* (London, 2005); and
for discussion of the difficulties in understanding the experience of the
soldiers, J. Keegan, *The Face of Battle: A Study of Agincourt, Waterloo and
the Somme* (London, 1976), pp. 87–107.

For popular beliefs in France placing the (probably Roman) saints Crispin and
Crispian in Soissons – although in England it was believed they had lived
at Faversham in Kent – see D. H. Farmer (ed.), *The Oxford Dictionary of
Saints* (Oxford, 2003), pp. 124–5.

For France as the 'eldest daughter of the Church', and the king as *le roi très-
chrétien*, see C. Beaune, *Birth of an Ideology: Myths and Symbols of Nation in
Late-Medieval France* (Berkeley, 1991), pp. 172–80.

For the life and military career of Henry V, see C. T. Allmand, 'Henry V
(1386–1422)', *ODNB*, and *Henry V* (London, 1992); G. L. Harriss, *Shaping
the Nation: England, 1360–1461* (Oxford, 2005), pp. 588–94; and, with
particular emphasis on his religiosity, I. Mortimer, *1415: Henry V's Year of
Glory* (London, 2009).

For Henry's facial injury, sustained at the battle of Shrewsbury in 1403: S. J.
Lang, 'Bradmore, John (d. 1412)', in *ODNB*; Barker, *Agincourt*, pp. 29–30.

For the capture of the French king Jean II at the battle of Poitiers in 1356, and
the decision of his son, Charles V, to avoid the battlefield, see R. Vaughan,
Philip the Bold: The Formation of the Burgundian State (London, 1962, repr.
Woodbridge, 2002), pp. 2, 7.

For Charles VI's illness, see F. Autrand, *Charles VI* (Paris, 1986), pp. 290–5,
304–17; R. C. Gibbons, 'The Active Queenship of Isabeau of Bavaria,
1392–1417', PhD dissertation, University of Reading (1997), pp. 24–40.

For contemporary comment on Charles VI's appearance (including his
concern about his baldness), see E. Taburet-Delahaye (ed.), *Paris 1400: Les
Arts sous Charles VI* (Paris, 2004), p. 29.

Charles VI as *le bien-aimé*: Beaucourt, *Charles VII*, I, p. 55.

For the description of the dauphin, Louis of Guienne, see *Journal de Nicolas de Baye, greffier du parlement de Paris, 1400–1417*, 2 vols (Paris, 1885–8), II, p. 231, and R. Vaughan, *John the Fearless: The Growth of Burgundian Power* (London, 1966, repr. Woodbridge, 2002), p. 209.

Duke John of Burgundy was known as 'John the Fearless' because of his bravery and audacity in securing Burgundian victory against the Liègeois at the battle of Othée in 1408: Vaughan, *John the Fearless*, p. 63; Monstrelet, *Chronique*, I, pp. 371, 389.

For the role of the dukes of Burgundy in French government, and conflict between John of Burgundy and Louis of Orléans, see Vaughan, *Philip the Bold*, pp. 40–5, 56–8, and *John the Fearless*, pp. 30–44.

Badges of plane and club: Vaughan, *John the Fearless*, pp. 234–5; Taburet-Delahaye (ed.), *Paris 1400*, p. 140.

For contemporary accounts of the murder of Louis of Orléans (including eyewitness testimony), see Vaughan, *John the Fearless*, pp. 45–6, and for the conflict of the years thereafter, pp. 67–102.

For the duke's tower at his home in Paris, the Hôtel d'Artois, see Vaughan, *John the Fearless*, p. 85; Taburet-Delahaye, *Paris 1400*, p. 138.

'*the great all hated each other*': *Journal*, p. 43 (translated in *Parisian Journal*, p. 80).

For the absence from the battle of the duke of Burgundy and the late arrival of the duke of Orléans, and the likelihood that this was the royal council's decision, see Curry, *Agincourt: A New History*, pp. 150–1, 218–20.

Making peace within the French lines: see the accounts of Waurin and Le Févre in Curry, *Battle of Agincourt: Sources and Interpretations*, p. 157.

For the idea of the humble (rather than Shakespeare's 'happy') English few, see Henry V's speech before the battle in *Gesta Henrici Quinti*, trans. and ed. F. Taylor and J. S. Roskell (Oxford, 1975), pp. 78–9: '". . . by the God in Heaven upon Whose grace I have relied and in Whom is my firm hope of victory, I would not, even if I could, have a single man more than I do. For these I have here with me are God's people, whom He deigns to let me have at this time. Do you not believe", he asked, "that the Almighty, with these His humble few, is able to overcome the opposing arrogance of the French who boast of their great number and their own strength?"'

For the duke of Brabant, see Curry, *Agincourt: A New History*, pp. 221, 276–7.

The wretched day – *la mauvaise journée* or *la malheureuse journée* – was what French contemporaries soon called the battle: Curry, *Battle of Agincourt: Sources and Interpretations*, pp. 279, 345.

The field of blood (*agrum sanguinis*) is from *Gesta Henrici Quinti*, pp. 92–3.

1: THIS WAR, ACCURSED OF GOD

For the English interpretation of the battle, see *Gesta Henrici Quinti*: David and
Goliath, pp. 110–11; the few against the many, and the disparity in casualties,
pp. 94–7; the 'clerical militia', pp. 88–9; '*that mound of pity and blood*' and '*far
be it . . .*', pp. 98–9; fighting a just war, pp. 14–15; Harfleur's obstinate refusal
to let Henry in, pp. 34–7; the '*true elect of God*', pp. 2–3; '*our gracious king,
His own soldier*', pp. 88–9; severity of Henry's restrictions on the behaviour
of his troops, pp. 60–1, 68–9. Another cleric with royal connections, Thomas
Elmham, wrote that St George himself had been spotted on the battlefield,
fighting on the English side: Curry, *Battle of Agincourt: Sources and
Interpretations*, p. 48, and for Elmham's career, pp. 40–2.

For medieval theories of just war, see P. Contamine, 'La Théologie de la
guerre à la fin du Moyen Age: La Guerre de Cent Ans fut-elle une guerre
juste?', in *Jeanne d'Arc: Une époque, un rayonnement: Colloque d'Histoire
Médiévale, Orléans Octobre 1979* (Paris, 1982), pp. 9–21; J. M. Pinzino, 'Just
War, Joan of Arc, and the Politics of Salvation', in L. J. A. Villalon and D.
J. Kagay (eds), *The Hundred Years War: A Wider Focus* (Leiden and Boston,
2005), pp. 365–96. For Henry's claim to the French throne, see the family
tree and note on pp. xvi–xvii.

For the aims and audience of the *Gesta*, see *Gesta Henrici Quinti*, pp. xxiii–xxviii.

For the royal chaplain's account of the bishop of Winchester's speech in
parliament, and 'O God . . .', see *Gesta Henrici Quinti*, pp. 124–5.

For Thomas Basin's account of the battle, see T. Basin, *Histoire de Charles VII*,
2 vols, trans. and ed. C. Samaran (Paris, 1933–44), I, pp. 42–7; Curry, *Battle
of Agincourt: Sources and Interpretations*, p. 190.

For the monk of Saint-Denis, see *Chronique du religieux de Saint-Denys*, trans.
and ed. M. L. Bellaguet, 6 vols (Paris, 1839–52, repr. in 3, Paris, 1994), V, pp.
578–81; Curry, *Battle of Agincourt: Sources and Interpretations*, p. 340.

For Burgundian contact with Henry V before 1415, see Vaughan, *John the
Fearless*, pp. 205–7.

For the *Histoire de Charles VI* of Jean Juvénal des Ursins, see J. A. C. Buchon
(ed.), *Choix de chroniques et mémoires relatifs à l'histoire de France* (Orléans,
1875), p. 519; Curry, *Battle of Agincourt: Sources and Interpretations*, p. 131.

For Fenin, see P. de Fenin, *Mémoires*, ed. E. Dupont (Paris, 1837), p. 67; Curry,
Battle of Agincourt: Sources and Interpretations, p. 119.

For the Burgundian view of Armagnac cowardice at the battle, see, for
example, *Le pastoralet*, a savage indictment of Armagnac crimes in the form
of an allegorical poem. Its author has no hesitation in characterising the

Burgundians as the lionhearted 'Léonois', who would 'rather give up their souls than flee', while the wolfish 'Lupalois', the greedy and duplicitous Armagnacs, turn tail without a second thought: Curry, *Battle of Agincourt: Sources and Interpretations*, pp. 352–3.

For John of Burgundy's appearance, see his portrait in the Royal Museum of Fine Arts in Antwerp: plate section and http://vlaamseprimitieven. vlaamsekunstcollectie.be/en/collection/john-the-fearless-duke-of-burgundy.

John of Burgundy's lands: Vaughan, *John the Fearless*, pp. 5–8, 237–8.

For the planned attack on Calais in 1406 (which did not, in the end, take place), see Vaughan, *John the Fearless*, pp. 38–41.

'*my lord has been and is as saddened . . .*': letter from the duke's treasurer Jean Chousat, see Vaughan, *John the Fearless*, p. 40, and for Chousat's career, pp. 121–4.

'*very distressed by the deaths . . .*': *Journal*, p. 66 (trans. *Parisian Journal*, pp. 96–8).

For the character of the dauphin Louis (including his tendency to sleep all day and carouse all night), and his death, see *Journal de Nicolas de Baye*, II, pp. 231–2; *Journal*, pp. 66–7 (trans. *Parisian Journal*, p. 97); *Chronique du religieux*, V, pp. 586–9.

'*the use on either side of injurious or slanderous terms . . .*': Vaughan, *John the Fearless*, p. 200.

The count of Armagnac's wisdom and foresight: *Chronique du religieux*, V, pp. 584–5.

The count of Armagnac in sole charge of the kingdom, and as cruel as Nero: *Journal*, pp. 69, 92 (trans. *Parisian Journal*, pp. 98–9, 115).

For the cabinet of curiosities at Hesdin, see R. Vaughan, *Philip the Good: The Apogee of Burgundy* (London, 1970, repr. Woodbridge, 2002), pp. 137–9.

For the Council of Constance, and Gerson and Cauchon, see Vaughan, *John the Fearless*, pp. 210–12.

For the duke of Gloucester as a hostage, and '*What kind of conclusion . . .*', see *Gesta Henrici Quinti*, pp. 169–75.

For Burgundy and Hainaut, see Vaughan, *John the Fearless*, pp. 212–13; B. Schnerb, *Armagnacs et Bourguignons: La Maudite Guerre, 1407–1435* (Paris, 1988, repr. 2009), pp. 225–6.

For the deaths of the dauphin Jean and Count William of Hainaut (who was married to John of Burgundy's sister), and for the presence of the new thirteen-year-old dauphin Charles in Paris from 1416, see Schnerb, *Armagnacs et Bourguignons*, pp. 226–8; Vaughan, *John the Fearless*, pp. 212–13; Juvénal des Ursins in Buchon (ed.), *Choix de chroniques*, p. 533; *Chronique du religieux*, VI, pp. 58–61.

For the breach between the dukes of Burgundy and Anjou, see Vaughan, *John the Fearless*, pp. 247–8.

For John of Burgundy's open letter, see Vaughan, *John the Fearless*, pp. 215–16; Schnerb, *Armagnacs et Bourguignons*, p. 234.

'*Paris was now suffering . . .*': *Journal*, p. 80 (trans. *Parisian Journal*, p. 105).

Innuendo about Isabeau: see, for example, *Chronique du religieux*, III, pp. 266–7. For discussion of the rumours about the queen, see R. Gibbons, 'Isabeau of Bavaria, Queen of France: The Creation of an Historical Villainess', in *Transactions of the Royal Historical Society*, ser. 6, VI (1997), pp. 51–73, and for sexual slurs on powerful women, see H. Castor, *She-Wolves: The Women Who Ruled England Before Elizabeth* (London, 2010), pp. 31–3.

For Isabeau, see Gibbons, 'Active Queenship', chs 5 and 6; Vaughan, *John the Fearless*, p. 221; Schnerb, *Armagnacs et Bourguignons*, pp. 239–41.

For Henry V's conquests in Normandy, see J. Barker, *Conquest: The English Kingdom of France in the Hundred Years War* (London, 2009), pp. 8–18.

'*Some people who had come to Paris . . .*': *Journal*, p. 83 (trans. *Parisian Journal*, p. 107).

For Martin V's envoys, see Schnerb, *Armagnacs et Bourguignons*, p. 247; Vaughan, *John the Fearless*, pp. 221–2.

For the events of 29 May and 12 June, including the terrible weather, see *Journal*, pp. 87–98 (trans. *Parisian Journal*, pp. 111–19); *Chronique du religieux*, VI, pp. 230–7, 242–51.

Parisians wearing Burgundian crosses of St Andrew: *Journal*, p. 90 (trans. *Parisian Journal*, p. 113).

'*God save the king . . .*': *Journal*, p. 89 (trans. *Parisian Journal*, p. 112).

'*Paris was in an uproar . . .*': *Journal*, pp. 90–1 (trans. *Parisian Journal*, p. 113).

For the description of the count of Armagnac and other southern captains as 'foreigners': *Journal*, p. 67 (trans. *Parisian Journal*, p. 98).

'*like sides of bacon . . .*': *Journal*, p. 91 (trans. *Parisian Journal*, p. 114).

For the band of flesh, see Schnerb, *Armagnacs et Bourguignons*, p. 252; Beaune, *Birth of an Ideology*, p. 141.

For the entry into Paris of the duke of Burgundy and Queen Isabeau, see *Journal*, p. 104 (trans. *Parisian Journal*, p. 123); *Chronique du religieux*, VI, pp. 252–5; and an anonymous contemporary letter quoted in Vaughan, *John the Fearless*, pp. 226–7.

For Henry V's arrival outside Rouen, see Barker, *Conquest*, pp. 20–1.

For the dauphin's counsellors and supporters, see Beaucourt, *Charles VII*, I, pp. 60–7, 113–18; M. G. A. Vale, *Charles VII* (London, 1974), pp. 23–4; Schnerb, *Armagnacs et Bourguignons*, pp. 257–8.

'*one of the worst Christians in the world*': *Journal*, pp. 89–90 (trans. *Parisian Journal*, p. 113).

The dauphin as 'regent of France': Beaucourt, *Charles VII*, I, p. 120.

For the dauphin's court and the division of France, see Vaughan, *John the Fearless*, pp. 263–5; Vale, *Charles VII*, pp. 22–7.

For the fall of Rouen and the English advance, see Barker, *Conquest*, pp. 22–5.

'*No one did anything about it . . .*': *Journal*, p. 121 (trans. *Parisian Journal*, p. 135).

'*So the kingdom of France . . .*': *Journal*, p. 113 (trans. *Parisian Journal*, pp. 129–30).

France torn apart; see, for example, *Chronique du religieux*, VI, pp. 202–3, 322–5.

For the three-way negotiations and their failure: *Chronique du religieux*, VI, pp. 314–17, 324–48 (including the truce between the dauphin and the duke of Burgundy, pp. 334–45).

John of Burgundy as a servant of Lucifer: Vaughan, *John the Fearless*, pp. 230–1.

For the storms of the summer of 1419 and their interpretation, see *Chronique du religieux*, VI, pp. 332–3.

For the fall of Pontoise, and the arrival of refugees from the town in Paris, see *Journal*, pp. 126–8 (trans. *Parisian Journal*, pp. 139–40).

For events at Montereau, see the authoritative analysis of Vaughan, *John the Fearless*, pp. 274–86, and contemporary documents in *Mémoires pour servir à l'histoire de France et de Bourgogne* (Paris, 1729), pp. 271–91 (including details of Tanguy du Châtel's role in setting up the meeting, pp. 272–3, the duke's black velvet hat, p. 273, and the swordsman kneeling over the duke, pp. 274–5). The surviving eyewitness accounts of the murder (of which the most detailed is that of the duke's secretary, Jean Seguinat) differ significantly: some have the duke of Burgundy raised to his feet by the dauphin before the attack began, for example, and others report the intervention of a lord named Archambaud de Foix, who died as a result of head wounds sustained in the mêlée. Since it is not possible to reconcile this testimony into a single coherent narrative, I have sought instead to offer an evocation of the murder. The circumstantial evidence supports the Burgundian case that the dauphin was centrally involved in the Armagnac plan.

For the dauphin's ungainliness, see Vale, *Charles VII*, pp. 195, 203, 229.

For the dauphin's account of the duke's death, see *Mémoires pour servir à l'histoire de France*, pp. 298–9 (his initial letter addressed to the towns of France), and G. du Fresne de Beaucourt, 'Le Meurtre de Montereau', *Revue des questions historiques*, V (1868), pp. 220–2 (letter to Philip of Burgundy, including the suggestion that Philip should stay calm), 224–9.

See Beaucourt, *Charles VII*, I, pp. 173–8, for a dauphinist reading of the evidence.

Philip of Burgundy's distress: Vaughan, *Philip the Good*, p. 2.

For the duchess of Burgundy's comparison of the murder with Judas's betrayal of Christ, see *Mémoires pour servir à l'histoire de France*, p. 292 (letter to the duchess of Bourbon).

For the Burgundian response to their perception of the dauphin's guilt, see, for example, *Chronique du religieux*, VI, pp. 376–9.

'*where they are with their poor retinue . . .*': *Journal*, p. 135 (trans. *Parisian Journal*, p. 147).

For the activities of Philip of Burgundy and the dowager duchess Margaret in the autumn of 1419, see Vaughan, *Philip the Good*, pp. 3–4; Monstrelet, *Chronique*, III, pp. 358–62.

For the bitter winter, see *Journal*, pp. 129–32 (trans. *Parisian Journal*, pp. 142–4).

The dauphin's declaration of his commitment to peace: Schnerb, *Armagnacs et Bourguignons*, pp. 282–3.

The English as the lesser of two evils: *Journal*, p. 139 (trans. *Parisian Journal*, p. 150); *Chronique du religieux*, VI, pp. 376–9.

For the negotiations, and gathering at Troyes: Monstrelet, *Chronique*, III, pp. 363–4, 378–80, 388–9.

For the architectural history of Troyes Cathedral, see S. Murray, *Building Troyes Cathedral: The Late Gothic Campaigns* (Bloomington and Indianapolis, 1987), p. 35; S. Balcon, *La Cathédrale Saint-Pierre-et-Saint-Paul de Troyes* (Paris, 2001), p. 10.

For the terms of the treaty of Troyes, see Monstrelet, *Chronique*, III, pp. 390–402; *Chronique du religieux*, VI, pp. 410–31 ('*notre très-cher fils*', pp. 424–5; the 'so-called dauphin' and his crimes, pp. 428–9; Henry to bring the rebels back into line, pp. 416–17).

2: LIKE ANOTHER MESSIAH

For the sacred history of France, see Beaune, *Birth of an Ideology*: Clovis, pp. 70–89; the Holy Ampulla, p. 78; the *oriflamme* (which was in historical, rather than mythical, fact first carried into battle by Louis VI in the twelfth century), pp. 53–5, 78–9, 217. The three possible St Denises, who were conflated at different historical moments in different combinations, were Denis the Areopagite, who became bishop of Athens after being converted to Christianity by St Paul in the first century AD; a third-century Denis, bishop of Corinth; and a Denis who was sent to evangelise Gaul in the first or perhaps the third century and became bishop of Paris. The confusion over the saint's identity meant that the relics of St Denis kept reverently within the kingdom of France included two bodies and another separate skull: see pp. 21–32. For St Louis, pp. 90–104; the Trojan origins of Paris, pp. 226–44, 333–45; Paris as a new Athens, Rome and Jerusalem, p. 51; the French as the 'chosen people' of a holy land, pp. 172–81.

Henry V's device of a fox's brush: *Journal*, p. 139 (trans. *Parisian Journal*, p. 151).

For the Anglo-Burgundian treaty, confirmed by Henry V on 25 December 1419, see T. Rymer (ed.), 'Rymer's Foedera with Syllabus: December 1419', *Rymer's Foedera*, IX, British History Online, http://www.british-history.ac.uk/report.aspx?compid=115251.

Letters patent declaring the dauphin's guilt: *Chronique du religieux*, VI, pp. 384–5.

The Armagnac pamphlet is 'La réponse d'un bon et loyal françois au peuple de France': see N. Grévy-Pons (ed.), *L'Honneur de la couronne de France: Quatre libelles contre les Anglais* (Paris, 1990), pp. 123, 132.

For the fleurs-de-lis, see Beaune, *Birth of an Ideology*, pp. 197–8, 200–19; for St Michael, pp. 152–8.

For the dauphin's standards, banners and armour, see Beaucourt, *Charles VII*, I, p. 199.

The dauphin's physical weakness: G. Chastellain, *Oeuvres*, ed. K. de Lettenhove, 8 vols (Brussels, 1863–6), II, pp. 178, 181; Vale, *Charles VII*, pp. 34, 229.

'*we may all tilt and joust . . .*': *Journal*, p. 140 (trans. *Parisian Journal*, p. 151).

For the exhumation of John the Fearless, see Monstrelet, *Chronique*, III, pp. 404–5; J. Le Févre, *Chronique*, ed. F. Morand, 2 vols (Paris, 1876–81), II, p. 44.

For the English advance to Melun, see Barker, *Conquest*, pp. 31–2.

For the dauphin's armour and army, his palace of Mehun-sur-Yèvre and the count of Vertus, see Beaucourt, *Charles VII*, I, pp. 210–12, 215.

For the entry of '*our French lords*' into Paris, starvation in the city and wine flowing in the conduits, see *Journal*, pp. 144, 146 (trans. *Parisian Journal*, pp. 153, 155); Monstrelet, *Chronique*, IV, pp. 16–17.

Musicians playing for Catherine at Melun: Monstrelet, *Chronique*, III, pp. 412–13.

For the judicial sentence against the dauphin, see Beaucourt, *Charles VII*, I, pp. 217–18; Monstrelet, *Chronique*, IV, pp. 17–20.

Departure of Catherine and Henry for England: Barker, *Conquest*, p. 37.

For the dauphin sending pilgrims to Mont-Saint-Michel, see Beaucourt, *Charles VII*, I, p. 219.

For the Scots in France, see B. Chevalier, 'Les Écossais dans les armées de Charles VII jusqu'à la bataille de Verneuil', in *Jeanne d'Arc: Une époque, un rayonnement*, pp. 85–6.

For James I as Henry's prisoner, see E. W. M. Balfour-Melville, *James I, King of Scots, 1406–1437* (London, 1936), pp. 28–32, 80–3; Chevalier, 'Les Écossais', pp. 88–9.

For Clarence and Baugé, see Allmand, *Henry V*, pp. 158–9; G. L. Harriss, *Cardinal Beaufort: A Study of Lancastrian Ascendancy and Decline* (Oxford, 1988), pp. 103–4; G. L. Harriss, 'Thomas, duke of Clarence (1387–1421)', *ODNB*; Barker, *Conquest*, pp. 37–9; Walter Bower, *Scotichronicon*, ed. D. E. R. Watt and others, 9 vols (Aberdeen, 1987–98), VIII, pp. 118–19.

For the Scottish earls' letter to the dauphin, see Beaucourt, *Charles VII*, I, pp. 220–1.

'drunken, mutton-eating fools' and *'like another Messiah'*: Bower, *Scotichronicon*, VIII, pp. 112–15.

For Buchan as constable, see Beaucourt, *Charles VII*, I, pp. 222–3, and for the dauphin's armour and standard with an image of St Michael, p. 223n.

For the dauphin's advance and retreat, see Beaucourt, *Charles VII*, I, pp. 226–30, and for his letter to the people of Lyon explaining the difficulties his army faced, p. 461; J. H. Wylie and W. T. Waugh, *The Reign of Henry V*, III (Cambridge, 1929), pp. 330–2.

For the effects of the bad winter, and Henry's return to France, *Journal*, pp. 153–6 (trans. *Parisian Journal*, pp. 160–2).

Catherine's pregnancy: M. Jones, 'Catherine (1401–1437)', *ODNB*.

For the difficulties of the siege at Meaux, see *Journal*, p. 160 (trans. *Parisian Journal*, pp. 164–5); Allmand, *Henry V*, p. 164.

For the holy foreskin of Christ, see *Journal*, p. 376n; *Parisian Journal*, p. 356n; N. Vincent, *Holy Blood: King Henry III and the Westminster Blood Relic* (Cambridge, 2001), p. 170n.

For the birth of the future Henry VI, and the Parisian journal-writer's despair, see *Journal*, pp. 163–4 (trans. *Parisian Journal*, pp. 166–7); Allmand, *Henry V*, p. 167.

The fall of Meaux: Barker, *Conquest*, pp. 42–3.

For the hermit Jean de Gand, see R. Jacquin, 'Un précurseur de Jeanne d'Arc', *Revue des deux mondes* (1967), pp. 222–6.

For the wedding of the dauphin and Marie of Anjou, see Beaucourt, *Charles VII*, I, pp. 235–6.

For Henry and Catherine in Paris, see Monstrelet, *Chronique*, IV, pp. 99–101. For the Hôtel Saint-Pol, see *Parisian Journal*, p. 11.

For the unusually hot summer, see *Journal*, p. 175 (trans. *Parisian Journal*, p. 177).

For Henry's illness and death, see Allmand, *Henry V*, pp. 170–1, 173; Monstrelet, *Chronique*, IV, pp. 109–12.

For Henry's will of 1421 and codicils of 1422, see P. Strong and F. Strong, 'The Last Will and Codicils of Henry V', *English Historical Review*, 96 (1981), pp. 89, 98–9.

For the last journey of the king's body, and his funeral, see Allmand, *Henry V*, pp. 174–8; W. H. St John Hope, 'The Funeral, Monument, and Chantry Chapel of King Henry the Fifth', *Archaeologia*, 65 (1914), pp. 129–45, 184–5; P. Cochon, *Chronique normande*, ed. C. de Robillard de Beaurepaire (Rouen, 1870), pp. 288–90; Monstrelet, *Chronique*, IV, pp. 112–16. Monstrelet says the body was taken to Notre-Dame in Paris, but the Parisian journal-writer says that it bypassed Paris and was taken instead to Saint-Denis outside the city walls: *Journal*, p. 176 (trans. *Parisian Journal*, p. 178).

For Charles VI's death and funeral: *Journal*, pp. 177–80 (trans. *Parisian Journal*, pp. 179–82); *Chronique du religieux*, VI, pp. 486–99.

Henry feared and Charles loved: see, for example, *Chronique du religieux*, VI, pp. 480–3, 486–7.

For the duke of Gloucester as protector in England, see R. A. Griffiths, *The Reign of King Henry VI* (Berkeley and Los Angeles, 1981), pp. 19–24, 28–9.

For Bedford as regent in France, and popular disquiet at that development and Burgundy's absence from Paris, see *Journal*, p. 180 (trans. *Parisian Journal*, p. 183); Juvénal des Ursins in Buchon (ed.), *Choix de chroniques*, p. 572. For the sword Joyeuse, and the possibility that Bedford also took the *oriflamme*, see G. Thompson, '"Monseigneur Saint Denis", His Abbey, and His Town, under English Occupation, 1420–1436', in C. Allmand (ed.), *Power, Culture and Religion in France, c.1350–c.1550* (Woodbridge, 1989), p. 26.

For the duke of Burgundy at Henry and Catherine's wedding in black velvet, see Wylie and Waugh, *Reign of Henry V*, III, pp. 206, 224–5. For Burgundian interests and priorities in these years, see Vaughan, *Philip the Good*, pp. 6–8, 16–17, 27–8, 31–5; '*in the service of the king of France*', p. 17.

For Anne of Burgundy and the treaty of Amiens, see Vaughan, *Philip the Good*, p. 9. For the new duchess going everywhere with Bedford, see *Journal*, pp. 200, 230 (trans. *Parisian Journal*, pp. 201, 227). The comment that Anne and her sisters were as 'plain as owls' ('*laides comme des chouettes*') is quoted by Ernest Petit from unnamed manuscripts, including accounts and receipts of judicial fines, to demonstrate the unpopularity of John the Fearless and his family in Burgundy itself; it is possible, therefore, that this may not have been a universal or objective view of Anne's appearance: E. Petit, 'Les Tonnerrois sous Charles VI et la Bourgogne sous Jean Sans Peur (épisodes inédits de la Guerre de Cent Ans)', *Bulletin de la Société des Sciences Historiques et Naturelles de l'Yonne*, xlv (1891), p. 314. Anne's sister Margaret had previously been married to the dauphin's elder brother, Louis of Guienne: see above, p. 25. For Richemont, see below, pp. 67–8.

For Armagnac praise of Henry V and the story of St Fiacre, see Juvénal des Ursins in Buchon (ed.), *Choix de chroniques*, p. 571, adapted and adopted from the less partisan *Chronique du religieux*, VI, pp. 480–3. The Scottish chronicler Walter Bower had no hesitation in dubbing the Irish St Fiacre a Scot, and putting into the dying king's mouth an acknowledgement of his sin: 'Wherever I pursue the Scots alive or dead', Bower's Henry observes grimly, 'I find them in my beard . . .': Bower, *Scotichronicon*, VIII, pp. 122–3, 205n.

For the dauphin's piety, see Vale, *Charles VII*, p. 43, and for his enduring interest in astrology, pp. 43–4; also Beaucourt, *Charles VII*, VI, pp. 399–400.

For Germain de Thibouville, see *Le 'Recueil des plus célèbres astrologues' de Simon de Phares*, ed. J.-P. Boudet, I (Paris, 1997), pp. 552–3. Beaucourt (*Charles VII*, I, pp. 222–3) mistakenly says that it was John Stewart of Darnley, not the earl of Buchan, who was given his services.

For Charles calling himself king of France at the beginning of 1423, see *Journal*, p. 183 (trans. *Parisian Journal*, p. 185); and for the proclamation of his title at Mehun-sur-Yèvre, see Beaucourt, *Charles VII*, II, p. 55.

For the territories controlled by Charles in 1423, and the isolated Armagnac garrisons in Champagne, see Beaucourt, *Charles VII*, II, pp. 8–9.

For the accident at La Rochelle, see Beaucourt, *Charles VII*, I, pp. 240–1, and for the grant to Mont-Saint-Michel in April 1423 with explicit reference to the incident, see S. Luce, *Jeanne d'Arc à Domrémy: Recherches critiques sur les origines de la mission de la Pucelle* (Paris, 1886), pp. 87–93.

For the white cross as the badge of the kings of France (at least from the fourteenth century), see P. Contamine, *Guerre, état et société à la fin du Moyen Age: Etudes sur les armées des rois de France, 1337–1494* (Paris, 1972), pp. 668–9.

For St Michael adopted as patron saint by Charles, in opposition to St George of England, and the white cross as his emblem, see Beaune, *Birth of an Ideology*, pp. 163–6.

The battle of Cravant, and Charles's attempt to play it down: Beaucourt, *Charles VII*, II, p. 58, and the full text of the king's letter in Beaucourt, *Charles VII*, III, pp. 493–4; B. G. H. Ditcham, '"Mutton-Guzzlers and Wine Bags": Foreign Soldiers and Native Reactions in Fifteenth-Century France',

in Allmand (ed.), *Power, Culture and Religion*, p. 1; Vale, *Charles VII*, p. 33.
Unsurprisingly, there is a great deal of historiographical confusion between
John Stewart, earl of Buchan, the constable of France, and John Stewart of
Darnley (starting with Monstrelet, *Chronique*, IV, pp. 161–2). It was Buchan
who was the constable, and not at Cravant; Darnley who was at Cravant,
and who lost an eye and his liberty.

Buchan and Wigtown's journey to Scotland: Beaucourt, *Charles VII*, II, pp.
59–60; Chevalier, 'Les Écossais', p. 88.

Charles's letter to Tournai about Buchan's return: Beaucourt, *Charles VII*, II,
pp. 59–60.

Letter announcing the birth of the dauphin Louis: Beaucourt, *Charles VII*, II,
p. 60.

For the Scots arriving in France, and discussion of their numbers, see
Chevalier, 'Les Écossais', p. 88; Beaucourt, *Charles VII*, II, p. 63. For the earl
of Douglas's military past, see M. H. Brown, 'Douglas, Archibald, fourth
earl of Douglas, and duke of Touraine in the French nobility (*c.*1369–1424)',
ODNB; M. Brown, *The Black Douglases: War and Lordship in Late Medieval
Scotland, 1300–1455* (Edinburgh, 1998), pp. 105–6; W. Fraser, *The Douglas
Book* (Edinburgh, 1885), pp. 368, 372–3. For Douglas in France, and his
treatment of Tours, see Brown, *The Black Douglases*, pp. 220–2; Chevalier,
'Les Écossais', p. 91.

For the decision that Charles should not take part in the campaign, see
Beaucourt, *Charles VII*, II, pp. 70–1, and for Aumâle's previous success in
Normandy, pp. 58–9. For all other details of the Armagnac army, the road
to Verneuil and the battle itself, see M. K. Jones, 'The Battle of Verneuil (17
August 1424): Towards a History of Courage', in *War in History*, 9 (2002),
pp. 375–411.

For the observation that no one could tell who was winning, see *Journal*, pp.
197–8 (trans. *Parisian Journal*, p. 198).

The Burgundian chronicler with the English army was Jean Waurin, who
noted the significance of Bedford's robe at Ivry: J. de Waurin, *Anchiennes
cronicques d'Engleterre*, ed. E. Dupont, 3 vols (Paris, 1858–63), I, p. 255, and
for Bedford's prowess, p. 267 (translated in J. de Waurin, *A Collection of the
Chronicles and Ancient Histories of Great Britain, now called England, from AD
1422 to AD 1431*, trans. E. L. C. P. Hardy (London, 1891), pp. 68, 76–7).

For Bedford's return to Paris and the year's vintage, see *Journal*, p. 200 (trans.
Parisian Journal, p. 201).

For the burial of the earls of Douglas and Buchan, and the blockade of the
Scots garrison at Tours, see Bower, *Scotichronicon*, VIII, pp. 126–7; Ditcham,

"'Mutton Guzzlers and Wine Bags'", pp. 6–7; Brown, *The Black Douglases*, p. 223.

3: DESOLATE AND DIVIDED

For the dukes of Bedford and Burgundy in Paris in the autumn and winter of 1424, and Burgundy's return to '*his own country*', see *Journal*, pp. 201–2 (trans. *Parisian Journal*, pp. 202–3); also Monstrelet, *Chronique*, IV, pp. 208–9; Beaucourt, *Charles VII*, II, pp. 364.

For Philip of Burgundy's appearance, and his badge, see Vaughan, *Philip the Good*, pp. 127, 143.

'*a city which had loved him so well*': *Journal*, p. 165 (trans. *Parisian Journal*, p. 168).

Fines for calling the dauphin 'king' or the Armagnacs 'French': B. J. H. Rowe, 'Discipline in the Norman Garrisons under Bedford, 1422–35', *English Historical Review*, 46 (1931), p. 205; Barker, *Conquest*, p. 74. Repeat offenders, Bedford said, could expect to have their tongues pierced, their foreheads branded and, if they still persisted, all their possessions confiscated. English France also included the duchy of Gascony in the south-west, which had been in English hands (albeit now in reduced size) since the twelfth century.

For Charles's various pronouncements on his forthcoming victory in 1423–4, see Beaucourt, *Charles VII*, II, pp. 58–64.

'*At that time the English ...*': *Journal*, p. 190 (trans. *Parisian Journal*, p. 191).

For Gloucester and Jacqueline, see G. L. Harriss, 'Humphrey, duke of Gloucester (1390–1447)', *ODNB*, and M. Atkins, 'Jacqueline, suo jure countess of Hainault, suo jure countess of Holland, and suo jure countess of Zeeland (1401–1436)', *ODNB*; and for the course of events in the Low Countries, Vaughan, *Philip the Good*, pp. 34–7.

For diplomatic exchanges between Bourges and Dijon in 1424, see Vaughan, *Philip the Good*, p. 20; Beaucourt, *Charles VII*, II, pp. 357–8.

For Bedford and the Burgundians at Verneuil, see Jones, 'The Battle of Verneuil', pp. 403–5.

For the text of the truce of September 1424, see U. Plancher, *Histoire générale et particulière de Bourgogne*, 4 vols (Dijon, 1739–81), IV, pp. xliv–xlv.

For the conflict between Gloucester and Burgundy, see Vaughan, *Philip the Good*, pp. 37–9. Burgundy's challenge to Gloucester, and Gloucester's acceptance, can be found in Monstrelet, *Chronique*, IV, pp. 216–22. For the description of Philip's preparations by Jean Le Févre, the duke's herald, see Le Févre, *Chronique*, II, pp. 106–7; for an extract from the accounts detailing Philip of Burgundy's expenditure, see L. de Laborde, *Les Ducs de Bourgogne*, 3 vols (Paris, 1849–52), I, pp. 201–4.

For Jacqueline's capture and escape, and the following war, see Vaughan, *Philip the Good*, pp. 39–42 and ff.

The dukes of Brittany did sometimes hold the earldom of Richmond, in the sense of the lands in England, but their use of the title – however contested it might be by the English – did not depend on the possession of those estates. For Richemont at Agincourt, see G. Gruel, *Chronique d'Arthur de Richemont*, ed. A. le Vavasseur (Paris, 1890), p. 18. For all other details here, see E. Cosneau, *Le Connétable de Richemont, Artur de Bretagne, 1393–1458* (Paris, 1886), pp. 1–74.

For Richemont's rapprochement with the Armagnacs, see Cosneau, *Connétable*, pp. 84–92; Beaucourt, *Charles VII*, II, pp. 77–87.

For Yolande, her family and her plans, see G. de Senneville, *Yolande d'Aragon: La Reine qui a gagné la Guerre de Cent Ans* (Paris, 2008), esp. pp. 67–70, 104–10, 123, 127–43.

Yolande's private correspondence with Philip of Burgundy: Beaucourt, *Charles VII*, II, p. 353.

Yolande's return from Provence and visits to Brittany in 1424–5: Beaucourt, *Charles VII*, II, pp. 61, 64, 71–3, 352–3; Senneville, *Yolande*, pp. 172–9.

For the removal from the Armagnac court of Louvet and du Châtel, see Beaucourt, *Charles VII*, II, pp. 84–104.

'*the good advice and counsel of our dearest and most beloved mother*': Cosneau, *Connétable*, p. 508.

For the schism, see A. Black, 'Popes and Councils', in C. Allmand (ed.), *The New Cambridge Medieval History, Volume VII c.1415–c.1500* (Cambridge, 1998), pp. 65–9.

For Marie Robine, see M. Tobin, 'Le Livre des révélations de Marie Robine (+1399): Étude et édition', in *Mélanges de l'École Française de Rome, Moyen-Age, Temps Modernes*, 98 (1986), pp. 229–64; A. Vauchez, 'Jeanne d'Arc et le prophétisme féminin des XIVe et XVe siècles', in *Jeanne d'Arc: Une époque, un rayonnement*, pp. 163–4; R. Blumenfeld-Kosinski, *Poets, Saints and Visionaries of the Great Schism* (Pennsylvania State University, 2006), pp. 81–6, and for the young cardinal Pierre de Luxembourg, pp. 75–8. Marie Robine made her journey to Avignon after the death of Pierre de Luxembourg in July 1387 and before the death of Pope Urban IV in October 1389, so 1388 is the most likely date.

For Jeanne-Marie de Maillé, see Vauchez, 'Jeanne d'Arc et le prophétisme féminin', pp. 162–3; Blumenfeld-Kosinski, *Poets, Saints and Visionaries*, pp. 91–3.

For the Armagnac call to arms, and Yolande and the royal council's financial retrenchment, see Beaucourt, *Charles VII*, II, pp. 121–3.

For grants to Darnley, see Vale, *Charles VII*, p. 33; Beaucourt, *Charles VII*, II, p. 131, and III, p. 511.

For Bedford's return to England, and his lieutenants in France, see Barker, *Conquest*, pp. 87–8.

For difficulties getting rid of Jean Louvet, see Beaucourt, *Charles VII*, II, pp. 90–101.

For Pierre de Giac, see Beaucourt, *Charles VII*, II, pp. 103, 123–5, 132–7 (with Richemont's letter pp. 134–5). Guillaume Gruel says that Giac was removed by the advice of Yolande of Aragon: Gruel, *Chronique d'Arthur de Richemont*, p. 48.

For Le Camus de Beaulieu, see Beaucourt, *Charles VII*, II, pp. 140–2.

For La Trémoille, see Beaucourt, *Charles VII*, II, pp. 142–6.

Yolande leaving court: Beaucourt, *Charles VII*, II, p. 146.

The battle of the blind, the greasy pole and the *Danse Macabre*: *Journal*, pp. 203–5 (trans. *Parisian Journal*, pp. 204–6, and for the etymology of the name '*Danse Macabre*', p. 204n).

Bedford's return to Paris and dreadful weather in the spring of 1427: *Journal*, pp. 213–14 (trans. *Parisian Journal*, pp. 212–13).

For the Anglo-Breton treaty and the fighting at Montargis and Sainte-Suzanne, see Barker, *Conquest*, p. 89; Beaucourt, *Charles VII*, II, pp. 28–9, 389; J. Chartier, *Chronique de Charles VII*, ed. V. de Viriville, 3 vols (Paris, 1858), I, pp. 54–6.

Richemont's rebellion and Charles's response: Beaucourt, *Charles VII*, II, pp. 149–73.

For the campaign that led to the siege of Orléans, see Barker, *Conquest*, pp. 96–8; M. K. Jones, '"Gardez mon corps, sauvez ma terre" – Immunity from War and the Lands of a Captive Knight: The Siege of Orléans (1428–29) Revisited', in M.-J. Arn (ed.), *Charles d'Orléans in England* (Cambridge, 2000), pp. 9–26.

'*a thorough soldier . . .*': *Journal*, p. 212 (trans. *Parisian Journal*, p. 211).

For the topography and defences of Orléans, see K. DeVries, *Joan of Arc: A Military Leader* (Stroud, 1999, new edn 2011), pp. 27, 54–5.

Salisbury's report of the campaign, in a letter to the mayor and aldermen of London, 5 September 1428: J. Delpit (ed.), *Collection générale des documents français*, I (Paris, 1847), pp. 236–7.

For the English bombardment and Salisbury's death, see the 'Journal du siège
d'Orléans' in Quicherat, *Procès*, IV, pp. 96–100; Monstrelet, *Chronique*, IV,
pp. 298–300; Bower, *Scotichronicon*, VIII, pp. 128–9; K. DeVries, 'Military
Surgical Practice and the Advent of Gunpowder Weaponry', *Canadian
Bulletin of Medical History*, 7 (1990), pp. 136, 139.

For Suffolk strengthening the blockade, see DeVries, *Joan of Arc: A Military
Leader*, pp. 56–7; and for reinforcements under Scales and Talbot, 'Journal
du siège' in Quicherat, *Procès*, IV, p. 103.

'believing that, if it were lost . . .': Monstrelet, *Chronique*, IV, p. 301.

Charles's response to the siege, and the petition of the estates-general:
Beaucourt, *Charles VII*, II, pp. 170–5.

The duke of Burgundy's visit to Paris: *Journal*, p. 225 (trans. *Parisian Journal*,
p. 222). For Burgundy's concerns in the Low Countries, see Vaughan, *Philip
the Good*, pp. 48–9.

For the duke of Alençon and Yolande at Chinon, see Beaucourt, *Charles VII*,
II, p. 170, and for Richemont at Parthenay, see Gruel, *Chronique d'Arthur de
Richemont*, pp. 66–7.

'too long and boring': Monstrelet, *Chronique*, IV, p. 301.

For details of the Battle of the Herrings, see S. Cooper, *The Real Falstaff:
Sir John Fastolf and the Hundred Years' War* (Barnsley, 2010), pp. 53–6
(including his identification of the battle site as Rouvray-Sainte-Croix
rather than Rouvray-Saint-Denis); Monstrelet, *Chronique*, IV, pp. 310–14;
Journal, pp. 230–3 (trans. *Parisian Journal*, pp. 227–9).

'if a hair of them escaped . . .': *Journal*, pp. 231–2 (trans. *Parisian Journal*, p. 228).

'How dreadful it is . . .': *Journal*, p. 233 (trans. *Parisian Journal*, p. 229).

For the injury to the Bastard of Orléans, and the other survivors, see 'Journal
du siège' in Quicherat, *Procès*, IV, p. 124.

For the king's fortunes going from bad to worse, see Monstrelet, *Chronique*, IV,
pp. 310, 313.

For the possibility that the king might flee to Scotland or Castile, or retreat
to the Dauphiné, and the debate about tactics, see Beaucourt, *Charles VII*,
II, pp. 175–6. It has sometimes been suggested that the later reporting of
these rumours is after-the-fact exaggeration to emphasise the significance
of God's intervention at Orléans, but it is clear both that the loss of the
town would have been a major blow to the Armagnac position and that
contemporaries believed the king to be under serious threat. See, for
example, the letter sent on 10 May 1429 from Bruges by the Italian merchant
Pancrazio Giustiniani to his father in Venice, in which he says that, if the
English were to take Orléans, they would easily make themselves lords of

France, and that Charles would be reduced to begging for his bread: A. Morosini, *Chronique: Extraits relatifs à l'histoire de France*, ed. and trans. G. Lefèvre-Pontalis and L. Dorez, 4 vols (Paris, 1898–1902), III, pp. 16–17.

'*that the persecutions of war, death and famine . . .*': from an anonymous Flemish chronicle, in J.-J. de Smet (ed.), *Recueil des chroniques de Flandre*, III (Brussels, 1856), p. 405.

The date of Joan's arrival at Chinon is not completely certain. According to the testimony in 1456 of Jean de Metz and Bertrand de Poulengy, who accompanied her, the journey took eleven days, and the most specific statement – that of Jean de Metz – suggests that they set off 'around the first Sunday in Lent', which in 1429 was 13 February. An eleven-day journey beginning on that Sunday would have brought them to Chinon on 23 February, which is the date given by the relatively well-informed and almost contemporaneous account of the clerk of La Rochelle. That is therefore the date I have adopted (cf. Tisset's discussion in *Condamnation*, II, pp. 55–6n; Vale, *Charles VII*, p. 46; L. J. Taylor, *The Virgin Warrior: The Life and Death of Joan of Arc* (New Haven and London, 2009), pp. 38–9, 222n). Bertrand de Poulengy, however, seems to offer a slightly different chronology, which implies that they left a little later, and other writers have suggested that she arrived at Chinon as late as 4 March (see, for example, Taylor, *Joan of Arc*, p. 10), or 6 March (the date given by the chronicler of Mont-Saint-Michel, for which see *Chronique du Mont-Saint-Michel (1343–1468)*, ed. S. Luce, I (Paris, 1879), p. 30). For the account of the clerk of La Rochelle, see J. Quicherat, 'Relation inédite sur Jeanne d'Arc', *Revue historique* (1877), p. 336; for the statements of Jean de Metz and Bertrand de Poulengy, see Duparc, *Nullité*, I, pp. 290, 306 (translated into French in Duparc, *Nullité*, III, pp. 278, 293, and into English in Taylor, *Joan of Arc*, pp. 272, 276–7).

Joan's dark hair ('*cheveux noirs*') is reported in the detailed description given by the clerk of La Rochelle: see Quicherat, 'Relation inédite sur Jeanne d'Arc', p. 336. For her clothes and cropped hair, see also the account of Mathieu Thomassin in Quicherat, *Procès*, IV, p. 304; for her companions, see the testimony of Jean de Metz in Duparc, *Nullité*, I, p. 290 (trans. French in Duparc, *Nullité*, III, p. 278; English in Taylor, *Joan of Arc*, p. 272).

4: THE MAID

For Joan writing to the king from Sainte-Catherine-de-Fierbois, see her own testimony in 1431: Tisset, *Condamnation*, I, p. 51 (trans. French in Tisset,

Condamnation, II, p. 55; English in Hobbins, *Trial*, p. 55, and Taylor, *Joan of Arc*, p. 144).

For Joan's first visits to Robert de Baudricourt and to the duke of Lorraine, and her eventual journey to Chinon, see testimony given in 1456: Duparc, *Nullité*, I, 289–91 (Jean de Metz), 296 (Durand Laxart), 305–7 (Bertrand de Poulengy), 378 (Marguerite La Touroulde) (trans. French in Duparc, *Nullité*, III, pp. 277–8, 283–4, 292–3, and IV, p. 61; for Metz, Laxart and Poulengy in English, see Taylor, *Joan of Arc*, pp. 271–4, 276–7). See also Joan's own testimony in 1431: Tisset, *Condamnation*, I, pp. 48–51 (trans. French in Tisset, *Condamnation*, II, pp. 47–56; English in Hobbins, *Trial*, pp. 54–5, and Taylor, *Joan of Arc*, pp. 142–40). The timing and precise details of these events are confused because of discrepancies between these various accounts: see Tisset's discussion in *Condamnation*, II, pp. 49–52nn.

For Baudricourt not taking Joan seriously to start with, see also the later reports of Jean Chartier, in Quicherat, *Procès*, IV, p. 52, and the 'Journal du siège d'Orléans', in Quicherat, *Procès*, IV, p. 118.

For Ermine de Reims, the 'discernment of spirits' and the referral of her case to Jean Gerson, see Blumenfeld-Kosinski, *Poets, Saints and Visionaries*, pp. 89–91; D. Elliott, 'Seeing Double: John Gerson, the Discernment of Spirits, and Joan of Arc', *American Historical Review*, 107 (2002), pp. 27–8, 39–43.

For Joan's black and grey outfit, see the clerk of La Rochelle in Quicherat, 'Relation inédite sur Jeanne d'Arc', p. 336; for her red dress and help with clothes and equipment from the people of Vaucouleurs, see Duparc, *Nullité*, I, pp. 289–90 (Metz), 296 (Laxart), 298 (Catherine, wife of Henri le Royer), 299 (Henri le Royer), 306 (Poulengy) (trans. French in Duparc, *Nullité*, III, pp. 277–8, 283–7, 293; Metz, Laxart, Catherine le Royer and Poulengy in English in Taylor, *Joan of Arc*, pp. 271–2, 274, 275–6).

For Colet de Vienne, see Duparc, *Nullité*, I, p. 290 (Metz) (trans. French in Duparc, *Nullité*, III, p. 278; English in Taylor, *Joan of Arc*, p. 272); Tisset, *Condamnation*, II, p. 53n.

The dangers of the route: Jean de Metz and Bertrand de Poulengy said that they sometimes travelled at night for fear of meeting English or Burgundian soldiers. See Duparc, *Nullité*, I, pp. 190, 306 (trans. French in Duparc, *Nullité*, III, pp. 278, 293; English in Taylor, *Joan of Arc*, pp. 272, 276).

For the likely role of René of Anjou and Yolande in facilitating Joan's arrival at court, see Vale, *Charles VII*, pp. 49–51; Taylor, *Virgin Warrior*, pp. 34–5.

For Joan's arrival, her meeting with the king (there are conflicting reports of how soon, but Joan herself said it was the day of her coming to Chinon), and the nature of her mission, see Joan's own testimony in 1431, in Tisset,

Condamnation, I, pp. 51–3 (trans. French in Tisset, *Condamnation*, II, pp. 55–6; English in Hobbins, *Trial*, pp. 55–6, and Taylor, *Joan of Arc*, p. 144), and evidence given in 1456, in Duparc, *Nullité*, I, pp. 317 (Bastard of Orléans), 326 (Raoul de Gaucourt), 329 (Guillaume de Ricarville), 330 (Regnauld Thierry), 362 (Louis de Coutes) (trans. French in Duparc, *Nullité*, IV, pp. 2–3, 11, 14, 15, 46–7, and the Bastard and Coutes in English in Taylor, *Joan of Arc*, pp. 277–8, 294); also the testimony, recorded in French, of Jean d'Aulon in Duparc, *Nullité*, I, p. 475 (trans. English in Taylor, *Joan of Arc*, p. 339). In 1456 Jean Pasquerel and Simon Charles both gave more extensive accounts of Joan's meeting with the king – Pasquerel saying that the king declared that she had told him secrets no one else knew, and Simon Charles that she had recognised the king despite his attempts to conceal himself among other members of the court. However, neither Pasquerel nor Simon Charles was present at Chinon to witness this encounter. It is clear both that they were keen to echo Joan herself in suggesting that her arrival had a miraculous quality – in 1431, she said that 'when she entered her king's chamber, she recognised him among the others by the counsel of her voice, which revealed him to her' – and that they may have conflated her first encounter with the king with a later, more public presentation at court, for which see below, pp. 99, 270. See Duparc, *Nullité*, I, pp. 389–90 (Pasquerel), 399–400 (Charles) (trans. French in Duparc, *Nullité*, IV, pp. 71–2, 81–2; English in Taylor, *Joan of Arc*, pp. 311–12, 317–18); for Joan's testimony, see Tisset, *Condamnation*, I, pp. 51–2 (trans. French in Tisset, *Condamnation*, II, p. 56; English in Hobbins, *Trial*, p. 55, and Taylor, *Joan of Arc*, p. 144).

For Joan addressing the king as 'Dauphin' because he was not yet crowned, see the testimony in 1456 of François Garivel: Duparc, *Nullité*, I, p. 328 (trans. French in Duparc, *Nullité*, IV, p. 13; English in Taylor, *Joan of Arc*, p. 286). In other testimony she is sometimes said to have called him 'dauphin' and sometimes 'king'; in her letters, she always referred to him as king: see pp. 98, 122.

Her mission: note that no one who knew Joan in Domrémy or Vaucouleurs said that she talked of relieving the siege at Orléans. Instead, they remembered her saying that she would save France from the English and take the king to be crowned at Reims. Those witnesses in 1456 who had been inside the besieged town in the spring of 1429 remembered hearing that she was coming to save them, but it makes psychological sense, given their own overwhelming need, that that might have been their conclusion at the time and their memory after the fact. What seems more likely is that the specific task of relieving Orléans was added to the general ones of repelling the

English and securing the king's coronation once Joan had access to more detailed information at Chinon about the progress of the war. This was not how she herself presented the evolution of her mission during her trial in 1431, but her evidence on the subject was neither internally consistent nor wholly plausible. See, for witnesses from Domrémy and Vaucouleurs, Duparc, *Nullité*, I, pp. 278 (Jean Waterin), 290–1 (Metz), 293 (Michel le Buin), 296 (Laxart), 298 (Catherine le Royer), 305 (Poulengy) (trans. French in Duparc, *Nullité*, III, pp. 265, 277–8, 280, 283, 285, 292–3; Metz, Laxart, Catherine le Royer and Poulengy in English in Taylor, *Joan of Arc*, pp. 271–6); for Joan's testimony in 1431, below, chs 9 and 10; and see below, pp. 269–70, for evidence suggesting that the relief of Orléans was adopted as a test of her mission during her interrogation at Poitiers.

For de Baudricourt suggesting that Joan's family should give her a few slaps, see the testimony in 1456 of Durand Laxart: Duparc, *Nullité*, I, p. 296 (trans. French in Duparc, *Nullité*, III, p. 283; English in Taylor, *Joan of Arc*, p. 274). Deborah Fraioli and Larissa Juliet Taylor both suggest that Joan was also met with derision by those around the king at Chinon, but the sources they cite refer to her initial reception at Vaucouleurs; by the time she arrived at court – perhaps thanks to Yolande's intervention – the message she brought was already being considered seriously: see D. Fraioli, *Joan of Arc: The Early Debate* (Woodbridge, 2000), p. 7, and the chronicle of Jean Chartier in Quicherat, *Procès*, IV, p. 52; Taylor, *Virgin Warrior*, p. 42, and Duparc, *Nullité*, I, pp. 377–8 (La Touroulde) (trans. French in Duparc, *Nullité*, IV, p. 61).

'excessive, overeager . . .': from Jean Gerson's *On the Proving of Spirits* (*De probatione spirituum*) in Fraioli, *Early Debate*, p. 18n.

For Joan's clothes, see R. Wirth (ed.), *Primary Sources and Context concerning Joan of Arc's Male Clothing*, Historical Academy (Association) for Joan of Arc Studies (2006), p. 1 and note 1.

For the Old Testament prohibition on cross-dressing, see Deuteronomy 22:5 – 'A woman shall not wear that which pertaineth unto a man, neither shall a man put on a woman's garment: for whosoever doeth these things is an abomination unto the Lord thy God'.

For arguments between Gerson and Cauchon at Constance, see above, p. 26.

For Armagnac scholars from the university of Paris reconvening at Poitiers in the kingdom of Bourges, see R. G. Little, *The Parlement of Poitiers: War, Government and Politics in France, 1418–1436* (London, 1984), pp. 104–5.

For Gerson's exile and settlement at Lyon, see B. P. McGuire, *Jean Gerson and the Last Medieval Reformation* (Pennsylvania State University, 2005), ch. 10; and for his principles for the discernment of spirits as laid out in

On Distinguishing True from False Revelations (1401), *On the Proving of Spirits* (1415) and *On the Examination of Doctrine* (1423), see Elliott, 'Seeing Double', pp. 28–9, 42–3.

For Joan's physical examination by ladies of the court, see the testimony of Jean Pasquerel in Duparc, *Nullité*, I, p. 389 (trans. French in Duparc, *Nullité*, IV, p. 71; English in Taylor, *Joan of Arc*, p. 311). This is hearsay, since Pasquerel was not at Chinon when Joan arrived, but is entirely plausible as a first step before any further spiritual examination, and the identity of the ladies he names supports his story, since their husbands were both at Chinon with the king. Pasquerel also says that Joan was examined twice. For what seems to have been the second occasion, at Poitiers, see pp. 97, 270.

For the correspondence with Jacques Gélu, which exists now only in seventeenth-century summaries, see M. Forcellin, *Histoire générale des Alpes Maritimes ou Cottiènes*, II (Paris, 1890) pp. 313–16; and discussion in Fraioli, *Early Debate*, pp. 16–23.

For Joan's lodgings at Chinon, see the testimony of Louis de Coutes in Duparc, *Nullité*, I, p. 362 (trans. French in Duparc, *Nullité*, IV, p. 47; English in Taylor, *Joan of Arc*, p. 90).

For the investigations at Poitiers, see Fraioli, *Early Debate*, ch. 3; Little, *Parlement of Poitiers*, pp. 94–108 (though note that he sees the process as political rather than theological); C. T. Wood, 'Joan of Arc's mission and the lost record of her interrogation at Poitiers', in B. Wheeler and C. T. Wood (eds), *Fresh Verdicts on Joan of Arc* (New York, 1996), pp. 19–28 (though note that he reaches the opposite conclusion to the one I propose here about the nature of Joan's mission: he suggests that the relief of Orléans, but not the coronation at Reims, was part of Joan's mission from the beginning).

No transcript of the inquiry at Poitiers survives. Instead, we have a short summary, which was widely publicised, of the conclusions reached by the clerics. For its text (quoted here and below: '*in two ways . . .*', '*She has conversed . . .*', '*For to doubt or discard . . .*', '*The king . . . should not prevent . . .*', and calling Joan 'the Maid'), see Quicherat, *Procès*, III, pp. 391–2, and various English translations in Fraioli, *Early Debate*, pp. 206–7; Hobbins, *Trial*, pp. 217–18; Taylor, *Joan of Arc*, pp. 72–4.

For the unlikelihood that the raising of the siege of Orléans, which was more than 150 miles away from Domrémy, formed part of Joan's mission from the beginning, see above, pp. 267–8. For the argument that it emerged as her 'sign' during the investigation at Poitiers, see Fraioli, *Early Debate*, p. 33, citing the account of Pope Pius II, written probably in 1459 – evidence that is supported by the testimony given in 1456 by the captain of Chinon, Raoul

NOTES

de Gaucourt, and Joan's squire, Jean d'Aulon: Duparc, *Nullité*, I, pp. 326, 475–6 (Gaucourt trans. French in Duparc, *Nullité*, IV, pp. 11–12; d'Aulon trans. English in Taylor, *Joan of Arc*, pp. 339–40). Note, however, that other testimony gives other versions. Joan's own account of her sign in 1431 is full of discrepancies and grows under pressure into something much more elaborate: see below, chs 9 and 10.

For Archbishop Gélu's worries about ridicule, see Forcellin, *Histoire générale*, p. 314.

For the second check on Joan's virginity under the supervision of Yolande, see the testimony of Jean d'Aulon in Duparc, *Nullité*, I, p. 476 (trans. English in Taylor, *Joan of Arc*, pp. 339–40).

For the text of Joan's letter to the English, see Tisset, *Condamnation*, I, pp. 221–2, or Quicherat, *Procès*, I, pp. 240–1, and various English translations in Hobbins, *Trial*, pp. 134–5; Taylor, *Joan of Arc*, pp. 74–6; Fraioli, *Early Debate*, p. 208. See also discussion in Fraioli, *Early Debate*, ch. 5.

For the story given by the clerk of La Rochelle of Joan's public presentation to the king, see Quicherat, 'Relation inédite sur Jeanne d'Arc', pp. 336–7. He, like Jean Pasquerel and Simon Charles in 1456, believed this to be Joan's first meeting with the king, before her interrogation at Poitiers, but it seems more likely, following the testimony of other witnesses (see above, pp. 266–7), that the first meeting took place in private, and that this public encounter happened only once the decision had been made to test Joan's mission at Orléans: cf. Taylor, *Virgin Warrior*, pp. 46–7.

Copies of the Poitiers Conclusions reached as far afield as Scotland and Germany, and may have been dispatched as an 'official circular': see Little, *Parlement of Poitiers*, pp. 108–11.

For the chronogram and prophecies, and the Latin poem *Virgo puellares* (which also reached Germany and Scotland), see Fraioli, *Early Debate*, pp. 61–6; Taylor, *Virgin Warrior*, pp. 47–8; Taylor, *Joan of Arc*, pp. 77–8 (comment and translation); Quicherat, *Procès*, IV, p. 305.

The story of Joan's sword also comes in different versions. Joan herself said in 1431 that she thought it was buried not very deep in the ground near the altar (in front or behind, she was not sure), and that when the clerics rubbed it, the rust immediately fell off it – though of course she was not there to witness its unearthing. She said she knew from her voices that it was there; her voices are not mentioned in sources before the trial, so the clerk of La Rochelle and the 'Journal du siège d'Orléans', for example, report simply that she knew it would be found there. I quote the clerk of La Rochelle because his account suggests a non-miraculous means by which that might

270

have been possible: if the sword was kept in a coffer that had been opened within living memory, Joan could have heard of it when she stopped at the church on her way to Chinon. But in fact that is also possible if the sword were buried. Legend had it that the great warrior Charles Martel had given his sword to the church at Sainte-Catherine-de-Fierbois after his eighth-century victory against the invading Moors, and other soldiers had left weapons there as offerings, so it may well have been a church full of swords with stories attached to them. As Joan's myth developed, it would eventually be said that the sword she carried was that of Charles Martel himself. See the clerk of La Rochelle in Quicherat, 'Relation inédite sur Jeanne d'Arc', pp. 331, 337–8; Joan's testimony in Tisset, *Condamnation*, I, pp. 76–7 (trans. French in Tisset, *Condamnation*, II, pp. 75–6; English in Hobbins, *Trial*, pp. 67–8, and Taylor, *Joan of Arc*, pp. 155–6); for the 'Journal du siège', see Quicherat, *Procès*, IV, p. 129; and for discussion see Taylor, *Virgin Warrior*, pp. 51–2, and B. Wheeler, 'Joan of Arc's Sword in the Stone', in Wheeler and Wood (eds), *Fresh Verdicts*, pp. xi–xv.

For St Catherine – who was also usually depicted with the wheel that failed to kill her – and her cult in France and specifically at Fierbois, see Beaune, *Birth of an Ideology*, pp. 127–32.

For Joan's armour, which cost the large sum of a hundred *livres tournois*, and the painting of her banners, see the extract from the accounts of the king's treasurer for his wars in Quicherat, *Procès*, V, p. 258. The painter is named as 'Hauves Polvoir', which is probably the Scots name 'Hamish Power': see discussion in Beaucourt, *Charles VII*, VI, p. 415.

Contemporary descriptions of Joan's banners vary in detail, but all agree on the white ground and the fleurs-de-lis. For Joan's version, see her testimony in 1431 in Tisset, *Condamnation*, I, p. 78 (trans. French in Tisset, *Condamnation*, II, p. 77; English in Hobbins, *Trial*, p. 69, and Taylor, *Joan of Arc*, p. 157); for that of Jean Pasquerel, see Duparc, *Nullité*, I, p. 390 (trans. French in Duparc, *Nullité*, IV, pp. 72–3; English in Taylor, *Joan of Arc*, p. 312).

For Joan moving to Tours, and her squire, pages and chaplain, see Duparc, *Nullité*, I, 362–3 (Coutes), 388–9 (Pasquerel), 476–7 (d'Aulon) (Coutes and Pasquerel trans. French in Duparc, *Nullité*, IV, pp. 46–7, 70–1; all three trans. English in Taylor, *Joan of Arc*, pp. 294–5, 310–11, 340).

For the likelihood of Joan's military training during these weeks, see, for example, Taylor, *Virgin Warrior*, pp. 49–50.

For the duke of Alençon, see his testimony in Duparc, *Nullité*, I, pp. 381–2 (trans. French in Duparc, *Nullité*, IV, pp. 64–5; English in Taylor, *Joan of Arc*, pp. 304–5).

For the involvement of La Hire and de Rais as well as Yolande and de Loré in
gathering supplies and troops, see the testimony of the Bastard of Orléans:
Duparc, *Nullité*, I, p. 318 (trans. French in Duparc, *Nullité*, IV, p. 3; English
in Taylor, *Joan of Arc*, p. 278).

Gerson's treatise: this is the Latin text known as *De quadam puella*, for which
see Quicherat, *Procès*, III, pp. 411–21, and English translations in Fraioli,
Early Debate, pp. 199–205, and Taylor, *Joan of Arc*, pp. 112–18. The
authorship, timing and intention of this work have all been the subject of
debate. For the argument that it is the work of Gerson, see Fraioli, *Early
Debate*, pp. 25, 41–3, and note that it was included in the first ever printed
edition of Gerson's writings in 1484. The argument that that attribution was
erroneous rests to a large extent on the suggestion that it does not 'sound'
like Gerson, and that its cautious argument differs from the support for
Joan expressed in *De mirabili victoria*, another treatise believed to have
been written by Gerson (for which, see pp. 112–3, 275–6). In considering
variations in the style of argument, it may be important to remember both
that Gerson characteristically wrote at great speed, and that these were the
very last months of his life (see McGuire, *Jean Gerson*, pp. 251, 253, 318–19).
The differences between *De quadam puella* and *De mirabili victoria* may
also be explicable in terms of their dating. The date of *De quadam puella*
is uncertain, but it talks of Joan riding in armour and carrying a standard,
which suggests that it was written after the interrogation at Poitiers, during
the period when she was preparing for military action. Fraioli argues that
it should be located before the Poitiers inquiry (*Early Debate*, pp. 24–5),
largely on the basis that it appears to be a contribution to a theological
debate that is not yet settled; but, given that Orléans was to be Joan's test,
the theological debate was very much alive in the weeks between Poitiers
and Orléans, when the Poitiers Conclusions were being circulated and Joan
was being equipped for war, but the outcome of her mission was not yet
known. The absence from the text of any reference, implicit or explicit, to
victory at Orléans means that it seems plausible to suggest that Gerson,
having heard at Lyon of Joan's arrival at Chinon, the inquiry at Poitiers
and the preparations for her intervention at Orléans, did indeed write the
even-handed *De quadam puella* during these weeks in late March and April
– and that he might subsequently have reached a more positive judgement
on her mission in *De mirabili victoria* once her test at Orléans had vindicated
her claims in May. (Note, however, that there remains the difficulty of a
sentence in *De quadam puella* remarking that towns and castles submit to
the king because of Joan; again, this makes a date before Poitiers much less

likely, and Craig Taylor argues (*Joan of Arc*, p. 112) that it must indicate instead that the text was written later, in the summer of 1429. However, the equivocal position adopted in *De quadam puella* would not easily fit with a summer date in terms of the evolution of theological responses to Joan over these months; such a date is also especially hard to reconcile with Gerson's authorship, if the latter is accepted, since it is likely that he wrote the much more positive *De mirabili victoria* in May, and died on 12 July.)

'*false French*': a phrase used in the 'Journal du siège d'Orléans' to describe the Parisians who fought alongside the English at the Battle of the Herrings: Quicherat, *Procès*, IV, p. 119.

For the delegation to the duke of Burgundy (and note that Poton de Xaintrailles had previously fought for Burgundy in Hainaut against the duke of Gloucester), see Morosini, *Chronique*, III, pp. 16–23; Little, *Parlement of Poitiers*, pp. 93–4; 'Journal du siège' in Quicherat, *Procès*, IV, pp. 130–1; Monstrelet, *Chronique*, IV, pp. 317–19.

For the duke of Burgundy's movements in April, see *Journal*, pp. 233–4 (trans. *Parisian Journal*, pp. 230–1).

For the return of Xaintrailles with a Burgundian herald, see 'Journal du siège' in Quicherat, *Procès*, IV, pp. 146–7.

For stories about the Maid circulating in Orléans, see the testimony of the Bastard of Orléans in Duparc, *Nullité*, I, pp. 316–17 (trans. French in Duparc, *Nullité*, IV, pp. 2–3; English in Taylor, *Joan of Arc*, pp. 277–8), and, for example, that of Guillaume de Ricarville: Duparc, *Nullité*, I, p. 329 (trans. French in Duparc, *Nullité*, IV, p. 14).

'*she prohibits murder . . .*' from *De quadam puella* (see above, p. 272, for discussion on authorship): Quicherat, *Procès*, III, p. 412, and English translations in Fraioli, *Early Debate*, p. 199, and Taylor, *Joan of Arc*, p. 113.

For Joan sleeping in her armour, see the testimony of her page, Louis de Coutes, who says she was bruised as a result: Duparc, *Nullité*, I, p. 363 (trans. French in Duparc, *Nullité*, IV, p. 48; English in Taylor, *Joan of Arc*, p. 295).

For 26 April as the likely date of the departure from Blois, see DeVries, *Joan of Arc: A Military Leader*, p. 66 at n. 58.

5: LIKE AN ANGEL FROM GOD

For the loss of soldiers whose contract had come to an end, see Barker, *Conquest*, p. 115.

For the departure of the Burgundians, see above, p. 102.

For the interception of the wine, pork and venison intended for the English, see the 'Journal du siège' in Quicherat, *Procès*, IV, p. 143.

For the priests leading the Armagnac forces, and their formation, see Duparc, *Nullité*, I, pp. 318–19 (Bastard), 391–2 (Pasquerel) (trans. French in Duparc, *Nullité*, IV, pp. 3–5, 73–4; English in Taylor, *Joan of Arc*, pp. 278–80, 312–13); 'Journal du siège' in Quicherat, *Procès*, IV, pp. 150–3. The details of their arrival at Orléans are once again inconsistent, for example about how much of the journey took place by river and how much by land: for discussion, see DeVries, *Joan of Arc: A Military Leader*, pp. 66–9.

For the response of the English soldiers to Joan, see, for example, Duparc, *Nullité*, I, pp. 363–4 (Coutes), 394 (Pasquerel) (trans. French in Duparc, *Nullité*, IV, pp. 48, 76; English in Taylor, *Joan of Arc*, pp. 295, 314).

For Henry V outside Harfleur, see above, p. 20.

For Joan's entry into Orléans, see the 'Journal du siège' in Quicherat, *Procès*, IV, pp. 152-3; Duparc, *Nullité*, I, pp. 319 (Bastard), 331 (Jean Luillier) (trans. French in Duparc, *Nullité*, IV, pp. 5, 16; English in Taylor, *Joan of Arc*, pp. 280, 287); DeVries, *Joan of Arc: A Military Leader*, pp. 69–70.

Joan's anger: Duparc, *Nullité*, I, pp. 318–20 (Bastard), 363 (Coutes) (trans. French in Duparc, *Nullité*, IV, pp. 4–5, 48; English in Taylor, *Joan of Arc*, pp. 279–80, 295).

For the behaviour of Joan's soldiers, see, for example, the testimony of the Bastard of Orléans in Duparc, *Nullité*, I, p. 319 (trans. French in Duparc, *Nullité*, IV, p. 4; English in Taylor, *Joan of Arc*, p. 279).

'*The king . . . should not prevent . . .*': from the Poitiers Conclusions, for which, see above, pp. 97, 269.

For the events of 30 April, including Joan's confrontation with the English, see 'Journal du siège' in Quicherat, *Procès*, IV, pp. 154–5; Duparc, *Nullité*, I, pp. 320 (Bastard), 363–4 (Coutes) (trans. French in Duparc, *Nullité*, IV, pp. 5, 48; English in Taylor, *Joan of Arc*, pp. 280, 295).

For the Bastard's departure for Blois, and Joan familiarising herself with the town, see 'Journal du siège' in Quicherat, *Procès*, IV, pp. 155–6; Jean Chartier in Quicherat, *Procès*, IV, pp. 55–6; Duparc, *Nullité*, I, pp. 319–20 (Bastard), 477–8 (d'Aulon) (Bastard trans. French in Duparc, *Nullité*, IV, p. 5; both trans. English in Taylor, *Joan of Arc*, pp. 280, 341).

For the procession in Joan's honour, see DeVries, *Joan of Arc: A Military Leader*, p. 73.

For the Bastard's return and the assault on Saint-Loup, see 'Journal du siège' in Quicherat, *Procès*, IV, pp. 157–8; Chartier in Quicherat, *Procès*, IV, pp. 56–7.

For Joan's mood and her eating, see Duparc, *Nullité*, I, pp. 364 (Coutes), 392 (Pasquerel) (trans. French in Duparc, *Nullité*, IV, pp. 48–9, 74–5; English in Taylor, *Joan of Arc*, pp. 296, 314).

For the text of Joan's third letter to the English, and the response of the English soldiers, see the testimony in 1456 of her confessor Jean Pasquerel: Duparc, *Nullité*, I, pp. 393–4 (trans. French in Duparc, *Nullité*, IV, pp. 75–6; English in Taylor, *Joan of Arc*, pp. 84, 314).

For the events of 5–8 May, see 'Journal du siège' in Quicherat, *Procès*, IV, pp. 159–64; Chartier in Quicherat, *Procès*, IV, pp. 60–3; Perceval de Cagny in Quicherat, *Procès*, IV, pp. 7–10; Duparc, *Nullité*, I, pp. 320–1 (Bastard), 331–2 (Luillier), 364–6 (Coutes), 394–5 (Pasquerel), 480–4 (d'Aulon) (all except d'Aulon trans. French in Duparc, *Nullité*, IV, pp. 6–7, 17, 49–50, 76–8; all trans. English in Taylor, *Joan of Arc*, pp. 280–1, 287–8, 296–7, 315–16, 343–5). I have sought to convey the broad outline of events, but note that, once again, the timing and details – including Joan's own movements and the question of whether there was disagreement over strategy between her and the other commanders – are confused and inconsistent between the different accounts: for discussion, see DeVries, *Joan of Arc: A Military Leader*, pp. 75–87.

For Monstrelet's report on the English decision to withdraw, see Monstrelet, *Chronique*, IV, p. 322.

For the celebrations in Orléans on 7 and 8 May, including the citizens embracing the soldiers as if they were their children, see 'Journal du siège' in Quicherat, *Procès*, IV, pp. 166–7.

For the letter of Pancrazio Giustiniani, the Italian merchant in Bruges, see Morosini, *Chronique*, III, pp. 43–54 (trans. English in Taylor, *Joan of Arc*, pp. 87–8).

For Jean Dupuy's addition to his *Collectarium historiarum*, see Taylor, *Joan of Arc*, pp. 89–91, and discussion in Fraioli, *Early Debate*, ch. 9.

For the Latin text of Gerson's *De mirabili victoria* (or *De puella Aurelianensi*), see Quicherat, *Procès*, III, pp. 298–306, and Duparc, *Nullité*, II, pp. 33–9 (part trans. English in Fraioli, *Early Debate*, appendix IV, and Taylor, *Joan of Arc*, pp. 78–83). Again, there has been debate about the authorship of the treatise, and Fraioli argues that it is not by Gerson (*Early Debate*, ch. 8). However, it was confidently attributed to Gerson during the nullification trial of 1456, and dated to 14 May 1429 – in other words, just after the raising of the siege of Orléans (Duparc, *Nullité*, II, p. 33); Gerson was also named as the author by Pancrazio Giustiniani in a letter of 20 November 1429, written to accompany a copy of the treatise which he was sending to Italy (see Morosini, *Chronique*, III, pp. 234–5), while Gerson's modern biographer says the attribution is certain, citing Daniel Hobbins's work on the manuscripts (McGuire, *Jean Gerson*, p. 401 n. 89). Craig Taylor thinks it odd that there is no explicit reference to the victory at Orléans (*Joan of Arc*, p. 78), but the text does implicitly refer to a miraculous event. See also Dyan Elliott's discussion in 'Seeing Double', pp. 44–7.

For the king's letter to the town of Narbonne, see Quicherat, *Procès*, V, pp. 101–4 (part trans. English in Taylor, *Joan of Arc*, pp. 86–7).

For Joan and the Bastard going to meet the king, and debates about what to do next, see 'Journal du siège' in Quicherat, *Procès*, IV, pp. 167–8; Eberhard de Windecken in Quicherat, *Procès*, IV, pp. 496–7; the Bastard's testimony in Duparc, *Nullité*, I, p. 321 (trans. French in Duparc, *Nullité*, IV, p. 7; English in Taylor, *Joan of Arc*, p. 281).

For the king's lack of money, see, for example, Guy de Laval's letter in Quicherat, *Procès*, V, p. 109.

Guy de Laval reported his encounter with Joan to his mother in a letter written on 8 June 1429: Quicherat, *Procès*, V, pp. 106–11 (part trans. English in Taylor, *Joan of Arc*, pp. 92–3).

For events at Jargeau, see 'Journal du siège' in Quicherat, *Procès*, IV, pp. 167–73; Cagny in Quicherat, *Procès*, IV, pp. 12–13; Chartier in Quicherat, *Procès*, IV, pp. 64–5; DeVries, *Joan of Arc: A Military Leader*, pp. 98–102.

For Meung, Beaugency and Patay, see 'Journal du siège' in Quicherat, *Procès*, IV, pp. 174–8; Cagny in Quicherat, *Procès*, IV, pp. 14–16; Chartier in Quicherat, *Procès*, IV, pp. 65–9; and, for the English perspective, see the eyewitness account of Jean Waurin in *Collection of the Chronicles*, trans. Hardy, pp. 179–88. See also discussion in DeVries, *Joan of Arc: A Military Leader*, pp. 102–3, 105–15.

For Richemont, see Gruel, *Chronique d'Arthur de Richemont*, pp. 70–4, and the testimony of the duke of Alençon in Duparc, *Nullité*, I, pp. 385–6 (trans. French in Duparc, *Nullité*, IV, pp. 68–9; English in Taylor, *Joan of Arc*, pp. 308–9).

'*by the renown of Joan the Maid . . .*' and '*And by these operations . . .*': Waurin, *Collection of the Chronicles*, trans. Hardy, pp. 183, 188.

For the English retreat from towns to the north of the Loire, see, for example, 'Journal du siège' in Quicherat, *Procès*, IV, p. 178.

6: A HEART GREATER THAN ANY MAN'S

For the duke of Orléans's gift to Joan, see Quicherat, *Procès*, V, pp. 112–14. Quicherat notes that the colours of the dukes of Orléans had originally been crimson and bright green, which darkened first after the murder of Duke Louis, and then to green so dark that it was almost black after the capture of his son at Azincourt.

For Gerson's comment on Joan's clothes, see *De quadam puella* in Quicherat, *Procès*, III, p. 412: '*Ubi autem de equo descendit, solitum habitum [mulierbrem] reassumens, fit simplicissima, negotiorum saecularium quasi innocens agnus imperita.*' Note that *mulierbrem* does not appear in Quicherat's text, but see Fraioli, *Early Debate*, pp. 28–9. For English versions, see Fraioli, *Early Debate*, p. 199, and Taylor, *Joan of Arc*, p. 113, which translate *habitum* as 'manners' and 'nature' rather than 'clothes'. Fraioli justifies this on the grounds that 'the latter disagrees with all the facts we know about Joan, who maintained male dress continually from Vaucouleurs' (*Early Debate*, p. 29n) – but in fact we have no definitive evidence that Joan did maintain male dress continually from Vaucouleurs, and, even if she did, Gerson, who had never seen her, might have believed otherwise. The word *habitus* is frequently used in texts referring to Joan's male clothes, and it therefore seems plausible that the word here, as elsewhere, carries the double sense of clothes and comportment: see, for example, discussion in K. Sullivan, *The Interrogation of Joan of Arc* (Minneapolis, 1999), p. 50.

For the wine and ring described by Guy de Laval, see Quicherat, *Procès*, V, pp. 107, 109 (trans. English in Taylor, *Joan of Arc*, p. 93). His grandmother Anne de Laval, to whom Joan sent the gold ring, had once been married to Bertrand du Guesclin, the great hero of an earlier stage of the wars against the English: Quicherat, *Procès*, V, pp. 105–6n.

For Joan and Alençon with the king, and discussion about Richemont and the campaign to come, see 'Journal du siège' in Quicherat, *Procès*, IV, pp. 168–9, 178–9; Chartier in Quicherat, *Procès*, IV, pp. 69–71; Cagny in Quicherat, *Procès*, IV, pp. 17–18; testimony of the Bastard of Orléans in Duparc, *Nullité*, I, pp. 323–4 (trans. French in Duparc, *Nullité*, IV, p. 9; English in Taylor, *Joan of Arc*, p. 283); Beaucourt, *Charles VII*, II, pp. 221–3.

For Fastolf at Janville, see 'Journal du siège' in Quicherat, *Procès*, IV, pp. 177–8.

For the military summons issued by the king, see Little, *Parlement of Poitiers*, pp. 114–15; see also Joan's letter to the people of Tournai, calling on them to come to the coronation at Reims, in Quicherat, *Procès*, V, pp. 123–5 (trans. English in Taylor, *Joan of Arc*, pp. 93–4).

For the king's letter sent ahead to Troyes, for example, see the seventeenth-century précis of Jean Rogier in Quicherat, *Procès*, IV, p. 287.

For Auxerre, see 'Journal du siège' in Quicherat, *Procès*, IV, pp. 180–1.

For the course of events at Troyes, see 'Journal du siège' in Quicherat, *Procès*, IV, pp. 181–4; Chartier in Quicherat, *Procès*, IV, pp. 72–6; the clerk of La Rochelle in Quicherat, 'Relation inédite', pp. 341–2; and especially Jean Rogier's account, compiled in the early seventeenth century from the town registers of Reims, in Quicherat, *Procès*, IV, pp. 284–302, including Joan's letter (pp. 287–8), the response of the people of Troyes (pp. 288–91), their later letter to Reims (pp. 295–6), and the letter from the brother of the captain of Reims (pp. 296–7).

For Brother Richard in Paris, see *Journal*, pp. 233–7 (trans. *Parisian Journal*, pp. 230–5); for his presence and conversion to Joan's cause at Troyes, see Quicherat, 'Relation inédite', p. 342; Jean Rogier's account in Quicherat, *Procès*, IV, p. 290; cf. Joan's testimony in 1431 in Tisset, *Condamnation*, I, p. 98 (trans. Tisset, *Condamnation*, II, pp. 94–5; English in Hobbins, *Trial*, pp. 80–1, and Taylor, *Joan of Arc*, p. 169).

Joan the Braggart: the French word is *coquard* (Quicherat, *Procès*, IV, p. 290), which – with its apparent derivation from *coq*, or cockerel – also seems to play in a derogatory sense on Joan's masculine self-presentation. The squire who reported to the brother of the captain of Reims compared Joan to 'Madame d'Or' (Quicherat, *Procès*, IV, p. 297), a female fool at the court of the duke of Burgundy: see Le Févre, *Chronique*, II, p. 168.

For the letter from the people of Châlons to those of Reims, and the king at Sept-Saulx, see the account of Jean Rogier in Quicherat, *Procès*, IV, pp. 298–9.

For the king's arrival in Reims and the coronation, see 'Journal du siège' in Quicherat, *Procès*, IV, pp. 184–6; the clerk of La Rochelle in Quicherat, 'Relation inédite', pp. 343–4; Cagny in Quicherat, *Procès*, IV, pp. 19–20; Chartier in Quicherat, *Procès*, IV, pp. 77–8.

For the cathedral's labyrinth (which was destroyed in the eighteenth century), see R. Branner, 'The Labyrinth of Reims Cathedral', *Journal of the Society of Architectural Historians*, 21 (1962), p. 18.

For the trumpets sounding so loudly that the vaults might shatter, see the report of three Angevin gentlemen to the queen and her mother Yolande, in a letter written on the day of the coronation itself: Quicherat, *Procès*, V, pp. 127–31.

For discussion of the coronation ceremony, see R. Jackson, *Vive le Roi! A History of the French Coronation* (Chapel Hill, 1984), pp. 34–6.

'*Noble king, God's will is done*': 'Journal du siège' in Quicherat, *Procès*, IV, p. 186.

For the presence of Joan's family at Reims, see Duparc, *Nullité*, I, pp. 255 (Jean Morel, her godfather, who saw her at Châlons, and it seems plausible that he went on to Reims), 296 (Durand Laxart, her cousin by marriage, sometimes referred to in the testimony of 1456 as her uncle) (both trans. French in Duparc, *Nullité*, III, pp. 243, 284; Laxart in English in Taylor, *Joan of Arc*, p. 274); R. Pernoud, *Joan of Arc: By Herself and Her Witnesses* (London, 1964), pp. 125–6; Taylor, *Virgin Warrior*, p. 93.

For La Trémoille's contact with the Burgundian court in late June and early July, see Beaucourt, *Charles VII*, II, pp. 401–2.

For Joan's letter to the duke of Burgundy, see Quicherat, *Procès*, V, pp. 126–7 (trans. English in Taylor, *Joan of Arc*, pp. 95–6). Her first letter to the duke is lost, but we know of its existence from the reference in this one.

For the duke of Burgundy's arrival in Paris, see *Journal*, p. 240 (trans. *Parisian Journal*, p. 237). He had been asked to come by Bedford because of the reverses of the previous weeks: see Monstrelet, *Chronique*, IV, p. 333.

For Bedford's attitude to Joan, see p. 208.

For Bedford's letter requesting reinforcements and King Henry's coronation, see H. Nicolas (ed.), *Proceedings and Ordinances of the Privy Council of England*, III (London, 1834), pp. 322–3.

For Bedford and Burgundy in Paris and the ceremony of 14 July, see *Journal*, pp. 240–1 (trans. *Parisian Journal*, pp. 237–8); the journal of Clément de Fauquembergue, the clerk of the Paris *parlement*, in Quicherat, *Procès*, IV, p. 455; Monstrelet, *Chronique*, IV, pp. 333–4.

For English payments to the duke of Burgundy, see J. Stevenson (ed.), *Letters and Papers Illustrative of the Wars of the English in France*, II, part I (London, 1864), pp. 101–11; Vaughan, *Philip the Good*, p. 17.

For Burgundian envoys at Reims, see Beaucourt, *Charles VII*, II, pp. 403–4.

For the continued Armagnac advance towards Paris, see 'Journal du siège' in Quicherat, *Procès*, IV, p. 187; Chartier in Quicherat, *Procès*, IV, p. 78.

Gerson's death: see McGuire, *Jean Gerson*, p. 319.

For Alain Chartier's *Epistola de puella*, see Quicherat, *Procès*, V, pp. 131–6 (quotations from pp. 134, 135), and English translation in Taylor, *Joan of Arc*, pp. 108–12.

For Christine de Pizan's *Ditié de Jehanne d'Arc*, see Quicherat, *Procès*, V, pp. 3–21 (quotation from p. 11), and English translation in Taylor, *Joan of Arc*, pp. 98–108.

For Joan's letter to the people of Reims, see Quicherat, *Procès*, V, pp. 139–40, and English translation in Taylor, *Joan of Arc*, pp. 118–19.

7: A CREATURE IN THE FORM OF A WOMAN

For Bedford's report of the duke of Burgundy to the royal council, which has a definite air of protesting too much, see Beaucourt, *Charles VII*, II, p. 403n.

For the Armagnac delegation to Arras, which arrived in the first few days of August, see Beaucourt, *Charles VII*, II, pp. 405–7; Monstrelet, *Chronique*, IV, pp. 348–9; Vaughan, *Philip the Good*, pp. 21–2.

For the presence of Anne of Burgundy, duchess of Bedford, at her brother's court, see *Journal*, p. 241 (trans. *Parisian Journal*, p. 238); Morosini, *Chronique*, III, pp. 186–7; Beaucourt, *Charles VII*, II, pp. 407–8.

For the reinforcement of the defences of Paris, see *Journal*, p. 239 (trans. *Parisian Journal*, p. 236); DeVries, *Joan of Arc: A Military Leader*, p. 130.

For Bedford's return with new troops, see *Journal*, p. 242 (trans. *Parisian Journal*, p. 238); journal of Clément de Fauquembergue in Quicherat, *Procès*, IV, p. 453; Nicolas (ed.), *Proceedings and Ordinances of the Privy Council*, III, pp. 322–3; J. H. Ramsay, *Lancaster and York: A Century of English History*, I (Oxford, 1892), pp. 401–2.

For Bedford's letter from Montereau, see Monstrelet, *Chronique*, IV, pp. 340–4, and English translation in Taylor, *Joan of Arc*, pp. 119–22.

For Brother Richard riding with the Armagnacs, see *Journal*, pp. 242–3 (trans. *Parisian Journal*, pp. 238–9).

For the encounter at Montepilloy, see Monstrelet, *Chronique*, IV, pp. 344–7; Cagny in Quicherat, *Procès*, IV, pp. 21–3; Chartier in Quicherat, *Procès*, IV, pp. 82–4; 'Journal du siège' in Quicherat, *Procès*, IV, pp. 192–6.

For Bedford moving to defend Normandy, see Beaucourt, *Charles VII*, II, p. 34; Barker, *Conquest*, pp. 133–4.

For the submission of Compiègne and Beauvais to the Armagnacs, see 'Journal du siège' in Quicherat, *Procès*, IV, pp. 190, 196–7.

For the negotiations at Arras and Compiègne, see Beaucourt, *Charles VII*, II, pp. 405–10; Monstrelet, *Chronique*, IV, pp. 348–9; Vaughan, *Philip the Good*, pp. 21–2.

For the letter from the count of Armagnac and Joan's response, see Tisset, *Condamnation*, I, pp. 225–6, and English translation in Taylor, *Joan of Arc*, pp. 122–3.

For Joan's move from Compiègne to occupy Saint-Denis, see Cagny in Quicherat, *Procès*, IV, pp. 24–5; Thompson, '"Monseigneur Saint Denis"', pp. 27–8.

For the king moving to Saint-Denis and Joan to La Chapelle with all her captains, see Cagny in Quicherat, *Procès*, IV, pp. 25–6; Chartier in Quicherat, *Procès*, IV, pp. 85–6; 'Journal du siège' in Quicherat, *Procès*, IV, pp. 197–8.

For the defences of Paris, see DeVries, *Joan of Arc: A Military Leader*, pp. 141–2.

For the summons issued by Bedford, see Stevenson (ed.), *Letters and Papers*, II, part I, pp. 118–19.

For the Armagnac assault on Paris, including '. . . *these men were so unfortunate*', and Joan's shouted exchange with the soldiers defending the walls, see *Journal*, pp. 244–5 (trans. *Parisian Journal*, pp. 240–1); also the journal of Clément de Fauquembergue in Quicherat, *Procès*, IV, pp. 456–8; Cagny in Quicherat, *Procès*, IV, pp. 26–7; Chartier in Quicherat, *Procès*, IV, pp. 86–8; 'Journal du siège' in Quicherat, *Procès*, IV, pp. 197–9; DeVries, *Joan of Arc: A Military Leader*, pp. 143–6.

For Charles's letter to Reims, 13 September 1429, see Beaucourt, *Charles VII*, III, pp. 518–19; and for the financial difficulties of his government, see 'Journal du siège' in Quicherat, *Procès*, IV, p. 200; Beaucourt, *Charles VII*, II, p. 239n.

For Joan the next day, see Cagny in Quicherat, *Procès*, IV, pp. 27–9; Chartier in Quicherat, *Procès*, IV, p. 88; DeVries, *Joan of Arc: A Military Leader*, pp. 146–7.

Collecting the dead: *Journal*, p. 246 (trans. *Parisian Journal*, p. 241).

Quotations from Gerson's *De mirabili victoria*: Duparc, *Nullité*, II, p. 39, and English translations in Elliott, 'Seeing Double', p. 47; Taylor, *Joan of Arc*, p. 83; Fraioli, *Early Debate*, p. 212.

The treatise *De bono et malu spiritu* was definitely written before 22 September, when the university of Paris paid for a copy. Its author is unknown, but he was a member of the university responding to Gerson's *De mirabili victoria*. For its Latin text and a French translation see N. Valois (ed.), 'Un nouveau témoignage sur Jeanne d'Arc: Réponse d'un clerc parisien à l'apologie de la Pucelle par Gerson (1429)', in *Annuaire-Bulletin de la Société de l'Histoire de France*, 43 (1906), pp. 161–79; English translation in Taylor, *Joan of Arc*, pp. 125–30, and see discussion in Elliott, 'Seeing Double', pp. 47–50.

Jean Chartier reported that the armour Joan left at Saint-Denis was the very armour in which she had been injured: Quicherat, *Procès*, IV, p. 89.

For Joan's journey back to the Loire valley, see 'Journal du siège' in Quicherat, *Procès*, IV, p. 201.

'*And thus was the will . . .*': Cagny in Quicherat, *Procès*, IV, p. 29.

For Bedford's return to Paris, and the fines imposed on Saint-Denis, see *Journal*, pp. 246–7 (trans. *Parisian Journal*, p. 242).

For the extension of the Armagnac–Burgundian truce to include Paris, Burgundy's arrival in the capital, and Burgundian negotiations with both sides, see Beaucourt, *Charles VII*, II, pp. 411–13; Stevenson (ed.), *Letters and Papers*, II, part I, pp. 126–7; *Journal*, pp. 247–8 (trans. *Parisian Journal*, pp. 242–3). The Parisian journal-writer believed that the duke of Burgundy became regent of France, and that the duke of Bedford's authority would now be limited to Normandy; this was not true, but emphasises how important the gesture of making Burgundy the governor of Paris was for the city's inhabitants.

For Bedford's private suggestion that April might see a new campaign rather than peace, see Monstrelet, *Chronique*, IV, p. 362.

For Henry VI's English coronation, see Griffiths, *Reign of King Henry VI*, p. 190.

For Alençon wanting Joan with him, and being refused: Cagny in Quicherat, *Procès*, IV, pp. 29–30.

For Perrinet Gressart, see A. Bossuat, *Perrinet Gressart et François de Surienne* (Paris, 1936), pp. 113–19; Barker, *Conquest*, pp. 137–8.

For the siege of Saint-Pierre-le-Moûtier, see the testimony of Jean d'Aulon in Duparc, *Nullité*, I, pp. 484–5 (trans. English in Taylor, *Joan of Arc*, pp. 345–6); DeVries, *Joan of Arc: A Military Leader*, pp. 151–6; and re timing, Morosini, *Chronique*, III, pp. 229–30n.

For Joan's letter to Riom, see Quicherat, *Procès*, V, pp. 147–8 (where Quicherat notes that he saw a fingerprint and a black hair caught in the wax of the seal), and English translation in Taylor, *Joan of Arc*, pp. 130–1.

For Pancrazio Giustiniani's letter of 20 November, see Morosini, *Chronique*, III, pp. 228–37.

8: I WILL BE WITH YOU SOON

For the siege of La Charité, including comment on the cold, see the account of the Berry herald in Quicherat, *Procès*, IV, p. 49; also Cagny in Quicherat, *Procès*, IV, p. 31; Chartier in Quicherat, *Procès*, IV, p. 91; DeVries, *Joan of Arc: A Military Leader*, pp. 157–8.

For the king at Mehun-sur-Yèvre, see Beaucourt, *Charles VII*, II, p. 265.

The tax exemption for Domrémy: Quicherat, *Procès*, V, pp. 137–9.

For the ennoblement of Joan and her family, granted at Mehun-sur-Yèvre in December 1429, see Quicherat, *Procès*, V, pp. 150–4.

Joan's movements are relatively hard to track in January and February 1430, but see itinerary in Pernoud and Clin, *Joan of Arc: Her Story*, p. 271.

For the deliberations of the town council of Tours about Joan's request for financial support for the wedding of the painter's daughter, see Quicherat, *Procès*, V, pp. 154–6.

For Philip of Burgundy's marriages and illegitimate children, see Vaughan, *Philip the Good*, pp. 8, 54–7; for the Order of the Golden Fleece, pp. 57, 160–2. Isabel of Portugal's mother was Philippa of Lancaster, eldest daughter of John of Gaunt. For Jean Le Févre's astonishing account of the wedding celebrations, see Le Févre, *Chronique*, II, pp. 158–72; for the Order of the Golden Fleece, pp. 172–4.

For Burgundy refusing the Garter, and his statement of independence, see C. A. J. Armstrong, 'La Double Monarchie, France-Angleterre et la maison du Bourgogne (1420–1435): Le Déclin d'une alliance', in *Annales de Bourgogne*, 37 (1965), pp. 105–6; Chastellain, *Oeuvres*, II, pp. 10–11.

For Anne of Burgundy at the wedding, see Le Févre, *Chronique*, II, pp. 166–7.

For St Michael in the Salisbury breviary, see Bibliothèque Nationale de France MS 17294 f. 595v, available online via Gallica at http://gallica.bnf.fr/ark:/12148/btv1b8470142p/f1200.image; P. Contamine, 'La "France anglaise" au XVe siècle: Mythe ou réalité?', in *La 'France anglaise' au Moyen Age, actes du IIIe Congrès National des Sociétés Savantes (Poitiers, 1986)*, I (Paris, 1988), p. 27.

For La Hire seizing Château Gaillard on 24 February, see Barker, *Conquest*, pp. 142–3.

For the Armagnac attack on Saint-Denis, see *Journal*, p. 251 (trans. *Parisian Journal*, p. 246).

For Burgundy becoming count of Champagne, and contracting to serve King Henry for two months, see Vaughan, *Philip the Good*, pp. 17–18; Armstrong, 'Double Monarchie', p. 90; Beaucourt, *Charles VII*, II, p. 418.

For the founding membership of the Order of the Golden Fleece, see Le Févre, *Chronique*, II, pp. 173–4.

For Hugues de Lannoy and his campaign for anti-Armagnac action, see Vaughan, *Philip the Good*, pp. 22–4; Beaucourt, *Charles VII*, II, pp. 415–17.

For Burgundian–Armagnac jousting at Arras, see Monstrelet, *Chronique*, IV, pp. 376–7; Chastellain, *Oeuvres*, II, pp. 18–26.

For the complexities of Burgundian interests and entanglements in the Low Countries, see Vaughan, *Philip the Good*, pp. 48–52, 57–60.

For English preparations for Henry VI's coronation campaign, see Barker, *Conquest*, pp. 144–5.

For Joan's letters to Reims, see Quicherat, *Procès*, V, pp. 159–62, and translations in Taylor, *Joan of Arc*, pp. 131–2, 133–4.

For Joan's letter to the Hussites, see Quicherat, *Procès*, V, pp. 156–9, and translation in Taylor, *Joan of Arc*, pp. 132–3.

For Catherine de La Rochelle, see Tisset, *Condamnation*, I, pp. 103–6 (trans. French in Tisset, *Condamnation*, II, pp. 99–100; English in Hobbins, *Trial*, pp. 83–4, and Taylor, *Joan of Arc*, pp. 172–3).

Joan's movements in April are once again not easy to track, but see Cagny in Quicherat, *Procès*, IV, p. 32; Chartier in Quicherat, *Procès*, IV, pp. 91–2; DeVries, *Joan of Arc: A Military Leader*, pp. 162–3.

For Armagnac raids on Paris, and '*the duke of Burgundy was expected daily*', see *Journal*, p. 253 (trans. *Parisian Journal*, p. 247).

For Compiègne, its defences and its significance, see Barker, *Conquest*, p. 146; DeVries, *Joan of Arc: A Military Leader*, p. 164.

For Henry VI's arrival and entourage, see Griffiths, *Reign of King Henry VI*, pp. 190–1; Barker, *Conquest*, pp. 144–5.

For Pierre Cauchon, see F. Neveux, *L'Évêque Pierre Cauchon* (Paris, 1987), pp. 70–82, 85–6; Monstrelet, *Chronique*, IV, p. 389.

Negotiations for peace were supposed to start on 1 April, but the duke of Burgundy refused to come, and the English asked for a postponement until 1 June: Beaucourt, *Charles VII*, II, pp. 418–20.

For Burgundy's muster at Péronne and his journey south, see Monstrelet, *Chronique*, IV, pp. 378–84.

For Charles's letter to the towns of Armagnac France on 6 May, see Beaucourt, *Charles VII*, II, p. 423.

It is very difficult to establish a clear chronology of military events during these weeks, but for Franquet d'Arras, see Monstrelet, *Chronique*, IV, pp. 384–5; Tisset, *Condamnation*, I, pp. 150–1 (trans. French in Tisset, *Condamnation*, II, p. 130; English in Hobbins, *Trial*, p. 103, and Taylor, *Joan of Arc*, pp. 190–1).

For Poton de Xaintrailles, see Monstrelet, *Chronique*, IV, p. 382.

For Joan at Soissons, see the account of the Berry herald in Quicherat, *Procès*, IV, pp. 49–50.

For Joan at Crépy and Compiègne, the fighting and her capture, see Cagny in Quicherat, *Procès*, IV, pp. 32–4; Monstrelet, *Chronique*, IV, pp. 386–8.

There has been much discussion over the years about whether the closing of the gate of Compiègne was the result of treachery, but there is no clear evidence that it was, and no plausible reason to think it, given that Compiègne did not subsequently fall. For detailed discussion, see DeVries, *Joan of Arc: A Military Leader*, pp. 166–74.

For Duke Philip's meeting with Joan, and Monstrelet's failure to recall what was said, see Monstrelet, *Chronique*, IV, p. 388.

The duke's letter announcing Joan's capture: Quicherat, *Procès*, V, pp. 166–7; see also Vaughan, *Philip the Good*, p. 186.

For Joan in the custody of Jean de Luxembourg at Beaulieu-les-Fontaines, see Monstrelet, *Chronique*, IV, p. 389.

For a précis of the archbishop's letter to Reims, see Quicherat, *Procès*, V, pp. 168–9.

For the letters from the university of Paris and the vicar-general of the inquisitor in English France to the duke of Burgundy, and another letter from the university of Paris to Jean de Luxembourg, see Tisset, *Condamnation*, I, pp. 4–9.

For the thinking behind the trial, see Hobbins, *Trial*, pp. 20–1.

For Burgundy's difficulties and commitments in the summer of 1430, see Vaughan, *Philip the Good*, pp. 24–5, 63–4; Barker, *Conquest*, pp. 152–3.

For Cauchon's role and the decision to ransom Joan, see Neveux, *L'Évêque Pierre Cauchon*, pp. 86, 135–6.

For Henry's arrival in Rouen, see Cochon, *Chronique normande*, pp. 312–13.

For the situation in Normandy, the reconfiguring of the royal council during the young king's visit, and the counsellors' attitude to Joan's trial, see A. Curry, 'The "Coronation Expedition" and Henry VI's Court in France, 1430 to 1432', in J. Stratford (ed.), *The Lancastrian Court* (Donington, 2003), pp. 40–2; Harriss, *Cardinal Beaufort*, p. 202; Barker, *Conquest*, pp. 150–1.

For Cauchon's payment for the negotiations, see Quicherat, *Procès*, V, pp. 194–5.

For the English raising money to buy Joan from the Burgundians, see Quicherat, *Procès*, V, pp. 178–92.

For Pieronne in Paris, see *Journal*, pp. 259–60 (trans. *Parisian Journal*, pp. 253–4).

For Joan's escape attempts, see Tisset, *Condamnation*, I, pp. 145, 153, 155–6 (trans. French in Tisset, *Condamnation*, II, pp. 127, 131, 133; English in Hobbins, pp. 100–1, 103–5, and Taylor, *Joan of Arc*, pp. 187, 191–3); and see below, pp. 176, 178, 181–2, 290.

For the letters from the university of Paris to Cauchon and King Henry, see Tisset, *Condamnation*, I, pp. 11–14 (Latin letter to Cauchon trans. French in

Tisset, *Condamnation*, II, pp. 13–14; both letters trans. English in Hobbins, *Trial*, pp. 38–9).

For King Henry's edict, see Tisset, *Condamnation*, I, pp. 14–15 (trans. English in Hobbins, *Trial*, pp. 40–1, and Taylor, *Joan of Arc*, pp. 135–6).

For Joan in Rouen by Christmas Eve, see Pernoud and Clin, *Joan of Arc: Her Story*, p. 101.

9: A SIMPLE MAID

The interrogations that took place during Joan's trial were so wide-ranging and repetitive, and her answers at times so elliptical and contradictory, that it is impossible here to cover everything contained in the whole transcript. Instead, I have sought to give a flavour of the exchanges, a sense of the central theological issues, and the main contours of Joan's developing responses.

For the opening of the session of 21 February, and the list of those in attendance, see Tisset, *Condamnation*, I, pp. 32–3 (trans. French in Tisset, *Condamnation*, II, pp. 32–3, and notes on personnel; English in Hobbins, *Trial*, pp. 46–7).

For the university's sense of its own importance, the narrowing of its intellectual outlook as it became a partisan institution as a result of the civil war, and the principles of academic discourse, see Sullivan, *Interrogation*, pp. 2–6.

For the session of 9 January, see Tisset, *Condamnation*, pp. 2–3 (trans. French in Tisset, *Condamnation*, II, pp. 4–5; English in Hobbins, *Trial*, pp. 34–5).

For the process of inquisition initiated by public infamy, see Hobbins, *Trial*, pp. 16–22.

'*the report has now become well known . . .*': Tisset, *Condamnation*, I, p. 1 (trans. French in Tisset, *Condamnation*, II, p. 1; English in Hobbins, *Trial*, p. 33).

For the care taken to follow proper procedure, the possibility of saving Joan's soul, and the vacancy in the see of Rouen, see Neveux, *L'Evêque Pierre Cauchon*, pp. 137–9.

For the hearings from 9 January to 20 February, and their personnel, see Tisset, *Condamnation*, I, pp. 3–32 (trans. French in Tisset, *Condamnation*, II, pp. 4–32; English in Hobbins, *Trial*, pp. 34–46).

Joan summoned '*to answer truly . . .*': Tisset, *Condamnation*, I, pp. 33–4 (trans. French in Tisset, *Condamnation*, II, pp. 33–4; English in Hobbins, *Trial*, pp. 47–8).

Joan's response to the summons, and the judges' decision not to allow her
to hear mass: Tisset, *Condamnation*, I, pp. 35–6 (trans. French in Tisset,
Condamnation, II, pp. 35–6; English in Hobbins, *Trial*, p. 48).

Examination of her virginity, under the supervision of the duchess of Bedford:
see testimony in 1456 in Duparc, *Nullité*, I, pp. 360 (Jean Monnet), 379 (Jean
Marcel), 432 (Jean Massieu) (all trans. French in Duparc, *Nullité*, IV, pp. 45,
62, 112; Massieu in English in Taylor, *Joan of Arc*, p. 333).

Exchange between Cauchon and Joan over the question of the oath: Tisset,
Condamnation, I, pp. 37–9 (trans. French in Tisset, *Condamnation*, II, p. 37;
English in Hobbins, *Trial*, pp. 49–50, and Taylor, *Joan of Arc*, pp. 137–8).

For details of the first day's interrogation (Wednesday 21 February), see
Tisset, *Condamnation*, I, pp. 40–2 (trans. French in Tisset, *Condamnation*, II,
pp. 38–42; English in Hobbins, *Trial*, pp. 50–1, and Taylor, *Joan of Arc*, pp.
138–9). Joan explained that she was known at home as Jeannette, and then
from when she came to court as Jeanne. Later in the trial, on Saturday 24
March, she said that her surname was d'Arc or Rommée, and that girls in
her region took their mother's surname (which, in this case, would therefore
mean that she was Jeanne Rommée): see Tisset, *Condamnation*, I, p. 181
(trans. French in Tisset, *Condamnation*, II, p. 148; English in Hobbins, *Trial*,
p. 116, and Taylor, *Joan of Arc*, p. 204).

For the second day's interrogation (Thursday 22 February), see Tisset,
Condamnation, I, pp. 42–54 (quotations from pp. 45–6, 50, 53) (trans. French
in Tisset, *Condamnation*, II, pp. 43–57; English in Hobbins, *Trial*, pp. 51–6,
and Taylor, *Joan of Arc*, pp. 140–5).

For the third session (Saturday 24 February), see Tisset, *Condamnation*, I,
pp. 54–68 (quotations from pp. 56, 59, 61–2, 67) (trans. French in Tisset,
Condamnation, II, pp. 57–68; English in Hobbins, *Trial*, pp. 56–63, and Taylor,
Joan of Arc, pp. 145–51). Where there are slight variations between the French
minute and the Latin transcript in these pages, I have preferred the French
text, since its meaning seems clearer: see, for example, Tisset, *Condamnation*,
I, p. 62, where the Latin has Joan say that the light comes 'in the name of the
voice', whereas in French she says that the light 'comes before the voice'.

Clerics struggling to find a seat: when the first inquiry into the trial process
took place in 1450, a friar named Guillaume Duval testified that he had
attended one session with another friar named Isambard de la Pierre. Neither
of them, he said, had been able to find a seat, so they had sat on the carpet
near to Joan herself in the midst of the assembly. The session these two
men attended (assuming that the 'Jean Duval' listed in the trial transcript
of 1431 is a clerical error for 'Guillaume') took place in the same chamber

on 27 March, when around twenty fewer clerics were present than on 24 February, so it seems safe to assume that on this earlier occasion latecomers might have had to stand. For the testimony of Guillaume Duval, see P. Doncoeur and Y. Lanhers (ed. and trans.), *L'Enquête ordonnée par Charles VII en 1450 et le codicile de Guillaume Bouillé* (Paris, 1956), pp. 46–7; for Duval's attendance in 1431, see Tisset, *Condamnation*, I, p. 185 (trans. French in Tisset, *Condamnation*, II, p. 152; English in Hobbins, *Trial*, p. 119), and for the identification of Jean with Guillaume, see Tisset, *Condamnation*, II, p. 398.

For the trial as a case of the discernment of spirits, see Sullivan, *Interrogation*, pp. 32–41.

For Gerson warning against the possibility that women and the unlearned might claim the gift of discernment for themselves, see Elliott, 'Seeing Double', pp. 29–30, 33–5, 37–8, and, for the need for prudence and humility in seeking counsel in such cases, pp. 39–40.

For the parish prayers on which Joan drew in her answer about being in a state of grace, see Tisset, *Condamnation*, II, p. 63 n. 1.

For the theological issues relating to the tree of the fairies, see Sullivan, *Interrogation*, pp. 7–20.

For the fourth session (Tuesday 27 February), see Tisset, *Condamnation*, I, pp. 68–79 (quotations from pp. 69, 72–5) (trans. French in Tisset, *Condamnation*, II, pp. 69–79; English in Hobbins, *Trial*, pp. 63–70, and Taylor, *Joan of Arc*, pp. 151–8).

For saints, angels, and the need for a sign, see Sullivan, *Interrogation*, pp. 23–32, 35–41, 61–4; see also K. Sullivan, '"I do not name to you the voice of St Michael": The Identification of Joan of Arc's Voices', in Wheeler and Wood (eds), *Fresh Verdicts*, pp. 85–112.

For the nature and tactics of the interrogation, see Sullivan, *Interrogation*, pp. 82–99; Hobbins, *Trial*, pp. 13–17.

For the theological implications of a woman wearing men's clothes, see Sullivan, *Interrogation*, pp. 42–54; S. Schibanoff, 'True Lies: Transvestism and Idolatry in the Trial of Joan of Arc', in Wheeler and Wood (eds), *Fresh Verdicts*, pp. 31–60.

For the fifth session (Thursday 1 March), see Tisset, *Condamnation*, I, pp. 80–90 (quotations from pp. 84, 88) (trans. French in Tisset, *Condamnation*, II, pp. 79–89; English in Hobbins, *Trial*, pp. 70–7, and Taylor, *Joan of Arc*, pp. 159–66).

For the last day of public interrogation (sixth session, Saturday 3 March), see Tisset, *Condamnation*, I, pp. 90–109 (quotations from pp. 104, 106) (trans. French in Tisset, *Condamnation*, II, pp. 89–102; English in Hobbins, *Trial*, pp. 77–85, and Taylor, *Joan of Arc*, pp. 166–74).

For the appointment of Jean de La Fontaine to lead the next phase of
questioning, see Tisset, *Condamnation*, I, pp. 109–10 (trans. French in Tisset,
Condamnation, II, pp. 102–3; English in Hobbins, *Trial*, pp. 85–6).

For the first session in Joan's prison cell (Saturday 10 March), see Tisset,
Condamnation, I, pp. 110–18 (quotations from p. 117, where I have preferred
the French reading) (trans. French in Tisset, *Condamnation*, II, pp. 103–9;
English in Hobbins, *Trial*, pp. 86–9).

For the second session in prison (Monday 12 March), see Tisset, *Condamnation*,
I, pp. 121–9 (trans. French in Tisset, *Condamnation*, II, pp. 111–16; English in
Hobbins, *Trial*, pp. 93–4, and Taylor, *Joan of Arc*, pp. 178–82).

For the third session in prison (Tuesday 13 March), see Tisset, *Condamnation*, I,
pp. 133–42 (quotation from p. 136) (trans. French in Tisset, *Condamnation*, II,
pp. 119–24; English in Hobbins, *Trial*, pp. 95–9, and Taylor, *Joan of Arc*,
pp. 182–6).

For the fourth, fifth and sixth sessions in prison (Wednesday 14, Thursday 15,
Saturday 17 March), see Tisset, *Condamnation*, I, pp. 143–79 (quotation from
p. 166) (trans. French in Tisset, *Condamnation*, II, pp. 126–46; English in
Hobbins, *Trial*, pp. 99–114, and Taylor, *Joan of Arc*, pp. 186–203).

For the decision made on Passion Sunday, discussion of procedure, and
d'Estivet's seventy articles (which he began to read on Tuesday 27 March
and continued on Wednesday 28), see Tisset, *Condamnation*, I, pp. 179–286
(quotation from pp. 191–2) (trans. French in Tisset, *Condamnation*, II, pp.
146–242; English in Hobbins, *Trial*, pp. 114–55).

For turning the seventy articles into twelve, plus the opinions of the
theologians and the lawyers, see Tisset, *Condamnation*, I, pp. 289–327
(quotation from p. 298) (trans. French in Tisset, *Condamnation*, II, pp.
244–84; English in Hobbins, *Trial*, pp. 156–66, and Taylor, *Joan of Arc*, pp.
207–12).

For the rigour with which the trial was conducted, see Hobbins, *Trial*, pp.
16–19, 21–4, 26.

For the concern of the judges for the fate of Joan's soul, see Sullivan,
Interrogation, pp. 106–13, 120–8.

10: FEAR OF THE FIRE

For Joan's illness, see Tisset, *Condamnation*, I, pp. 328–9 (trans. French in
Tisset, *Condamnation*, II, pp. 285–6; English in Hobbins, *Trial*, pp. 166–7).

For the visit to Joan's cell on 31 March, see Tisset, *Condamnation*, I, pp. 286–9 (trans. French in Tisset, *Condamnation*, II, pp. 242–4; English in Hobbins, *Trial*, pp. 155–6, and Taylor, *Joan of Arc*, pp. 205–6).

For Joan's escape attempts, see the interrogations of 14 and 15 March: Tisset, *Condamnation*, I, pp. 143–5, 153, 155–6, 164 (quotation from p. 156) (trans. French in Tisset, *Condamnation*, II, pp. 126–7, 131, 133, 137; English in Hobbins, *Trial*, pp. 100, 103–5, 108, and Taylor, *Joan of Arc*, pp. 187, 191–3, 196). Joan and her interrogators spoke always of her 'leap' from the tower, but the Burgundian 'Chronicle of the Cordeliers', written around 1432, instead describes an escape attempt in which whatever she was using to lower herself from the tower broke, thus causing her fall: see Taylor, *Joan of Arc*, p. 237.

For St Catherine resisting the interrogation of pagan scholars, see Taylor, *Virgin Warrior*, p. 26.

For exchanges between Joan and her judges about the possibility that she could hear mass if she would put on women's clothes, see Tisset, *Condamnation*, I, pp. 156–8, 167–8, 182–3 (trans. French in Tisset, *Condamnation*, II, pp. 133–4, 139–40, 149–50; English in Hobbins, *Trial*, pp. 105–6, 110, 117, and Taylor, *Joan of Arc*, pp. 193–4, 198–9, 204–5).

For the visit to Joan's cell on Wednesday 18 April, see Tisset, *Condamnation*, I, pp. 327–33 (quotations from pp. 329, 330, 332) (trans. French in Tisset, *Condamnation*, II, pp. 284–8; English in Hobbins, *Trial*, pp. 166–9).

For Cauchon's birth probably in 1371, see Neveux, *L'Evêque Pierre Cauchon*, p. 7.

For the session on Wednesday 2 May, see Tisset, *Condamnation*, I, pp. 333–48 (quotations pp. 337, 342–3, 346–7) (trans. French in Tisset, *Condamnation*, II, pp. 288–301; English in Hobbins, *Trial*, pp. 169–78).

For the threat of torture on Wednesday 9 May, see Tisset, *Condamnation*, I, pp. 348–50 (quotation from p. 349) (trans. French in Tisset, *Condamnation*, II, pp. 301–2; English in Hobbins, *Trial*, pp. 178–9). The following session on 12 May consisted of the judges' deliberations about whether or not they should proceed to the use of torture: see Tisset, *Condamnation*, I, pp. 350–2 (trans. French in Tisset, *Condamnation*, II, pp. 302–4; English in Hobbins, *Trial*, pp. 179–80). In the session after that, on 19 May, Cauchon and fifty-one advisers met to consider the opinions on the case sent by the faculties of theology and canon law at the university of Paris: Tisset, *Condamnation*, I, pp. 352–74 (trans. French in Tisset, *Condamnation*, II, pp. 304–25; English in Taylor, *Joan of Arc*, pp. 213–16, and summary in Hobbins, *Trial*, pp. 180–4).

For the final hearing (Wednesday 23 May), see Tisset, *Condamnation*, I, pp. 374–85 (quotations from pp. 376, 380, 383–4) (trans. French in Tisset,

Condamnation, II, pp. 325–35; English in Hobbins, *Trial*, pp. 184–90).

For Pierre Maurice's age, see Tisset, *Condamnation*, I, p. 418 (trans. French in Tisset, *Condamnation*, II, p. 364; English in Hobbins, *Trial*, p. 205); for his career, see Tisset, *Condamnation*, II, p. 417.

For proceedings at Saint-Ouen, and events afterwards, on Thursday 24 May, see Tisset, *Condamnation*, I, pp. 385–94 (quotation from p. 386), (trans. French in Tisset, *Condamnation*, II, pp. 335–43; English in Hobbins, *Trial*, pp. 190–2, and Taylor, *Joan of Arc*, pp. 216–19).

For Joan previously asking to be taken to the pope (on 17 March and 2 May), see Tisset, *Condamnation*, I, pp. 176, 343 (quotation from p. 343) (trans. French in Tisset, *Condamnation*, II, pp. 144, 298; English in Hobbins, *Trial*, pp. 113, 176, and, for 17 March, Taylor, *Joan of Arc*, p. 202).

For the executioner waiting with his cart, see the testimony of Guillaume Manchon in 1456: Duparc, *Nullité*, I, pp. 425, 427 (trans. French in Duparc, *Nullité*, IV, pp. 106, 108; English in Taylor, *Joan of Arc*, pp. 328, 330).

For the discovery of Joan's relapse and the visit to her cell on Monday 28 May, see Tisset, *Condamnation*, I, pp. 395–9 (quotation from p. 398) (trans. French in Tisset, *Condamnation*, II, pp. 344–6; English in Hobbins, *Trial*, pp. 196–8, and Taylor, *Joan of Arc*, pp. 220–2); and see discussion of Joan's distressed state in Sullivan, *Interrogation*, pp. 131–9.

For discussion of Joan's resumption of male clothing, see Hobbins, *Trial*, pp. 24–6, and above, pp. 225–6, for the suggestion in 1456 that she might have found herself under threat or coercion, albeit that the stories varied in their detail. Certainly, the fact that men's clothes were still available to her in her cell suggests that someone had an interest in the possibility of her relapse.

For the hearing of Tuesday 29 May, see Tisset, *Condamnation*, I, pp. 399–408 (trans. French in Tisset, *Condamnation*, II, pp. 346–53; English in Hobbins, *Trial*, pp. 198–9).

For the visit to Joan's cell on the morning of Wednesday 30 May, see the witness statements compiled on 7 June in Tisset, *Condamnation*, I, pp. 416–22 (quotation from p. 418) (trans. French in Tisset, *Condamnation*, II, pp. 362–8; English in Hobbins, *Trial*, pp. 204–9). Many historians have been reluctant to accept the evidence contained in these statements, on the grounds that they were recorded eight days after the event and not signed by the notaries. Larissa Juliet Taylor, for example, mentions them only in an endnote, to say that 'additions to the trial transcript were made on June 7 but *not* signed by the trial notaries, including a falsified confession' (her emphasis, *Virgin Warrior*, p. 236n). However, this is an endnote appended to a part of Taylor's text entirely derived from witness statements given twenty-five years after the event, in the context of a no less politicised inquiry than that of 1431. The absence of the notaries' signatures can straightforwardly be explained by the fact that they were not there to witness the meeting of 30 May; and they were not there to witness it because, in the terms by which the trial was conducted, this was a pastoral visit concerned with saving Joan's soul, not a judicial one, since the fate of her body was already decided. Certainly, the judges and the English had an interest in Joan being seen to renounce her claims, and the fact that these statements were taken down and added to the trial transcript is undoubtedly significant, but if their account of Joan's words were wholly falsified – a suggestion for which there is no evidence – it is hard not to believe that the confession put into her mouth would have been, on the one hand, more fulsome and dramatic, and, on the other, less psychologically detailed and convincing. As a whole, the description of Joan on her last morning derived from these testimonies seems to me to be consistent with the distress evident in her last formal interview on 28 May. It presents a psychologically plausible account of her voices and visions: for example, several witnesses at the nullification trial spoke of her love for the ringing of bells (see pp. 234, 238). It also presents a plausible explanation of her story of her 'sign' as an angel presenting a golden crown to the king – something which has not become a part of her myth in the same way as the communication she claimed with Saints Catherine, Margaret and Michael, precisely because it seems to strain credulity too far. Joan's acknowledgement of error also helps to explain why she was allowed that morning to make confession and take communion, an unusual privilege for a relapsed heretic. I see no reason not to take the evidence recorded on 7 June as seriously, and carefully, as the rest of the evidence from the two trials. See discussion in Hobbins, *Trial*, pp. 12–13; Sullivan, *Interrogation*, pp. 71–81, 139–48.

For the official transcript of Joan's final sentencing on 30 May, see Tisset, *Condamnation*, I, pp. 408–14 (quotation from p. 410) (trans. French in Tisset, *Condamnation*, II, pp. 353–60; English in Hobbins, *Trial*, pp. 199–202, and Taylor, *Joan of Arc*, pp. 222–4).

For the cap Joan wore to the stake, see the journal of Clément de Fauquembergue in Quicherat, *Procès*, IV, p. 459, and English translation in Taylor, *Joan of Arc*, p. 228.

For the English soldiers, and Joan saying the name of Jesus amid the flames, see, for example, testimony given in 1450: Doncoeur and Lanhers (eds), *L'Enquête ordonnée par Charles VII*, pp. 38–9 (Isambard de la Pierre), 44–5 (Martin Lavenu), 51 (Guillaume Manchon), 56 (Jean Massieu).

11: THOSE WHO CALLED THEMSELVES FRENCHMEN

For Bedford's move to Paris and the convoy of supplies, see *Journal*, pp. 261–2 (trans. *Parisian Journal*, pp. 255–6); J. Stevenson (ed.), *Letters and Papers Illustrative of the Wars of the English in France*, II, part II (London, 1864), pp. 424–6.

For Bedford on campaign, see Ramsay, *Lancaster and York*, p. 431.

For Henry VI's letters to the emperor and to the lords and cities of France, see Tisset, *Condamnation*, I, pp. 423–30 (trans. French in Tisset, *Condamnation*, II, pp. 368–76; English in Hobbins, *Trial*, pp. 209–11, and second letter in Taylor, *Joan of Arc*, pp. 225–8). Griffiths suggests (*Reign of King Henry VI*, p. 220) that the duke of Bedford wrote the text, but that seems unlikely given how little he had to do with the process of the trial, and that he was not in Rouen in June, where the letters were dated.

For Jean Graverent's sermon in Paris, and the account of Joan's execution, see *Journal*, pp. 266–72 (trans. *Parisian Journal*, pp. 260–5).

For the writing up of the Latin transcript of the trial, see Hobbins, *Trial*, pp. 5–6, 8–13. Cauchon addressed the transcript 'to all who will read the present letters or public instrument': Tisset, *Condamnation*, I, p. 1 (trans. French in Tisset, *Condamnation*, II, p. 1; English in Hobbins, *Trial*, p. 33).

For the letter from Bruges to Venice reporting St Catherine's words, see Morosini, *Chronique*, III, pp. 348–57.

For the letter of the archbishop of Reims, see Quicherat, *Procès*, V, pp. 168–9, and above, p. 160.

For comment and information about William the Shepherd collected from the Parisian journal and the chronicles of Jean Le Févre, Monstrelet, the Berry herald and Jean Chartier, see Quicherat, *Procès*, V, pp. 169–73.

For the fall of Louviers and Château Gaillard to the English, see Barker, *Conquest*, pp. 151, 169–70.

For King Henry's entry into Paris, see *Journal*, pp. 274–6 (trans. *Parisian Journal*, pp. 268–71); F. W. D. Brie (ed.), *The Brut, or the Chronicles of England*, I (London, 1906), pp. 459–60; Monstrelet, *Chronique*, V, pp. 2–4; G. L. Thompson, *Paris and Its People under English Rule: The Anglo-Burgundian Regime, 1420–1436* (Oxford, 1991), pp. 199–205, 244–6; Curry, '"Coronation Expedition"', p. 49.

For the death of William the Shepherd, as reported by Jean Le Févre, see Quicherat, *Procès*, V, p. 171.

For the coronation and feast, see *Journal*, pp. 277–8 (trans. *Parisian Journal*, pp. 271–2); Brie (ed.), *The Brut*, I, pp. 460–1; Monstrelet, *Chronique*, V pp. 5–6.

For tension at the coronation, and arguments afterwards, see Monstrelet, *Chronique*, V, p. 5; *Journal*, pp. 277–9 (trans. *Parisian Journal*, pp. 271–3).

For decreasing English familiarity with the French language, and the divergence between English pronunciation of French and that of the Parisians, see Thompson, *Paris*, pp. 214–16.

For Henry VI leaving Paris, and the wintry weather, see *Journal*, pp. 279–80 (trans. *Parisian Journal*, pp. 273–4); Curry, '"Coronation Expedition"', pp. 50–1.

For Philip of Burgundy's angry letter on the subject of Compiègne, written in November 1430, see Vaughan, *Philip the Good*, pp. 24–5. The duke blamed inadequate funding despite the large sums he had already received and his generous monthly pension from the English king: see pp. 17–18.

Philip was welcomed into Brussels as the new duke of Brabant on 8 October 1430: Vaughan, *Philip the Good*, p. 52.

For Burgundy's absence from the coronation, see Armstrong, 'Double Monarchie', pp. 105–6.

For Burgundian–Armagnac truces sealed in September and December 1431, see Vaughan, *Philip the Good*, p. 26; Plancher, *Histoire générale et particulière de Bourgogne*, IV, documents 79, 90, 93; Beaucourt, *Charles VII*, II, p. 442.

For the conspiracies of 1432 and Bedford's failure at Lagny, see Barker, *Conquest*, pp. 180–6.

For the death of Anne of Burgundy, see *Journal*, pp. 289–90 (trans. *Parisian Journal*, p. 282); also Monstrelet, *Chronique*, V, pp. 44–5. The polyphonic singing – which was 'most moving', according to the journal-writer – was a particular skill perfected by English musicians in the early fifteenth century: Harriss, *Shaping the Nation*, pp. 328–9.

For Albergati as an 'angel of peace', see Beaucourt, *Charles VII*, II, p. 440.

For English concerns about treaties made during Henry's minority, see Griffiths, *Reign of King Henry VI*, p. 192.

For details of the Auxerre conference, and the preceding diplomacy, see Beaucourt, *Charles VII*, II, pp. 443–52.

'*and they had done nothing . . .*': *Journal*, p. 290 (trans. *Parisian Journal*, pp. 282–3).

For the marriage of Bedford to Jacquetta de Luxembourg, see Monstrelet, *Chronique*, V, pp. 55–6; Armstrong, 'Double Monarchie', pp. 108–9; Barker, *Conquest*, pp. 189–90.

For events at Saint-Omer, see Monstrelet, *Chronique*, V, pp. 57–8; Armstrong, 'Double Monarchie', p. 109; Barker, *Conquest*, p. 190.

For Yolande, the treaty with Brittany and rapprochement with Richemont, see

Beaucourt, *Charles VII*, II, pp. 279–84; Cosneau, *Connétable*, pp. 189–91; Vale, *Charles VII*, p. 71.

For the coup against La Trémoille, see Beaucourt, *Charles VII*, II, pp. 297–8; Cosneau, *Connétable*, pp. 200–1; Chartier, *Chronique*, I, pp. 170–1.

For the fighting in 1433–4, see Barker, *Conquest*, pp. 191–2, 196–209.

'*The war grew worse and worse . . .*' and '*they might as well have been dead*': *Journal*, pp. 299–300 (trans. *Parisian Journal*, pp. 289–90).

For Bedford's memorandum of 1434, see H. Nicolas (ed.), *Proceedings and Ordinances of the Privy Council of England*, IV (London, 1835), pp. 223–4; excerpt in Taylor, *Joan of Arc*, p. 239.

For the dreadful winter of 1434–5, see *Journal*, pp. 302–3 (trans. *Parisian Journal*, pp. 292–3); Brie (ed.), *The Brut*, I, p. 571.

For snow sculptures in Arras, see Vaughan, *Philip the Good*, p. 67; for '*la grande Pucelle*' and Joan passing through Arras in 1430, see J. van Herwaarden, 'The appearance of Joan of Arc', in J. van Herwaarden (ed.), *Joan of Arc: Reality and Myth* (Hilversum, 1994), pp. 22–3 and nn.

For the conference at Nevers: Beaucourt, *Charles VII*, II, pp. 514–17; Vaughan, *Philip the Good*, p. 67; Monstrelet, *Chronique*, V, pp. 107–9.

For the hostility of the Holy Roman Emperor, and his declaration of war on the duke of Burgundy in December 1434, see Vaughan, *Philip the Good*, pp. 67–72.

For the congress of Arras, see J. G. Dickinson, *The Congress of Arras, 1435* (Oxford, 1955), chs 6 and 7; Beaucourt, *Charles VII*, II, pp. 523–59; Harriss, *Cardinal Beaufort*, pp. 247–52; Vaughan, *Philip the Good*, pp. 98–101.

For the hangings in the hall of the abbey, see A. de la Taverne, *Journal de la paix d'Arras* (Paris, 1651), p. 6.

For attendance at the congress, see Monstrelet, *Chronique*, V, pp. 132–8 (with Monstrelet's brave attempts at spelling difficult English surnames and place-names), 150–1; Chartier, *Chronique*, I, pp. 185–92.

For the warmth of interaction between the Burgundians and Armagnacs, and the unhappiness of the English, see Monstrelet, *Chronique*, V, pp. 143–4.

For Suffolk's release and ransom, see J. Watts, 'Pole, William de la, first duke of Suffolk (1396–1450)', *ODNB*.

For Beaufort's efforts, including his sweaty conversation, see Taverne, *Journal de la paix*, p. 71; Harriss, *Cardinal Beaufort*, p. 251.

For torrential rain when the English left, see Taverne, *Journal de la paix*, p. 79; for the embroidery on the sleeves of the cardinal's men, see 'Le Livre des trahisons de France' in *Chroniques relatives à l'histoire de la Belgique*, ed. K. de Lettenhove (Brussels, 1872), p. 210.

For Burgundian justifications for abrogating the treaty of Troyes, see
Dickinson, *Congress of Arras*, pp. 174–7.

Requiem mass for John the Fearless: Beaucourt, *Charles VII*, II, p. 544.

For Bedford's death on 14 September, and news reaching Arras, see J.
Stratford, 'John, duke of Bedford (1389–1435)', *ODNB*; Beaucourt, *Charles
VII*, II, p. 546.

For the ceremony at Saint-Vaast on 21 September, see Dickinson, *Congress of
Arras*, pp. 179–85; Monstrelet, *Chronique*, V, p. 183.

For the court at Bourges waiting for news from Arras, see Beaucourt, *Charles
VII*, II, p. 308; for the birth of baby Philip at Tours on 4 February 1436, and
the identity of his godfather, see Beaucourt, *Charles VII*, III, p. 33.

For the Armagnac campaigns in Normandy and around Paris in late 1435 and
early 1436, see Barker, *Conquest*, pp. 231–8.

For the attempt at defending Paris by the three bishops, see *Journal*, pp. 312–13
(trans. *Parisian Journal*, pp. 300–1); Thompson, *Paris*, pp. 228–34.

For the entry of the Armagnac forces into Paris, see *Journal*, pp. 314–18 (trans.
Parisian Journal, pp. 302–6); Thompson, *Paris*, pp. 235–6.

For Parisian disenchantment by the autumn, see *Journal*, p. 327 (trans. *Parisian
Journal*, p. 312).

For the king's entry into Paris, see Monstrelet, *Chronique*, V, pp. 301–7; T.
Godefroy (ed.), *Le Cérémonial françois* (Paris, 1649), pp. 654–8; *Journal*, pp.
334–6 (trans. *Parisian Journal*, pp. 319–20); Vale, *Charles VII*, pp. 198–201.

For the exhumation of the count of Armagnac, see Monstrelet, *Chronique*, V,
p. 307.

For King Charles's court remaining in the castles of the Loire, see, for
example, Beaucourt, *Charles VII*, III, pp. 56–7.

For fading English hopes, and new English leaders, see Barker, *Conquest*, pp.
235, 246–9.

Problems at the French court, including the resistance of 1437 and connections
between the *écorcheurs* and the duke of Bourbon: Beaucourt, *Charles VII*, III,
pp. 41–8.

For the military reforms of November 1439, see Beaucourt, *Charles VII*, III,
pp. 384–416.

For the revolt of 1440, known as the Praguerie, see Beaucourt, *Charles VII*, III,
pp. 115–42 ('*humility and obedience*', quotation from royal letters patent, pp.
133–4); Vale, *Charles VII*, pp. 76–82.

For the death of Yolande and the rise of Agnès Sorel, see Vale, *Charles VII*, pp.
91–3.

For Henry VI, see J. Watts, *Henry VI and the Politics of Kingship* (Cambridge,

1996), chs 4 and 5.

For negotiations led by the earl of Suffolk in 1444–5, see Watts, 'Pole, William de la', *ODNB*; Harriss, *Shaping the Nation*, pp. 576–7; Barker, *Conquest*, pp. 316–19, 323–37.

For the collapse of the English position and the French advance, see Harriss, *Shaping the Nation*, pp. 577–83; Barker, *Conquest*, chs 22–5.

For Cherbourg, see Barker, *Conquest*, pp. 398–9.

For the text of the letter from the council at Rouen in 1441, see Stevenson (ed.), *Letters and Papers*, II, part II, pp. 603–7.

For the surrender of the town of Rouen on 16 October, and the surrender of Beaufort in the castle on 29 October, see Barker, *Conquest*, pp. 390–1.

For the king's entry into Rouen, see Godefroy (ed.), *Le Cérémonial françois*, pp. 659–63.

For Joan's ashes being thrown into the river, see the 'Chronicle of the Cordeliers' in Taylor, *Joan of Arc*, p. 238.

12: SHE WAS ALL INNOCENCE

'*It seemed to the Greeks an impossible thing*': see Bertrandon de la Broquière, *Le Voyage d'outremer*, ed. C. Schefer (Paris, 1892) p. 165.

For celebrations on 8 May at Orléans, and the *Mystère du siège d'Orléans*, see, for example, Quicherat, *Procès*, V, pp. 79–82, 285–99.

For Gilles de Rais and his extravagant expenditure on the play, see E. Bossard, *Gilles de Rais, maréchal de France, dit Barbe-Bleue (1404–1440)* (Paris, 1886), pp. 94–116; J. Benedetti, *Gilles de Rais* (London, 1971), pp. 128, 132–3; E. Odio, 'Gilles de Rais: Hero, Spendthrift, and Psychopathic Child Murderer of the Later Hundred Years War', in L. J. A. Villalon and D. J. Kagay (eds), *The Hundred Years War (Part III): Further Considerations* (Leiden/Boston, 2013), pp. 167–8, and, for de Rais's later career, 170–85.

For all documents relating to the career of 'Claude des Armoises', see Quicherat, *Procès*, V, pp. 321–36 (quotation from the accounts of the town of Orléans, p. 331); *Journal*, pp. 354–5 (trans. *Parisian Journal*, pp. 337–8). See also V. de Viriville (trans. and ed.), *Procès de condamnation de Jeanne d'Arc* (Paris, 1867), pp. lxix–lxxi; and Pernoud, *Joan of Arc: By Herself and Her Witnesses*, pp. 242–7.

For the king's letter to Guillaume Bouillé, 15 February 1450, see Doncoeur and Lanhers (eds), *L'Enquête ordonnée par Charles VII*, pp. 33, 35, and English translation in Taylor, *Joan of Arc*, pp. 259–60.

For Bouillé, see Doncoeur and Lanhers (eds), *L'Enquête ordonnée par Charles VII*, p. 58.

De la Pierre said 'the English' threatened to throw him into the Seine, while Duval named the earl of Warwick: Doncoeur and Lanhers (eds), *L'Enquête ordonnée par Charles VII*, pp. 36–7, 46–7.

For testimony concerning English pressure on the trial process, see Doncoeur and Lanhers (eds), *L'Enquête ordonnée par Charles VII*, pp. 36–7 (de la Pierre), 40–1 (Jean Toutmouillé), 42–5 (Lavenu), 46-7 (Duval), 48 (Manchon), 54 (Massieu).

For Manchon's testimony concerning Loiseleur the spy, see Doncoeur and Lanhers (eds), *L'Enquête ordonnée par Charles VII*, p. 48. Note that Loiseleur was present among the clerics in many of the hearings at which Joan appeared (see Hobbins, *Trial*, pp. 57, 63, 70, 77, 178), so that, unless he was in deep disguise when he visited her cell (as was later, rather implausibly, suggested, for which, see pp. 241, 303–4), she must have known that he was involved in the trial process.

'*Farewell! It is done*': Doncoeur and Lanhers (eds), *L'Enquête ordonnée par Charles VII*, pp. 42–3. De la Pierre (pp. 36–7) also mentioned this comment, but gave Cauchon's words as 'Farewell! Farewell! Be of good cheer. It is done.'

For testimony concerning Joan's resumption of male clothing, see Doncoeur and Lanhers (eds), *L'Enquête ordonnée par Charles VII*, pp. 36–7 (de la Pierre), 40–1 (Toutmouillé), 44–5 (Lavenu), 54 (Massieu).

For testimony concerning Joan's death, see Doncoeur and Lanhers (eds), *L'Enquête ordonnée par Charles VII*, pp. 38–9 (de la Pierre), 51 (Manchon), 55–6 (Massieu).

For testimony concerning the executioner, see Doncoeur and Lanhers (eds), *L'Enquête ordonnée par Charles VII*, pp. 38–9 (de la Pierre), 44–5 (Lavenu).

For the testimony of Jean Beaupère, see Doncoeur and Lanhers (eds), *L'Enquête ordonnée par Charles VII*, pp. 56–7.

For Bouillé's treatise, see Doncoeur and Lanhers (eds), *L'Enquête ordonnée par Charles VII*, pp. 65–119, and, for his keenness to exonerate Joan, pp. 66–9.

For Raoul Roussel, see Doncoeur and Lanhers (eds), *L'Enquête ordonnée par Charles VII*, p. 11; Vale, *Charles VII*, p. 61; Godefroy (ed.), *Le Cérémonial françois*, pp. 661–3.

For d'Estouteville, his commission from the pope, and reopening the inquiry, see Vale, *Charles VII*, pp. 62–3; Pernoud and Clin, *Joan of Arc: Her Story*, p. 151.

'*greatly concerns your honour and estate*': Vale, *Charles VII*, p. 63; Taylor, *Joan of Arc*, pp. 260–1.

For Jean Bréhal, see Vale, *Charles VII*, pp. 63–4.

For the articles of accusation drafted in 1452 (first twelve, then twenty-seven), see Duparc, *Nullité*, I, pp. 177–9, 191–6 (trans. French in Duparc, *Nullité*, III, pp. 167–9, 181–5; the twenty-seven articles trans. English in Pernoud and Clin, *Joan of Arc: Her Story*, pp. 152–5).

For the witness statements of 1452, see Duparc, *Nullité*, I, pp. 181–90, 196–244 (trans. French in Duparc, *Nullité*, III, pp. 170–9, 185–232).

For de la Pierre's story of the English soldier, see Duparc, *Nullité*, I, pp. 224–5 (trans. French in Duparc, *Nullité*, III, p. 212).

For testimony defending the reliability of the trial transcript, see Duparc, *Nullité*, I, pp. 197, 199 (Nicolas Taquel), 207 (Massieu), 215, 217 (Manchon), 223 (de la Pierre), 228 (Richard de Grouchet), 232–3 (Pierre Miget), 234 (Lavenu), 243 (Jean Fave) (trans. French in Duparc, *Nullité*, III, pp. 187–8, 196, 203, 205, 211, 216, 219–20, 222, 231).

For testimony that Joan answered well, see Duparc, *Nullité*, I, pp. 198 (Taquel), 208 (Massieu), 213 (Guillaume du Désert), 216 (Manchon), 229 (Grouchet), 239 (Thomas Marie), 241 (Riquier) (trans. French in Duparc, *Nullité*, III, pp. 187, 197, 201, 204, 217, 227, 229).

For testimony that Cauchon was of the English party (though note that explicit statements to this effect came in response to one of the twelve articles which asked the question explicitly in that form; the twenty-seven articles were worded differently, asking about English threats and pressure, and therefore received more nuanced answers), see Duparc, *Nullité*, I, pp. 181 (Manchon), 184 (Miget), 185 (de la Pierre), 189 (Lavenu), 203 (Nicolas de Houppeville), 214 (Manchon again), 221 (de la Pierre again) (trans. French in Duparc, *Nullité*, III, pp. 171, 173, 175–6, 178, 192, 203, 209).

For Cauchon standing up to the English cleric at Saint-Ouen, see Duparc, *Nullité*, I, pp. 200 (Pierre Bouchier), 227 (André Marguerie), 231 (Miget) (trans. French in Duparc, *Nullité*, III, pp. 189, 215, 219).

For Nicolas Caval remembering very little, see Duparc, *Nullité*, I, pp. 211–12 (trans. French in Duparc, *Nullité*, III, pp. 199–200).

For Bréhal gathering expert opinions, see Duparc, *Nullité*, II, ch. 8 (a collection of texts which includes Gerson's *De mirabili victoria* and Bouillé's treatise of 1450).

For Talbot, Castillon, and the English loss of Gascony, see A. J. Pollard, 'Talbot, John, first earl of Shrewsbury and first earl of Waterford (*c.*1387–1453)', *ODNB*; Harriss, *Shaping the Nation*, pp. 584–5.

For Roussel's death, see Tisset, *Condamnation*, II, p. 422; for d'Estouteville's appointment as archbishop of Rouen, see Pernoud, *Joan of Arc: By Herself and Her Witnesses*, p. 263.

Charles as *le roi très-victorieux*: see Doncoeur and Lanhers (eds), *L'Enquête ordonnée par Charles VII*, pp. 68–9, for Guillaume Bouillé addressing the king in 1450 as '*rex victoriosissimus*'. See also the inscription on his portrait, plate section.

For the sack of Constantinople, see E. Zachariadou, 'The Ottoman World', in Allmand (ed.), *New Cambridge Medieval History VII*, pp. 824–5.

For Bréhal's journey to Rome and the papal letter of 1455, see Duparc, *Nullité*, I, pp. 18–20 (trans. French in Duparc, *Nullité*, III, pp. 16–18; English in Taylor, *Joan of Arc*, pp. 262–4); Pernoud, *Joan of Arc: By Herself and Her Witnesses*, p. 264. For the advice of Jean de Montigny that Joan's family should act as plaintiffs, see Duparc, *Nullité*, II, p. 312.

For the ceremony of 7 November 1455, see Duparc, *Nullité*, I, pp. 8–11 (trans. French in Duparc, *Nullité*, III, pp. 7–10; Isabelle's petition in English in Taylor, *Joan of Arc*, pp. 264–5).

For Isabelle living at Orléans, see Pernoud, *Joan of Arc: By Herself and Her Witnesses*, p. 264.

For the crowd gathering, and the family's discussion with the commissioners, see Duparc, *Nullité*, I, pp. 11–16 (trans. French in Duparc, *Nullité*, III, pp. 10–14).

For the hearing in the episcopal court on 17 November and the commissioners' decision to proceed, see Duparc, *Nullité*, I, pp. 16–41 (trans. French in Duparc, *Nullité*, III, pp. 14–36).

Appointment of promoter and notaries: Duparc, *Nullité*, I, pp. 64–6 (trans. French in Duparc, *Nullité*, III, pp. 58–9).

Scrutiny of Manchon's French minute of the trial and the investigation of 1452: Duparc, *Nullité*, I, pp. 67–70 (trans. French in Duparc, *Nullité*, III, pp. 61–3).

For the 101 articles, see Duparc, *Nullité*, I, pp. 111–50 (trans. French in Duparc, *Nullité*, III, pp. 103–44).

Most of the articles of inquiry on which the witnesses were to be examined do not survive, apart from those for the investigation in Joan's home region, for which see Duparc, *Nullité*, I, pp. 250–1 (trans. French in Duparc, *Nullité*, III, pp. 238–9; English in Taylor, *Joan of Arc*, pp. 255–6).

For the older villagers remembering Joan as dutiful and hardworking 'Jeannette', see Duparc, *Nullité*, I, pp. 252–4 (Jean Morel, her godfather, whose comment is on p. 253), 257–8 (Béatrice, widow of Estellin), 259–60 (Jeannette, wife of Thévenin), 261–2 (Jean Moen), 263–4 (Jeannette, widow of Thiesselin), 266–7 (Thévenin le Royer), 267–8 (Jaquier de Saint-Amant), 269 (Bertrand Lacloppe), 270–2 (Perrin Drappier), 278–9 (Gérardin d'Épinal) (trans. French in Duparc, *Nullité*, III, pp. 240–2, 245–6,

247–8, 249–50, 251–2, 254–5, 255–6, 257, 258–9, 266–7; Morel and Béatrice
in English in Taylor, *Joan of Arc*, pp. 267–9).

Hauviette's memories of Joan as her friend: Duparc, *Nullité*, I, p. 276 (trans.
French in Duparc, *Nullité*, III, p. 264).

For the boys teasing Joan, and her kneeling in the fields when she heard
the bells, see Duparc, *Nullité*, I, pp. 277 (Jean Waterin), 280–1 (Simonin
Musnier), 287 (Colin, son of Jean Colin) (trans. French in Duparc, *Nullité*,
III, pp. 265, 268, 275). Her godfather Jean Morel also said that she was
teased: Duparc, *Nullité*, I, p. 253 (trans. French in Duparc, *Nullité*, III, p.
241; English in Taylor, *Joan of Arc*, p. 268).

For the testimony of Perrin Drappier, see Duparc, *Nullité*, I, p. 271 (trans.
French in Duparc, *Nullité*, III, p. 259).

Those who remembered Laxart saying that he had lied to Joan's father:
Duparc, *Nullité*, I, pp. 283 (Isabelle, wife of Gérardin), 285 (Mengette, wife
of Jean Joyart), 288 (Colin) (trans. French in Duparc, *Nullité*, III, pp. 271,
273, 276).

For the testimony of Durand Laxart, see Duparc, *Nullité*, I, pp. 295–7 (trans.
French in Duparc, *Nullité*, III, pp. 282–4; English in Taylor, *Joan of Arc*, pp.
273–4).

For Catherine and Henri le Royer, see Duparc, *Nullité*, I, pp. 298, 299–300
(trans. French in Duparc, *Nullité*, III, pp. 285, 286–7; Catherine in English in
Taylor, *Joan of Arc*, p. 275).

For the testimony of Jean de Metz and Bertrand de Poulengy, see Duparc,
Nullité, I, pp. 289–92, 304–7 (trans. French in Duparc, *Nullité*, III, pp. 276–
9, 291–4; English in Taylor, *Joan of Arc*, pp. 271–3, 275–7).

For the lack of carnal impulses, see Duparc, *Nullité*, I, pp. 325 (Bastard), 378
(La Touroulde), 387 (Alençon), 486 (d'Aulon) (all apart from d'Aulon
trans. French in Duparc, *Nullité*, IV, pp. 10, 61, 70; the Bastard, Alençon
and d'Aulon in English in Taylor, *Joan of Arc*, pp. 284, 309, 347). The royal
squire Gobert Thibaut said he had heard soldiers who had fought alongside
Joan say that, if they did have carnal desires, the feelings went away when
they thought of her: Duparc, *Nullité*, I, p. 370 (trans. French in Duparc,
Nullité, IV, p. 54).

'*the secret malady of women*': see the testimony of d'Aulon in Duparc, *Nullité*,
I, p. 486 (trans. English in Taylor, *Joan of Arc*, p. 347).

Simon Charles and the call of nature: Duparc, *Nullité*, I, p. 402 (trans. French
in Duparc, *Nullité*, IV, p. 84).

Joan as an innocent: see the testimony of Marguerite La Touroulde in Duparc,
Nullité, I, 378 (trans. French in Duparc, *Nullité*, IV, pp. 61–2).

Her confidence on the battlefield: see the testimony of Alençon in Duparc, *Nullité*, I, pp. 387–8 (trans. French in Duparc, *Nullité*, IV, p. 70; English in Taylor, *Joan of Arc*, p. 310).

For her intolerance of swearing in general, see Duparc, *Nullité*, I, pp. 327 (Gaucourt), 330 (Ricarville), 339 (André Bordes), 340 (Renaude, widow of Huré), 370 (Thibaut), 373 (Simon Beaucroix), 409 (Pierre Milet) (trans. French in Duparc, *Nullité*, IV, pp. 12, 15, 23, 25, 54, 57, 90; Beaucroix in English in Taylor, *Joan of Arc*, p. 301). Louis de Coutes said she had reproved the duke of Alençon for swearing, and the theologian Seguin Seguin recalled her chastising La Hire: Duparc, *Nullité*, I, pp. 367, 473 (trans. French in Duparc, *Nullité*, IV, pp. 51, 152; English in Taylor, *Joan of Arc*, pp. 298, 338).

For Joan chasing women away from the camp, see Duparc, *Nullité*, I, pp. 367 (Coutes), 373–4 (Beaucroix), 387 (Alençon), 409 (Milet) (trans. French in Duparc, *Nullité*, IV, pp. 51, 57, 69–70, 90; Coutes, Beaucroix and Alençon in English in Taylor, *Joan of Arc*, pp. 298, 302, 309).

For Joan's sparing appetite: Duparc, *Nullité*, I, pp. 327 (Gaucourt), 329 (Ricarville), 364 (Coutes), 408 (Colette, wife of Pierre Milet) (trans. French in Duparc, *Nullité*, IV, pp. 12, 15, 49, 89; Coutes in English in Taylor, *Joan of Arc*, p. 296).

For Joan refusing to eat stolen food, see Duparc, *Nullité*, I, pp. 373 (Beaucroix), 396 (Pasquerel) (trans. French in Duparc, *Nullité*, IV, pp. 57, 78; English in Taylor, *Joan of Arc*, pp. 302, 316).

For Joan forbidding plunder and protecting churches, see Duparc, *Nullité*, I, pp. 330 (Regnauld Thierry), 373 (Beaucroix), 409 (Milet) (trans. French in Duparc, *Nullité*, IV, pp. 15, 57, 90; Beaucroix in English in Taylor, *Joan of Arc*, p. 302).

For Joan asking her troops to confess their sins: Duparc, *Nullité*, I, pp. 338 (Pierre Compaing), 363 (Coutes), 373 (Beaucroix), 391 (Pasquerel) (trans. French in Duparc, *Nullité*, IV, pp. 23, 47, 57, 73; Coutes and Pasquerel in English in Taylor, *Joan of Arc*, pp. 295, 313).

Joan's pity for those who died without absolution: Duparc, *Nullité*, I, pp. 366 (Coutes), 392 (Pasquerel) (trans. French in Duparc, *Nullité*, IV, pp. 50, 75; English in Taylor, *Joan of Arc*, pp. 297, 314).

'*she did God's work*': Duparc, *Nullité*, I, p. 402 (trans. French in Duparc, *Nullité*, IV, p. 84).

For the Bastard and the miracle of the wind, see Duparc, *Nullité*, I, pp. 318–19 (trans. French in Duparc, *Nullité*, IV, pp. 4–5; English in Taylor, *Joan of Arc*, pp. 279–80).

For Pasquerel and the miracle of the water, see Duparc, *Nullité*, I, pp. 391–2 (trans. French in Duparc, *Nullité*, IV, p. 74; English in Taylor, *Joan of Arc*, p. 313).

For Alençon's memory of Joan saving his life, see Duparc, *Nullité*, I, pp. 384–5 (trans. French in Duparc, *Nullité*, IV, pp. 67–8; English in Taylor, *Joan of Arc*, p. 307). For the duke's illness and bitterness by the 1450s, see Vale, *Charles VII*, pp. 159–60.

For Jean Barbin's memory of the comments of Jean Érault, see Duparc, *Nullité*, I, p. 375 (trans. French in Duparc, *Nullité*, IV, p. 59; English in Taylor, *Joan of Arc*, p. 303). In the surviving text that records Marie Robine's visions, there is one that speaks of a burning wheel with weapons (for which, see above, p. 72), but no mention of a Maid to come. In other words, the only mention of this version of the prophecy is here, in Barbin's memory of what Érault had said twenty-five years earlier.

For the Bastard's memory of Joan asking for the bells to be rung, and her description of her voice, see Duparc, *Nullité*, I, pp. 323–4 (trans. French in Duparc, *Nullité*, IV, pp. 8–9; English in Taylor, *Joan of Arc*, pp. 283–4).

For Jean d'Aulon's conversation with Joan about her revelations, see Duparc, *Nullité*, I, pp. 486–7 (trans. English in Taylor, *Joan of Arc*, pp. 347–8).

For Joan's conversation with Seguin Seguin, see Duparc, *Nullité*, I, pp. 471–2 (trans. French in Duparc, *Nullité*, IV, pp. 150–1; English in Taylor, *Joan of Arc*, pp. 337–8).

For Nicolas Caval's even briefer statement, see Duparc, *Nullité*, I, p. 451 (trans. French in Duparc, *Nullité*, IV, pp. 130–1).

For the statement of Jean de Mailly, see Duparc, *Nullité*, I, pp. 353–5 (trans. French in Duparc, *Nullité*, IV, pp. 37–9). De Mailly had been a counsellor to King Henry, represented the duke of Burgundy at Arras in 1435 and received King Charles into Noyon in 1443: Tisset, *Condamnation*, II, pp. 414–15.

For the testimony of Thomas de Courcelles, see Duparc, *Nullité*, I, pp. 355–9 (trans. French in Duparc, *Nullité*, IV, pp. 40–4; English in Taylor, *Joan of Arc*, pp. 292–4).

For the testimony of Guillaume Manchon, see Duparc, *Nullité*, I, pp. 415–28 (trans. French in Duparc, *Nullité*, IV, pp. 96–109; English in Taylor, *Joan of Arc*, pp. 321–31).

For Loiseleur disguising himself as St Catherine, see the testimony of Pierre Cusquel in Duparc, *Nullité*, I, pp. 451–4 (trans. French in Duparc, *Nullité*, IV, pp. 131–3). Cusquel was a townsman of Rouen, now in his fifties, who claimed that as a young man he had been brought to meet Joan in her

cell twice by the man it seems he then worked for, the master of works at
Rouen Castle – visits which, if they took place as he claimed, must have
been unsanctioned, and reinforce the sense of Joan's vulnerability to
those who had access to her in the castle. Cusquel's statement is mostly
hearsay, including the far-fetched story about Loiseleur, and gives a sense
that he (unlike many of the other witnesses) was thrilled to find himself
involved in such significant events, both Joan's captivity and, now, her
rehabilitation. He himself had talked to Joan, he declared, and advised her
to speak carefully, since her life was at stake. It is Cusquel who reports that,
on the day of Joan's death – an execution he could not bear to witness, he
said, because his heart was so overcome with pity for a woman unjustly
condemned – he encountered the king of England's secretary on his way
back from the execution and heard him say 'We are all undone, for a saint
has been burned!' This is one of the most often cited comments concerning
the immediate reaction to Joan's death, but, in the context of the rest of
Cusquel's testimony, it needs to be treated with caution; certainly, it had
grown in the telling since Cusquel testified at the earlier hearing of 1452:
Duparc, *Nullité*, I, pp. 187–8 (trans. French in Duparc, *Nullité*, III, pp.
176–9).

For the sentence of nullification of 7 July 1456, see Duparc, *Nullité*, II, pp.
602–12 (quotations from pp. 608–9) (trans. French in Duparc, *Nullité*, IV,
pp. 221–30; extract in English in Taylor, *Joan of Arc*, pp. 348–9).

For Charles in the Loire valley, and his health, see Vale, *Charles VII*, pp. 134,
172–3.

For the dauphin's rebellion and the arrest of the duke of Alençon, see Vale,
Charles VII, pp. 154–62, 166–70.

EPILOGUE

For the process of Joan's canonisation, see H. A. Kelly, 'Joan of Arc's Last
Trial: The Attack of the Devil's Advocates', in Wheeler and Wood (eds),
Fresh Verdicts, pp. 205–36; T. Wilson-Smith, *Joan of Arc: Maid, Myth and
History* (Stroud, 2006), pp. 183–4, 196–9; report of Joan's beatification by F.
M. Wyndham in the *Tablet*, 10 April 1909, http://archive.thetablet.co.uk/
article/10th-april-1909/7/the-beatification-of-joan-of-arc-its-history-
with-; Warner, *Joan of Arc*, pp. 259–60.

'*She is a saint*': Wilson-Smith, *Joan of Arc*, p. 184.

'*Joan of Arc has shone like a new star . . .*': Wilson-Smith, *Joan of Arc*, p. 198.

For the comments of Pope Benedict XVI in 2011, captured on film, see http://
www.catholicherald.co.uk/multimedia/2011/01/26/st-joan-of-arc-an-
inspiration-for-public-service/.

For Joan's letter to the English, see above, p. 98.

'*Joan is above all the saint of reconciliation . . .*': Pernoud, *Joan of Arc: By
Herself and Her Witnesses*, p. 277.

For the testimony of Aimon de Macy, see Duparc, *Nullité*, I, p. 404–6 (trans.
French in Duparc, *Nullité*, IV, pp. 86–8; English in Taylor, *Joan of Arc*, pp.
319–21).

Select Bibliography

PRIMARY SOURCES

A Parisian Journal, 1405–1449, trans. and ed. J. Shirley (Oxford, 1968).

Basin, T., *Histoire de Charles VII*, 2 vols, trans. and ed. C. Samaran (Paris, 1933–44).

Boudet, J.-P. (ed.), *Le 'Recueil des plus célèbres astrologues' de Simon de Phares*, I (Paris, 1997).

Bower, W., *Scotichronicon*, ed. D. E. R. Watt and others, 9 vols (Aberdeen, 1987–98).

Brie, F. W. D. (ed.), *The Brut, or the Chronicles of England*, I (London, 1906).

Broquière, B. de la, *Le Voyage d'outremer*, ed. C. Schefer (Paris, 1892).

Buchon, J. A. C. (ed.), *Choix de chroniques et mémoires relatifs à l'histoire de France* (Orléans, 1875).

Chartier, J., *Chronique de Charles VII*, ed. V. de Viriville, 3 vols (Paris, 1858).

Chastellain, G., *Oeuvres*, ed. K. de Lettenhove, 8 vols (Brussels, 1863–6).

Chronique du Mont-Saint-Michel (1343–1468), ed. S. Luce, I (Paris, 1879).

Chronique du religieux de Saint-Denys, trans. and ed. M. L. Bellaguet, 6 vols (Paris, 1839–52, repr. in 3, Paris, 1994).

Chroniques relatives à l'histoire de la Belgique, ed. K. de Lettenhove (Brussels, 1872).

Cochon, P., *Chronique normande*, ed. C. de Robillard de Beaurepaire (Rouen, 1870).

Curry, A., *The Battle of Agincourt: Sources and Interpretations* (Woodbridge, 2000).

Delpit, J. (ed.), *Collection générale des documents français*, I (Paris, 1847).

Doncoeur, P., and Lanhers, Y. (ed. and trans.), *L'Enquête ordonnée par Charles VII en 1450 et le codicile de Guillaume Bouillé* (Paris, 1956).

Duparc, P. (trans. and ed.), *Procès en nullité de la condamnation de Jeanne d'Arc*, 5 vols (Paris, 1977–88).

Fenin, P. de, *Mémoires*, ed. E. Dupont (Paris, 1837).

Gesta Henrici Quinti, trans. and ed. F. Taylor and J. S. Roskell (Oxford, 1975).

Godefroy, T. (ed.), *Le Cérémonial françois* (Paris, 1649).

Grévy-Pons, N. (ed.), *L'Honneur de la couronne de France: Quatre libelles contre les Anglais* (Paris, 1990).

Gruel, G., *Chronique d'Arthur de Richemont*, ed. A. le Vavasseur (Paris, 1890).

Hobbins, D. (trans. and ed.), *The Trial of Joan of Arc* (Cambridge and London, 2005).

Journal de Nicolas de Baye, greffier du parlement de Paris, 1400–1417, ed. A. Tuetey, 2 vols (Paris, 1885–8).

Journal d'un bourgeois de Paris, 1405–1449, ed. A. Tuetey (Paris, 1881).

Le Févre, J., *Chronique*, ed. F. Morand, 2 vols (Paris, 1876–81).

Mémoires pour servir à l'histoire de France et de Bourgogne (Paris, 1729).

Monstrelet, E. de, *La Chronique d'Enguerran de Monstrelet*, ed. L. Douët-d'Arcq, 6 vols (Paris, 1857–62).

Morosini, A., *Chronique: Extraits relatifs à l'histoire de France*, ed. and trans. G. Lefèvre-Pontalis and L. Dorez, 4 vols (Paris, 1898–1902).

Nicolas, H. (ed.), *Proceedings and Ordinances of the Privy Council of England*, III and IV (London, 1834–5).

Quicherat, J. (ed.), *Procès de condamnation et de réhabilitation de Jeanne d'Arc*, 5 vols (Paris, 1841–9).

Quicherat, J., 'Relation inédite sur Jeanne d'Arc', *Revue historique* (1877), 327–44.

Rymer, T. (ed.), *Foedera* (1704–35), IX, via British History Online at http://www.british-history.ac.uk.

Smet, J.-J. de (ed.), *Recueil des chroniques de Flandre*, III (Brussels, 1856).

Stevenson, J. (ed.), *Letters and Papers Illustrative of the Wars of the English in France*, II, parts I and II (London, 1864).

Strong, P. and Strong, F., 'The Last Will and Codicils of Henry V', *English Historical Review*, 96 (1981), 79–102.

Taverne, A. de la, *Journal de la paix d'Arras* (Paris, 1651).

Taylor, C. (ed. and trans.), *Joan of Arc: La Pucelle* (Manchester, 2006).

Tisset, P., and Lanhers, Y. (trans. and ed.), *Procès de condamnation de Jeanne d'Arc*, 3 vols (Paris, 1960–71).

Valois, N. (ed.), 'Un nouveau témoignage sur Jeanne d'Arc: Réponse d'un clerc parisien à l'apologie de la Pucelle par Gerson (1429)', in *Annuaire-Bulletin de la Société de l'Histoire de France*, 43 (1906), 161–79.

Waurin, J. de, *Anchiennes cronicques d'Engleterre*, ed. E. Dupont, 3 vols (Paris, 1858–63).

Waurin, J. de, *A Collection of the Chronicles and Ancient Histories of Great Britain, now called England, from AD 1422 to AD 1431*, trans. E. L. C. P. Hardy (London, 1891).

SECONDARY SOURCES

Allmand, C. T., 'Henry V (1386–1422)', *Oxford Dictionary of National Biography*.

Allmand, C. T., *Henry V* (London, 1992).

Allmand, C. T., (ed.), *Power, Culture and Religion in France, c.1350–c.1550* (Woodbridge, 1989).

Allmand, C. T. (ed.), *The New Cambridge Medieval History, Volume VII c.1415–c.1500* (Cambridge, 1998).

Armstrong, C. A. J., 'La Double Monarchie, France-Angleterre et la maison de Bourgogne (1420–1435): Le Déclin d'une alliance', in *Annales de Bourgogne*, 37 (1965), 81–112.

Arn, M.-J. (ed.), *Charles d'Orléans in England* (Cambridge, 2000).

Atkins, M., 'Jacqueline, suo jure countess of Hainault, suo jure countess of Holland, and suo jure countess of Zeeland (1401–1436)', *Oxford Dictionary of National Biography*.

Autrand, F., *Charles VI* (Paris, 1986).

Balcon, S., *La Cathédrale Saint-Pierre-et-Saint-Paul de Troyes* (Paris, 2001).

Balfour-Melville, E. W. M., *James I, King of Scots, 1406–1437* (London, 1936).

Barker, J., *Agincourt: The King, the Campaign, the Battle* (London, 2005).

Barker, J., *Conquest: The English Kingdom of France in the Hundred Years War* (London, 2009).

Beaucourt, G. du Fresne de, 'Le Meurtre de Montereau', *Revue des questions historiques*, V (1868), 189–237.

Beaucourt, G. du Fresne de, *Histoire de Charles VII*, 6 vols (Paris, 1881–91).

Beaune, C., *Birth of an Ideology: Myths and Symbols of Nation in Late-Medieval France* (Berkeley, 1991).

Beaune, C., *Jeanne d'Arc* (Paris, 2004).

Benedetti, J., *Gilles de Rais* (London, 1971).

Black, A., 'Popes and Councils', in Allmand (ed.), *New Cambridge Medieval History VII*, 65–86.

Blumenfeld-Kosinski, R., *Poets, Saints and Visionaries of the Great Schism* (Pennsylvania State University, 2006).

Boissonade, P., 'Une étape capitale de la mission de Jeanne d'Arc', *Revue des questions historiques*, 3rd ser. XVII (1930), 12–67.

Bossard, E., *Gilles de Rais, maréchal de France, dit Barbe-Bleue (1404–1440)* (Paris, 1886).

Bossuat, A., *Perrinet Gressart et François de Surienne* (Paris, 1936).

Bouzy, O., *Jeanne d'Arc en son siècle* (Paris, 2013).

Branner, R., 'The Labyrinth of Reims Cathedral', *Journal of the Society of Architectural Historians*, 21, no. 1 (1962), 18–25.

Brown, M. H., 'Douglas, Archibald, fourth earl of Douglas, and duke of Touraine in the French nobility (*c.*1369–1424)', *Oxford Dictionary of National Biography*.

Brown, M., *The Black Douglases: War and Lordship in Late Medieval Scotland, 1300–1455* (Edinburgh, 1998).

Brown, M., 'French Alliance or English Peace? Scotland and the Last Phase of the Hundred Years' War, 1415–53', in Clark (ed.), *Conflicts, Consequences and the Crown in the Late Middle Ages*, 81–99.

Castor, H., *She-Wolves: The Women Who Ruled England Before Elizabeth* (London, 2010).

Chevalier, B., 'Les Écossais dans les armées de Charles VII jusqu'à la bataille de Verneuil', in *Jeanne d'Arc: Une époque, un rayonnement*, 85–94.

Clark, L. (ed.), *Conflicts, Consequences and the Crown in the Late Middle Ages* (Woodbridge, 2007).

Clin, M.-V., 'Joan of Arc and her doctors', in Wheeler and Wood (eds), *Fresh Verdicts on Joan of Arc*, 295–302.

Contamine, P., *Guerre, état et société à la fin du Moyen Age: Etudes sur les armées des rois de France, 1337–1494* (Paris, 1972).

Contamine, P., 'La Théologie de la guerre à la fin du Moyen Age: La Guerre de Cent Ans fut-elle une guerre juste?', in *Jeanne d'Arc: Une époque, un rayonnement*, 9–21.

Contamine, P., 'La 'France anglaise' au XVe siècle: Mythe ou réalité?', in *La 'France anglaise' au Moyen Age*, 17–29.

Contamine, P., Bouzy, O. and Hélary, X., *Jeanne d'Arc: Histoire et dictionnaire* (Paris, 2012).

Cooper, S., *The Real Falstaff: Sir John Fastolf and the Hundred Years' War* (Barnsley, 2010).

Cosneau, E., *Le Connétable de Richemont, Artur de Bretagne, 1393–1458* (Paris, 1886).

Curry, A., 'The "Coronation Expedition" and Henry VI's Court in France, 1430 to 1432', in Stratford (ed.), *The Lancastrian Court*, 29–52.

Curry, A., *Agincourt: A New History* (Stroud, 2005, repr. 2010).

DeVries, K., 'Military Surgical Practice and the Advent of Gunpowder Weaponry', *Canadian Bulletin of Medical History*, 7 (1990), 131–46.

DeVries, K., 'A Woman as Leader of Men: Joan of Arc's Military Career', in Wheeler and Wood (eds), *Fresh Verdicts on Joan of Arc*, 3–18.

DeVries, K., *Joan of Arc: A Military Leader* (Stroud, 1999, new edn 2011).

Dickinson, J. G., *The Congress of Arras, 1435* (Oxford, 1955).

Ditcham, B. G. H., '"Mutton-Guzzlers and Wine Bags": Foreign Soldiers and Native Reactions in Fifteenth-Century France', in Allmand (ed.), *Power, Culture and Religion*, 1–13.

Duparc, P., 'La délivrance d'Orléans et la mission de Jeanne d'Arc', in *Jeanne d'Arc: Une époque, un rayonnement*, 153–8.

Elliott, D., 'Seeing Double: John Gerson, the Discernment of Spirits, and Joan of Arc', *American Historical Review*, 107 (2002), 26–54.

Farmer, D. H. (ed.), *The Oxford Dictionary of Saints* (Oxford, 2003).

Forcellin, M., *Histoire générale des Alpes Maritimes ou Cottiènes*, II (Paris, 1890).

Fraioli, D., 'L'image de Jeanne d'Arc: Que doit-elle au milieu littéraire et religieux de son temps?', in *Jeanne d'Arc: Une epoque, un rayonnement*, 191–6.

Fraioli, D., *Joan of Arc: The Early Debate* (Woodbridge, 2000).

Fraser, W., *The Douglas Book* (Edinburgh, 1885).

Gibbons, R., 'Isabeau of Bavaria, Queen of France: The Creation of an Historical Villainess', *Transactions of the Royal Historical Society*, ser. 6, VI (1997), 51–73.

Gibbons, R. C., 'The Active Queenship of Isabeau of Bavaria, 1392–1417', PhD dissertation, University of Reading (1997).

Griffiths, R. A., *The Reign of King Henry VI* (Berkeley and Los Angeles, 1981).

Guillemain, B., 'Une carrière: Pierre Cauchon', in *Jeanne d'Arc: Une époque, un rayonnement*, 217–25.

Harriss, G. L., *Cardinal Beaufort: A Study of Lancastrian Ascendancy and Decline* (Oxford, 1988).

Harriss, G. L., 'Thomas, duke of Clarence (1387–1421)', *Oxford Dictionary of National Biography*.

Harriss, G. L., 'Humphrey, duke of Gloucester (1390–1447)', *Oxford Dictionary of National Biography*.

Harriss, G. L., *Shaping the Nation: England, 1360–1461* (Oxford, 2005).

Jackson, R., *Vive le Roi! A History of the French Coronation* (Chapel Hill, 1984).

Jacquin, R., 'Un précurseur de Jeanne d'Arc', *Revue des Deux Mondes* (1967), 222–6.

Jeanne d'Arc: Une époque, un rayonnement: Colloque d'Histoire Médiévale, Orléans Octobre 1979 (Paris, 1982).

Jones, M., 'Catherine (1401–1437)', *Oxford Dictionary of National Biography*.

Jones, M. K., 'The Battle of Verneuil (17 August 1424): Towards a History of Courage', *War in History*, 9 (2002), 375–411.

Jones, M. K., '"Gardez mon corps, sauvez ma terre" – Immunity from War and the Lands of a Captive Knight: The Siege of Orléans (1428–29) Revisited', in Arn (ed.), *Charles d'Orléans in England*, 9–26

Keegan, J., *The Face of Battle: A Study of Agincourt, Waterloo and the Somme* (London, 1976).

Kelly, H. A., 'Joan of Arc's Last Trial: The Attack of the Devil's Advocates', in Wheeler and Wood (eds), *Fresh Verdicts on Joan of Arc*, 205–36.

La 'France anglaise' au Moyen Age, actes du IIIe Congrès National des Sociétés Savantes (Poitiers, 1986), I (Paris, 1988).

Laborde, L. de, *Les Ducs de Bourgogne*, 3 vols (Paris, 1849–52).

Lang, S. J., 'Bradmore, John (d. 1412)', *Oxford Dictionary of National Biography*.

Leguai, A., 'La "France bourguignonne" dans le conflit entre la "France française" et la "France anglaise" (1420–1435)', in *La 'France anglaise' au Moyen Age*, 41–52.

Lethel, F.-M., 'La soumission à l'Église militante: un aspect théologique de la condamnation de Jeanne d'Arc', in *Jeanne d'Arc: Une époque, un rayonnement*, 182–9.

Lewis, P. S., 'La "France anglaise" vue de la France française', in *La 'France anglaise' au Moyen Age*, 31–9.

Little, R. G., *The Parlement of Poitiers: War, Government and Politics in France, 1418–1436* (London, 1984).

Luce, S., *Jeanne d'Arc à Domrémy: recherches critiques sur les origines de la mission de la Pucelle* (Paris, 1886).

McGuire, B. P., *Jean Gerson and the Last Medieval Reformation* (Pennsylvania State University, 2005).

Mortimer, I., *1415: Henry V's Year of Glory* (London, 2009).

Murray, S., *Building Troyes Cathedral: The Late Gothic Campaigns* (Bloomington and Indianapolis, 1987).

Neveux, F., *L'Évêque Pierre Cauchon* (Paris, 1987).

Odio, E., 'Gilles de Rais: Hero, Spendthrift, and Psychopathic Child Murderer of the Later Hundred Years War', in Villalon and Kagay (eds), *The Hundred Years War (Part III)*, 145–84.

Oxford Dictionary of National Biography, ed. H. C. G. Matthew and B. Harrison (Oxford, 2004), online edn, ed. L. Goldman (2010).

Pernoud, R., *Joan of Arc: By Herself and Her Witnesses* (London, 1964).

Pernoud, R., and Clin, M.-V., *Joan of Arc: Her Story*, trans. and revised J. DuQuesnay Adams (New York, 1998).

Petit, E., 'Les Tonnerrois sous Charles VI et la Bourgogne sous Jean Sans Peur (épisodes inédits de la Guerre de Cent Ans)', *Bulletin de la Société des Sciences Historiques et Naturelles de l'Yonne*, xlv (1891), 247–315.

Peyronnet, G., 'Un problème de légitimité: Charles VII et le toucher des écrouelles', in *Jeanne d'Arc: Une époque, un rayonnement*, 197–202.

Pinzino, J. M., 'Just War, Joan of Arc, and the Politics of Salvation', in Villalon and Kagay (eds), *The Hundred Years War: A Wider Focus*, 365–96.

Plancher, U., *Histoire générale et particulière de Bourgogne*, 4 vols (Dijon, 1739–81).

Pollard, A. J., 'Talbot, John, first earl of Shrewsbury and first earl of Waterford (c.1387–1453)', *Oxford Dictionary of National Biography*.

Ramsay, J. H., *Lancaster and York: A Century of English History*, I (Oxford, 1892).

Rowe, B. J. H., 'Discipline in the Norman Garrisons under Bedford, 1422–35', *English Historical Review*, 46 (1931), 194–208.

St John Hope, W. H., 'The Funeral, Monument, and Chantry Chapel of King Henry the Fifth', *Archaeologia*, 65 (1914), 129–86.

Schibanoff, S., 'True Lies: Transvestism and Idolatry in the Trial of Joan of Arc', in Wheeler and Wood (eds), *Fresh Verdicts on Joan of Arc*, 31–60.

Schnerb, B., *Armagnacs et Bourguignons: La Maudite Guerre, 1407–1435* (Paris, 1988, repr. 2009).

Senneville, G. de, *Yolande d'Aragon: La Reine qui a gagné la Guerre de Cent Ans* (Paris, 2008).

Stratford, J., 'John, duke of Bedford (1389–1435)', *Oxford Dictionary of National Biography*.

Stratford, J. (ed.), *The Lancastrian Court* (Donington, 2003).

Sullivan, K., '"I do not name to you the voice of St Michael": The Identification of Joan of Arc's Voices', in Wheeler and Wood (eds), *Fresh Verdicts on Joan of Arc*, 85–112.

Sullivan, K., *The Interrogation of Joan of Arc* (Minneapolis, 1999).

Taburet-Delahaye, E., (ed.), *Paris 1400: Les Arts sous Charles VI* (Paris, 2004).

Taylor, L. J., *The Virgin Warrior: The Life and Death of Joan of Arc* (New Haven and London, 2009).

Thompson, G. L., '"Monseigneur Saint Denis", His Abbey, and His Town, under English Occupation, 1420–1436', in Allmand (ed.), *Power, Culture and Religion*, 15–35.

Thompson, G. L., *Paris and Its People under English Rule: The Anglo-Burgundian Regime, 1420–1436* (Oxford, 1991).

Tobin, M., 'Le livre des révélations de Marie Robine (+1399): Étude et édition', in *Mélanges de l'École Française de Rome, Moyen-Age, Temps Modernes*, 98 (1986), 229–64.

Vale, M. G. A., *Charles VII* (London, 1974).

Vale, M., 'Jeanne d'Arc et ses adversaires: Jeanne, victime d'une guerre civile?' in *Jeanne d'Arc: Une époque, un rayonnement*, 203–16.

Valois, N., 'Conseils et prédictions adressés à Charles VII, en 1445', *Annuaire-Bulletin de la Société de l'Histoire de France*, XLVI (1909), 201–38.

van Herwaarden, J., 'The appearance of Joan of Arc', in van Herwaarden (ed.), *Joan of Arc: Reality and Myth*, 19–74.

van Herwaarden, J. (ed.), *Joan of Arc: Reality and Myth* (Hilversum, 1994).

Vauchez, A., 'Jeanne d'Arc et le prophétisme féminin des XIVe et XVe siècles', in *Jeanne d'Arc: Une époque, un rayonnement*, 159–68.

Vaughan, R., *Philip the Bold: The Formation of the Burgundian State* (London, 1962, repr. Woodbridge, 2002).

Vaughan, R., *John the Fearless: The Growth of Burgundian Power* (London, 1966, repr. Woodbridge, 2002).

Vaughan, R., *Philip the Good: The Apogee of Burgundy* (London, 1970, repr. Woodbridge, 2002).

Villalon, L. J. A., and Kagay, D. J. (eds), *The Hundred Years War: A Wider Focus* (Leiden and Boston, 2005).

Villalon, L. J. A., and Kagay, D. J. (eds), *The Hundred Years War (Part III): Further Considerations* (Leiden and Boston, 2013).

Vincent, N., *Holy Blood: King Henry III and the Westminster Blood Relic* (Cambridge, 2001).

Viriville, V. de (trans. and ed.), *Procès de Condamnation de Jeanne d'Arc* (Paris, 1867).

Warner, M., *Joan of Arc: The Image of Female Heroism* (London, 1981).

Watts, J., *Henry VI and the Politics of Kingship* (Cambridge, 1996).

Watts, J., 'Pole, William de la, first duke of Suffolk (1396–1450), *Oxford Dictionary of National Biography*.

Wheeler, B., 'Joan of Arc's Sword in the Stone', in Wheeler and Wood (eds), *Fresh Verdicts on Joan of Arc*, xi–xvi.

Wheeler, B., and Wood, C. T. (eds), *Fresh Verdicts on Joan of Arc* (New York, 1996).

Wilson-Smith, T., *Joan of Arc: Maid, Myth and History* (Stroud, 2006).

Wirth, R. (ed.), *Primary Sources and Context concerning Joan of Arc's Male Clothing*, Historical Academy (Association) for Joan of Arc Studies (2006).

Wood, C. T., 'Joan of Arc's mission and the lost record of her interrogation at Poitiers', in Wheeler and Wood (eds), *Fresh Verdicts on Joan of Arc*, 19–28.

Wylie, J. H., and Waugh, W. T., *The Reign of Henry V*, III (Cambridge, 1929).

Zachariadou, E., 'The Ottoman World', in Allmand (ed.), *New Cambridge Medieval History VII*, 812–30.

Acknowledgements

The debts I've incurred in the writing of this book begin with my agent and my editors, without whom I wouldn't have had the chance to tell Joan's story. I couldn't ask for more thoughtful guidance or boundless support than that provided by Patrick Walsh, with the able assistance of Alex Christofi and Carrie Plitt. Nor could I hope for wiser or more insightful editors than Walter Donohue and Terry Karten. To them, and to the brilliant teams at Faber in the UK and HarperCollins in the US who have brought the book into being, I am immensely grateful.

For their generosity in sharing references, advice and encouragement, I owe huge thanks to Dan Jones, my friend in the fifteenth century as well as the twenty-first; to Rowena Archer, Hannah Skoda and the students taking the 'Joan of Arc' Special Subject in Oxford University's History Faculty, who welcomed me to one of their illuminating seminars; and to Richard Beadle and Jenny Stratford, on whose expertise it is a privilege to call. I have benefited too from discussing Joan with Lucy Swingler, Lucy Parker, Ross Wilson and Jacqui Hayden, brilliant storytellers in another medium. I am sorry that I couldn't use Arabella Weir's inspired title for the book, but she has been with me every step of the way, as have Jo Marsh, Katie Brown and Thalia Walters, and I can only hope that they and every one of my friends and family know how much difference they make.

My parents, Gwyneth and Grahame Castor, have been an unfailing source of support of all kinds, practical, emotional and intellectual. Julian Ferraro, my first and most necessary reader, has both held the fort and helped. The book is for Luca, our gorgeous both held the fort and helped. The book is for Luca, our gorgeous boy, to thank him for his patience, and in the hope that he might like it.

Helen Castor
London, 2014

Index

Subentries are in chronological order

day of interrogation, 173–5; fifth day of interrogation, 175; sixth day of interrogation, 175–6; interrogations in prison, 176–8, 181; accounts of voices, 170–1, 173–4, 186, 192, 193; account of sign of angel with crown, 4, 176–8, 193; articles of accusation against her, 179–80; illness, 181; refusal of Cauchon's offer, 182–3; admonition by court, 184–5; threatened with torture, 185–6; final session, 186–8; at the scaffold, 188–90; appeal to Rome, 189–90; sentenced to be burned, 190; submission and confession, 190–1; sentence of imprisonment, 190–1; changes of clothes, 191–2, 226; recantation, 192–3; final attempts at persuasion, 193; death sentence to be carried out, 193–4; death, 1, 194, 198, 226–7, 239–40, 241; body, 198, 221, 227; record of her trial, 2, 198–9; memories of, 2–3, 4–5, 222–4, 233–42, 246; impersonator, 223; inquiries into her trial, 234–31; new trial, 231; petition of her family, 231–2; inquiry into her trial, 232–3; verdict of innocence, 241–2; recognised as saint, 2, 243–5; feast day, 244
Juvénal des Ursins, Jean, archbishop of Reims, 22, 231

La Charité-sur-Loire, 147–8, 149, 176, 200
La Hire (Étienne de Vignolles): Montargis victory, 77, 81; Orléans defence, 81; Battle of the Herrings, 83–5; forces for Joan, 101; Joan's arrival at Orléans, 105–6; capture of Augustins, 109; end of Orléans siege, 111; Jargeau siege, 114; pursuit of English, 117; Montepilloy battle, 136; arrival at Saint-Denis, 140; capture of Château Gaillard, 152; capture of

Louviers, 200; entry into Paris, 215; memories of Joan, 236
La Rochelle, dauphin at, 56, 59
La Trémoille, Georges de: relationship with Richemont, 75–6, 78, 82, 116, 120; marriage, 76; relationship with king, 76, 78, 116, 120; Burgundian diplomacy, 128; at coronation of Charles, 127; Montepilloy battle, 136; direction of Joan, 146; as witness to Joan's sign, 176; arrest and exile, 206–7, 217
La Trémoille, Jean de, 63, 75–6, 128, 153
Lagny-sur-Marne: Joan at, 144, 155, 175, 203; beheading, 157, 178; siege lifted, 203
Lannoy, Hugues de, 153
l'Archier, Richard, 235
Laval, Guy de, 114, 119, 127, 140
Lavenu, Martin, 194, 225, 226, 227, 229
Laxart, Durand, 234
Le Camus de Beaulieu, 75
le Maçon, Robert, 32, 75, 93, 123–4
le Maistre, Jean, 167, 179, 186, 192, 193
le Royer, Henri, 234–5
l'Isle-Adam, lord de, 214
Loiseleur, Nicolas, 225, 240–1
Lorraine, duke of, 89, 90, see also René of Anjou
Louis, dauphin (later Louis XI), 58, 59, 70, 215, 218, 242
Louis IX, king, 42
Louis de Coutes, page, 100
Louis de Luxembourg, bishop and chancellor, 205, 214, 220, 227
Louis of Guienne, dauphin, 10–11, 13–14, 25, 29
Louvet, Jean, 32, 36, 71, 74–5
Louviers, fall to English, 200
Luxembourg, see Jacquetta de Luxembourg, Jean de Luxembourg, Louis de Luxembourg

gundian occupation (1418), 31–2, 214; arrival of Henry V, Philip of Burgundy and Charles VI, 45–6; entertainments, 76–7; Bedford's return, 77; university, 92–3, 161; Duke Philip's visit, 129–31; handover issue, 132; defences, 134, 140–1; assault on, 141–2; Armagnac raids, 155; theologians demand surrender of Joan, 161, 163; Pieronne burned for heresy, 163; arrival of Henry VI, 200–1; sufferings from Armagnacs, 207, 208; winter weather (1434-5), 209; Armagnac entry, 214–15, 223; entry of King Charles, 215, 217; petition of Joan's mother, 231–2

Paris, bishops of, 202, 214, 231

Parthenay, citadel, 78, 82

Pasquerel, Jean, 100, 154, 237

Patay, battle, 117–18, 119, 137

Petit, Jean, 12, 26

Pieronne, follower of Brother Richard, 163

Pius X, pope, 244

Poitiers: battle (1356), 10, 20; Joan questioned, 95–6, 99

Poulengy, Bertrand de, 235–6

Provins, Charles VI at, 34

Quicherat, Jules, 243

Raymond, page, 100

Regnault de Chartres, archbishop of Reims: examination of Joan, 95; Troyes strategy, 123; Reims entry, 125–6; coronation of Charles, 126–7; embassy to Philip of Burgundy, 134, 138; direction of Joan, 146; view of Joan's capture, 160–1; as witness to Joan's sign, 176, 177; response to Joan's fate, 200; Nevers conference, 210; Arras conference, 211

Reims: Burgundian occupation (1417), 29; cathedral, 56, 82; coronation planned, 120–1; letters from Troyes, 124–5; entry of Charles, 125–6; coronation of Charles, 126–8, 131

René of Anjou, duke of Bar and Lorraine, 69–70, 90, 127, 136, 219

Richard, Brother: preachings in Paris, 121–2, 136; at Troyes, 121, 122; won over by Joan, 122, 125, 136; brings letter from Joan, 122–3; seeks Joan's opinion, 154–5; follower burned, 163; Joan's interrogation, 175

Richemont, Arthur, count of: Azincourt battle, 14, 15, 67; prisoner of English, 15, 67; release, 67; marriage, 55, 67, 68, 210; constable of France, 68–9, 71, 73; campaign (1426), 74; relationship with king, 74–5, 78, 82, 120, 206; military failures, 77–8; troops, 116–17, 120; meeting with Joan, 116–17; Joan's petition to king, 120; refused permission to attend coronation, 127; restored to royal favour, 206; Arras conference, 211; at Paris, 214; royal entry into Paris, 215; action against rebels, 218

Roucy, count of, 14, 15

Rouen: Charles VI at (1415), 14, 16; Burgundian advance (1418), 30; English advance (1418), 32; fall to English (1419), 34; Bedford's government, 63, 64; Armagnac threat, 137; arrival of Henry VI, 162; arrival of Joan, 164; trial of Joan, 165; archbishopric, 166; Armagnac attack, 213–14; surrender, 220, 224; entry of King Charles, 220–1, 224

Roussel, Raoul, archbishop of Rouen, 227–8, 230

Rouvray, battle (Battle of the Herrings), 84–5, 86, 101, 115, 117, 137